Nuclear Powered Baseball

Articles inspired by The Simpsons episode Homer at the Bat

Edited by Emily Hawks and Bill Nowlin

Associate editors: Russ Lake and Len Levin

Society for American Baseball Research, Inc.
Phoenix, AZ

Nuclear-Powered Baseball
Articles Inspired by The Simpsons episode, "Homer At the Bat"
Edited by Emily Hawks and Bill Nowlin
Associate editors: Russ Lake and Len Levin

Copyright © 2016 Society for American Baseball Research, Inc.
All rights reserved. Reproduction in whole or in part without permission is prohibited.

ISBN 978-1-943816-11-8
(Ebook ISBN 978-1-943816-10-1)

Cover and book design: Gilly Rosenthol
Original cover art by Bob Krieger

All photography courtesy of the National Baseball Hall of Fame, unless otherwise indicated.
Photographs on pages 32 and 53 are by Brad Mangin, National Baseball Hall of Fame Library.

Society for American Baseball Research
Cronkite School at ASU
555 N. Central Ave. #416
Phoenix, AZ 85004
Phone: (602) 496-1460
Web: www.sabr.org
Facebook: Society for American Baseball Research
Twitter: @SABR

TABLE OF CONTENTS

Introduction *by Emily Hawks*..1

The Making of "Homer at the Bat" *by Erik Malinowski* 3

The Burns-Smithers Question *by Bradley Woodrum* 8

Wade Boggs *by Steve West*...17

Jose Canseco *by Geoffrey Dunn* 23

Roger Clemens *by Frederick C. Bush* 35

Ken Griffey Jr. *by Emily Hawks*..49

Don Mattingly *by James Lincoln Ray* 60

Steve Sax *by Alan Cohen*...77

Mike Scioscia *by Susan Lantz* 84

Ozzie Smith *by Charles F. Faber* 95

Darryl Strawberry *by Shawn Morris*..99

Cap Anson *by David Fleitz* 107

Mordecai "Three Finger" Brown *by Cindy Thomson*...............................114

Jim Creighton *by John Thorn* 119

Honus Wagner *by Jan Finkel* 124

Pie Traynor *by James Forr*..131

Harry Hooper *by Paul Zingg and E. A. Reed* 149

Nap Lajoie *by David Jones and Stephen Constantelos*..............................154

Gabby Street *by Joseph Wancho* 159

Joe Jackson *by David Fleitz* 165

Homer Simpson *by Bill Nowlin* 172

"Homer at the Bat"—the game *by Bill Nowlin* 179

Ryan Tosses No-Hitter; Cash Wields Table Leg *by Gregory H. Wolf*....182

The New Springfield Nine *by Jonah Keri* 185

The Simpsons Baseball Edition *by Joe Posnanski* 189

Baseball People Mentioned in The Simpsons 194

Contributors 197

THE "HOMER PROJECT"

If you were a child who grew up with a TV in your household, chances are good that you also had a TV family: a family you looked forward to spending your time with in the evenings, and, in a strange way, felt a part of. In the 1950s and 1960s, you might have felt a kinship with Beaver Cleaver, sharing a dinner table with Ward, June, and Wally while rolling your eyes at that sycophant Eddie Haskell. If your childhood occurred a decade later, you might've blended in with the Brady clan, wishing you could be as "groovy" as Marsha, or as "far out" as Greg. Maybe you were a child of the 1980s and got an early taste of dinner table bipartisanship with the Keatons.

But if, like me, you were a child of the 1990s, there is a good chance that your TV family was two-dimensional, in the form of Homer, Marge, Bart, Lisa, and Maggie. That decade, the Simpsons were ubiquitous, and you'd be hard-pressed to go anywhere without seeing an "Eat My Shorts" or "D'oh!" screen-printed tee. I spent countless evenings in the colorful town of Springfield following the wily hijinks of Bart and rooting for the hapless but good-hearted Homer.

Unsurprisingly (else I would likely not be editing this book!), when I wasn't watching *The Simpsons* in my youth, I was tirelessly watching baseball. So when the Season Three episode "Homer at the Bat" aired on February 20, 1992, I was over the moon. To see so many of the biggest MLB stars of the day in Simpsonian animated form—Ken Griffey, Jr., Ozzie Smith, and Jose Canseco, just to name a few—seemed the most exciting thing in the world to this '90s kid. And the fact that they all lent their own voices to the parts seemed even cooler. It may have also been one of my first glimpses into baseball's early days. As a kid, I had no idea that Mr. Burns' dream squad—comprised of colorful names like Shoeless Joe Jackson, Pie Traynor, and Napoleon Lajoie—actually referenced real players. Those seemed like decidedly fabricated names to me!

When I became more involved with the SABR BioProject, I had a conversation with Bill Nowlin, a veteran at editing many great biography compilations. He'd just finished editing the book *Van Lingle Mungo: The Man, The Song, the Players*. I told him that if I were ever to compile a biography book, I'd want it to center on my favorite Simpsons episode, and told him about "Homer at the Bat." Bill's reply was simply, "Let's do it." And from there, the "Homer Project" was born.

The biographies compiled here take the players well beyond their two-dimensional caricatures, and present a well-rounded view of their lives in baseball. We've also included a few very entertaining takes on the now-famous "Homer at the Bat" episode from prominent baseball writers Jonah Keri, Erik Malinowski, and Bradley Woodrum. As an added bonus, we've also included Joe Posnanski's piece on the Season 22 sabermetric-themed episode, "MoneyBART."

This project has been loads of fun to edit for this '90s kid, and I hope you as a reader enjoy it, no matter who your TV family happens to be.

—Emily Hawks

NUCLEAR-POWERED BASEBALL

As the subtitle explains, and as described in Emily Hawks's Introduction, this book was inspired by the "Homer at the Bat" episode of *The Simpsons*. We started work on it in February 2014, and we gave it the working title "The Homer Project." We considered *17 Men Out*, but that seemed a little too obscure. We did realize that the game in the actual episode was a softball game, but we decided not to get sidetracked in that direction. *The Homer Project* itself might have worked, but in the end we decided to go with *Nuclear-Powered Baseball*.

It was great fun working on this book, and writing my first fictional bio—though some of the actual ballplayers I have written up for BioProject have elements that seem stranger than fiction in their true-life stories. In that vein, please note that the writers for *The Simpsons* were more than glad to borrow here and there from real-life baseball. Please see Gregory Wolf's game account, "Ryan Tosses No-Hitter; Cash Wields Table Leg."

—BN

THE MAKING OF "HOMER AT THE BAT," THE EPISODE THAT CONQUERED PRIME TIME 20 YEARS AGO TONIGHT

By Erik Malinowski

On February 20, 1992, more American homes tuned into *The Simpsons* than they did *The Cosby Show* or the Winter Olympics from Albertville, France. A foul-mouthed cartoon on a fourth-place network bested the Huxtables and the world's best amateur athletes. Fox over NBC and CBS—its first-ever victory in prime time. New over old.

Why the shift? Well, the Olympic programming that night featured no marquee events, and *Cosby* was just two months away from ending its eight-season run. Meanwhile, *The Simpsons*, airing just its 52nd episode out of 500 (and counting), had put forth its most ambitious effort to date, an episode called "Homer at the Bat." Months of work went into corralling nine baseball players, a cross-section of young stars and established veterans, to guest-star as members of a rec-league softball team.

Sam Simon, the co-creator of *The Simpsons*, originally pitched the idea, and it was put into words by John Swartzwelder, a charter member of the show's writing staff, who would eventually pen 59 episodes, more than anyone else. On a staff full of fantasy baseball junkies, Swartzwelder was the über-geek, a fanatic who had rented out stadiums for hours at a time so he and his close friends could play ball. (Years after Swartzwelder's departure from the show, it's easy to see his influence endures. During the episode's roundtable DVD commentary, the word "Swartzweldian" is used with a deference and awe usually reserved for long-dead Nobel Laureates.)

If you're somehow unfamiliar with the episode, the premise was relatively simple: Mr. Burns's company softball team, having lost 28 of 30 games the previous season, goes on an incredible run when Homer starts hitting, well, homers with his WonderBat, carved from the fallen branch of a lightning-struck tree. (Sound familiar?) As the season winds down, it becomes a two-team race for the pennant: Springfield vs. Shelbyville. While dining at the Millionaires' Club with the owner of the Shelbyville Power Plant, a cocky Burns agrees to a handshake bet worth (you guessed it) $1 million.

To fix the game and secure his victory, Burns orders Smithers to enlist ballplayers like Cap Anson, Honus Wagner, and Jim Creighton. (Swartzwelder's choice of Creighton was particularly inspired. The ace pitcher for the Brooklyn Excelsiors in the 1850s and '60s, Creighton supposedly didn't strike out once while batting during the 20 games of the 1860 season. Creighton died two years later. He was 21.) Upon learning that his entire suggested lineup is dead, Burns instructs Smithers to come back with real ballplayers. And so he sets off across the country: nabbing Jose Canseco at a card convention, accosting a Graceland-touring Ozzie Smith, nearly getting shot in the woods by Mike Scioscia, and stopping by Don Mattingly's pink suburban house to interrupt his dish-washing.

Before "Homer at the Bat," *The Simpsons* had used guest stars only sporadically—and never more than four of them in a single show, that I can remember.

Recognizable voices popped up now and then, but no athlete had appeared until Magic Johnson on October 17, 1991, five episodes into the third season. (Exactly three weeks later, Johnson held a press conference to announce he was HIV-positive and would immediately retire from the NBA.)

Now it was using nine guests, some of whom were obvious baseball Hall of Famers. The end result was not only an iconic piece of pop culture but a loving satire of baseball that looks downright prescient today, here on the other side of the Mitchell Report. Our heroes got drunk in bars, ingested odd substances because they were told to, and mindlessly clucked like diseased poultry. "Homer at the Bat" felt vaguely forbidden, like an animated addendum to Ball Four. This was the side of the sport we never saw.

We couldn't pull our eyes away then. We still can't.

* * *

Despite all the planning and prep, "Homer at the Bat" wasn't easy to put together. Of the players with guest-starring roles, only the Dodgers' Darryl Strawberry and Mike Scioscia were local. The script was pretty much locked down by summer 1991, but the writers and producers had to wait throughout the season for players to swing through Los Angeles to play the Dodgers or the California Angels so they could record their lines.

Aside from the Yankees' twofer of Don Mattingly and Steve Sax, each athlete coming to the Fox studios was booked for a single voiceover session, which often got cramped when friends and family tagged along. Ken Griffey Jr., then 21 and easing into his third season in the majors, showed up in early August with his father and Mariners teammate, who was a few months from retirement. (In the show's DVD commentary, showrunner Mike Reiss recalls Griffey Jr. laboring through his lines and getting increasingly upset. He "looked like he was going to beat the crap out of me," Reiss says.)

St. Louis Cardinals shortstop Ozzie Smith stopped by in early September with his Bart-impersonating son Nikko, who himself wound up on Fox television 14 years later as an *American Idol* finalist. "I knew he was a *Simpsons* fan and had the Bart thing down pretty good," Smith told me, "but I didn't know he could do *anything* like that." Smith also made sure to work through his script beforehand, unlike his peeved centerfielder. "I worked on those lines, even though there wasn't really a whole lot of them," he says. "I just wanted to get the inflections in the right place."

Steve Sax, who retired three years after "Homer at the Bat" and did time as a financial adviser before becoming a life coach and motivational speaker, acknowledges a sizable debt to the show. (The writing staff's early preference for second base was Chicago's Ryne Sandberg.) "Sometimes, fans would yell, 'Hey, how's Homer?'" Sax told me. "I know they weren't talking about me hitting home runs, but it was a lot better than the stuff I used to hear."

Before *The Simpsons*, Sax was best known for a much-publicized case of the fielding yips that had dogged him throughout the '80s. His brief TV fame seemed to remove that period of his 14-year career from fans' minds. "Today, I still get people that ask me, 'What was it like to be on *The Simpsons*?' not, 'What was it like to face Nolan Ryan?'" (Actually, it's a legit question. Sax hit .265 lifetime against the Express. In their first matchup in April 1982, the rookie went 2-for-4 with a RBI triple. So, please, the next time you pass Steve Sax on the streets of Sacramento, ask him about Nolan Ryan.)

Sax's affability at the recording session also stuck with some members of the staff, with one later admitting (half-jokingly, maybe) that the "closest I ever came to falling in love with a man was Steve Sax. He was so handsome, so sweet."

Showrunner Al Jean has said the players who committed were more than happy to do the show. Well, *almost* of all of them. "They were all really nice," Jean said on the DVD commentary, "except for one whose name rhymes with Manseco."

* * *

Aside from the logistics of recording nine separate guest roles, plot lines had to be rewritten on the fly. Jose Canseco's scene originally called for him and Mrs. Krabappel to engage in *Bull Durham*-inspired extramarital shenanigans. Canseco's wife rejected the scene, and the staff had to do a last-minute Saturday afternoon rewrite when Oakland came south on a mid-August road trip.

Instead of Lothario, Canseco got to play hero, rushing into a woman's burning house to rescue her baby, then cat, followed by a player piano, washer, dryer, couch and recliner combo, high chair, TV, rug, kitchen table and chairs, lamp, and grandfather clock. Requesting the new sequence turned out to be the wiser move. Canseco and his wife had nearly divorced earlier that year before reconciling, and a week before "Homer at the Bat" aired, Canseco was arrested by Miami police for chasing down and ramming his wife's BMW twice with his red Porsche at 4:30 a.m. After the chase ended, he allegedly got out of his car, came over to his wife's driver-side window, and spit on it.

The Don Mattingly of "Homer at the Bat" hit even closer to the mark. In August 1991, Yankees management ordered the team captain to cut his hair shorter. He refused, was benched by manager Stump Merrill, and fined $250, including $100 for every subsequent day that he didn't cut his hair. "I'm overwhelmed by the pettiness of it," Mattingly told reporters. "To me, long hair is down my back, touching my collar. I don't feel my hair is messy."

Six months later, when "Homer at the Bat" aired, Mattingly's storyline centered around Mr. Burns's insane interpretation of his first baseman's "sideburns." Mattingly is booted from the team, muttering as he walks away, "I still like him better than Steinbrenner."

Most fans assumed that the show had cribbed from real-life events. In fact, Mr. Burns's sociopathic infatuation with sideburns was inspired by showrunner Al Jean's grandfather, who owned a hardware store in the '70s and would constantly berate his employees for their excessive follicular growth. Mattingly had recorded his dialogue a full month before his dustup with the Yankees.

Wade Boggs, who would labor through the worst year of his Hall of Fame career in 1992, was supposed to engage in a belching contest with Barney. As a player, Boggs was known for (among other pursuits) indulging in a bit o' drink from time to time; lore has it that he once drank dozens of beers during a team flight. Boggs tried to play down the story during a 2005 appearance on *Pardon the Interruption*—"It was a few Miller Lites," he claimed—but his occasional forays into boozy karaoke give the legend at least a little plausibility. For reasons now lost to history, the belching contest was scrapped in favor of a beer-fueled argument over who was England's greatest prime minister.

Still, rewriting plot lines was simple compared with getting the look of the players correct. The show's artists had never before had to tackle such a wide range of new faces on their animation cels. The show's biggest guest star to that point, Michael Jackson, posed no such challenge, as he voiced a morbidly obese white man. Matt Groening later said that "caricaturing real, living people" was the toughest challenge at the time, but they pulled it off, nailing features like Clemens's frat-boy spike, Strawberry's kiss-ass grin, and Canseco's chemistry-experiment-gone-wrong physique.

Beyond these aesthetic and creative challenges, *The Simpsons* were in the midst of fighting off a ginned-up national outrage over the show. A backlash was on. Retailers became saturated with growing piles of *Simpsons* merchandise, and some licensing deals were abruptly dropped. Elementary schools from Ohio to Orange County started banning Bart Simpson T-shirts that had been deemed offensive. The show even became a point of contention during the 1992 presidential election. George H.W. Bush, struggling to boost his bona fides with conservatives, took the stage at the annual convention of National Religious Broadcasters on January 27, three weeks before "Homer at the Bat" aired.

Bush ran through the usual Republican talking points, emphasizing "sanctity of life," working hard, sacrifice, and so forth. He then pivoted and started hammering nameless folks who would promote injustice and incivility.

"I speak of decency, the moral courage to say what is right and condemn what is wrong," Bush said. "And we need a nation closer to *The Waltons* than *The Simpsons*." The partisan crowd inside the Sheraton Washington Hotel roared with laughter, but it was priceless publicity that put the show square in the national conversation.

Bush, meanwhile, repeated the shot in August at the Republican National Convention. This time, it backfired. Though the next scheduled episode was a repeat, the *Simpsons* staff cobbled together a new show open in just three days. In it, the family gathers around the TV to watch Bush's address, and Bart wryly observes how they're just like the Waltons: "We're praying for an end to the Depression, too."

Bush really should've picked his battles more carefully. His wife was criticized in 1990 for calling the show "the dumbest thing I had ever seen." In return, "Marge Simpson" wrote her a letter in reply, explaining how she was deeply hurt by the comments. The situation was put to rest with the First Lady, amazingly, writing a letter back to the fictional TV mom, apologizing for her "loose tongue." It's hard to fathom now, two decades later, with the show ensconced in a family-hour time slot, but *The Simpsons* was once dangerous.

* * *

"Homer at the Bat" was not remotely close to what you might consider a typical *Simpsons* episode. You have Chief Wiggum (sounding more like a Edward G. Robinson rip-off than a fully formed character) acting responsibly, ordering his team to stop shooting in the air in post-home run celebration. Ralph, of all people, outwits Bart at picking players for sandlot baseball. Lisa, normally so moralistic and holier-than-thou, taunts Darryl Strawberry and brings him to tears. These weren't the conventional character patterns that had worked so well, and one could see why cast members Harry Shearer and Julie Kavner openly hated Swartzwelder's script.

Then there's the title of the episode, borrowed from "Casey at the Bat," the titular character being the ultimate symbol of baseball failure. In the end, Homer wins his team the pennant, albeit through inexplicable and unconventional means. But to see Homer excelling at *anything* flies in the face of the standard *Simpsons* script. In 22 minutes, he morphs from underdog to hero, and the contrast with the character we know from the rest of the series is more unnerving than welcome. The show was about inverting TV tropes. Homer's ineptitude was as vital to the show as Fred MacMurray's pipe was to *My Three Sons*. So when Homer smacks a bottom-of-the-ninth grand slam with his team down three runs, how the hell are we supposed to process that? Homer doesn't fail miserably; Bart doesn't quip his way out of trouble; Lisa doesn't roll her eyes in judgment. It was like watching some avant-garde, one-night-only experiment in ad hoc television.

Ratings might have had a little to do with that. Chasing *Cosby* was a priority for the Fox suits, and a splashy ensemble of ballplayers was likely to bring in big numbers. If the show had to tweak its own formula a little to do so, it was still young enough that it wouldn't look desperate; there were no sharks to jump, at that point. Die-hards might cringe a little, but in retrospect the episode looks a lot like a well-timed, what-the-hell swing for the fences.

And for all the "very special episode" feel of "Homer at the Bat," it certainly doesn't go easy on its targets. This wasn't Mel Allen doing bloopers on *This Week in Baseball*. Nor was this the game "designed to break your heart." This was a far more bemused look at the putative national pastime. Coaches' inspirational talk is often clichéd gibberish? You bet. Ballplayers sometimes drink too much and get into barroom trouble? Hell yeah, they do. Acute radiation poisoning, cranial gigantism, and pits of eternal darkness? Meet your 2011 Red Sox. And because there were actual, living ballplayers in the show, every manic twist carried the added fillip that we were looking in on something we weren't supposed to see, something funny and unauthorized. This was *Ball Four*'s demented stepson.

When the show aired in 1992, baseball was on the verge of a remarkable transformation. You could see hints of it in "Homer at the Bat." There is a meta-commentary on rising player salaries—Canseco's $50,000 game check to play softball would've been a raise, not a pay cut, as he claimed. Two years earlier, remember, the last of owner collusion cases had been settled, setting the stage for the 1994 strike. Two of the Springfield Nine, Canseco and Clemens, would be closely associated with PED use in years to come.

And maybe there's even a whiff of the jock-nerd culture war that would overtake baseball a decade later. With the bases loaded and the score tied 43-43 in the bottom of the ninth, Mr. Burns benches Strawberry, who has hit nine home runs in the game to this point. Burns explains to his increasingly incredulous star—and viewers at home, by extension—that he's pulling him for a right-handed batter, since a left-handed pitcher is on the mound. (Never mind that the Shelbyville pitcher is clearly shown holding the ball in his right hand just seconds before.) "It's called playing the percentages," Burns explains. "It's what smart managers do to win ballgames." The joke would come full circle in 2010, when the patron saint of sabermetrics, Bill James, appeared on a *Moneyball*-inspired episode and exuberantly took credit for making baseball "as much fun as doing your taxes."

"Homer at the Bat" was proof you could see baseball in all its silliness and still love the game. Even the stars who were both target and participant in the spoof remember the episode fondly. Ozzie Smith is generally regarded as the greatest defensive shortstop in baseball history. He has played in three World Series, and he's earned election to the Hall of Fame—and yet he still gets questions from fans about *The Simpsons* whenever he does a card show or some other event. He can't escape it, but with no hesitation, he reckons his tumble into the Springfield Mystery Spot to be one of the highlights of his career.

"It ranks right up there, and people are still talking about it today," Smith says. "*The Simpsons* are a part of Americana, so to be part of an episode that featured all of those ballplayers from a special time? I guess it'll go down in history."

This story originally appeared on Deadspin.com (February 20, 2012).

THE BURNS-SMITHERS QUESTION

By Bradley Woodrum

On February 20, 1992, America's most important cartoon sitcom, *The Simpsons*, aired an episode entitled "Homer at the Bat." The episode featured nine guest stars, all active major leaguers. It became the first *Simpsons* episode to win its time slot.

The fascinating cultural impact of that episode is a well-trod and well-worthy road. Let's instead turn our eyes to the ever-lasting ache of baseball fans, the itch that spawned sabermetrics and advanced baseball analytics: Let's construct impossible hypothetical situations between players divided by eons of baseball evolution.

Let's find out which was better: the Burns team or the Smithers team.

The Rosters

The episode begins with Homer rallying his coworkers to join a down-on-its-skill company softball team. Homer promises to provide a secret weapon, and a funny montage homaging and riffing on *The Natural* ensues. When Homer's lightning-bat-guided softball team begins winning, the company owner, Mr. Burns, and his loyal stooge, Mr. Smithers, place a $1 million wager on their team against a fellow aristocrat's company team.

Naturally, as is consistent with *literally* the roots of professional baseball, Mr. Burns immediately sets out to load the roster of his amateur softball team with professional baseball stars.

Just a few ticks before the seven-minute mark, Mr. Burns reveals his roster of ringers:

- SP Mordecai Brown
- C Gabby Street
- 1B Cap Anson
- 2B Nap Lajoie
- 3B Pie Traynor
- SS Honus Wagner
- LF Joe Jackson
- CF Harry Hooper
- RF Jim Creighton

The attentive reader will find it quite difficult to find statistics for Jim Creighton on FanGraphs or Baseball Reference. That's not because Creighton is an invented person, but because he played in the Amateur Era. He died three years before the end of the Civil War (at the age of 21). As Mr. Smithers notes: "In fact, your right fielder has been dead for 130 years."

Well, make it 152 years this October.

In a fit of frustration, Mr. Burns sends Smithers out to find a new, *living* team of ringers within the next 24 hours. This proves to be quite doable, perhaps as a byproduct of Springfield bordering Ohio, Nevada, Maine, and Kentucky as a rare feature of geographical serendipity. Smithers makes short work of assembling an updated roster:

- SP Roger Clemens
- C Mike Scioscia
- 1B Don Mattingly
- 2B Steve Sax
- 3B Wade Boggs
- SS Ozzie Smith
- LF Jose Canseco
- CF Ken Griffey Jr.
- RF Darryl Strawberry

We cannot help but ask—given that Mr. Burns offered a lineup including six Hall-of-Famers (plus the great Joe Jackson, who is/was HOF material, 'cept for all that Black Sox business) and Mr. Smithers offered a lineup of nine All-Stars and two Hall-of-Famers (plus Griffey, who will be soon, and Clemens, who should be, eventually)—which team was better?

You, like me, are no doubt making the obvious conclusions: Well, if one team had six Hall-of-Famers and the other has only twoish, then the Burns team is clearly better. All-Stars are great, but plenty flash-in-the-pan types can find themselves in the Midseason Classic. The Hall of Fame tends to be more choosy than friendly.

Looking at career wins above replacement (WAR) from FanGraphs, we can see the first obstacle:

Career WAR, Burns Anachronisms vs. Smithers Contemporaries			
Burns Anachronisms	WAR	Smithers Contemporaries	WAR
SP Mordecai Brown*	46.9	SP Roger Clemens	139.5
C Gabby Street	0.5	C Mike Scioscia	28.5
1B Cap Anson	91.2	1B Don Mattingly	40.7
2B Nap Lajoie	102.2	2B Steve Sax	22.6
3B Pie Traynor	37.8	3B Wade Boggs	88.3
SS Honus Wagner	138.1	SS Ozzie Smith	67.6
LF Joe Jackson	60.5	LF Jose Canseco	42.1
CF Harry Hooper	52.3	CF Ken Griffey Jr.	77.3
RF Jim Creighton	0.0	RF Darryl Strawberry	41.5
Total	529.5	Total	548.1

*RA9 Wins 70.7

"Three Finger" Brown's historical ability to beat his fielding independent pitching (FIP) numbers pushes his team's value just above that of the Smithers team. But these players aren't being called upon to play 10 seasons of baseball, just one all-important softball game. And since we've resurrected dead players, why not bring them back at their peaks?

Peak Season WAR, Burns Anachronisms vs. Smithers Contemporaries			
Burns Anachronisms	WAR	Smithers Contemporaries	WAR
SP Mordecai Brown*	6.9	SP Roger Clemens	10.8
C Gabby Street	1.7	C Mike Scioscia	5.5
1B Cap Anson	7.2	1B Don Mattingly	7.2
2B Nap Lajoie	9.4	2B Steve Sax	4.5
3B Pie Traynor	4.7	3B Wade Boggs	8.9
SS Honus Wagner	11.8	SS Ozzie Smith	6.7
LF Joe Jackson	9.3	LF Jose Canseco	7.6
CF Harry Hooper	4.6	CF Ken Griffey Jr.	9.7
RF Jim Creighton	0.0	RF Darryl Strawberry	6.5
Total	55.6	Total	67.4

*RA9 Wins 10.7

The Three-Finger bonus here doesn't push the Burns team far enough to catch the peak years of the Smithers All-Stars. The problem here, though, is that the Smithers team wasn't composed of dead players; they couldn't be revived at their peak ability. These were active players with a season just a few months away. In other words, we don't need projection systems to estimate how these guys would do in the year 1993. Which is unfortunate for them, because they didn't do well:

Avg WAR Vs 1993 WAR, Burns Anachronisms Vs. Smithers Contemporaries			
Burns Anachronisms	WAR/ season	Smithers Contemporaries	1993 WAR
SP Mordecai Brown*	3.0	SP Roger Clemens	4.1
C Gabby Street	0.1	C Mike Scioscia	0.0
1B Cap Anson	4.8	1B Don Mattingly	2.9
2B Nap Lajoie	5.9	2B Steve Sax	-0.3
3B Pie Traynor	2.7	3B Wade Boggs	3.3
SS Honus Wagner	7.1	SS Ozzie Smith	2.6
LF Joe Jackson	6.4	LF Jose Canseco	0.0
CF Harry Hooper	3.1	CF Ken Griffey Jr.	8.4
RF Jim Creighton	0.0	RF Darryl Strawberry	-1.0
Total	33.0	Total	20.0

*RA9 Wins 4.5

The Burns team jumps back into the lead! Even without Mordecai's ERA-whooping talents, the average (or prorated, in this instance) performance from the Burns team decimates what turns out to be a rather down year for all but the great Ken Griffey Jr. Yes, it's obviously not fair to compare a single season to an average of seasons, but since Mr. Burns does not give us a single season to give context to his expectations, we have to assume his roster was built on the general impressions left by these historic players. And since his players' careers don't all overlap, we have to either pick an arbitrary date or expect an average of their career performances.

The Context Problem

The astute reader may be thinking: "Why is Jim Creighton receiving 0 WAR in each of these comparisons?"

Other readers who possess the ability to read the minds of fellow internetters may be answering: "Because he had zero plate appearances in the majors, therefore 0 WAR. It's obvious!"

But it isn't so obvious. Attributing 0 WAR to Creighton is fine if we also attribute him zero plate appearances, but he's going to get at least four in this hypothetical game. And in those charts above, all the other position players are getting 600. Giving Creighton 0 WAR assumes a replacement-level performance, which is a problematic assumption.

The non-Hall-of-Famers on the Burns team, well, they frankly aren't that great. Jackson was a gift to humanity, yes, but Gabby Street was a "Feh" catcher with a brief career in the majors, and though Creighton may have been the best player of his era, he basically didn't play baseball. He essentially played four-sided cricket.

Which brings us to the problem of context. Let's say Mr. Burns splurged on a time machine. And after pumping the velocitator and levering the deceleratrix, he transported himself to the peak age of each of his players. These peak players, now competing against early Steroid Era players, how would they fare?

Steroids or nay, the physical and sport sciences have vastly improved training systems over the last century. So how good would Honus Wagner or Joe Jackson be if they just appeared in 1992 to face contemporary All-Stars?

"We don't know, obviously," says Dave Cameron, managing editor of FanGraphs, "but I think the reality is probably not very good. The players of yesteryear didn't have to face the same velocity; they didn't have to face the pitch types; they didn't have to face a lot of the things they would have to face today. I think if you took straight that player and that skill level and what he was used to facing in the [1920s] and put him in the [1990s], he probably wouldn't be very good."

The Steroid Era gets a bad rap, I think. In my humble opinion, the worst performance-enhancing blight in the history of baseball was the systematic rejection of African-American and non-white athletes through baseball's so-called "Golden Age." The fact that Jackie Robinson, age 27, eviscerated Triple-A pitching in 1946 and immediately became an MVP candidate in his first season in the major leagues; the fact that Satchel Paige, at age 41 and with no time spent in the minor leagues beforehand, became an above-average swingman and reliever; the fact that Irish players were denied starting positions for no reason other than their names suggests the pool of talent in the early years, the level of competition, was artificially suppressed.

Winning the WAR game is not sufficient when the key concept behind WAR—the replacement level—is not even close to equal. A team of Dan Johnson, Scott Moore, Matt Palmer, and a bevy of other Triple-A frequenters would theoretically obliterate a lineup of similar fringe-major-league talent from 1930.

"What might [Honus] Wagner have done in the 1979 American League, given a livelier ball but tougher competition?" Dick Cramer asked in the 1980 publication of SABR's *Baseball Research Journal* ("Average Batting Skill Through Major League History"). Cramer's research suggested Wagner's stellar 1908 season would have been merely great, not otherworldly, in 1979: "[Adjusting] Wagner's 1908 stats gives a 1979 BA of .292 and [SLG] of .551. (In 600 ABs, he would have, say 30 homers, 10 triples, 35 doubles). Wagner's stolen base crown and 10th place tie in walks translate directly to similar positions in the 1979 stats. That's impressive batting production for any shortstop, and a '1979 Honus Wagner' would doubtless be an All-Star Game starter!"

In 1908, Wagner had a filthy .354/.415/.542 slash and a 194 wRC+. Drop that to a .292/.353/.551 slash or thereabouts and indeed, we're still impressed. In Cramer's research, we are seeing the quality of league talent increasing by 0.1 percent per season in terms of the statistics he observed. If we wanted to get daring and suppose that talent build applied to linear weights hitting metrics too, we'd say Wagner could manage a 178 wRC+ or thereabouts if he had his 1908 season in 1993.

That's peak Wagner, his best offensive season. But it does not consider the veritable arms race (heehee) with respect to velocity and pitch types. Wagner faced the spitball, yes, but he did not face 90-mph pitches—and certainly no 100-mph pitches. The major-league skill level certainly increased during Wagner's 20-year career, but that came in such subtle increments that he—and those around him—were able to adjust relatively easily. Transporting him to the 1990s would give him baseball's equivalent of decompression sickness.

But if Burns has a time machine, why not bring a 23-year-old Wagner to 1989 and give him a few years to train up for the softball game. What then? Is baseball talent born or is it built? Is it nature or nurture?

"I think a lot of it is nurture, honestly," says Cameron. "If you give [the Burns players] time in the minor leagues, let them get used to facing that velocity in college or whatever, so that becomes their norm, where they're seeing 94 [mph] all the time instead of 86, and you give them video technology so they can do video scouting—I think the talent they had, if you nurtured it the way current players have, they would still be all-time greats."

For the sake of projection simplicity—and in-game competitiveness—let's say that Burns brings his roster to the present day and trains them up in modern baseball, seasoning them in the minors for a year or two. That would theoretically leave only the Cramer adjustment—the 0.1 percent per year penalty in hitting ability—and some guesswork on the defensive abilities. (We're also assuming that the contemporary players don't fall victim to the many misfortunes they do in the episode, but you probably already guessed that.)

But Jim Creighton. What do we do with the league's first star? Creighton is a fascinating guy. He is often believed to be the first professional baseball player —remember when I mentioned Burns' hiring of ringers being consistent with the roots of pro ball? When the Brooklyn Excelsiors paid him to join their roster in 1859, the world of baseball was strictly and proudly amateur. Creighton, in truth, was the original ringer.

He was also one of the first to live out the old baseball maxim: "If you aren't cheating, you aren't trying." But Creighton's game was not Mattingly's or Sax's game. Creighton—both the game's best pitcher and hitter—played ball in an era where it was illegal to bend the wrist when pitching (though he was accused of doing exactly that), and his hitting stance and motion—the very oddity that ultimately killed him — was more in line with cricket techniques than anything like a baseball hitter's swing.

Just listen to the fatal batting motion John Thorn describes: "Creighton had swung so mighty a blow—in the manner of the day, with hands separated on the bat, little or no turn of the wrists, and incredible torque applied by the twisting motion of the upper body—that it was reported he ruptured his bladder."

Imagine that action: Stiff wrists and hands separated. Consider this hit from Sachin Tendulkar, famed Indian batsman, during his epic 175-run game. (No, I don't know what that means either.)

[see Sachin's batting in a video that accompanies the original version of this article on Hardball Times at: http://www.hardballtimes.com/the-burns-smithers-question/]

Creighton's swing action definitely fits the occasional cricket swing or maybe a baseball drop bunt. A year or two might simply not be enough time to train Jim Creighton to be a pro player.

The Pitching Conundrum

Let's address that pachyderm in the office: Wasn't this a slow pitch softball team? Wouldn't Mordecai Brown's famous sinker not sink? Wouldn't Roger Clemens' famous fastball not fastball? Well, we know from the practice footage that Roger Clemens is throwing hard. But is it underhand?

Footage shows Clemens throws so hard his pitch rips Homer's Wonderbat asunder. And, earlier in the episode when playing against the police team, we clearly see an underhand fast pitch.

So they were playing against hard pitches, but were they overhand pitches? We can see from Darryl Strawberry's home run during the critical game, the opposing team was definitely pitching underhand, slow pitch.

But then there's this problem in the penultimate scene: While receiving a delightfully over-complicated signal from Mr. Burns, our hero—Homer Simpson—gets pegged in the face bone with what appears to be a fast, quite linear pitch.

So are they throwing underhand or overhand? Is it slow pitch or fast? Since when does a slow pitch league award bases on a HBP? The Amateur Softball Association (ASA) 2014 rulebook has only one mention of HBP from what I can tell (Rule 7, Section 5F) which says it's a ball, but only for specific, slow-pitch league types. There are two possibilities for this game-ending HBP to make sense: (a) The league is indeed a (underhand) fast pitch league, or (b) the league has a special HBP rule. Given there are far more underhand fast pitch deliveries early and late in the episode, we have to assume this is a fast pitch league, so that could mean good things for our impressive pitchers.

Would Brown and Clemens have an advantage over Joe Beerleague when it comes to underhand pitching? As a veteran of many a terrible softball team, I can confirm there is a special skill necessary to be an accurate and effective slow-pitch pitcher, much less a fast-pitch pitcher.

Those with less experience in slow pitch may not realize: (a) The distance from mound to plate is a fairly incredible distance to underhand a ball—it's probably the furthest one would ever choose to underhand toss anything—and (b) just as with baseball, pitchers employ a variety of grips and wrist actions to add spin to the ball. Obviously, the effect is muted with slow-pitch rules, but good pitchers will still have a variety of pitch types—maybe even a knuckleball.

What we need to know is whether Clemens and Brown could somehow translate their pitching ability to softball games. Brown was originally a third baseman; maybe there's reason to think he could field his position well. And maybe given the physical oddity of his right hand, he could manage some unusual spin and drop on his pitches. Given the footage in the episode, we can also assume Clemens' arm strength translated in hard, accurate underhand throwing.

Believe no illusions, though. The methods of underhand and overhand pitching are quite different. Since we know these players had some serious training time, I think it's reasonable these Hall of Fame-quality pitchers could learn how to pitch effectively with the new motion.

Management

The final component of these teams is their managers. Presumably, Burns would manage the time machine team, Smithers the living team. What do we know about these managers? Well, Burns uses dated workout mechanisms (ab jigglers, rowing machines, steam boxes, and so on); he has little grasp on modern baseball (as demonstrated by his roster); and has a penchant for bunting.

And while he didn't know modern players, when he actually sat down to fill out his lineup full of them, he put his best hitter sixth in the order.

Yes, it's a team full of great players, but Griffey has to be higher than sixth—certainly higher than a later-career Don Mattingly. Moreover, Burns pushes a toxic brain tonic on his players, and he pinch-hit for Darryl Strawberry! He's aggressive, eager to win, and thoroughly incompetent.

We don't know much about Smithers' managerial preferences. He is a go-getter—having signed nine star baseball players in just 24 hours—but without any real responsibilities, he does not show any particular sports leadership abilities. We'll have to assume his managerial abilities are just average. He's going to set his lineup according to batting average, steals and home runs.

The Simulation

I thought about a dozen different ways to do this. I thought about using Markov chains, running simulations through different websites, making custom OOTP rosters, and ultimately decided on something uncommon. Instead of running these lineups through 100 simulated games, I would do one game. Just one game. And in the spirit of Dungeons and Dragons, I would let chance decide the master strokes and the dungeon master (me, in this instance) decide the details.

The methodology will be simple: For the Burns team, I will take career average PA result rates (walk percentage, singles percentage, etc.) and then use a simple Cramer 0.1 percent adjustment (as discussed above). I will then take the PA rates for each of the Smithers players, using their 1992 statistics. Why 1992? Because I want to give them a chance, and because this game theoretically took place close enough to that season that they would still be near that ability level.

Then, using a random number generator, I will calculate the results of their PAs and construct a box score. Once a pitcher has gone through the lineup five times, he will tire and be replaced with a reliever (Jim Creighton for the Burns team; Jose Canseco for the Smithers team—because Jose actually pitched an inning in 1993). The reliever will be less effective than the starter (Creighton will be 30 percent worse than Brown; Jose will be 50 percent worse than Clemens—because Creighton actually was a pitcher and Jose was not). Lastly, and most importantly, Homer Simpson will be on the bench for the Smithers team, and Otto Neu will be on the bench for the Burns team. They'll enter the game in right field as a double switch if/when the starting pitcher leaves. Creighton will be a league average hitter. And because this is softball, I'm reducing the odds of an out by 10 percent for every player (encouraging offensive production), and no one will hit into double plays (because the bases are closer together).

What follows here is the much anticipated, much preambled Burns-Smithers game.

Top of the First Inning

Joe Jackson walks to the plate. He taps clay off his shoes with his bat, Black Betsy. He winks at the umpire and the fans squirm uncomfortably in their seats. The bat is 48 ounces, 36 inches long, and not a regulation softball bat.

Clemens winds and hurls, and Jackson smacks a hard liner at Griffey, deep in center field. Nap Lajoie's up second, but bounces and out back to the pitcher. Cap Anson steps to the plate. He looks at Ozzie Smith at short, at Griffey in center and Strawberry in right, and mutters something under his curled mustache. He ropes a hard single to right, and then Honus Wagner knocks a single to left.

Impressed with his sheer lack of sideburns, Mr. Burns has Gabby Street batting No. 5. Street waggles his bat, readies himself, and then whiffs on three straight pitches. The threat is ended, and the game is on.

Bottom of the Third Inning

After mustering next to nothing through the first two innings, the Smithers Contemporaries send No. 9 hitter Roger Clemens to the plate. Clemens looks out of his element with a bat in his hand, but he manages to drop a duck-snort single front of Jackson in left. Ozzie Smith comes to the plate and chops an infield single to Wagner's right. Wagner kicks the dirt and slings his barely-a-glove on the ground, saying, "I was too bum on that last play."

Steve Sax pops out to Gabby Street and the No. 3 hitter, Griffey, sends a loud, echoing out to Creighton in right field. Canseco walks to the plate after having walked in the second inning. "Three Finger" Brown squints in at Gabby, then slings a dipping sinker that doesn't dip enough. Canseco rips the ball over Pie Traynor's head for a two-run double. Contemporaries fans go wild, but Canseco's teammates appeared reserved. Don Mattingly then dunks an RBI single into center field, and the Contemp's lead 3-0 after three innings.

Top of the Fifth Inning

Center fielder Harry Hooper leads off with a ground ball single through the right side of the infield. Creighton comes up, but leaves the bat on his shoulder as he watches a complicated sign from Mr. Burns. When the sign has finished, Creighton has already drawn ball four.

Mordecai Brown bunts the runners into scoring position, then Jackson, Lajoie, and Anson rip back-to-back-to-back singles—small-ball style. The away team fans raise their voices in hope as the Burns Anachronisms tie the game 3-3.

Bottom of the Seventh Inning

The Contemporaries start the seventh with Clemens leading off. Knowing that Simpson has a better chance at hitting a home run, Smithers takes a gamble and sends the All-Star from Sector 7G to the plate. But without his Wonderbat, Homer finds himself outmatched against the three-digit hurler from Indiana.

The lineup wraps around and Ozzie Smith cracks a single to right, followed by a Sax single to left. With runners on the corners, Griffey's bad day continues: He pops out to Lajoie—infield fly rule—to mount his outing to an 0-for-4 showing.

Canseco leans into a borderline pitch, and suddenly the bases are loaded, two outs, bottom of the seventh. And Donny at the bat.

Mattingly works a 3-2 count, then smashes the ball hard! It disappears into the blue Springfield sky, then reappears through the clouds. The fans hold their breath. Joe Jackson is sprinting to the left field wall. Just the sounds of his footfalls in the crisp, green grass—no talking, no breathing, just Jackson in a dead sprint.

He scales the wall. He reaches up. He stretches his glove high over his head.

"Batter out!"

Top of the Eighth Inning

With Clemens out of the game, the Contemporaries turn to Canseco. He looks athletic enough to control the mound, but his pitches come in slow, looping arcs—not unlike the Shelbyville pitching staff.

Street and Traynor start the inning with back-to-back walks. Smithers starts looking around the field for another pitcher. Strawberry makes eye contact, but shakes his head.

It's Canseco or bust at this point.

Harry Hooper receives the three-fold, double-reverse, secret Saturday pie handshake signal from Mr. Burns. It means he needs to bunt. Hooper drops a beauty—the ball chops hard in front of the plate, and by the time Scioscia collects it, he can go only to first.

One out, two runners in scoring position. Creighton eases up to the dish. "Bowl one down the center, if you've the gumption," he says. Canseco assumes it was French-Canadian or some such.

A fastball off the corner. "Throw a drop-ball or changepiece, and I'll smack it clear to Yonkers and back," Creighton taunts.

Scioscia gives Canseco the sign: Fastball, outside. Canseco throws a slider. It doesn't slide enough. Creighton lasers the ball into center field and snaps his belt in one great, violent motion. Two runs score. The Anachronisms fans are throwing their derbies and bonnets into the air.

Burns calls Mordecai Brown to the dugout as the crowd settles to a murmur.

"I'm bringing in the big guns," Mr. Burns says. He waves to Otto Neu.

Neu has no discernable face. You know the type. He stands so-and-so tall and weighs about you guessed it. Mordecai looks Neu up and down and doesn't know what he sees. Mordecai remarks to Joe Jackson in the on-deck circle, "He can't possibly be a better hitter than me."

But Neu strides to the plate and settles into the right-handed batter's box. A bloop single to right! Runners on the corners!

Joe Jackson tips his cap to Neu, then hits a lazy fly to right. Lajoie grounds out to Ozzie at short, and the game is 5-3, heading into the bottom half.

Bottom of the Eighth Inning

Creighton is on the mound. Otto Neu is standing in right field, looking vaguely like a blur of obscurity. Creighton fires his last warmup throw, and it's obvious to Boggs, the inning's first hitter, that they've gone from Mordecai's mid-80s fastballs to a high-70s fastball, with no secondary offerings.

Boggs redistributes the first pitch into right center for a leadoff double. The Contemporaries fans are on their feet, chanting "Darryl! Darryl!" but in a supportive way.

Strawberry swings at an inside fastball and grunts "Beane!" as he fires a single into right field. Otto Neu boots the ball, and Boggs scores on a trot. The Anachronisms' lead is down to 5-4.

"Mikey-Mikey, *clap-clap, clapclapclap*!"

The home crowd is ready for a miracle. Scioscia hits a high chopper to third base. Traynor moves to his left, but the ball squirts just past those weird little gloves they used to play with. Runners on the corners!

Simpson comes up for his second at-bat. Creighton is stretching and rubbing his stomach. The first pitch is outside, but Homer swings anyway. A deep fly to right, and the game is tied, 5-5!

Bottom of the Ninth Inning

It wouldn't be on TV if it didn't come to the bottom of the ninth, or so my spreadsheet apparently thinks.

The Anachronisms went quietly in the top half, but now Griffey is looking to snap his 0-fer with a leadoff hit. He lines a single off Lajoie's glove and he's got the inning started!

Canseco dumps a weak single into left, but a strong throw from Jackson keeps Griffey at second. Creighton appears to be struggling on the mound.

Mattingly chops a grounder up the middle and Wagner has to eat it for an infield single. Boggs steps to the plate and promptly lines the ball hard, but right at Honus, who collects it for an easy out.

The crowd is chanting "Darryl! Darryl!" again. He works the count to 3-1 and the fans of both teams are on their feet. A walk wins it.

Jim Creighton readies himself. He twirls a fastball, and it's down the middle. Strawberry rockets the ball into deep left-center. It bounds hard on the grass and pops over the fence — ground-rule double! Game over!

Smithers disappears into the clubhouse as Mr. Burns hurls his cap at the infield. He's jawing with the umpire as the Contemporaries mob Strawberry between first and second. It's final in Springfield: The Smithers Contemporaries 6, the Burns Anachronisms 5.

Thanks for coming out to the ballpark.

Box Scores

Burns Anachronisms										
Away	*1st*	*2nd*	*3rd*	*4th*	*5th*	*6th*	*7th*	*8th*	*9th*	*FINAL*
Joe Jackson	OUT		OUT		1B	OUT		OUT		1/5
Nap Lajoie	OUT		OUT		1B		OUT	OUT		1/5
Cap Anson	1B			OUT	1B		OUT		OUT	2/5
Honus Wagner	1B		2B	OUT		OUT		OUT		2/5 with 2B
Gabby Street	OUT			OUT	OUT			BB	OUT	0/4 with BB
Pie Traynor		OUT		OUT		OUT		BB		1/3 with BB
Harry Hooper		OUT			1B	BB		OUT		1/3 with BB
Jim Creighton		OUT			BB	OUT		1B		1/3 with BB
Mordecai Brown			OUT		OUT	BB		n/a		0/2 with BB
PH — Otto Neu								1B		1/1
RUNS	0	0	0	0	3	0	0	2	0	5

Smithers Contemporaries										
Home	*1st*	*2nd*	*3rd*	*4th*	*5th*	*6th*	*7th*	*8th*	*9th*	*FINAL*
Ozzie Smith	OUT		1B	OUT			1B	OUT		2/5
Steve Sax	OUT		OUT		OUT		1B	OUT		1/5
Ken Griffey Jr.	OUT		OUT		OUT		OUT		1B	1/5
Jose Canseco		BB	2B		OUT		HBP		1B	2/3 with 2B
Don Mattingly		OUT	1B			OUT	OUT		1B	2/4
Wade Boggs		OUT	OUT			OUT		2B	OUT	1/5 with 2B
Darryl Strawberry		BB		1B		1B		1B	2B	4/4 with 2B
Mike Scioscia		OUT		OUT		OUT		1B		1/4
Roger Clemens			1B	OUT			n/a	n/a		1/2
Homer Simpson								OUT	OUT	0/2
RUNS	0	0	3	0	0	0	0	2	1	6

This article originally appeared on March 31, 2014 on The Hardball Times, and is offered here with permission. The original article can be found at this address: http://www.hardballtimes.com/the-burns-smithers-question/ along with accompanying illustrations which, lacking permission from *The Simpsons*, we prefer not to print here.

WADE BOGGS

By Steve West

"That kid's got a hell of a stance! Everything's perfect! He ought to become a great hitter!" Legend has it that Ted Williams uttered these words while critiquing a photo of an 18-month-old boy.[1] He was absolutely right; that boy, Wade Boggs, went on to win several batting titles on his way to becoming one of the best hitters of all time in a Hall of Fame career.

Winfield "Win" Boggs was a Marine during World War II, and met Susan Graham, a mail-plane pilot, in 1945, marrying her just two weeks later. Win stayed in the military, serving as a pilot in the Air Force during the Korean War and moving his family around as military people often do. The couple had a son, Wayne, and daughter, Ann, and their third child, Wade Anthony Boggs, was born in Omaha, Nebraska, on June 15, 1958.

Wade loved the idea of being in a military family and having a regimented routine every day. This is something that would carry over to his entire baseball career, in which he would become known for doing set things at set times every day before a game.

Wade began playing baseball in Little League, receiving instruction from his father and several coaches. Win Boggs had retired from the military in 1967, and moved the family to Tampa, Florida, where he opened a fishing camp. At Henry B. Plant High School in Tampa, Wade played baseball and football. After he hit .522 as a junior, scouts began watching him play, and he switched from quarterback to kicker on the football team to avoid injury. He was good enough to become All-State in football and get a scholarship offer from the University of South Carolina.

In baseball Boggs had earned a reputation as a hitter, and pitchers wouldn't throw strikes to him. When he tried to hit balls out of the strike zone he struggled, until his father got him the book *The Science of Hitting* by Ted Williams. After reading the book he realized he had lost some of his patience at the plate, and took Williams's advice about not swinging at pitches out of the strike zone.[2] When this forced pitchers to throw strikes he hit everything, finishing the season hitting .485.

Scouts had seen Boggs struggle, and even when he hit they weren't sure if he had the necessary talent to play professional baseball. He didn't have much speed or range, and was rated poorly in most areas. The Major League Scouting Bureau called him a nonprospect. One scout wrote, "needs a lot of help with bat," and thought it would take more money than he was worth to persuade him to turn down the football scholarship. But that scout hadn't seen the drive that Boggs had to play baseball. Boston Red Sox scout George Digby had seen him play, and persuaded the team to select Boggs in the seventh round of the 1976 amateur draft. When the Red Sox offered $7,500, Boggs's father said "You're going to have to make a choice, son, college ball or pro ball."[3] An easy choice for the young baseball fan, Boggs signed and went to the minor leagues.

Boggs was assigned to Elmira (New York) of the Class-A (rookie season) New York-Penn League, where he hit .263 and was below team average in almost every category. But the Red Sox saw enough in him to promote him to Winston-Salem of the Class-A Carolina League in 1977. Boggs proceeded to hit .332 that year, and showed an excellent batting eye by walking much more often than he struck out, something he would do every year until he was 40 years old.

Boggs still moved slowly through the Red Sox system. He was slow and he didn't have much power; all he was showing was that batting average and the ability to earn bases on balls. "I was told in the minor leagues that I'll never play third in the big leagues. That I don't hit for power so I'm not going to play in the big leagues. I'm not fast enough. I was told so many different things."[4] What he did have was drive. "The only thing I ever wanted to do was play professional baseball and in the minors I was getting paid to play so I didn't get discouraged."[5]

He spent the 1978 and 1979 seasons at Bristol (Connecticut) of the Double-A Eastern League, followed by the 1980 and 1981 seasons at Pawtucket in the Triple-A International League. An event in baseball history that Boggs played in was the longest-ever professional baseball game, a 33-inning affair in 1981 between the Pawtucket Red Sox and the Rochester Red Wings that began on April 18 and, after being suspended in the wee hours of Easter morning, was finished on June 23. "When I doubled in the tying run in the 21st inning, I didn't know if the guys wanted to hug me or slug me," he said.[6] In 1981 he led the International League in hitting with a .335 average, and still didn't get called up in September. On the last day of the season, his manager, Joe Morgan, suggested that Boggs play first base in winter ball. He went to Puerto Rico to play, but because of injuries to others he ended up playing third base again. This time he hit .374, and the Red Sox couldn't ignore him any longer, adding him to the 40-man roster.

Boggs knew Debbie Bertucelli in high school, and they began dating. Shortly after his debut in the minor leagues he proposed, and they were married in December 1976. Two years later they had a daughter, Meagann, and eight years later a son, Brett (named for George Brett).

In 1982 Boggs was trapped behind reigning American League batting champion Carney Lansford, the Red Sox third baseman, but he had a good spring and manager Ralph Houk kept him as a utility infielder. It took a couple of extra days due to rainouts, but he made his major-league debut in the second game of a doubleheader at Baltimore on April 10, 1982. Boggs played first base and hit ninth, and didn't show anything against Orioles starter Dennis Martinez or reliever Sammy Stewart. "I hit four dribblers in the infield, all off changeups," he said.[7] He had a pinch-hit flyout a few days later, then sat for almost two weeks before again playing first base and batting ninth in the first game of a twi-night doubleheader in Chicago. This time, after a couple more groundouts, he came up and led off the eighth inning with a single off White Sox starting pitcher Richard Dotson. Boggs eventually came round to score, on Jim Rice's single, what proved to be the winning run in a 3-2 game.

Before the June 23 night game versus Detroit, and hitting only .258, Boggs had played in just 15 of the team's first 66 games. During that evening, Lansford tried for an inside-the-park home run, and suffered a severe ankle sprain in a collision with Tigers catcher Lance Parrish. Coming off the bench to replace Lansford, Boggs was hitless in two at-bats. his batting average dropping to .242. Houk said, "We'll find out about Boggs,"[8] and Boggs took the opportunity with both hands, playing in 89 of the team's last 96 games, hitting .358 while filling in for Lansford and playing first base when Carney returned a month later. That was enough to convince the Red Sox that he could do the job, and they traded Lansford to the Oakland Athletics after the season, giving Boggs the third-base job full-time. He would keep the job for the next 10 years.

Boggs finished a distant third behind Cal Ripken Jr. and Kent Hrbek for the American League Rookie of the Year award. But he knew he would be starting in the major leagues, and he would take the opportunity he had been given.

The comfort of being set as the everyday third baseman in 1983 gave Boggs a great deal of confidence. He spent the first month primarily in the leadoff position for the Red Sox, moved to fifth in the order for a couple of months, and spent the second half of the year hitting second. These moves never fazed him; he hit wherever he was put. Boggs was 6-feet-2 and weighed 190 pounds. He threw right-handed, but was a left-handed batter. He hit .397 in Fenway Park, hitting to the opposite field and taking advantage of the Green Monster, and hit .321 everywhere else. Boggs was consistent no matter what happened, and he was rewarded by comfortably winning his first American League batting title with a .361 average, which was 22 points better than runner-up Rod Carew (.349) of the California Angels. Boggs's .444 on-base percentage led both leagues.

He followed up in 1984 by hitting .325, which placed him third in the American League, then began a streak of four batting titles in a row, 1985 through 1988. Consistency was again the watchword, as in those four seasons Boggs's highest average was .368 and lowest was .357. His 240 hits in 1985 were the most in a major-league season since 1930. He led all of baseball in on-base percentage for five years in a row, through 1989. In 1985 he got his first of 12 consecutive All-Star selections, as the league recognized his hitting talent.

Boggs hit 24 home runs in 1987, more than double his total of any other years, seeming to indicate that he had more power potential than he usually employed, focused as he was on getting base hits and getting on base.

For all his efforts, and before Boggs arrived in Boston, the Red Sox had meandered around the middle or bottom of the AL East Division since 1980, until it all came together in 1986. Pitcher Roger Clemens came into his own, starting 14-0 as the Red Sox climbed to the top of the division. On May 14 they moved into a tie for first place in the division, and two days later they had the lead by themselves and never relinquished it for the rest of the season.

But a terrible disruption to the season occurred for Boggs on June 17, when his mother was killed by the driver of a cement truck who ran a red light. That driver was on work release from jail, and wasn't

Wade Boggs, five-time AL batting champ for the Boston Red Sox.

supposed to be there, and got off with a charge of running a red light. Boggs was devastated. It took him years to let the incident go.[9]

Boggs returned to baseball six days after his mother's death, and baseball gave him a relief from it. He had his routines, embracing everything he did on game day, and that helped keep him from thinking about his mother. He resumed hitting, the Red Sox kept winning, and they ended up back in the postseason for the first time since losing the 1975 World Series. A tough best-of-seven American League Championship Series with the California Angels ensued, the Red Sox trailing three games to one before rallying to win three in a row. Boggs hit just .233 in the series.

In the 1986 World Series, the Red Sox faced the New York Mets. Boggs fared a little better, hitting .290, but was not much of a factor until the 10th inning in Game Six, when he doubled and later scored to

Boggs in pinstripes

give the Red Sox a 5-3 lead. But in perhaps the most famous ending to a World Series game ever, Boggs was playing third base when the ball was hit to Bill Buckner, and watched it travel through his legs to lose the game. Boggs said, "The ball could've easily been hit to me and gone through my legs. Nobody is blaming anybody. It's fate."[10]

In Game Seven Boggs singled with two outs in the second inning to push the Red Sox to a 3-0 lead. But they couldn't hold the lead and the Mets took over in the late innings and won the World Series. Boggs sat in the dugout and cried, the world thinking he was crying because his team had lost. But Boggs later said that wasn't the case, that he had buried himself in baseball to forget about his mother's death, and now that baseball was over his mother had come flooding back in. "When it was over, I was thinking, 'Now I've got to go home and when I walk in the house, she's not going to be there.'"[11]

Boggs went home and commiserated with his father. Wade had decided that he would retire from baseball, because he wanted to spend more time with his family. Win persuaded him to carry on in baseball. "I told him life goes on, that he had to face up to his loss," Win said.[12]

Boggs returned to baseball and the Red Sox, and resumed hitting. He hit over .300 every year from 1982 to 1991, and in 1988 and 1990 the Red Sox won the AL East again, but both times they were swept by Oakland in the ALCS. Boggs hit .385 and .438 in the two series, but that wasn't enough to get his team to a single win.

Scandal began for the Boggs family in 1988, when it was revealed that Wade had a four-year affair with a woman named Margo Adams. She had sued him for millions of dollars in a palimony lawsuit, and began telling her story to anyone who would listen, including *Penthouse* magazine and the Phil Donahue daytime television show. She said she had traveled with Boggs on Red Sox road trips, and that the whole team knew about her. Any time he would be away from home he would try to arrange for her to be there; even when he left spring training (with permission) for a couple of days to record his voice for an episode of the TV show *The Simpsons*, he took her with him to Los Angeles.

As the scandal broke around the team, Boggs told his wife, Debbie, everything. It was his honesty that made her want them to stay together. "I never had that feeling (of wanting to leave him) because of the way Wade handled it. We had an agreement that he would tell me everything." The lawsuit was settled out of court and Boggs moved on, but to this day his name is always entwined with that of Adams.

In 1992 everything changed for Boggs. It was the worst year of his career; he hit only .259. He later blamed the Red Sox front office, saying that they had betrayed him in contract negotiations. He had a promise from Jean Yawkey, the Red Sox owner, for a five-year contract, because she wanted him to follow in the footsteps of Ted Williams and Carl

Yastrzemski as career-long Red Sox legends. But she died before the contract was signed, and when Boggs talked to the new management, all they were offering was a year and an option. Boggs felt slighted, lost his legendary focus, and struggled in his last season with the Red Sox before the team decided not to re-sign him and let him become a free agent.

Despite his carefully regimented lifestyle, Boggs managed to find himself in the headlines for odd reasons over the years. In 1988 he received a minor cut on the neck from a knife after an altercation outside a bar in Gainesville, Florida. Two men, possibly attempting to rob Boggs and his friends, threatened them with the knife and a gun. Boggs said that he "willed himself invisible" during the fight.[13] In another incident, Boggs fell out of the family Jeep and was run over by his wife, Debbie. Although he was not seriously injured, his arm had scrapes and bruises. Comedians across the country suggested that Debbie was getting payback for the Margo Adams situation.[14] Red Sox fans tended to love Boggs more for his many quirks.

The last line on Boggs's Hall of Fame plaque is "Legendary for his superstitions," and he was. Numerous stories tell of his different superstitions, whether it was wearing the same socks for every game, or fielding exactly 150 groundballs in practice each day. Every time he batted, he drew the Jewish word "chai," meaning good luck and life, in the dirt, to wish himself luck. Perhaps the best-known superstition Boggs had was eating chicken before each game every day, and he became known as "Chicken Man" because of it. Boggs even authored a book titled *Fowl Tips*, which presented various chicken recipes. He readily acknowledged his superstitions, saying in his Hall of Fame induction speech, "Believe me, I have a few superstitions, and they work."

In a surprising move, after so many years with the Red Sox, Boggs signed a three-year, $11-million contract to play for their archrivals, the New York Yankees. From being a Boston hero, he found himself returning to boos every game. His focus meant he was able to block it out, and resume his hitting. Again Boggs was back over .300 for his first four years with the Yankees.

The Yankees were on the rise, and Boggs wanted to be part of it. He enjoyed some good seasons with New York, and won a Gold Glove in both 1994 and 1995, but they missed the playoffs his first season, the entire 1994 postseason was wiped out by the players strike, and in 1995 they lost a classic best-of-five ALDS to the Seattle Mariners.

In 1996 the Yankees again made the playoffs, and Boggs struggled. He hit just .158 that postseason, losing playing time for hitting so poorly. His biggest moment was as a 10th-inning pinch-hitter in Game Four of the World Series, when he walked with two outs and the bases loaded to give the Yankees the go-ahead run. But the rest of the Yankees did well during the Series, coming back against the Atlanta Braves, and Boggs got his first World Series ring. In yet another iconic moment, he rode around Yankee Stadium on the back of a police horse as he celebrated.

In 1997 Boggs hit .292, split time, and ultimately lost his third-base job to Charlie Hayes. Boggs hit .429 in seven postseason at-bats, but New York again lost in the ALDS, this time to the Cleveland Indians, and his time with the Yankees was over.

Boggs returned home to Tampa, to play in his hometown for the expansion Tampa Bay Devil Rays. As a 40-year-old his time was over; he hit an anemic (for him) .280 in 1998 and finished out his career hitting .301 in 1999. He had been hanging on long enough to get his 3,000th hit, which came on August 7, and was ironically, given his lack of power throughout his career, a home run off Chris Haney of the Indians. A couple of weeks later he was done, ending his career with 3,010 hits and a career batting average of .328.

Boggs spent some time in the front office of the Devil Rays, acting as assistant general manager in 2000, then returning to the field as hitting instructor for the team in 2001. After that he took off the uniform for good.

Boggs was elected to the National Baseball Hall of Fame in 2005, his first year of eligibility, receiving 91.9 percent of the votes. Speaking about being elected, he said, "The only time the Hall of Fame ever came into my mind was probably the time I was rounding first going into second when I hit my home run for my 3,000th hit. I thought, 'Well, there's my ticket. If anybody wants to vote for me for Cooperstown then I've got the credentials to get in.'"[15]

There was controversy before Boggs's induction when it was reported that the Devil Rays had a part of his contract written so that when he went into the Hall of Fame his plaque would have a Devil Rays cap on it. Boggs denied that had happened, and noted that the Hall of Fame had the choice of what cap he would wear. As it happened, given his five batting titles with Boston, they put him in a Red Sox cap.

Boggs was widely known as a beer drinker, and in retirement undertook promotional tours for the Miller brewing company. His teammates have told stories about his drinking prowess, including stories of Boggs downing dozens of cans of beer on cross-country flights. Boggs did not downplay these stories, and it is fair to say that the stories of his consumption of beer have now reached legendary status.

After retiring from professional baseball, Boggs didn't stay unemployed for long. His son, Brett, was playing high-school baseball, and Wade became an assistant coach for the team while Brett was there. Brett moved on to play at the University of South Florida, where Wade would watch him play. As of 2015, Wade and Debbie lived in Tampa, where they both grew up.

SOURCES

Thanks to Dana Berry for getting this biography under way.

NOTES

1 Dan Shaughnessy, "Wade Boggs: 2005 Hall of Fame Inductee," *Boston Globe,* July 31, 2005.

2 Peter Gammons, "Pretty Fair for a Fowl Guy," *Sports Illustrated*, April 14, 1986.

3 Wade Boggs Hall of Fame Induction speech.

4 Shaughnessy.

5 Ibid.

6 Ira Berkow, "33 Innings, 882 Pitches and One Crazy Game," *New York Times,* June 24, 2006.

7 Shaughnessy.

8 Christopher L. Gasper, "Fact is, injuries can cost you a job in sports," *Boston Globe,* November 25, 2012.

9 Ian O'Connor, "Wade's World: Boggs, Dad bounce back after series of struggles," *New York Daily News,* October 16, 1996.

10 O'Connor.

11 Shaughnessy.

12 O'Connor.

13 Jack Curry, "Did someone say Boggs? Not in Boston," *New York Times,* March 18, 1993.

14 Dan Shaughnessy, "Leave it to Boggs to spice up spring," *Boston Globe,* March 31, 1991.

15 Ibid.

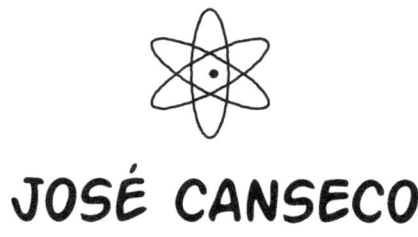

JOSÉ CANSECO

By Geoffrey Dunn

Perhaps no other player in major-league history has been blessed with as much talent and at the same time burdened by such erratic impulses as José Canseco.[1] Amassing borderline Hall of Fame numbers with 462 home runs and 1,407 runs batted in during a 17-year major-league career, the former American League Rookie of the Year (1986) and Most Valuable Player (1988) has found his name as often in the tabloids as in the sports pages.[2] In the aftermath of his 2005 tell-all memoir, *Juiced: Wild Times, Rampant 'Roids, Smash Hits & How Baseball Got Big*, in which Canseco admitted to personal steroid use and also named several other ballplayers who he claimed used performance-enhancing drugs as well, Canseco was reduced to a baseball pariah, cast aside to the distant margins of the national pastime.[3] "I was known as the godfather of steroids in baseball," he wrote unapologetically. "I introduced steroids into the big leagues back in 1985."[4] That he was more forthright than most in his chronicles of anabolic steroid use provided him with little solace after his career.

In 2007, when Canseco's name first appeared on the Hall of Fame ballot, he received only 1.1 percent of the vote from the Baseball Writers' Association of America—in spite of having been named to six All-Star teams,[5] garnering four Silver Slugger Awards, and compiling a then-unprecedented 40-homer, 40-stolen-base season in 1988 as he led the Oakland A's to the American League pennant. By the end of his career he was known in baseball circles simply as "The Chemist." While he continued to serve as fodder for late-night comedians, in many respects, his troubled life—and his roller-coaster career—can just as easily be viewed as an American tragedy.

José Canseco Capas Jr. was born on July 2, 1964, in Regla, a borough of Havana, Cuba, overlooking the city's shipyards.[6] His identical twin brother, Osvaldo "Ozzie" Canseco Capas, who would have a brief career in major-league baseball, was born two minutes before. Canseco's parents, José Jr. and Barbara, were both of recent Spanish lineage to Cuba and had an older daughter, Teresa, born a decade earlier. Canseco's father had worked in oil refineries in the United States during the 1950s and, the year following the birth of his twin sons, was able to secure his family's immigration to the United States, where the Canseco originally settled in Opa-locka, Florida, 15 miles northwest of Miami. In his various interviews and memoirs, Canseco identifies his father as a stern taskmaster who was highly critical of the two brothers as they worked their way through various youth leagues. He identifies himself frequently as "scrawny" throughout his youth and acknowledges that he played junior-varsity baseball at Coral Park Senior High School until his senior year, when he was scouted by his teammate's father, the former major-league pitcher Camilo Pascual. In 1982, following his high-school graduation when he was still only 17, Canseco was selected as a 15th-round draft choice by the Oakland A's.[7]

Canseco began his professional baseball career inauspiciously in Idaho Falls of the Pioneer League, batting .263 in 28 games, with only two home runs. In Miami of the Class-A Florida State League he batted .111 in six games. The following year, he started the season at Single-A Medford (Oregon) of the short-season Northwest League, where he batted .269 with 11 home runs, making the All-Star team, but also recorded 78 strikeouts in only 59 games. He

Canseco bashes one out for the Oakland A's.

finished out the season at Madison (Wisconsin) of the Single-A Midwest League, where he struggled to a .159 average with three home runs in 34 games.

The following year, 1984, Canseco was sent to Modesto, the A's "high" Single-A team, the top Class-A team of the California League, where he got off to a good start before receiving a call that his mother was dying in a Miami hospital from complications due to diabetes and hepatitis. In his memoirs, Canseco claims that his mother's death, coming when he was just 20 years old, was the catalyst that that led him to dedicate his life to becoming "the best athlete on the planet." He batted .276 at Modesto, with 15 homers and 73 runs batted in, and returned home from the offseason to Miami, where, he asserts, he began his first use of anabolic steroids with a friend from Coral Park Senior High, combined with vigorous weight training. As a result of his new regimen, Canseco put on several pounds of muscle and continued to grow in height.[8]

In 1985, still only 20 and following his initial use of steroids, Canseco had a breakout season, starting with Double-A Huntsville (Alabama) in the Southern League, where he batted .318 with 25 home runs in a mere 58 games. He was then moved up to Triple-A Tacoma of the Pacific Coast League, where he batted .348 with 11 home runs in 60 games and where his power was beginning to make headlines. At one point Canseco was batting .525 and had hit 500-foot home runs in games at Vancouver and Las Vegas. He hit another ball over the 32-foot right-center-field fence at Tacoma's Cheney Stadium. Suddenly he was being dubbed "the next Mickey Mantle." Tacoma's general manager, Stan Naccarato, echoed those sentiments in an interview sent out over the wire services by United Press International. "Everybody you talk to says he has Mantle's speed and Mantle's power," Naccarato declared. "There's electricity in the air."[9] Canseco received a late-September callup with the A's during which he batted .302 with five home runs, including a towering 480-foot drive onto the left-field roof at Comiskey Park in Chicago. After the season, "the rip-roaring, 21-year-old slugger" received *Baseball America's* Minor League Player of the Year Award.

The following spring, Canseco's rocket ship took off. In a telling spring-training profile of him appearing in March of 1986, the Associated Press noted, "When Oakland A's rookie outfielder José Canseco talks, people don't always listen. But when he hits, they fear for their lives." Triple-A Phoenix manager Jim Lefebvre compared him to sluggers Richie "Dick" Allen and Willie Stargell, with yet another nod to Mantle. A's hitting coach Bob Watson compared him to Roberto Clemente, Dale Murphy, and Reggie Jackson, "all rolled into one." All heady company. Karl Kuehl, then the A's director of player development, said his one concern was how Canseco would handle all the attention he was receiving. "He's been very good in the local theaters," Kuehl observed. "Now, he's going to Carnegie Hall."[10]

In truth, Canseco's rookie season on the A's more than matched his hype. Managed at the start of the season by Jackie Moore, replaced near midseason by interim skipper Jeff Newman, and then finally replaced by Tony La Russa in early July, the 1986 A's were a lackluster team with little offense (no starter batted over .285 that year) and mediocre pitching (no pitcher won more than 13 games). Canseco provided one of the few bright spots, storming to a unanimous selection by edging out the California Angels' Wally Joyner as the American League Rookie of the Year. Although batting only .240 with a thunderous 175 strikeouts, third most in the league, Canseco belted out 33 home runs (tied for fourth in the league) and had 117 runs batted in (good for second), along with 15 stolen bases. There was also some promise for the future: Under La Russa's tutelage, the A's went 45-34 to finish the season. Moreover, there was also another rookie who appeared on the A's roster briefly that year—playing as a third baseman—a 22-year-old from Southern California named Mark McGwire.

The following season, 1987, Canseco's star was eclipsed by his rookie teammate, McGwire, who had switched over to first base and batted cleanup in the A's lineup. While Canseco maintained solid power numbers—31 home runs and 113 runs batted in – McGwire surpassed him, generating huge amounts of press and crashing a record-breaking 33 home runs before the All-Star break. He destroyed the longtime rookie standard of 38 round-trippers with 49 home runs and was unanimously voted American League Rookie of the Year. The two sluggers soon became known as the "Bash Brothers," hitting 80 home runs between them and driving in 231 runs while also making the pounding of their celebratory forearm bump famous. The A's finished at an even .500 pace that year, good for only third in the American League West, but the '87 season set the stage for three straight World Series appearances and a world championship in the trio of seasons ahead.

Soon after McGwire's spectacular rookie campaign, according to Canseco, the glamour of the Bash Brothers took on an ominous undertone. In his memoirs, Canseco asserted that beginning in 1988, "Mark and I started talking about steroids again, and soon we started using them together. I injected Mark in the bathrooms at the Coliseum more times than I can remember. Sometimes we did it before batting practice, sometimes afterward."[11] (McGwire originally denied Canseco's charges; later asserted his Fifth Amendment rights before Congress; and, finally, in 2010, admitted to continued steroid usage throughout his career, beginning in the 1990s. (He continued to deny Canseco's allegations that he shot McGwire with syringes.)[12] Canseco has continuously contended that A's manager Tony La Russa was aware of McGwire's steroid use, which La Russa has denied, saying that he was not aware of McGwire's use until McGwire admitted it to him personally during a phone conversation in 2010 when La Russa hired his former slugger as a hitting coach for the St. Louis Cardinals.[13] "I'm tired of justifying what I've said," Canseco said about steroid use in baseball during the late 1980s and 1990s. "I've polygraphed, I've proven that I'm 100 percent accurate. I never exaggerated. I told it the way it actually happened. I'm the only one who has told it the way it actually happened. Major League Baseball is still trying to defend itself. It's strange. All I have is the truth, and I've proven that."[14]

Whatever was revealed to have gone on behind the scenes long afterward, on the ballfield during their three-year run from 1988-1990, the A's had one of the best three-year records of any baseball team over the last 30 years. They averaged 102 wins for each of the three seasons (for a remarkable .630 winning percentage during that period).

Canseco led things off in 1988 with a campaign for the ages. In April of that year, after getting off to a quick start, he declared: "I think I can have a 40-40 season. Let's go for a big time goal."[15] Canseco's prediction was more than a bit brash: He had never stolen more than 15 bases before in a year. But by June 2, only 51 games in, Canseco was leading the league with 13 home runs and was third in stolen bases with 17. "I'm trying to shake off the stereotype of just being a power hitter," he declared.[16] It was also a way of differentiating himself from McGwire and returning himself to the spotlight. Meanwhile, the

A's were operating on all pistons, at one point earlier in the season winning 18 out of 19 games (including 14 in a row) and extending a nine-game lead over the second-place Minnesota Twins.

By midsummer Canseco had captured the imagination of the entire country. He was moving from baseball star into the realm of cultural icon. *Vanity Fair*'s Annie Leibovitz photographed him shirtless for an American Express ad campaign. In a memorable midseason profile appearing in the *Washington Post*, baseball writer Thomas Boswell wrote of him: "After lockering next to Reggie Jackson last year, Canseco has incorporated the Spanish language version of 'The World According to Buck' into his act—how to play the outfield standing sideways, how to wear the tight uniform, how to gaze lovingly at the long homers and how to cook quotes like 'I don't expect to reach my pinnacle for a few years.'"[17] Canseco led all American league outfielders in votes for the All-Star Game, and manager Tom Kelly of the Twins let it be known he considered Canseco the best player in the game.[18] The game was played that year in Cincinnati. Canseco joined Dave Winfield and Rickey Henderson (both then on the Yankees) in the American League's starting lineup. Although Canseco went 0-for-4 in his starting role, Kelly played him for all nine innings of the annual showcase, initially in left field and then moving him to right.

Canseco came out hot again in the second half of the 1988 season. On September 18 he clubbed his 40th homer. The following day, the A's clinched the division title over the Twins by more than a dozen games, behind the pitching of the indomitable Dave Stewart, who picked up his 19th win. Then on Friday, September 23, Canseco banged out three hits, including his 41st home run, and stole two bases, to reach the 40-40 plateau. Canseco admitted after the game that when he made his prediction at the beginning of the season, he hadn't realized that no one had done it before. He had now created an exclusive club. "I'm greatly relieved at having done it," he declared. "I didn't want to go through the season and come up short and say I stuck my foot in my mouth."[19]

That fall would mark the first of three straight trips for Canseco and the A's to the fall classic. But in the week leading up to the American League Championship Series, the *Washington Post*'s Boswell, who had earlier heaped praise on Canseco in his midseason profile, appeared on Charlie Rose's middle-of-the-night television talk show *Nightwatch*. The conversation turned to the end-of-the-season pennant races and to Canseco's unprecedented 40-40 accomplishment. Canseco, Boswell declared, is "the most conspicuous example of a player who has made himself great with steroids." He also said that other players referred to steroids as "a Canseco milkshake."[20]

Boswell's charges against Canseco, vague and unsubstantiated as they were, marked the first time that steroid allegations in baseball had broken to the surface of the mainstream media. Ironically, Boswell's comments never appeared in the *Post*. His editor, George Solomon, would later contend: "You have to have your sources. You have to be 100 percent sure of what you print. At that point, we were not." What Boswell had said on television, Solomon declared, was strictly "Boswell's opinion."[21]

Nevertheless, the charges were explosive. Headlines echoing Boswell's remarks appeared across the country. Canseco was forced to deny the charges. "It's just not true," he declared. "It was an ignorant statement, and I usually don't pay attention to ignorant statements. There was no background and no basis to it."[22] Baseball's Establishment went into full defensive mode. La Russa, in the midst of getting his team prepared for the playoffs, immediately denied Boswell's allegations. So, too, did former A's slugger Reggie Jackson, who had retired from the game a year earlier and said that Boswell "had done a disservice to baseball."[23] But the damage had been done. According to Canseco, Pepsi pulled a $1 million endorsement away from him as a result of the controversy. When the A's appeared in Boston for the first games of the ALCS, Red Sox fans chanted "STER-oids! STER-oids!" when Canseco came to the plate.

The chanting didn't seem to intimidate Canseco. He belted a critical home run at Fenway Park in the A's opening 2-1 win over the Red Sox; he hit a two-run homer off Roger Clemens in the A's 4-3 Game Two victory; and after going 0-for-4 in Game Three, he went 3-for-4 in the clincher with another home run and two runs scored. For the series, he batted .313 with a .938 slugging percentage. He also declared what would become his mantra, albeit a deceitful one, for the next two decades. "If you guys saw what I went through during the offseason, you'd know where this body came from," Canseco said. "My brother and I work out about 3 hours a day, 6 days a week. We play volleyball in the sand to build up the legs, swim to build up the shoulders and back, and then lift weights."[24]

In the ensuing World Series, however, between the A's and the Los Angeles Dodgers, Canseco's—and the A's—bubble burst. In the very first game at Dodger Stadium, Canseco put the A's ahead 4-2 with a grand slam off Dodgers starter Tim Belcher, providing him with an auspicious start to the Series and giving the A's a lead, which they held, 4-3 going into the ninth inning. The A's brought in their star closer, Dennis Eckersley, needing only three final outs to secure the Game One victory. With two down and Mike Davis on second base, however, Kirk Gibson, who had been injured in the NLCS against the New York Mets, hobbled to the plate as a pinch-hitter. Gibson managed to work a 3-and-2 count and, based on a scouting report, was looking for a backdoor slider as Eckersley's next delivery. Gibson used his wrist and upper body strength to drive the pitch well over Canseco's head and into the right-field bleachers. It was one of the most momentous home runs in World Series history—and completely took the wind out of the A's sails, even though they had been widely favored to win the Series. Had Eckersley secured the save, Canseco would have been the hero; instead, he was all but forgotten as Gibson assumed the spotlight. The A's were cooked. The Dodgers closed out their world championship in five games, with Canseco going 0-for-17 the rest of the way for an .053 Series batting average. McGwire was just as feeble, going 1-for-17 with an .059 average. The "Bash Brothers" had become the "Crash Brothers."

If the World Series loss to the Dodgers had been a profound disappointment, the offseason was even worse for Canseco. In early February, headlines across US sports pages read that Canseco and the A's could not reach an agreement on his forthcoming contract—arbitration seemed inevitable. At the eleventh hour, however, his agent reached an agreement with the A's, resulting in the largest raise in baseball history to a one-year contract for $1.6 million. A's general manager Sandy Alderson was forced to acknowledge "the number he submitted was a fairly reasonable one."[25] It might have been a moment of triumph leading him into spring training. Instead, only days later, however, Canseco was arrested by Florida state troopers for driving his new Jaguar 125 miles per hour on Interstate 95. Canseco was cited for reckless driving, creating more headlines.[26] (He was found guilty and fined $500.)

From that point on, the bad press and the bad behavior never seemed to slow down. That same month Canseco was a no-show at a baseball-card convention in New York. A local radio station took to publishing a sign called a "Slam-O-Gram," featuring short derogatory blasts about the A's slugger (an early precursor to Twitter):

"Canseco—major league player, minor league human being."

"Canseco, MIP—Most Invisible Player."

The bad press continued. Canseco was stopped for running a red light in spring training, during which time he argued with police, and had three other traffic tickets that spring. He opened up the 1989 season with a stress fracture in his left wrist. By the third week of April, he hadn't had an at-bat. While getting treatment for his fracture at the University of California Medical Center in San Francisco, Canseco was arrested by campus police and FBI agents for being in possession of a loaded 9mm handgun on a state campus. In January an unidentified traveling companion of Canseco's had been stopped in Detroit for carrying a 15-shot, Italian-made handgun on an airline flight. Canseco seemed to be in freefall.

Alderson was terse in his response. "Oakland does not condone this event," he declared, "nor are we happy with the series of events. I am embarrassed for the organization."[27] Canseco, however, was anything but recalcitrant. He claimed he was carrying the gun for protection following anonymous threats he had received. "I'm no felon," he declared. "I am no criminal. I am no rapist. I am no murderer. They ought to spend more time apprehending criminals."[28] Canseco later pleaded no contest to misdemeanor charges and performed community service.[29]

By early May Canseco was on a 20-day rehab assignment with Double-A Huntsville, but quickly reinjured his wrist again and was forced to undergo surgery at the same medical center where he had been arrested on weapons charges. After more than a month of recuperation, Canseco returned to Huntsville again, and began his second rehab assignment.

Without ever having to come to bat in the American League that season, Canseco found himself winning a position in the American League's starting lineup in the All-Star Game. He publicly asserted his intent to play in the game, even though he was still in the middle of a rehab assignment in Huntsville. A's manager Tony La Russa, who had clearly become irritated with his wounded slugger, said that he was "concerned if he has his head on straight about what he's supposed to be doing, and that's to help us win the division." Canseco retorted that he didn't think the decision was in La Russa's "jurisdiction." Alderson interceded. "It's our decision when he comes off the disabled list," the GM declared, "and he has to be activated to play in the All-Star Game."[30] In the end, he did not play—the A's cited his injury—but he did receive yet another speeding ticket while recuperating during the All-Star break. More headlines. More tension with management. It was a dynamic that would repeat itself for the rest of his career.

The A's were a game and a half out at the All-Star break, and when Canseco finally returned to their lineup on July 13, he did so with a bang—2-for-3, with a home run, three RBIs, two runs scored and a stolen base, as the A's pounded the Blue Jays 11-7. They never looked back. The A's finished the season with 99 wins, seven games ahead of the Kansas City Royals and with the best record in baseball, while Canseco hit 17 home runs and had 57 RBIs in only 65 games, with a slugging average of .542. In the ensuing ALCS and World Series encounters with the Toronto Blue Jays and San Francisco Giants, the A's lost only a single game on their way to their first world championship since 1974. Canseco registered the signature moment of the ALCS—a towering 480-foot homer off former Cy Young Award winner Mike Flanagan into the fifth deck of Toronto's SkyDome—but the postseason stars of the Athletics were future Hall of Famer Rickey Henderson, who was named the MVP of the ALCS, and pitcher Dave Stewart, who was named World Series MVP after collecting two wins in the so-called Bay Bridge Series, which had been disrupted by the fatal Loma Prieta Earthquake. The 24-year-old Canseco batted a respectable .294 and .357 in the respective series, but he hit only a single homer in each and would have only three more postseason hits in his career. His baseball pinnacle had been reached much sooner than he anticipated.

It wasn't quite a downhill slide after that, but there would be far fewer heroics, no more Most Valuable Player awards—not even close. The A's stormed to their third successive American League West championship in 1990—Canseco had a respectable season with 37 home runs, 101 RBIs, and another berth on the All-Star team—but he collected only two hits against the Red Sox in the ALCS and a solo home run in the World Series, as the A's were swept by the underdog Cincinnati Reds in four games. That was the end of their triumphant run.

Canseco won the American League home run championship again in 1991 with 44. That same year the then-married outfielder also had a celebrated late-night rendezvous with pop star Madonna, one that made for tabloid headlines around the world. The *New York Post* dubbed him "Madonna's Bat boy." Yankee fans chanted "Ma-don-na!" when he came to the plate.[31] At the time, Canseco said that he and the diva were "just friends."[32] Later, he would claim that Madonna wanted to have a child with him. "She had a Cuban child and wanted another one," he told *Us* magazine. "She wanted to get married and have a child with me—she wanted a Cuban child." He said that when he first met her in California, "(S)he came over and said, 'What would you do if I kissed you?' and then sat on my lap and kissed me."[33]

By the following February Canseco was charged with "aggravated battery" for allegedly ramming his wife Esther's BMW with his Porsche. Before the start of the 1992 season, Canseco pleaded not guilty to charges of aggravated assault and later bargained a deal where he underwent counseling and fulfilled a community-service requirement—but Alderson and La Russa were done with him. Just before the September 1 trade deadline, the A's humiliated Canseco by trading him in the middle of a game (and while he was on his way to the on-deck circle) to the Texas Rangers for All-Star outfielder Ruben Sierra, pitchers Jeff Russell and Bobby Witt, and cash. Over the course of the ensuing decade, Canseco would play for a half-dozen teams—and even another stint with the A's after La Russa had left the team to manage St. Louis—but injuries and continued off-field challenges always seemed to get the best of him. In 1994, his final season with the Rangers, Canseco nearly returned to his peak form—he hit 31 home runs and had 90 RBIs in the strike-shortened season—but the Rangers sent him to Boston that December for outfielder Otis Nixon and part-time third baseman Luis Ortiz.

In 1998 Canseco produced memorable numbers at the age of 33 for the Blue Jays—a career-high 46 home runs, 107 runs batted in (albeit with a league-leading 159 strikeouts)—but he watched in the shadows as his former teammate Mark McGwire, now of the St. Louis Cardinals, and Sammy Sosa of the Chicago Cubs—both players that Canseco later identified as having used performance enhancing drugs—captured the imagination of the nation as they staged an epic battle chasing the seasonal home run record

José Canseco

of 61 by the Yankees' Roger Maris in 1961. McGwire hit 70 and Sosa 66—but they and Canseco all knew the record was tainted.

From that point on, Canseco's playing time and his performance diminished. Just 38 home runs shy of the coveted 500 mark, he signed with the Montreal Expos in 2002, but the Expos cut him during spring training after batting just .200 in 14 games, leaving him to sign a Triple-A contract with the White Sox. After batting a meager .172 with five home runs in 18 games with the Charlotte Knights, a frustrated Canseco simply failed to show up at the park one day. Later, his agent, Alan Nero, stated: "José felt that because of personal reasons and a strong desire on his part to spend more quality time with his young daughter, it was time to announce his retirement."[34] A week later, Canseco took a swipe at baseball and augured things to come. "There would be no baseball left if they drug-tested everyone today," he told the Associated Press. "It's completely restructured the game as we know it. That's why guys are hitting fifty or sixty or seventy home runs."[35] He staged desperate comeback attempts with various major-league and minor-league teams—including an open tryout with the Dodgers in 2004—but he never made it back to "The Show." As far as Major League Baseball was concerned, the José Canseco saga was finally over.

At least on the field. Canseco would continue to find himself in trouble with the law and surrounded by controversy, his name still constantly in the headlines. In 2003 he was sent to jail by an angry judge who felt that Canseco had not taken the terms of his probation for a 2001 nightclub brawl seriously enough. Canseco had failed to take anger-management courses and perform community service; he also tested positive for steroids, whose use had also been banned by the terms of his probation. In June he was arrested and placed in Broward County Jail without bond. In *Juiced*, he described the two-plus months he spent in custody as "the low point of my life."[36] He also claimed that he experienced a "nervous breakdown" while he was incarcerated after his ex-wife, Jessica, told him that she was "in love with somebody else." "I'm not using the term *nervous breakdown* lightly," he wrote. "It all became too much for me. It felt like something inside me was being crushed."[37] While he was in jail, his attorneys acknowledged that he was addicted to steroids, but their motion for a medical evaluation for their client was denied.[38] In August he was released from custody when a judge ruled that the state could not determine when Canseco had last taken steroids; Canseco also claimed in his memoir that "the chain of custody on my blood test was full of holes." From that point on, Canseco asserted that he would never set foot in Florida again.[39]

When his memoir *Juiced* was first published in 2005, it became an instant cause célèbre. *60 Minutes* featured a segment on the book, in which Mike Wallace interviewed Canseco. The baseball Establishment—and many baseball writers—took potshots at Canseco. They remained in serious denial. In the *Los Angeles Times*, longtime baseball writer Allen Barra proclaimed it "the worst sports book so far in three centuries." His longtime nemesis Boswell declared that "in baseball, when it's your word against Canseco's, they invoke the forfeit rule." Tom Verducci of *Sports Illustrated* echoed Boswell's attack by asserting that Canseco had "the kind of credibility not even nano-technology could find or measure."[40] But many fans were apparently beginning to come around to Canseco's perspective. On March 6 *Juiced* shot up to No. 1 on the *New York Times*' Best Seller List and spent a total of seven weeks on the coveted list. One aspect of *Juiced* that has long been overlooked, however, is the fact Canseco, in addition to naming names, was still openly advocating for steroid use in its pages. "Yes, you hear me right," he declared. "Steroids, used correctly, will not only make you stronger and sexier, they will also make you healthier. … Steroids will give you a better quality of life and also drastically slow down the aging process."[41]

On March 17, 2005, during the middle of the controversy surrounding *Juiced* and while the major leagues prepared for the coming season in spring training, several of the game's most memorable stars—Canseco, McGwire, Sosa, Alex Rodriguez, Rafael Palmeiro, and Curt Schilling—appeared before the House Government Reform Committee during the course of an all-day, nationally televised hearing. It was a stunning encounter. Canseco and McGwire were together in the same lineup for the first time since their days together with the Oakland A's, but no one could have anticipated the venue where they were now appearing. Both made headlines. In the end, McGwire stumbled unconvincingly through his testimony, refusing to answer the ultimate question: whether or not he used steroids. He also took a potshot at Canseco. "I don't intend to dignify Mr. Canseco's book," he declared. "It should be enough that you consider the source of the statements in the book, and that many inconsistencies and contradictions have already been raised." But when the time came to acknowledge his own participation, McGwire dodged the question. "I have been advised that my testimony here could be used to harm friends and respected teammates," he declared. "My lawyers have advised me that I cannot answer these questions without jeopardizing my friends, my family and myself. I intend to follow their advice."[42]

The force of public opinion seemed to be bending Canseco's way. As it would turn out, Canseco's testimony before Congress proved to be the most honest of all those who testified. On the other hand, McGwire's performance was universally slammed by the media. Dave Sheinin of the *Washington Post* declared that McGwire, "once the game's most celebrated slugger but now the face of the steroid scandal, [was] reduced to a shrunken, lonely, evasive figure whose testimony brought him to the verge of tears."[43]

In his follow-up book, *Vindicated*, Canseco named more names, went on the offensive against several sportswriters, and doubled-down on his charges against McGwire. Five years later, McGwire finally admitted to using steroids, though he denied ever using them with Canseco and claimed to have begun using them a half-decade later only as a response to injuries. Canseco was outraged by what he viewed as an incomplete, insincere admission. "I've defended Mark, I know a lot of good things about him," Canseco told ESPN. "I can't believe he just called me a liar. There's something very strange going on here. I even polygraphed that I injected him, and I passed it completely. So I want to challenge him on national TV to a polygraph examination. I want to see him call me a liar under a polygraph examination."[44] McGwire has never taken him up on his offer.

In the years since his retirement, Canseco asserted that he was forced out of the game and was "blackballed" by Major League Baseball. The one-time MVP has been forced to the margins of the national pastime and became something of a celebrity circus act on reality television programs. In 2003 he appeared in a TV special entitled *Stripper's Ball*, with porn star Jenna Jameson. He has also engaged in a variety of martial arts and boxing contests, and in 2009 he fought a former child star, 5-foot, 6-inch Danny Bonaduce, to a three-round draw at a bout held in Aston, Pennsylvania. A 2010 effort on Twitter to get Mets GM Sandy Alderson to invite him to spring training elicited no response.

Canseco's behavioral circus never abated. In 2011 he sent out a series of Twitter postings declaring his "love" for Lady Gaga, proclaiming he "would marry her in a second."[45] In 2012 he filed for bankruptcy, citing $1.7 million in debt against $21,000 in assets. That same year he was banned by the Mexican League, in which he was hoping to stage yet another comeback, for "refusing to take a doping test."[46] The following year, Canseco was named publicly—initially by himself via Twitter—as a suspect in a rape allegation by a fitness model (and the mother of six children) in Las Vegas. He made defamatory countercharges against his accuser via Twitter postings, in which he identified her by name. A month later, he was cleared of all charges by Las Vegas police investigators.[47] Later that year he was pulled over with his girlfriend, Leila Knight, and found with a diaper-clad goat in the back seat of their car. The following year, he blew off a portion of the middle finger on his left hand while cleaning his gold-plated Remington .45 handgun, and, a month later, allegedly threatened to kill Knight and her mother. Knight also contended that Canseco was still using the anabolic steroid Anavar to "stay big."[48]

In June of 2015, Canseco appeared at Dodger Stadium in what was clearly a publicity stunt aimed at his former Bash Brothers teammate Mark McGwire, the hitting coach of the Dodgers. Canseco was carrying a sign that read: "Sorry Mark—Read My Poem! Love José." The poem was posted online:

Roses are red
Violets are blue
I am sorry I wrote a book about you
The balls we hit used to fly
But to do so we had to lie
In our heyday the Bash Brothers stood tall
But the bigger you are, the harder you fall
I know I exposed your secret injections
I hope this apology doesn't find a rejection[49]

It wasn't exactly Shakespeare, and McGwire publicly rejected the overture. Nor was Canseco seeking conciliation with everyone he had outed in his two books. About Alex Rodriguez, he declared: "Fuck him. I can't stand that guy. He hit on my wife. I'd rather kick his ass."[50]

Only weeks later, Canseco was playing baseball in an independent league in Northern California. He signed a three-day contract with the Pittsburg Diamonds of the Pacific Association of Baseball Clubs. In a series against the San Rafael Pacifics, Canseco pitched, went 3-for-5 in the second game with an RBI, and in the final contest, started a bench-clearing scuffle when he was brushed back on successive pitches. "Hey, you never know, maybe next year I'll manage, maybe a commissioner, maybe a player/manager," Canseco asserted after the series. "Who knows? A whole lot could happen."[51] Indeed it could: In midsummer of 2015, Canseco generated national headlines once again by declaring that he intended to support newly transgendered Caitlyn Jenner by "dressing up and living as a woman for a week." His announcement immediately drew criticism, according to the *Washington Post*, for "misunderstanding transgender issues and even making fun of them." Canseco was not dissuaded by the criticism. "I wonder what I would look like as a woman," he Tweeted. "Move over Caitlyn." He indicated that he intended to carry out his intentions, in part, by appearing as a woman on his Internet show, "Spend a Day With José."[52]

In spite of these continued media stunts, Canseco contends that he still loves the game that once brought him fame and fortune. "I love baseball," he wrote in *Vindicated*. "Baseball is a great game. Maybe the greatest game ever."[53] But for the time being, as a profile of Canseco in *Sports Illustrated* noted, the closest he was likely to get to a baseball diamond was in an outlaw league or the lowest level of the minors.[54] He has expressed his regrets for writing his memoir and naming names, but the apologies would clearly not bring him an invitation anytime soon to official gatherings in Cooperstown. He remained

Canseco, poised and ready to pounce on a pitch.

"a Judas," in the words of author Howard Bryant, forever banished from the inner sanctums of the game he once dominated. "If José Canseco is ever in the Hall of Fame," one Hall of Fame player told Bryant, "there shouldn't be a Hall of Fame. He wasted more ability than most of us ever had."[55]

NOTES

1   Special thanks to Joel Domhoff, Mark Nisson, Emily Hawks, Bill Nowlin, and Marlene Vogelsang for their assistance and feedback on this piece.

2   For an interesting discussion about Canseco and the Hall of Fame, see "Jose Canseco and the Keltner List," by Ryan Wilkins, *Baseball Prospectus*, May 23, 2002. baseballprospectus.com/article.php?articleid=1483. The article came out before the official confirmations of Canseco's steroid use, and as such, it provides an interesting, more objective, perspective on his career without the steroid question being taken into account. Bill James's Hall of Fame Monitor has Canseco at 103, slightly higher than the 100 benchmark for a "likely Hall of Famer." James has otherwise been dismissive of Canseco; in *The New Bill James Historical*

NUCLEAR-POWERED BASEBALL

Baseball Abstract (New York: Free Press, 2010), 811-812, James merely mentions Canseco among other twins who have played major-league baseball. It's clearly a dig. He does, however, list Canseco at 36th among all-time right-fielders, ahead of the likes of Chuck Klein and Hall of Famer Harry Hooper. Later on, James also acknowledges that Canseco's RBI-per-game average of .764 ranks him 10th among *all outfielders* in baseball history.

3   Jose Canseco, *Juiced: Wild Times, Rampant 'Roids, Smash Hits & How Baseball Got Big* (New York: Regan Books: 2005); although his name did not appear on the book, it was later revealed that *Juiced* was ghost-written by Steve Kettman. Canseco published a sequel three years later entitled *Vindicated: Big Names, Big Liars, and the Battle to Save Baseball* (New York: Simon Spotlight Entertainment: 2008).

4   *Juiced*, 4.

5   Canseco was named to the American League All-Star team in 1986, 1988, 1989, 1990, 1992, and 1999.

6   As with most ballplayers from Spanish-speaking countries in the Caribbean, Canseco dropped his mother's maiden name (Capas) when coming to the United States. I have used the Spanish spelling of his first name, with an accent over the "é."

7   Biographical data collected from *Juiced*, 1-46.

8   *Juiced*, 49-55.

9   *Ukiah* (California) *Daily Journal*, July 21, 1985: 11.

10 "The A's Budding Superstar," *Santa Cruz* (California) *Sentinel*, March 9, 1986: 62.

11 *Juiced*, 74.

12 Tyler Kepner, "McGwire Admits That He Used Steroids," *New York Times*, January 11, 2010. Web edition.

13 Ann Killion, "Steroid Taint Didn't Extend to Managers," *San Francisco Chronicle*, December 12, 2013, web edition. Killion wrote: "If there were an all-steroid baseball team (Bonds in left, McGwire at first, Clemens on the mound — we can keep going), there's no doubt who the manager would be. It would be [Tony] La Russa, who managed the A's in the late '80s and early '90s Bash Brothers era, widely considered Ground Zero for rampant steroid use. Then La Russa went on to manage the St. Louis Cardinals, where McGwire made it fashionable to use steroids to break baseball's most hallowed records. Along the way to this week's Hall of Fame vote, La Russa has been a hypocritical steroid-era bully, pointing fingers at and calling out players he didn't like, even ones he managed, such as Canseco, while simultaneously angrily defending McGwire and others."

14 "Canseco: McGwire Not Fully Forthcoming," ESPN.com, January 12, 2010.

15 "Canseco Sets Lofty Goal," *Santa Cruz Sentinel*, June 3, 1988: 21.

16 Ibid.

17 Thomas Boswell, "Jose Canseco's 40-40 Vision Starting to Come Into Focus," *Washington Post*, August 19, 1988. In *Los Angeles Times* web edition.

18 "Bay Area Bombers: Canseco Has Come Long Way," *Santa Cruz Sentinel*, July 14, 1988: 13.

19 "Canseco Steals Into Baseball History," *Santa Cruz Sentinel*, September 25, 1988: B1-B3.

20 Associated Press, "Slugger Denies Use," *Kokomo* (Indiana) *Tribune*, September 30, 1988: 17.

21 Bryan Curtis, "The Steroid Hunt," Grantland.com, January 8, 2014.

22 Associated Press, "Slugger Denies Use," *Kokomo Tribune*, September 30, 1988: 17.

23 Ironically, Boswell would claim that La Russa had been one of his sources. "Slugger Denies Use." See also "The Steroid Hunt."

24 "Slugger Denies Use." John Weyler, "Canseco Leaves Strong Impression on Red Sox: He Gives Oakland Early Lead With Home Run, Tries to Deflect Steroid Charge," *Los Angeles Times*, October 6, 1988, web edition. Hal Brock, "Shocked Devils," *Gettysburg* (Pennsylvania) *Times*, October 8, 1988: B-1.

25 "Canseco Receives Largest Raise in Baseball History," *Hazelton* (Pennsylvania) *Standard-Speaker*, February 4, 1989: 20.

26 "Canseco Shows New Type of Speed," *Santa Cruz Sentinel*, February 12, 1989: 57.

27 "Canseco Arrested on Loaded Firearm Charge," *San Bernardino Sun*, April 22, 1989: 17.

28 "Canseco Needs a Wake-up Call," *Santa Cruz Sentinel*, April 23, 1989: 51.

29 *Santa Cruz Sentinel*, August 20, 1989: 28.

30 "Retired, Injured Players Among Most Popular," *Greenwood* (South Carolina) *Index Journal*, July 6, 1989: 12-14.

31 "New York Tabloid Links Jose, Madonna," *Santa Cruz Sentinel*, May 12, 1991: 16.

32 "Canseco, Madonna 'Just Friends,'" *Chicago Tribune*, May 13, 1991, web edition.

33 "Jose Canseco Claims Madonna Wanted His Baby, Magazine Sez," *New York Daily News*, July 10, 2008, web edition.

34 "Major League Player Conseco [sic] Retires as Charlotte Knight," *Greenwood Index Journal*, May 14, 2002: 9.

35 "Canseco Talks Steroids," *Gettysburg Times*, May 18, 2002: 13.

36 *Juiced*, 249.

37 *Juiced*, 254.

38 Catherine Wilson, "Lawyers: Canseco Has History of Steroid Abuse," *Salina* (Kansas) *Journal*, July 8, 2003: 13.

39 *Juiced*, 255.

40 All quotes from writers in response to *Juiced* are from Bryan Curtis, "The Steroid Hunt," Grantland.com, January 8, 2014, a fascinating historical account of how sportswriters failed to respond to steroid use in professional baseball.

41 *Juiced*, 3. For a balanced review of Canseco's memoir, see Bill Nowlin, "'Juiced' Slugger Goes to Bat for Steroids," *Boston Globe*, March 2, 2005, web edition.

42 Excerpts from McGwire's testimony appeared in the *Washington Post*, March 18, 2005: D6.

43 "Baseball Has a Day of Reckoning In Congress," *Washington Post*, March 18, 2005: A1.

44 "Canseco: McGwire Not Fully Forthcoming," sports.espn.go.com, January 12, 2010. sports.espn.go.com/mlb/news/story?id=4819250.

45 "Jose Canseco and Lady Gaga: A match made in Twitter heaven?, *Yahoo Sports*, May 26, 2011.

46 "Jose Canseco Banned by League," ESPN.com, March 9, 2012.

47 "Jose Canseco Cleared In Las Vegas Rape Case," Fox News Latino, June 10, 2013. latino.foxnews.com/latino/sports/2013/06/10/jose-canseco-cleared-in-las-vegas-rape-case/.

48 Christian Red, "Jose Canseco's Fiancée, Leila Knight, Dumps Former Slugger After He Allegedly Threatened to Kill Her and Her Mother," *New York Daily News*, November 24, 2014. Web edition.

49 Paul Sacca, "Jose Canseco Apologizes To MLB Players He Said Used Steroids In The Most Ridiculous And Hilarious Ways," BroBible.com, June 2, 2015.

50 Jake O'Donnell, "Jose Canseco Apologizes to Ped Users He Snitched on (Except A-Rod, Of Course)," SportsGrid.com, June 3, 2015. sportsgrid.com/mlb/jose-canseco-apologizes-to-ped-users-he-snitched-on/. Canseco also devotes an entire section to Rodriguez in *Vindicated*, in which he asserts that Rodriguez was obsessed with his wife and made sexual remarks about her repeatedly, pp. 180-190. "Try your luck with Google," he writes (189). "Put in *Alex Rodriguez* and *infidelity* and you'll get about 50,000 hits." ESPN reportedly refused to let Canseco read the poem on the air.

51 Nate Gartrell, "Jose Canseco Will Return to Play for Pittsburg Diamonds," *Vallejo* (California) *Times Herald*, July 8, 2015. Web edition.

52 Christian Red, "Jose Canseco to live as a woman for a week to support Caitlyn Jenner," *New York Daily News*, July 29, 2015, Internet edition; Cindy Boren, "Jose Canseco plans to live as a woman for a week to support Caitlyn Jenner," *Washington Post*, July 30, 2015, Internet edition. (Link to latest Canseco headline:latintimes.com/jose-canseco-dress-woman-week-support-caitlyn-jenner-332705).

53 *Vindicated*, 205.

54 Jack Dickey, "Jose Canseco," *Sports Illustrated*, July 6 and 13, 2015: 58-62.

55 Howard Bryant, *Juicing the Game: Drugs, Power, and the Fight for the Soul of Major League Baseball* (New York: Plume Book, 2006), Chapter 10, excerpted by ESPN.com.

ROGER CLEMENS

By Frederick C. Bush

Roger Clemens' last major-league start, on October 7, 2007 — for the New York Yankees against the Cleveland Indians, the very team against which he had made his major-league debut in May 1984 — ended with him limping off the mound after only 2⅓ innings with a hamstring injury. Clemens had already allowed the Indians one run in each of the first and second innings, and, after facing two batters in the top of the third, he could pitch no more. He was charged with a third run, though the Yankees came back to win the game 8-4 for their lone victory in this American League Division Series. Such an ending is not what a movie screenwriter would have scripted as the final chapter of "Rocket's" 24-year career, but at least one element of Clemens' last appearance was storybook in character: He struck out the final batter he faced, Indians catcher Victor Martinez.

In spite of the abrupt end to Clemens' evening and career, as he left the mound, it seemed a certainty that he would be inducted into the National Baseball Hall of Fame in Cooperstown, New York, as soon as he passed the five-year waiting period for eligibility. Few pitchers in the history of baseball could boast anything near to his accomplishments: a record seven Cy Young Awards, 354 victories, 4,672 strikeouts, seven-time ERA leader with a career 3.12 ERA, six-time 20-game winner, five-time strikeout leader, 46 shutouts in the era of relief specialists and closers, and two-time World Series champion. He was too much of a polarizing figure in his career to exceed Tom Seaver's record of being named on 98.8 percent of the Hall of Fame ballots, but he seemed certain to be a first-ballot selectee.

On December 13, 2007, little more than two months after Clemens' final Yankees start, doubt was cast over his future enshrinement among baseball's immortals when he was mentioned repeatedly in the Mitchell Report on the use of performance-enhancing drugs in baseball. In the years following the report, Clemens spent almost as much time in courtrooms as he spent on pitcher's mounds during his career. By the time his first year of eligibility for the Hall of Fame arrived in January 2013, he was named on only 37.6 percent of the ballots and, in his second year, that number declined to 35.4 percent while two of his contemporaries and fellow members of the 300-win club, Greg Maddux and Tom Glavine, were elected.

Clemens' life is the tale of a fanatically driven man who worked hard to achieve his dream of stardom and attained the pinnacle of success. Jorge Posada, Clemens' catcher with the Yankees, was complimentary when he said, "The only thing he wants to do is just win."[1] Cito Gaston, Clemens' manager with the Toronto Blue Jays until he was fired toward the end of the 1997 season, intended no such praise when he commented, "It's all about him, nobody else but him."[2] Clemens' ambition gained him both fans and detractors, helped him to achieve massive success, and ultimately contributed to his fall from grace.

William Roger Clemens was born on August 4, 1962, in Dayton, Ohio, the fifth child of Bill and Bess Clemens. He was only 5 months old when his mother took her children and left his father, with whom he claims to have spoken only once in his life, when he was 10 years old. Less than two years later, Bess married Woody Booher, whom Roger looked up to as a real father. But he became fatherless again at the age of 8 when Booher died of a heart attack.

While his mother provided Roger with an example of the work ethic he would adopt by laboring at several jobs to support her children, he came under the tutelage of his older brother Randy, whom he idolized. In high school Randy was a shortstop on the baseball team, the star shooting guard for the basketball team, and the king of his senior prom, leading Clemens to admit, "While I was growing up, Randy was the star as far as I was concerned."[3] Though the two brothers have become estranged, Randy's influence was immense as he "instill[ed] in his brother a simple philosophy: Either you're a winner or you're a failure."[4] It was a mantra that caused Clemens to question at times whether he was good enough to become the star athlete that both of them wanted him to be.

While Clemens' baseball career dwarfs his brother Randy's high-school athletic exploits, his initial attempts to emulate his elder sibling were less than encouraging. He played baseball, basketball, and football, but distinguished himself in none of these sports. In fact, the only notable event from his youth baseball exploits was that he split starts for his 1977 squad with Kelly Krzan, who was the first girl in Ohio to play on a boys' Little League team.

By the time Clemens was 15 and a high-school sophomore, Randy had married and moved to Sugar Land, Texas, a suburb 20 miles southwest of downtown Houston. Randy had failed to achieve athletic stardom of his own largely due to the development of a substance-abuse problem, but he now wanted to guide his younger brother's athletic career. After the two brothers received their mother's permission, Ohio-born-and-raised Roger Clemens made the sojourn to Texas, the state with which he has become identified.

Clemens enjoyed initial success by amassing a 12-1 record and helping Sugar Land's Dulles High School win a district title, but Randy was plotting a move to more competitive fields. After watching a tournament game between two of the Houston area's premier high-school teams, Bellaire and Spring Woods, Clemens decided that he wanted to play for the latter team. Bess Clemens had moved to Houston now as well, and she made sure that her son's wish was granted.

The time spent at Spring Woods High School was a mixed blessing: Clemens played for a coach, Charlie Maiorana, whom he credits for much of his knowledge about mechanics and conditioning, but he spent his junior year seeing little action on a team with two of the state's best pitching prospects. His determination showed as he became known for his workout regimen, especially his running, and he had his turn as Spring Woods' number-one starting pitcher during his senior year. Still, at that point in his life, the player who came to sit at number three on the major-league strikeout list still threw too softly to draw any notice from either professional or college scouts.

As a favor to Clemens, Maiorana called a colleague, Wayne Graham, the new coach at San Jacinto Junior College, to ask if he could pull any strings to get Clemens to his desired destination, the University

Clemens won two more Cy Young Awards as a Blue Jay.

of Texas in Austin. Graham could not accomplish that feat, but he did offer Clemens a scholarship to San Jacinto, which is where Clemens' fortunes were reversed. The failure to achieve high-school stardom resulted in the season that launched Clemens on the path to professional greatness.

The year 1981 was Wayne Graham's first season to coach at any college level, but he has become a legend by guiding San Jacinto to five national junior-college championships in six years (1985-1990)—a feat that earned him *Collegiate Baseball Magazine*'s Junior College Coach of the Century Award—and leading Houston's Rice University to the NCAA College World Series Championship in 2003. What Graham did with Clemens—turning a soft-tossing youth into a flamethrower—was an equally impressive accomplishment. He preached to Clemens that he needed to finish hard on his pitches or he would never have a chance to realize his dream of pitching in the major leagues, a message Clemens took to heart as he finished his sole season at San Jacinto with a 9-2 record while the college won the Texas Junior College Athletic Association championship. His coach's assessment was that "Roger began the year as one of the guys, and he ended it as an ace."[5]

Graham anticipated that Clemens would remain at San Jacinto for a second year, an expectation that was buoyed when Clemens turned down an offer from the New York Mets, who had selected him in the 12th round of the 1981 draft. Clemens went through the motions of throwing for Mets manager Joe Torre and pitching coach/legend Bob Gibson at Houston's Astrodome, but he had other plans in mind. He had been contacted by University of Texas Longhorns coach Cliff Gustafson, who was now interested in the improved pitcher. The opportunity to play at Texas had been Clemens' dream, and he pounced on it; however, he failed to contact Graham about his decision and alienated the man who had placed him on the road to stardom.

Clemens fulfilled expectations at Texas, although there were some hiccups along the way. The 1982 Longhorns began their season with a 33-game winning streak that was one win shy of tying the NCAA record. Clemens, who had begun the campaign 7-0, pitched in game number 34 but lost 4-3 to the University of Houston. It was later revealed that he had bursitis while pitching that game, and he missed the next two weeks of the season. He finished 12-2 with a 1.99 ERA, but Texas was eliminated from the College World Series by Wichita State.

The Longhorns suffered under the burden of high expectations in 1983 and plodded through an up-and down season. At one point, the driven Clemens became so frustrated by his personal mound setbacks that he was ready to quit the team, an example of the toll that the insecurity caused by Randy Clemens' "winner or failure" mentality took on him. While he was not yet a polished pitcher, he still demonstrated great potential. Houston Astros scout Gordon Lakey reported that Clemens' delivery was not compact enough, but he believed it could be helped and that Clemens would develop more leg drive and become a power pitcher.[6] Chicago White Sox scout Larry Monroe's report echoed that of Lakey as he wrote of Clemens: "Delivery is fluid but does not use body at all. Should be easily improved and no reason why he shouldn't be in low 90's. I'm surprised he doesn't have shoulder problems from standing up and just throwing. Some bend in legs and drive to plate would help velocity, life, and location."[7] Both scouts projected Clemens as a likely second-round draft pick. Owing to rare encouragement from the usually gruff Gustafson, Clemens persevered—he went 13-5 with a 3.04 ERA—and the Longhorns survived their inconsistency to make a return trip to the College World Series.

Before Clemens took the mound for his start against Oklahoma State in the College World Series on June 6, the Boston Red Sox selected him as the 19th player chosen in the major-league draft, a circumstance about which he said, "I was completely surprised. As far as I was concerned, Boston was a foreign country."[8] Five days after defeating Oklahoma State, Clemens capped his Texas career with a complete-game 4-3 victory over Alabama in the College World

Series Championship Game to put himself and his team on top of the collegiate baseball world before he departed Austin for Boston, having now been signed by Red Sox scout Danny Doyle. Of course, Clemens did not make it to the parent club straight out of college, but he did take the fast track through the Red Sox' minor-league system where he already exhibited character traits that became hallmarks of his career.

His first stop was with the Winter Haven Red Sox of the Class-A Florida State League, for whom he went 3-1 with a 1.24 ERA in four starts and where he established his reputation for pitching inside to hitters. Two days before his final Winter Haven start, Clemens had taken umbrage at the Lakeland Tigers' Ronald Davis taking out his Red Sox (and ex-University of Texas) teammate Mike Brumley at second base, a play on which Brumley was injured. Clemens pitched a 15-strikeout shutout against Lakeland in which he also retaliated for Brumley's injury by hitting Davis in the head in his first at-bat. Clemens claimed—as most pitchers do—that he had only wanted to brush Davis back and that the pitch had gotten away from him; however, he also claimed that he was prepared to fight, something for which Davis was in no condition as he collapsed and was taken to a hospital.

The split opinion among baseball observers as to whether Clemens merely pitched inside or was a headhunter mirrors the split in opinion about his character in general. Few players thought poorly of Don Drysdale or Nolan Ryan for pitching close inside, but these two pitchers were held in high regard while Clemens was often considered arrogant. Clemens fanned the flames of this negative reputation by both his actions and his words, never more infamously so than after winning the 1986 American League MVP Award. When informed that no less a luminary than Hank Aaron had asserted that pitchers should not receive the MVP, he retorted, "I wish he was still playing. I'd probably crack his head open to show him how valuable I was."[9]

After his debacle-marred gem, Clemens was promoted to the New Britain (Connecticut) Red Sox of the Double-A Eastern League and amassed a 4-1 record with a 1.38 ERA in seven starts, but he also continued to draw controversy. In the team's first-round playoff series, Reading Phillies manager Bill Dancy protested that Clemens was using a glove that had writing all over it and claimed that it was distracting. The home-plate umpire ordered Clemens to use a different glove—an order the pitcher complied with—but he began to curse at Clemens due to the grief he was getting from New Britain's bench. Clemens charged the umpire but stopped short of any physical contact. Instead he calmed down, borrowed a teammate's glove, and proceeded to dominate Reading. Charging umpires became another Clemens trait as his career progressed, but calming down did not. As he accumulated successes, his "winner or failure" mentality and its resultant insecurity morphed into hypercompetitive intensity on and off the mound.

New Britain dispatched the Phillies and faced the Lynn Sailors for the championship, which they won when Clemens pitched a 10-strikeout shutout in Game Four. After he had breezed through two levels of the minor leagues and won his second championship in three months, Clemens' baseball future looked bright. His personal life became equally so when he began to date Debra Lynn Godfrey, whom he had known in passing at Spring Woods High School, in the offseason. Godfrey was a fellow fitness fanatic who twice auditioned for the Dallas Cowboys cheerleaders squad, and the two of them worked out together regularly. They became engaged in May 1984 and were married in November of that year.

Before his engagement to Godfrey, Clemens made one final stop on his way to Boston. He took part in spring training with the parent club in the familiar surroundings of Winter Haven, Florida, but ended up being assigned to Pawtucket of the Triple-A International League to begin the season after posting a 6.60 ERA in Grapefruit League games. Clemens did not allow his disappointment to keep him from excelling at yet another level as he posted a 1.93 ERA in 46⅔ innings for Pawtucket. Enough

Both of Clemens' 20-K games were for the Red Sox.

was enough and, on May 11, 1984, Roger Clemens was officially called up by the Boston Red Sox.

On Tuesday, May 15, 1984, Clemens made his major-league debut against the Indians before a mere 4,004 fans at chilly Cleveland Stadium and learned that minor-league success does not always carry over instantly to the majors. He received no decision after surrendering 11 hits, three walks, and five runs (four earned) in 5⅔ innings, but what was alarming was that Indians baserunners had swiped six bases against him because, in the words of his catcher, Gary Allenson, "(a)t that point, he had no real concept of keeping opposing runners in check."[10] In his next start, against the Minnesota Twins on May 20, he pitched seven strong innings to earn his first major-league victory.

The remainder of Clemens' rookie season was not as memorable as the one put together by his National League counterpart, Dwight Gooden of the New York Mets, who finished with a 17-9 record and easily won the NL Rookie of the Year award. Clemens was up and down from start to start and later conceded that some people were beginning to question whether he might fall into the same category as David Clyde, the 1970s poster boy for young pitchers who had been rushed to the major leagues too quickly. That fear was put to rest by a 15-strikeout performance against the Kansas City Royals on August 21, but soon a new specter—that of injury—arrived to haunt the Red Sox and their fans. In his final start of the season, on August 31 against the Indians, Clemens registered seven of 11 outs by strikeout and then exited the game with a strained tendon in his right forearm. Though the injury was minor, Clemens was shut down for the year and finished a solid but unspectacular rookie campaign at 9-4 with a 4.32 ERA.

Clemens endured nagging injuries on his way to a 7-5/3.29 sophomore campaign in 1985. The low point of his season came on July 7 when he could not make his scheduled start against the California Angels due to what he described as "[...] an intensely sharp pain, as if someone stuck a knife in the back of my shoulder."[11] Clemens' early-career insecurity came to the fore again as he engaged in a clubhouse meltdown in Anaheim that day, and his fear of failure caused him to break down in tears while repeatedly asking, "Why me?" The next day he was placed on the 15-day disabled list due to shoulder inflammation and, though he returned to the rotation, he never recovered fully that year. On August 30 surgeon James Andrews removed a small piece of cartilage from Clemens' right shoulder in a 20-minute procedure. Clemens spent the offseason learning new exercises to strengthen his shoulder and waited for the 1986 season to come around.

The Red Sox started out slowly in 1986, but Clemens overcame his spring-training fears about his rehabilitated shoulder and charged out to a 3-0 record with a 1.85 ERA. His fourth start provided the harbinger of things to come as April 29, 1986, became the night on which Roger Clemens vaulted himself to stardom. Facing a free-swinging Seattle Mariners team that had struck out 166 times in 19 games, he turned in a record-setting performance by striking out 20 batters in a nine-inning, complete-game effort at Fenway Park. Clemens began the game in form by brushing back his former college teammate and role model Spike Owen with his second and third pitches of the night. Afterward, he denied throwing at Owen, but a conflicting account exists in which former Longhorns teammate Mike Capel dared him to plunk Owen on the day before the game.

Whatever the truth about Clemens' intent, the tone for the game was set and the Mariners were baffled for all but one pitch. Gorman Thomas launched Clemens' lone mistake for a solo home run and a 1-0 Mariners lead in the top of the seventh inning and, for a moment, it looked as though Clemens' brilliance might be for naught. Fortunately for Clemens and the Red Sox, Dwight Evans hit a three-run homer in the bottom of the inning for the final 3-1 margin of victory. From that point on, Clemens struck out four more batters to reach the record-breaking total of 20. He became an instant superstar and fulfilled a dream he claimed to have had when he was 12 by making the cover of *Sports Illustrated*'s May 12, 1986 issue, which carried the headline "Lord of the K's."[12]

After an 11-strikeout victory at Baltimore on June 27, Clemens was only the fifth pitcher in major-league history to start a season 14-0. He suffered his first loss on July 2 against the Toronto Blue Jays, but his 15-2 first-half record led Kansas City manager Dick Howser to name him the American League's starter in the All-Star Game, which would be held in his adopted hometown of Houston. The Red Sox, meanwhile, were in first place in the AL East with a 56-31 record and a seven-game lead at the break.

There was, however, a downside that accompanied all of this success, and it involved his relationship with the media and its burgeoning demands on his time. According to Clemens, "The attention I enjoyed and appreciated at first after breaking the strikeout record soon became stressful." He claimed that the press did not realize "how I needed to stay on my program and work."[13] For their part, the reporters began to perceive Clemens as alternately aloof or difficult, depending upon whether or not they could get any worthwhile quotes from the new star. Clemens correctly conceded that this period was "the first time I experienced some problems with the media,"[14] but it would not be the last.

The media crush of an All-Star Game that matched Clemens and fellow fireballer Dwight Gooden as the starters did not deter him from turning the event into yet another showcase for his talents. While Gooden surrendered two runs in three innings of work, Clemens retired all nine NL batters he faced, struck out two, and did not allow a single baserunner, a performance that earned him the game's MVP award. His newfound stardom also birthed a new arrogance that surfaced in the second half of the 1986 season.

In his July 30 start against the Chicago White Sox at Comiskey Park, Clemens had a new manner of meltdown after first-base umpire Greg Kosc made a disputed call that went against him. With two outs in the fifth inning, Red Sox first baseman Bill Buckner had flipped a Harold Baines grounder to Clemens, who thought he had beaten the runner to the bag. Instead, Kosc ruled that Clemens had missed first base and called Baines safe, which allowed what ended up being the winning run to score for the White Sox. Clemens charged at Kosc to argue the call and made incidental contact with the umpire, which resulted in his automatic ejection. Now he came completely unglued—he claimed to have hyperventilated twice during his rampage—and eventually was carried off the field by teammates Jim Rice and Don Baylor. Clemens was suspended for two games and fined, but his outlook on his punishment was revealing: In his autobiography, he stated, "As it turned out, all I lost was a day's pay—little more than $1,000—and $250" [for paying his teammates' (Bruce Hurst and Al Nipper) minor fines].[15] A fine was no great consequence to Clemens and, from this point on, he often alternated feats with fits over the course of his career.

The 1986 Red Sox rolled into the playoffs, with Clemens winning his last seven decisions, but Clemens' own postseason hopes seemed jeopardized when John Stefero's line drive hit his pitching elbow in his final regular-season start, against Baltimore on October 1. X-rays were negative and the swelling went down in time for Clemens to make his Game One start in the ALCS against the California Angels at Fenway. Clemens made three starts in Boston's hard-fought seven-game series against the Angels: Game One was forgettable as he surrendered eight runs (seven earned) in 7⅓ innings and Game Four resulted in a no-decision in 8⅓ innings during Boston's extra-inning loss, but in the clinching Game Seven he dominated the Angels and allowed only one run in seven innings to help send the Red Sox to the World Series for the first time since 1975.

World Series Game Two was a Clemens-versus-Gooden rematch, but neither pitcher lasted longer than five innings; a flu-ridden Clemens gave up four walks and three runs in 4⅓ innings of a game that Boston won 9-3. His second start came in Game Six, with the Red Sox holding a 3-2 edge in games, and he struck out eight while surrendering only two runs (one earned) in seven innings. The Red Sox had a 3-2 lead when Clemens was lifted from the game for a pinch-hitter in the eighth inning, but there was controversy over the timing of his exit. Clemens had torn open a blister and had begun bleeding, and manager John McNamara later claimed that Clemens had asked out of the game as a result, a contention that Clemens and several of his teammates denied. Game Six went down in Red Sox infamy as Calvin Schiraldi combined with Bob Stanley, Bill Buckner, and fate to lose to the Mets 6-5 in 10 innings. The Mets' 8-5 victory in Game Seven kept Clemens from putting the ultimate jewel in the crown of his 1986 season, a campaign during which he went 24-4 with a league-leading 2.48 ERA and became the first player to win the Cy Young Award, American League MVP Award, and All-Star Game MVP Award in the same season.

In addition to all of his on-field success, Roger and Debbie Clemens welcomed their first son, Koby, into the world on December 4, 1986. In what became a theme, Clemens gave all four of his sons names that begin with the letter "K"— Kory, Kacy, and Kody followed Koby—since it is the baseball scoring abbreviation for a strikeout.

The relationship between Clemens and the Red Sox took a downturn when Clemens walked out in the middle of spring training over a contract dispute. Commissioner Peter Ueberroth eventually negotiated an agreement between the team and its star, but the incident did not bode well for the future. The Red Sox had a miserable 1987 season, finishing at 78-84, though Clemens won his second consecutive Cy Young Award with a 20-9 record, 2.97 ERA, and seven shutouts.

In 1988 Clemens created a minor stir by deciding to pitch against the Angels in Anaheim rather than return to Houston for the birth of his second son, Kory. He earned a complete-game victory in that May 30 game on his way to an 18-12, 2.93, eight-shutout season. The Red Sox rebounded to win the AL East in 1988 but were swept in the ALCS by the Oakland Athletics, though Clemens pitched adequately in his Game Two start.

The biggest firestorm Clemens ignited that year came on December 5 when he gave an interview to a Boston television station in which he attacked anyone and everyone associated with the Red Sox, from management to teammates to fans. His complaint, "Travel, road trips and carrying your own luggage around isn't all that fun and glory,"[16] propagated the stereotype of the spoiled, pampered athlete and cast him in a negative light to fans.

Clemens did play for the Red Sox through the 1996 season, winning his third Cy Young in 1991 and leading the AL in ERA from 1990 to 1992, but he continued to be antagonistic with the media and, in turn, both the media and fans emphasized his shortcomings—real and perceived—more than his accomplishments.

One highly scrutinized event was a tantrum in Game Four of the 1990 ALCS in which the Athletics again swept the Red Sox. Clemens had pitched six shutout innings in Game One, but Boston had lost, and things were not going well at the outset of Game Four. With Oakland leading 1-0 and two outs in the second inning, Clemens began cursing from the mound at home-plate umpire Terry Cooney over balls and strikes and was ejected from the game. When Clemens realized that he had been tossed, he charged Cooney and pushed right-field umpire Jim Evans aside, an offense for which he was fined $10,000 and suspended for the first five games of the 1991 season.

Rather than lie low after such an ignominious end to the season, Clemens gained additional notoriety off the field when he and older brother Randy were arrested at a Houston nightclub on January 18, 1991. Randy had become involved in an altercation, and Roger was arrested for hindering the security guard—an off-duty police officer—who was attempting to arrest his brother. He was found "not guilty" of the charge, but his fame was now increasing for the wrong reasons.

In 1992 Clemens further strained his relationship with the Red Sox when he reported eight days late for spring training; however, he still registered another stellar campaign on the mound, finishing 18-11. After he posted his first losing record in 1993—11-14 with a 4.46 ERA—speculation renewed about how much longer Clemens would last. He pitched well in strike-shortened 1994, but in 1995 he had a bloated 4.18 ERA and again came up short in the postseason, though he received no decision in the Red Sox' ALDS Game One extra-inning loss to the Cleveland Indians.

While Clemens was in an up-and-down phase of his career on the mound and was in the process of alienating Boston fans and management, he was still popular enough with fans nationwide that he made several guest appearances as himself on different television shows. Clemens even showed a sense of humor by taking a role in the animated *The Simpsons* episode titled "Homer at the Bat." In the course of the story, Clemens—as himself—is hypnotized into thinking that he is a chicken and spends much of the episode squawking and clucking. His acting exploits also included the big screen, for which his most notable role was as an unnamed flamethrower who pitches to Ty Cobb in the 1994 film *Cobb*, based on Al Stump's biography of the Georgia Peach.

In 1996 Clemens posted his second losing record, 10-13, but had a more respectable 3.63 ERA and led the AL with 257 strikeouts. He momentarily turned back the clock 10 years by registering his second career 20-strikeout game, against Detroit at Tiger Stadium on September 18; it was also his 192nd victory, which tied him with Cy Young atop the Red Sox' all-time list. Nonetheless, Red Sox general manager Dan Duquette considered his 40-39 record for the team from 1993 through 1996 and questioned whether Clemens might be in the "twilight" of his career; he apparently did not see him as a player around whom to rebuild the team into a perennial contender. Clemens spurned Boston's contract offer and signed for three years and $24.75 million with the Toronto Blue Jays.

Toronto was far removed from its consecutive World Series victories of 1992-1993 and was not a contender during Clemens' stint with the team, but "Rocket" was not finished yet after all. Quite the contrary, the brief Blue Jays era of 1997-1998 was Clemens at his dominant best as he went a combined 41-13 with a 2.33 ERA and 563 strikeouts, winning the pitching Triple Crown—wins, ERA, strikeouts—in both years as well as his fourth and fifth Cy Young Awards. He also exacted revenge against the Red Sox in his first start as a Blue Jay at Fenway Park on July 12, 1997 when he pitched eight innings of one-run ball and struck out 16 batters.

In time, a cloud of suspicion gathered over this mid-30s pitching renaissance for two reasons: 1) The prevalence of performance-enhancing drugs (PEDs) in baseball by this time, and 2) the hiring of Brian McNamee as Toronto's strength and conditioning coach after the 1997 season. Baseball was in the midst of its PED era and—as was the case with most players—no public accusations were made against Clemens at the time; however, McNamee later claimed that he injected Clemens with the steroid Winstrol in 1998.

Clemens longed to pitch for a contender again and his trade request was granted on February 18, 1999, when Toronto traded him to the New York Yankees—an old adversary with whom he had engaged in numerous beanball wars—for starter David Wells, reliever Graeme Lloyd, and second baseman Homer Bush. As a Yankee, Clemens was back in the center of the baseball universe, but that was a mixed blessing as he turned in an inconsistent 14-10, 4.60 campaign.

The 1999 postseason began promisingly as Clemens pitched seven scoreless innings in the ALDS-clinching Game Three against the Texas Rangers, but the ALCS was another matter altogether as Clemens fizzled in his return to Fenway in a Game Three marquee matchup against Boston's new ace, Pedro Martinez. While Martinez pitched seven shutout innings and struck out 12, Clemens suffered the Yankees' only loss of the series and was battered for five runs in only two innings. As he left the mound in the bottom of the third, Boston fans taunted him by chanting "Where is Rog-er?" That game became a distant memory for Clemens after he won World Series Game Four against the Atlanta Braves with a 7⅔-inning, one-run performance that capped a Yankees sweep. The one prize, a World Series ring, that had eluded Clemens for his entire career was now his: "Tonight, I know what it's like to be a Yankee. I am blessed," he exulted.[17]

Prior to Game Two of the World Series at Atlanta's Turner Field, Clemens had been named—along with 29 other players—as a member of the All-Century Team. The 100 nominees for the team had been chosen by a panel of experts and had been presented at that year's All-Star Game, but it was the fans who had voted for the players. Clemens was the only active pitcher—and one of only four active players—voted onto the team, joining Cal Ripken Jr., Ken Griffey Jr., and Mark McGwire. This accolade and his first World Series championship appeared to validate Clemens' tunnel-vision tenacity in pursuit of his goals.

On the heels of reaching the pinnacle of professional success, Clemens experienced one of the lowest points in his personal life. In May 2000 his ex-sister-in-law Kathy, who had been married to his brother Randy and had been like a mother to him when he had first moved to Texas, was murdered in a home-invasion robbery in Houston. Kathy's son Marcus had adopted his father Randy's drug habit, and the robbery was tied to money and drugs. Roger blamed Randy's substance-abuse addiction for the couple's divorce, his nephew's drug addiction, and Kathy's murder, and he became alienated from the brother who had exerted such tremendous influence on his life, his outlook on the world, and his early career.

On the mound in 2000, Clemens posted a pedestrian 13-8 record and lost his two starts against Oakland in the ALDS, but he experienced a reversal of fortune from the previous year's ALCS in Boston in his Game Four start against the Seattle Mariners. In a game as dominant as any he had ever pitched, he set an ALCS record by striking out 15 batters in a one-hit shutout. It was an amazing performance for a 38-year old power pitcher that also served as an endorsement for Clemens' now-legendary workout regimen—one that players half his age were unwilling to attempt—which again fell under the auspices of Brian McNamee, who had joined the Yankees as an assistant strength coach in 2000.

Clemens turned in another eight shutout innings in World Series Game Two against the crosstown Mets, a Series the Yankees won in five games. The focus of the game, though, was a bizarre incident that occurred in the top of the first inning. Mets catcher Mike Piazza, whom Clemens had hit in the head with a pitch in a regular-season game on July 8, shattered his bat hitting a soft liner that squibbed foul into the Yankees dugout. Clemens picked up the barrel piece of the bat and threw it in Piazza's direction as he ran up the baseline. The shard almost hit Piazza, who was angered and exchanged words with Clemens as both benches emptied. Clemens was not ejected for his action and dominated the Mets with eight innings of shutout ball in which he allowed only two hits and no walks, and struck out nine. After the game, Clemens offered the implausible excuse that he had thought he had the ball, rather than the barrel of Piazza's bat, which still did not explain why he threw it toward Piazza rather than first baseman Tino Martinez. Nobody believed Clemens, and he was fined $50,000 for the incident.

In 2001, a season in which McNamee has claimed he injected Clemens with the steroids Sustanon 250 and Deca-Durabolin, Clemens raced out to a 12-1 record that garnered him his second career All-Star Game start. He took his record to 19-1 before his first attempt at win number 20 was placed on hold by the terrorist attacks against the United States on September 11, 2001. After America regrouped, and MLB resumed play on September 17 at the behest of President George W. Bush, Clemens finished the season 20-3 with a 3.51 ERA and earned his sixth Cy Young Award. The Yankees again made it to the World Series, and Clemens registered a 1.35 ERA over 13⅓ innings in two starts against the Arizona Diamondbacks. He engaged in a Game Seven duel against Curt Schilling that the Yankees lost when Luis Gonzalez looped an RBI single off Mariano Rivera to win the game in the bottom of the ninth inning.

Clemens was solid, though no longer spectacular, with the Yankees in 2002-2003. He did reach both the 300-win and 4,000-strikeout milestones in a 5-2 victory over the St. Louis Cardinals at Yankee Stadium on June 13, 2003, becoming the first pitcher to hit both landmarks in the same game. He had said repeatedly that he was retiring after the 2003 season, so when he walked off the mound of Miami's Pro Player Stadium after pitching seven innings of three-run ball in World Series Game Four on October 22, 2003, everyone assumed it was his swan song. There was no fairytale ending to his story, though, as the Yankees fell to the Florida Marlins in six games.

Clemens' retirement lasted little more than 2½ months. Shortly after Yankees free agent, friend, and fellow Houstonian Andy Pettitte signed to play for the Houston Astros, Clemens joined him and the pair set Houston abuzz with the hope that they could help franchise icons Jeff Bagwell and Craig Biggio reach the promised land of the World Series before they too reached retirement age.

Although 2004 was his first year in the National League, Clemens registered the same results he had through most of his career: He posted an 18-4 record, 2.98 ERA, and 218 strikeouts for which he won his record-extending seventh Cy Young Award, joining Gaylord Perry, Randy Johnson, and Pedro Martinez as the only pitchers to win the award in both leagues. He also started his third All-Star Game—this time for the NL—in his adopted hometown of Houston,

Cys 6 and 7 were for the Yankees, as was his one World Series title.

where he had started his first All-Star Game for the AL 18 years earlier.

The Astros were the NL wild-card team in 2004, and Clemens started the franchise toward its first-ever postseason-series victory in 43 seasons of existence by winning NLDS Game One against the Atlanta Braves. Against the St. Louis Cardinals in the NLCS, he won Game Three but lost the decisive Game Seven; however, he received none of the criticism he had often endured in Boston and New York when he had fallen short in the postseason. He could do no wrong in his hometown and was becoming a Texas legend on a par with his boyhood idol Nolan Ryan.

Clemens returned to the Astros in 2005 and added to his increasingly larger-than-life exploits. At the age of 43, he led the majors with a 1.87 ERA and might have won an eighth Cy Young Award had he received more run support to improve his 13-8 record. On September 14, in a decision reminiscent of his choice to pitch on the day of his son Kory's birth, Clemens defeated the Florida Marlins after his mother, Bess, died that morning. In response to those who questioned his decision, Clemens replied that his mother had made him promise to pitch and that the game was important to the Astros' playoff hopes. It was clear that he was still as driven to win as he had always been.

The Astros were the NL wild-card entry again in 2005 and faced the Atlanta Braves once more. Clemens lost Game Two, but for Houston fans his status grew to mythological proportions three days later in Game Four. On October 9, after the Astros had exhausted their bullpen by the 15th inning of their marathon contest against the Braves, Clemens came to the rescue and pitched three scoreless innings. He earned the win when Chris Burke ended the game with a solo homer in the bottom of the 18th, and the Astros advanced to the NLCS. As if pitching on short rest were not enough, Clemens had also demonstrated a bit of batting acumen when he laid down a perfect sacrifice bunt in the bottom of the 15th.

In the NLCS, the Astros met another familiar opponent — the Cardinals — whom they defeated in six games to reach their first World Series, with Clemens contributing a victory in Game Three. The magic ran out in the World Series, though, as he exited Game One with a sore hamstring after allowing three runs in only two innings. The Chicago White Sox swept the Astros, and Clemens seemed likely to retire permanently.

Alas, he could not stay away from the game, and he lost much of the goodwill he had engendered in 2005 by appearing willing to sell himself to the highest bidder as he engaged in talks with numerous teams. The so-called "family-friendly" clause that had allowed Clemens to remain home for road trips during which he was not scheduled to pitch — and which he insisted upon to the end of his career — now had some people questioning whether his true motive was team success or money. In the end, he signed with the Astros on May 31 and still posted a 2.30 ERA in 113⅓ innings over 19 starts, but the team failed to make the playoffs.

Clemens played the same "Will he or won't he pitch?" game at the start of the 2007 season before announcing his return to the New York Yankees from owner George Steinbrenner's luxury box during the seventh-inning stretch of a Yankees-Mariners game on May 6. He posted a mediocre 6-6, 4.18 line over 99 innings before limping off the Yankee Stadium mound with yet another hamstring injury in the Yankees' October 7 ALDS game against Cleveland.

Once his career was finally over, the countdown to Clemens' Hall of Fame induction began. Whether media members and fans liked him or not — and there were plenty of people in both camps — his statistics pointed to him being one of the best pitchers ever to play the game. Even so, the voters who cast ballots for players to gain entry into the National Baseball Hall of Fame are told to take a player's character into account, and all sorts of skeletons fell out of Clemens' closet upon the release of the Mitchell Report.

First, there were Brian McNamee's allegations of steroid use. Clemens vehemently denied McNamee's accusations and, under the advice and guidance of his lawyer Rusty Hardin, went on the offensive. On January 6, 2008, Clemens filed a defamation suit against McNamee. Though Clemens eventually dropped his suit, McNamee filed his own defamation suit against Clemens in 2008, which dragged on for almost seven years before McNamee received an out-of-court settlement to be paid by Clemens' insurer — not Clemens himself — in March 2015.

The same day that Clemens filed his lawsuit in Houston, CBS-TV's investigative news show *60 Minutes* aired a Mike Wallace interview of Clemens. In the interview Clemens claimed that McNamee had only injected him with vitamin B12 and the painkiller Lidocaine, an assertion that was dubious to many viewers and which made him the butt of countless pain-in-the-butt jokes.

The next day Clemens and Hardin held a press conference in Houston and played a recording of a recent phone conversation between Clemens and McNamee that was to prove Clemens' innocence. The tape proved nothing as McNamee sounded both too desperate and too cautious to say anything that might incriminate him. Clemens fielded questions from the media, but grew increasingly aggravated and angry as the conference continued. When asked if he thought McNamee's allegations would affect his chances at being elected to the Hall of Fame, his retort, "I don't give a rat's ass about the Hall of Fame,"[18] was another statement no one believed, and he soon stormed out of his own press conference.

On February 13, 2008, Clemens was called to testify before a congressional committee in Washington, where he continued to profess his innocence. Some of his testimony contradicted a sworn statement made by Andy Pettitte, who claimed Clemens had told him that McNamee injected him with human growth hormone (HGH). Clemens responded that Pettitte had "misremembered" [sic] their conversation and that he had told Pettitte it was his wife, Debbie, whom McNamee had injected with HGH. There were enough inconsistencies in Clemens' testimony that a drawn-out legal process resulted in an August 19, 2010, grand-jury indictment for making false statements to Congress. His first trial, in July 2011, quickly resulted in a mistrial, while his second trial ended with his acquittal on June 18, 2012.

Along with the steroid allegations and their attendant legal troubles, Clemens was also accused of having extramarital affairs with numerous women. The two most notable names were those of the late country singer Mindy McCready and pro golfer John Daly's ex-wife Paulette. Clemens denied these accusations as well, but McCready and Paulette Daly neither confirmed nor denied them, which gave them implicit affirmation in many people's minds.

All of this dirty laundry was aired in the media in the immediate aftermath of the Mitchell Report, but two books contributed further to the decline of Clemens' reputation: Jeff Pearlman's unauthorized biography *The Rocket That Fell to Earth*, and *New York Daily News*' Sports Investigative Team's *American Icon: The Fall of Roger Clemens and the Rise of Steroids in America's Pastime*. Pearlman's book portrays Clemens in such a consistently negative light that it is easy to dismiss it as one-sided, but the *Daily News* team's research into McNamee's claims casts serious doubt on Clemens' assertion of innocence. The facts remain, however, that Roger Clemens never tested positive for PEDs and that he was acquitted of all charges of lying to Congress.

Nonetheless, the repercussions of the allegations have resulted in a lack of support for Clemens' Hall of Fame candidacy. If he is ultimately enshrined, it is entirely possible that a Veterans Committee will have determined his fate after his initial 10-year period of eligibility has passed. His new road to baseball immortality involves rehabilitation of his former reputation as a hard-working star, which will be an arduous process since everything he does now is greeted with suspicion and cynicism, a circumstance that was in evidence when he pitched two games with the independent Atlantic League's Sugar Land Skeeters in 2012.

Sugar Land, where Clemens lived when he first moved to Texas, received a national publicity boost during the Skeeters' inaugural season when Clemens pitched in two games in August and September 2012. His motive for doing so was suspect, however, as he had just been acquitted of lying to Congress in June and needed positive publicity during his first time on the Hall of Fame ballot. Some media members believed that Clemens was attempting a late-season MLB comeback to push back his Hall of Fame eligibility by five years in the hope his legal troubles would blow over and that he would be a first-ballot selectee. Clemens denied such claims, but his comment—"I probably overextended myself a little bit. I wanted to see where I was at"[19]—after his August 25 start for the Skeeters was interpreted to mean that he was gauging his comeback status.

By his second start, on September 7, the Skeeters had signed Clemens' oldest son, Koby, a catcher, and father and son formed the battery against the Long Island Ducks. This time, the 50-year-old Clemens clearly left open the possibility of a major-league comeback attempt when he said, "I would have to get ready. It would be fun. There's no reason why I couldn't do it next year."[20] Though he had pitched well in both games—and no doubt enjoyed being the center of attention for his pitching rather than his court appearances—this was unaffiliated minor-league ball and his fastball had topped out at 88 MPH, which was hardly the dominant stuff he had once had in his prime.

In the end, Clemens chose to go out as a hometown hero and a winner after his appearances for the Skeeters rather than to risk going out as a failure in one last major-league stint. As of 2015, he and Debbie reside in Houston, where they work to benefit children through the Roger Clemens Foundation and where he also serves as a special assistant to the Astros' general manager.

Clemens' work with the Astros and his induction into the Red Sox Hall of Fame at Fenway Park on August 14, 2014, prior to Boston's game against the Astros, show that there is still a place for him in baseball. The March 2015 settlement in the McNamee case may eventually allow Clemens to move past constant discussion of the steroid allegations against him, though the court of public opinion is unlikely to change its judgment. Clemens did not attend the McNamee settlement, saying, "I was not present, nor would have I participated in paying one dime. Everyone knows my stance on the subject."[21] The fact that he had been named on only 37.5 percent of the Hall of Fame ballots in January 2015 demonstrated that the Hall of Fame voters have not changed their stance in regard to Clemens either.

SOURCES

Baseballhall.org

Baseball-Reference.com

Boston Globe

CBC Sports

Chicago Tribune

Clemens, Roger, with Peter Gammons. *Rocket Man* (Lexington, Massachusetts: The Stephen Greene Press, 1987).

ESPN.com

Hartford Courant

Houston.astros.mlb.com

Houston Chronicle

Lexington (Kentucky) *Herald-Leader*

New York Daily News

New York Times

Pearlman, Jeff. *The Rocket That Fell to Earth* (New York: Harper, 2009).

Riceowls.com

The Sporting News

Sports Illustrated

Sugarlandskeeters.com

Texassports.com

Thompson, Teri, et al. *American Icon* (New York: Knopf, 2009).

Yankeeography: Pinstripe Legends, "Roger Clemens," (2011, A&E Home Video), DVD.

NOTES

1   *Yankeeography*: Pinstripe Legends.

2. CBC Sports, "Clemens lambasted by Blue Jays' Gaston," http://www.cbc.ca/sports/baseball/clemens-lambasted-by-blue-jays-gaston-1.817361, accessed July 27, 2014.

3. Roger Clemens with Peter Gammons, *Rocket Man*, 20.

4. Jeff Pearlman, *The Rocket That Fell to Earth*, 13.

5. Pearlman, 39.

6. Gordon Lakey, "Houston Astros Free Agent Report—William Roger Clemens," scouts.baseballhall.org/report?reportid=01373&playerid=clemer002, accessed April 11, 2015.

7. Larry Monroe, "Chicago White Sox Free Agent Report—Roger Clemens," scouts.baseballhall.org/report?reportid=00948&playerid=clemer002, accessed April 11, 2015.

8. Clemens with Gammons, 33.

9. Mark Story, "22 things you should know about 'Rocket,'" web.archive.org/web/20060615043527/http://www.kentucky.com/mld/kentucky/sports/14749611.htm, accessed August 3, 2014.

10. Pearlman, 76.

11. Clemens with Gammons, 52.

12. si.com/vault/cover/1986/05/12, accessed April 11, 2015.

13. Clemens with Gammons, 75.

14. Ibid.

15. Clemens with Gammons, 110-111.

16. Pearlman, 132.

17. Jeff Jacobs, "From Ruth To Clemens, Monumental Dynasty," articles.courant.com/1999-10-28/sports/9910280137_1_yankee-stadium-25th-world-series-babe-ruth-s-monument, accessed July 30, 2014.

18. Mike Lupica, "Either Roger Clemens or Brian McNamee will tell lies on the Hill," nydailynews.com/sports/baseball/yankees/roger-clemens-brian-mcnamee-lies-hill-article-1.311566, accessed December 12, 2014.

19. ESPN.com, "Roger Clemens shines in return," espn.go.com/mlb/story/_/id/8303548/roger-clemens-impressive-comeback-sugar-land-skeeters, accessed December 15, 2014.

20. Associated Press, "Roger Clemens solid in outing," espn.go.com/mlb/story/_/id/8350222/roger-clemens-solid-again-second-outing-sugar-land-skeeters, accessed December 15, 2014.

21. ESPN.com news services, "Defamation suit vs. Clemens settled," espn.go.com/mlb/story/_/id/12509911/roger-clemens-brian-mcnamee-reach-settlement-2008-defamation-lawsuit, accessed March 19, 2015.

KEN GRIFFEY JR.

By Emily Hawks

While the honor of having the sweetest swing in baseball may seem like it's a subjective one, few would disagree that Ken Griffey Jr. possessed the sweetest swing there ever was. He was a natural, and his inborn abilities coupled with his youthful enthusiasm ignited an entire city's passion for baseball. Behind the center-field wall at Seattle's Safeco Field, beneath the feet of the fans donning backwards baseball caps as a tribute to "The Kid," one can find two special bricks installed when the stadium opened in 1999. The brick on the left reads "Trey + Taryn Griffey," and the brick on the right, "The House Their Father Built." It wouldn't be long after the mortar had dried that Griffey would leave for what he had hoped would be a storybook return to his hometown of Cincinnati. But frequent trips to the disabled list stifled the talents of one of the greatest center fielders to play the game, and Griffey's carefree attitude seemed to dissipate along with his playing time. Still, although it is tempting to contemplate what could have been were it not for those injuries, it is still gratifying to marvel at what was. Griffey's effortless home-run swings, dazzling center-field catches, and 1,000-watt smile lit up the game for an entire generation of baseball fans, and few would dispute that he saved baseball in Seattle.

George Kenneth Griffey Jr. was born on November 21, 1969, in Donora, Pennsylvania to parents George Kenneth Sr. and Alberta, better known as Birdie. He shared a birthday and a birthplace with Stan Musial, who was born exactly 49 years earlier in Donora, a former steel town 20 miles south of Pittsburgh on the Monongahela River. Griffey was followed 18 months later by a younger brother, Craig, as well as a sister, Lathesia, two years after Craig.

With Griffey Sr., a baseball star himself, the younger Ken Griffey grew up in major-league clubhouses, often spotted in a miniature Reds uniform at Riverfront Stadium surrounded by stars like Pete Rose and Johnny Bench. For the Griffeys, it was about family time. "My dad didn't care if we watched him play baseball," said Junior. "He cared about spending quality time with us."[1]

Junior's time in the clubhouse with his dad would also influence his own eventual path in the major leagues. When Griffey Sr. was with the Yankees, manager Billy Martin requested through one of his coaches that Griffey's kids be removed from the clubhouse after they'd been playing in the stadium corridors with the other players' kids before and after a blowout loss. Though 14 kids had joined them, Martin allegedly only wanted the Griffeys gone.[2] From that moment, Griffey Jr. had distaste for the Yankees, and ultimately vowed never to play for them. "I don't forget things like that," he said. "And I never will."[3]

It wasn't long before the standout high-school athlete piqued the interest of major-league scouts. One such scout was Tom Mooney. Mariners owner George Argyros had directed general manager Hal Keller to promote his then-chauffeur Mooney to the scouting staff in 1984, and Mooney went on to cover Ohio, Michigan, and Indiana for the Mariners. After an abysmal last-place finish in 1986, the Mariners had the first pick in the 1987 draft, and their selection was still very much in the air. In the spring of 1987 Mariners director of scouting Roger Jongewaard joined Mooney to watch Griffey's Moeller High School team play in a new community park in Cincinnati. The park had a grove of trees roughly 20 yards beyond the outfield fence. In his second at-

Griffey with his signature sweet swing

bat, Griffey lobbed one high into right field and well over the fence. "Which tree did it hit?" Jongewaard asked. "Roger," said Mooney, "it went over the trees."[4] High-profile baseball names were also taking note. "I saw Ken Griffey Jr. in high school at Moeller High in Cincinnati and he was the best prospect I've ever seen in my life," said Bobby Cox, then general manager of the Atlanta Braves. `"There was nobody even close to him; he was outstanding."[5]

Still, Mariners ownership was hesitant to take on another high schooler after their 1986 first-round pick, Pat Lennon, had flopped. Also, Griffey had failed a psychological test that baseball teams used to forecast a player's behavior and character. In fact, his test result was the worst the Mariners had ever seen.[6] While Griffey was averse to retaking the test, he desperately wanted to be the number-one pick in the draft. "The thing in our favor was that he knew everyone would remember who the No. 1 pick was,"

Mooney recalled. "He was very proud of that and wanted to show his dad."[7] So Mooney re-administered the test one afternoon at the Griffey house. This time Griffey had an average result. More importantly, though, Mooney saw firsthand in Griffey's home how he interacted with his mother, grandmother, brother, and friends. He declared him a normal kid, and the endorsement trickled up to the front office. Argyros remained skeptical, but he reluctantly agreed to selecting Griffey after Griffey and his agent agreed to sign for just $160,000. When agent Brian Goldberg told Griffey he might be leaving tens of thousands of dollars on the table, Griffey replied, "I'll make up for that later. Let's be No. 1."[8]

In spite of a seemingly bright future, Griffey struggled with turmoil in his teenage years. "It seemed like everyone was yelling at me in baseball, then I came home and everyone was yelling at me there," said Griffey. "I got depressed. I got angry. I didn't want to live."[9] In the summer of 1987, Griffey was playing for the Bellingham Mariners of the short-season Class-A Northwest League. While on the team bus one day, Griffey got into a dispute with the teenage sons of the bus driver. One of them had reportedly expressed racial epithets toward Griffey, while another allegedly threatened him with a gun. Griffey recalled, "Growing up back home I never had to deal with anything like that."[10] When he returned home to Ohio that fall, he was regularly staying out until the early-morning hours, often worrying his mother. Griffey Sr. decided that his son should either pay rent or get his own place. Griffey Jr. recalled, "I was confused. I was hurting and I wanted to cause some hurt for others." He had contemplated suicide many times, and on one fateful day in January 1988 he followed his thoughts with action. A 17-year-old Griffey ingested 277 aspirin, and wound up in an intensive-care unit in Mount Airy, Ohio. Shortly thereafter, a frightened and angry Griffey Sr. arrived at the hospital and a fight commenced. Though Birdie was distressed, she knew the primary source of conflict and angst for Junior originated with Senior, and opted to stay out of the fray. Eventually Griffey Jr. moved into his own condo. While the arguments continued between father and son, an increased understanding began to develop between the two of them.

Griffey quickly ascended the minor leagues. His first hit with the Bellingham team in 1987 was a home run, and he finished his first professional season in Low A, batting .313 in 54 games. In 1988, after he clubbed 74 hits in just 58 games for San Bernardino of the Class-A California League, the team retired his jersey. He was promoted to Vermont of the Double-A Eastern League later that season, and the mere 17 games there would be his last as a full-time minor leaguer.

Griffey joined the big-league club in Tempe, Arizona, for spring training in 1989, and it didn't take long for him to make a splash in the Cactus League. He hit .359 that spring and compiled a 15-game hitting streak. He also set Mariners preseason records in three categories with 32 hits, 49 total bases, and 20 RBIs.[11] He had extra incentive to make the Opening Day squad, as his father told him, "This could be my last season, so you had better make the team."[12] The baseball world quickly took note. Prior to the 1989 season, *Baseball America* ranked Griffey the best number-one draft pick since the draft's inception in 1966. While an Opening Day roster spot seemed like a foregone conclusion, manager Jim Lefebvre couldn't resist giving Griffey a hard time. "At the end of spring training, he called me into his office," Griffey recalled. "He goes through, like, five minutes of stuff like 'These decisions are so tough,' 'You know, we've got a lot of veterans that have earned their chance,' then at the end, he sticks out his hand from across his desk and says, 'You're my starting center fielder.' ... And he had managed to keep a straight face the whole time."[13]

Like Lefebvre, Griffey's teammates also couldn't help but give the rookie a razzing about his big promotion. The Mariners had one last exhibition game in Las Vegas prior to the season opener in Oakland, and it happened to fall on April Fools' Day. "I walk into the clubhouse, and everyone's talking about a big trade we just made for Dale Murphy. Which would mean he's our new center fielder, not me," remembered Griffey. "So I make that long walk to Lefebvre's office, and he says, 'I guess you've heard about the big trade we made?' And again, he goes on and on, then finally he says, 'Do you know today's date?'"[14]

Griffey made his major-league debut on April 3, 1989, at the Oakland Coliseum, facing Athletics ace Dave Stewart. "We got to Oakland, and man, I'm nervous," Griffey recalled. "Dave Stewart's on the mound, and he could have rolled the ball up there, I would have swung."[15] In spite of his nerves, Griffey hammered a 375-foot double to left-center in his first at-bat on the second pitch he saw. "He was scary all night long," remarked Oakland manager Tony La Russa. "The young man has a world of talent. ... He's going to be something to contend with."[16] One week later, in his home debut at the Kingdome, Griffey hit his first major-league home run, launching the first pitch he saw from White Sox pitcher Eric King into the left-field seats.[17] Griffey's quick success led to a near-instantaneous fan following in Seattle. Just over a month after his debut, a Seattle-area trading-card company launched a Ken Griffey Jr. candy bar. Demand quickly soared, and ultimately nearly one million bars were purchased.[18] Ironically, Griffey was allergic to chocolate.[19]

By late July, Griffey was a leading candidate for the American League Rookie of the Year award, batting .287 with 13 homers and 45 RBIs. But on July 25 he suffered a fracture in his right hand, purportedly after falling while coming out of the shower in his Chicago hotel room.[20] However, club officials later admitted that the injury occurred when Griffey slammed his hand in anger against a hotel-room wall during an argument with a girlfriend.[21] The incident suggested to Mariners management that Griffey still had a lot of maturing to do. Griffey, who was raised by his mother and grandmother, often struggled with homesickness. "He was the only player I've ever dealt with where I'd have to call his mother," said Mariners GM Woody Woodward.[22] He missed nearly a month of playing time as he healed. After returning to the lineup on August 20, Griffey finished out the year with an additional three home runs and 16 RBIs, and ended the season batting .264. He finished third in AL Rookie of the Year voting. He did receive one first-place vote, presumably from Bob Finnigan of the *Seattle Times*, who wrote, "I will vote for Ken Griffey Jr. ... He has brought to the Mariners an exuberance long missing. ... Seeing Griffey play almost every day, there is no way I cannot vote for him."[23]

As the 1989 season came to a close, Griffey's future in Seattle seemed bright. He pondered the possibility of his father joining him in Seattle. "Nothing would make him happier than to be in one game with me," said Griffey.[24]

While Griffey had become known for his swing, he was also increasingly becoming known for his glove. On April 26, 1990, with Randy Johnson on the mound, Yankees right fielder Jesse Barfield, having homered off Johnson in his first at-bat, was aiming for a repeat, and with a loud crack of the bat he launched Johnson's offering deep to left-center. Griffey ran to the fence, gave it a quick glance, and dug a spike into the soft padding, hoisting his shoulders above the 7-foot-3 wall at Yankee Stadium. With his perfectly timed leap, he robbed Barfield of what would have been his 200th home run. Griffey's wide grin could be seen even before he landed. His father, who was seated next to Barfield's wife in the stands, commented, "I think (the smile) was for me."[25]

Though the Griffeys had already made history in 1989, becoming the first father-son combination to play in the major leagues in the same season, that storyline was eclipsed in 1990. Griffey Sr. was released by the Reds on August 18 and was picked up by the Mariners on the 29th, a move the Mariners hoped would help the younger Griffey mature. "A big reason we signed his father was so he would be with him," said Jongewaard.[26]

On August 31 the two Griffeys became the first father and son tandem in major-league history to play in a game on the same team, with Griffey Sr. in left and Griffey Jr. in center. That evening the two hit back-to-back singles in the bottom of the first. "I wanted to cry or something," said Junior after the game. "It just seemed like a father-son game, like we were out playing catch in the backyard. But we were actually playing a real game."[27]

The fairytale culminated two weeks later on September 14 in a game against the California Angels in Anaheim. In the first inning, Griffey Sr., facing Angels starter Kirk McCaskill, hammered an 0-and-2 pitch 402 feet over the center-field wall. He was greeted at home plate by his son. "I felt for him then," said Senior. "I knew he would be thinking home run. I could see it in his eyes when I crossed the plate."[28] What Senior saw in Junior's eyes soon became reality. Junior came to the plate, and ran the count to 3-and-0. He was given the green light by third-base coach Bill Plummer and followed his dad's lead with a 388-foot shot over the left-field wall. Senior reacted with a quiet clap of his hands in the dugout and waited for his son by the bat rack while his teammates climbed the dugout steps for high fives. Junior looked for his father in the dugout, and the two shared a smile and an embrace. "It's about time," Griffey Sr. told his son.[29] The father-son duo played 51 games together before Senior retired the following year. Many credited Senior's presence for a change in Junior's demeanor. One clubhouse aide noted, "He toned down when Senior got there. He went from a brash and outspoken kid to someone more respectful of elders. He really quieted down a lot."[30]

Griffey Jr. wrapped up the 1990 season batting .300 with 22 homers and 80 RBIs. He was named to the American League All-Star squad and earned his first Gold Glove. The future appeared bright for the young phenom.

In 1991 Griffey continued to dazzle. He was elected to the American League All-Star squad as the top vote-getter in the junior circuit. Griffey was still finding his way, however, and often struggled with the high expectations set for him and criticism by fans and the media. Just before the All-Star break, *Seattle Times* columnist Steve Kelley published an open letter to Griffey criticizing him for not giving his all. He accused Griffey of playing to be a multi-

Griffey's backwards cap style was copied by fans everywhere.

millionaire rather than a Hall of Famer, not running out groundballs and taking a lackadaisical approach in the outfield. Kelley drew talent comparisons to Willie Mays, citing Mays as a player who always strived to reach his full potential and condemning Griffey as one who squandered his talents.[31] Griffey fired back the next day. "People have no idea why I play," he said. "My thing is I don't like to be criticized. I hate for people to say I don't do this right or that right. How do they know?" To fans' sky-high expectations, Griffey responded, "I'm still learning what I can do. I'm driven. … I'll never hit 40 home runs in a year. … Numbers are not everything, only if they help the team win." Griffey was also grappling with the impending reality of his father's retirement. "That's why I've been struggling, because I don't want him to go."[32]

Griffey silenced his critics in the second half, batting .373 with 13 home runs and 64 RBIs, and he had much more fun doing it. He credited teammate Harold Reynolds with his turnaround. "We were in Toronto right before the break and Harold sat me down," Griffey said. "He told me I wasn't having any fun. He was right."[33] Griffey took home another Gold Glove as well as the American League Silver Slugger award that season after batting .327. For the first time in franchise history, the Mariners finished with a winning record. Griffey was having more fun off the field as well. After the season he appeared, in animated form, on an episode of *The Simpsons* titled "Homer at the Bat." He also collaborated with Seattle-area rapper Kid Sensation to co-write and record a rap song titled "The Way I Swing."

By 1992 there was little doubt as to who was the centerpiece of the Mariners. Third baseman Mike Blowers noted, "There was a lot of pressure on him, not just fans, but from veterans in the clubhouse."[34] The pressures of big-league stardom coupled with a tumultuous ownership group constantly threatening to sell or relocate the team were difficult for a sensitive Griffey. Still, he managed another stellar season, hitting .308 with 27 homers and 103 RBIs, and winning another Gold Glove. He was also the MVP of the All-Star game, ending a triple short of a cycle. Opposing NL manager Bobby Cox marveled, "He doesn't have a ceiling that I can see."[35]

After the season finished, Griffey married his girlfriend of three years, Melissa Gay, a Seattle-area native, in a ceremony in Kirkland, Washington.

In 1993 Griffey's power began to take center stage. He clubbed his 100th homer on June 15, becoming the sixth-youngest player to reach that milestone. After being named to his fourth consecutive All-Star team, he became the first player to homer off the B&O warehouse in Baltimore's Camden Yards, hitting a 445-foot shot during the Home Run Derby.[36] On July 28 he tied the major-league record for consecutive home-run games, homering for an eighth consecutive day, this time into the third deck of the Kingdome. Griffey finished the season leading the American League in total bases (359), winning his second Silver Slugger Award, and finishing fifth in MVP voting. He added a fourth Gold Glove to his trophy case.

In January 1994 Griffey became a father when Melissa gave birth to a baby boy, Trey Kenneth Griffey, at a Seattle-area hospital. "He has a full head of hair," said a proud Griffey. "I mean, he came out with an Afro."[37] Those around him noted the calming influence Griffey's family had on him, and his family became the center of his world. "They're the two most important things in my life," Griffey said of Melissa and Trey.[38]

Griffey's power streak continued in 1994. He clubbed his 30th home run of the season into the Kauffman Stadium fountains in Kansas City on June 17, tying Babe Ruth's record for home runs before July 1. "That's one of the hardest hit balls I've ever seen," remarked Seattle manager Lou Piniella.[39] Griffey went on to surpass Ruth's record with home runs on June 22 and June 24. He was named to his fifth consecutive All-Star squad, shattering Rod Carew's record for All-Star votes (4,292,740 in 1977) with a staggering 6,079,688-vote tally.[40] True to form, Griffey credited his father for the votes. "To have his name. … It was a little bit easier for people to look at me and recognize what my dad has done."[41] Then the players' strike put an end to Griffey's stellar season. As baseball shut its doors on August 11, Griffey finished with 40 home runs, the highest tally in the AL. He added another Gold Glove and Silver Slugger to his résumé, and finished second in AL MVP voting. He also bolstered his acting résumé, making cameos in the movie *Little Big League* and the hit TV show *The Fresh Prince of Bel-Air*. Griffey ventured into the video-game business, partnering with Mariners owner Nintendo to develop a series of video games bearing his name.

After baseball resumed in 1995, the Mariners went on to have a season permanently etched in franchise lore, and Griffey played a central role. On May 26, in a game against Baltimore in the Kingdome, he made a catch that would feature in highlight reels for decades to come, scaling the center-field wall to make a backhanded grab of a Kevin Bass bid for an extra-base hit. The dazzling play would ultimately become known as the "Spiderman" catch. However, Griffey suffered a broken left wrist on the play, and missed 73 games. He returned to the roster on August 15, and on August 24 he delivered one of the most crucial home runs of the season. The Mariners were in the heat of the wild-card race, and were trailing the Yankees 7-6 in the bottom of the ninth. After Joey Cora hit a single to tie it, Griffey strode to the plate with two outs and clubbed a two-run homer off closer John Wetteland. From there, the Mariners went on a tear through late August and September, securing their first-ever AL West division championship.[42]

The 1995 ALDS pitted the Mariners against the wild-card champion Yankees. The Mariners had home-field advantage, meaning they would open the series in the Bronx (prior to 1998, the ALDS had a 2-3 rather than a 2-2-1 format). Game One went to the men in pinstripes, though Griffey gave a solid effort, going 3-for-5 with two home runs. The Mariners fell to the Yankees again in Game Two in a heartbreaking 15-inning marathon, losing 7-5 in spite of Griffey's clubbing another home run, going 2-for-6. The series headed back to Seattle, with the Yankees needing just one win for the series victory. Back on their home Astroturf, the Mariners battled back, winning the next two games and forcing a decisive Game Five.

The Yankees' Game One victor David Cone held the Mariners to two runs through seven innings, leaving them trailing, 4-2. Griffey faced Cone with one out in the eighth, sending a fastball into the second deck of the Kingdome, for his fifth homer of the series—a division series record. The Yankees' lead was cut to 4-3, and Seattle tied the tense contest to send Cone to the showers before the inning ended. After dramatic relief appearances by the Yankees' Jack McDowell and the Mariners' Randy Johnson, the Mariners fell behind 5-4 in the 11th. In the bottom of the inning a confident Griffey came to the plate with Joey Cora on base. He ripped a McDowell fastball into center for a single, advancing Cora to third. Edgar Martinez came to the plate and bashed a fastball into the left-field corner. Cora scored easily to tie the game, and all 57,411 eyes in the Kingdome turned to Griffey, who represented the winning run. "I saw that (Gerald) Williams was playing toward left-center," Griffey said. "When I saw the ball land near the line, I ran as fast as I could for as long as I could. When I got to third, Sammy (Perlozzo) said, 'Keep going!' So I did."[43] Griffey slid home safely, and was quickly dogpiled by his teammates as they took home the Mariners first-ever division series championship. Griffey's smile was so bright that it could be seen from the Kingdome rafters. The Mariners went on to lose to the Indians in six games during the ALCS, but their division championship remains etched in fans' memories as the quintessential Mariners moment.

The excitement continued that offseason for Griffey when he and Melissa added a daughter to their family. When Taryn Kennedy Griffey was born, her father noted, "We've added a track star to the family," he said. "I can tell."[44]

On January 31, 1996, Griffey became baseball's highest-paid player when he signed a four-year, $34 million deal. He clubbed his 200th homer on May 21 at just 26 years old. He enjoyed a huge game against the Yankees on May 24, hitting three homers, scoring five runs, and driving in six. He finished the 1996 season fourth in AL MVP voting, adding another All Star selection (7), Gold Glove (7), and Silver Slugger (4) to his résumé. His popularity soared, and a Nike campaign promoting Griffey as a presidential candidate was ubiquitous. "Griffey in '96" began appearing on TV commercials, T-shirts, and even bumper stickers.[45]

In 1997 construction began on a new Mariners ballpark. Before ground had even been broken, the stadium was being billed as "The House That Griffey Built." By design, Griffey was the only player to fly up for the groundbreaking ceremony during spring training. "It was the right thing for me," he said. "I thought it was important that I go."[46]

Griffey led the Mariners to their second American League West Division championship in the 1997 season. He scored an American League-leading 125 runs and bashed a staggering 56 home runs, while leading the majors with 147 RBIs. In addition to garnering what was becoming his standard All-Star-Gold Glove-Silver Slugger trifecta, he was named the unanimous MVP of the American League, snagging all 28 first-place votes. For Griffey, the award was vindication against his toughest critics. "All my life in professional baseball, people said, 'He could be better,'" Griffey said. "This award means a lot."[47]

On April 13, 1998, Griffey hit his 300th homer. Only Hall of Famer Jimmie Foxx had reached this milestone at a younger age. That same season, he left Foxx in the dust, hitting his 350th home run on September 25 and reaching that plateau at nearly a year younger than Foxx was at the time he achieved it. Griffey was named to his ninth All-Star team in July, this time at the hitter-friendly Coors Field in Denver, and disappointed fans when he opted not to participate in the Home Run Derby. He cited a plethora of reasons, including the Mariners' travel schedule, a sore wrist, and a poor performance in the prior year's derby. Yet after the boos rained down over him as he stepped out for American League batting practice, Griffey was taken aback. "I don't like to get booed," he said.[48] Minutes later, Griffey re-emerged from the clubhouse with his signature backwards cap and a bat in his hand, ready to participate. "If they want to see me in the home-run competition, the fans, there's 4 million reasons why I did it, for them."[49] Griffey made it worth their while, hitting eight homers in the first round, eight more in the second, then beating Jim Thome in the final round, securing the Home Run Derby crown. Griffey finished the 1998 season by matching his prior-season home run total of 56. He finished fourth in AL MVP voting.

The 1999 season marked the end of an era in Seattle, in what would turn out to be more ways than one. In July the Mariners moved out of the Kingdome—their home since the franchise's inception in 1977. Griffey hit the last home run ever to be hit in the Kingdome, on June 27. He tallied 198 home runs in the Kingdome, more than any other player. He was selected to his 10th All-Star Game in July, and won his second straight Home Run Derby title, this time at Fenway Park. He moved into his new home, Safeco Field, two days later. Many were concerned that Griffey's offense would be stifled in the new, larger outdoor stadium, and that Griffey—whose contract was set to expire after the following season—would flee to more hitter-friendly pastures. In his 42 games at Safeco that summer, Griffey hit .278 with 14 homers.

Griffey was one of 100 players nominated as potential vote-getters for the All-Century team in July. During the 1999 World Series, it was announced that Griffey was one of 30 players selected to the team.

In November the Mariners announced that Griffey had turned down an eight-year deal worth in excess of $135 million, and had requested to be traded to a team closer to his hometown of Orlando, Florida. Griffey, a 10-and-5 player with 10 years of major-league service and five with the same team, had the power to reject any trade the Mariners proposed. In December Griffey announced that his short list had narrowed to just one team: the Cincinnati Reds.

On February 10, 2000, Griffey's day of reckoning had arrived. He was traded to the Reds for pitcher Brett Tomko, outfielder Mike Cameron, infielder Antonio Perez, and minor-league pitcher Jake Meyer. The Reds signed Griffey to a nine-year, $112.5 million contract. "Well, I'm finally home," Griffey said in his first press conference at Cinergy Field. As he had in the past, Griffey left money on the table for what he felt was the right decision. "This is my hometown. I grew up here. It doesn't matter how much money you make; it's where you feel happy. Cincinnati is the place where I thought I would be happy."

In Griffey's first season with the Reds, he hit 40 home runs and drove in 118 runs. While few would have expected it, 2000 would turn out to be his best Reds season. Later in the season, during a confrontation with broadcaster Marty Brennaman, Griffey admitted to having played hurt all year with a sore hamstring.[50] It was a harbinger of things to come.

On Opening Day 2001, Griffey sat out for the first opener in his career with a sore hamstring. He went on the disabled list on April 29. In July Griffey's former teammate and then-ESPN analyst Harold Reynolds criticized the Reds' decision to play a recovering Griffey when they were out of contention. "They gave me the green light to play," Griffey retorted. "If I blow out, I blow out. But I am going to do it under my own terms."[51]

Six games into the 2002 season, the Reds were facing the Expos at home when Griffey was caught in a rundown between third and home. He slipped and twisted his right knee, tearing his patella. Season-ending surgery was contemplated, but Griffey decided to rehab instead. He played 70 games that season, hitting .264 with eight home runs.

One bright spot for Griffey that season was the welcoming of adopted son Tevin Kendall in May. Since Melissa had been adopted, the Griffeys always wanted to adopt a child into their family. It was challenging finding the right match, as prospective birth parents were trying to extract favors from the Griffeys once they discovered their identities. However, this time it worked out perfectly, and the Griffeys became a family of five, with all three children sharing the same initials.[52]

Ugly rumors plagued Griffey the following offseason, with reports that Reds GM Jim Bowden and

Griffey hit 630 home runs in the big leagues.

manager Bob Boone were conspiring to trade Griffey, considering his acquisition a flop. Griffey, always sensitive to criticism, responded with a combination of the silent treatment and dismissive defiance: "I don't play for a GM, I don't play for a manager. I don't play for an owner. I love playing baseball because I love playing baseball."[53]

Griffey's bad luck continued in 2003; on July 17 he suffered a season-ending injury rounding first base on a double. He underwent surgery to repair a ruptured ankle tendon. It was the latest in a laundry list of injuries that year that included a dislocated shoulder, which would be surgically repaired in August, tears to both hamstrings, and the aggravation of his previously torn patella.[54]

Griffey returned in 2004, and on Father's Day, with both his parents in attendance, he hit his 500th home run, against the Cardinals in St. Louis.[55] On August 4 Griffey tore his hamstring while making a sliding play in the outfield. He had season-ending surgery on August 16.

Griffey bounced back in 2005, hitting 35 home runs with 92 RBIs. He was ultimately sidelined by an ankle injury in September, but won the National League Comeback Player of the Year Award, voted in by the fans. "This award is one I'll cherish forever," he said.[56]

As the 2007 season commenced, Griffey asked Commissioner Bud Selig for permission to wear Jackie Robinson's retired number 42, 60 years to the day after Robinson broke the color barrier in baseball. He had also sought the approval of Robinson's widow, Rachel. Ten years earlier, Griffey had worn number 42 with the encouragement of the Jackie Robinson Foundation, to honor Robinson on the day his number was retired by all of baseball. Selig agreed, and extended the opportunity to all other major leaguers as well. "This is a wonderful gesture on Ken's part and a fitting tribute to the great Jackie Robinson," said Selig.[57] Several other players followed suit, and the practice soon became a tradition for players, coaches, and umpires around the league each April 15, Jackie Robinson Day in baseball. The idea originated with Griffey, who said, "It's just my way of giving that man his due respect."[58]

In June, Griffey returned to Safeco Field for the first time since his trade. He was ambivalent about his return, fearing he might be greeted with a chorus of boos.[59] On June 23 the Mariners held a pregame ceremony to welcome back Griffey and his family. A sellout crowd greeted him with a four-minute standing ovation; there wasn't a boo heard in the house. The normally stoic Griffey let his guard down during his speech, and appeared to choke back tears. "Never could I imagine it would be like this coming back," he said in his speech. "I met my beautiful wife here. Two out of my three kids were born here. This place will be home. I didn't realize how much I missed being in Seattle."[60] After a sentimental weekend, the wheels were put in motion for a Seattle return.

Before that, though, Griffey would make a pit stop with the Chicago White Sox. After hitting his 600th home run on June 9, 2008, with the Reds, Griffey was dealt to the White Sox at the July 31 trade deadline with cash for pitcher Nick Masset and infielder Danny Richar. The White Sox made the playoffs that year, partly due to a spectacular defensive play Griffey made during a tie-breaking 163rd game on September 30 against the Minnesota Twins at US Cellular Field. Griffey threw a strike from center to home in the fifth inning and the Twins' Michael Cuddyer was out at the plate. The White Sox won, 1–0, advancing to the Division Series, which they lost to the Tampa Bay Rays in four games.

A free agent after the 2008 season, Griffey was agonizing over his choice between joining the Braves and the Mariners. Though initially leaning towards Atlanta, which was closer to his Orlando home, ultimately he chose Seattle. He was reportedly persuaded by Willie Mays, the man who was the reason he wore number 24 with the Mariners. Mays emphasized Griffey's legacy with the Mariners franchise, as did Griffey's daughter Taryn, who urged him to go to the Mariners and never have any regrets about how he finished his career.[61]

Griffey made a strong impact on the Mariners' clubhouse in 2009, and his lighthearted antics were reminiscent of his younger self. He could be found playing pranks on teammates during road trips, or teasing and tickling a normally composed Ichiro Suzuki during batting practice. "His humor and presence is something I feel only he can do," Ichiro said. "Everybody considers him to be a genius as a player, but he's a genius in that respect as well."[62]

Though his bat was fairly quiet in 2009—he hit just .214—the Mariners brought Griffey back in 2010 largely for his clubhouse influence. On May 10 a report surfaced that Griffey had missed an at-bat because he was asleep in the clubhouse.[63] Manager Don Wakamatsu had also been limiting Griffey's playing time due to poor performance. The storybook return began to appear tarnished. On June 2, in the midst of a four-game set at home versus the Twins, Griffey quietly packed up and left in the middle of the night, driving cross-country back to his home in Orlando. He issued a statement through the team, "While I feel I am still able to make a contribution on the field ... I will never allow myself to become a distraction."[64] With that, Griffey had played his last major-league game.

Griffey finished his career with 2,781 hits, including 630 home runs. He was a 13-time All-Star and garnered 10 Gold Gloves, seven Silver Sluggers, and one AL MVP Award. He would later be inducted into both the Mariners' and Reds' Halls of Fame. While Griffey's on-field accolades speak for themselves, he considered his proudest accomplishment in life being a good father. He could often be seen at the University of Arizona cheering on his son Trey, a football star, and Taryn, a basketball standout. Griffey is also a pilot and a photography enthusiast. As former teammate Harold Reynolds explained, "I have always believed that Junior's No. 1 goal in life was to be a dad like his dad. That's what he wanted to do, more than hitting all the home runs and more than going to the Hall of Fame. Junior loves his kids."[65]

Note: Statistics from Baseball-Reference.com unless otherwise noted

NOTES

1. Jeff Savage, *Sports Great Ken Griffey, Jr.* (New York: Enslow Publishers, 2000), 16.
2. Filip Bondy, "Baseball; Griffey Enjoys Clobbering Yankees," *New York Times*, July 25, 1991.
3. Bob Finnegan, "Junior in Pinstripes? Not as Long as George is Around—Griffey Still Irked Over Slights by Steinbrenner When He Was a Kid," *Seattle Times*, October 5, 1995.
4. Art Thiel, *Out of Left Field: How the Mariners Made Baseball Fly in Seattle* (Seattle: Sasquatch Books, 2003), 25.
5. Hal Bodley, "Griffey's Son the Brightest of Stars," *USA Today*, July 15, 1992.
6. Art Thiel, 27.
7. Ibid.
8. Art Thiel, 30.
9. Bob Finnegan, "Young Cry For Help—At 17, Griffey Jr. Attempted Suicide; Now He Warns Others," *Seattle Times*, March 15, 1992.
10. Ibid.
11. Larry Stone, *Ken Griffey, Jr: The Home Run Kid* (New York: Skyhorse Publishing, 2013), 6.
12. "Baseball America Rates Seattle's Griffey Best No. 1 Pick Ever; Second Generation—Griffey, Alomar—Head Big League Prospects." *Baseball America* news release, April 5, 1989.
13. Josh Lewin, *You Never Forget Your First* (Herndon, Virginia: Potomac Books, 2014), 66-67.
14. Ibid.
15. Ibid.
16. Mark Kreidler, "Griffey Jr. wastes no time getting into the swing of things," *San Diego Union*, April 5, 1989.
17. Ken Wheeler, "Mariners Come to Life at Home; Knock Off White Sox 6-5," *The Oregonian* (Portland), April 11, 1989.
18. Steve Christilaw, "Edmonds Businessman Gets a Big HR—Amazing Success of Griffey Bar Surprises Creator," *Seattle Times*, May 24, 1989.
19. "Griffey Jr. Allergic to His Own Candy Bar," *Baltimore Sun*, May 8, 1989.
20. Jim Street, "Griffey's in Drydock After Slip in Shower," *The Sporting News*, August 7, 1989.
21. Art Thiel, 34.
22. Ibid.
23. Bob Finnigan, "MVP Up for Grabs; Not Top Rookie," *Seattle Times*, October 1, 1989.
24. Bob Sherwin, "Mariner Review: Griffey Captivates Seattle," *Seattle Times*, September 27, 1989.

25. Bob Sherwin, "'The Kid' Provides Another Dazzler for Highlight Films," *Seattle Times*, April 27, 1990.
26. Art Thiel, 34.
27. Larry Schwartz, "Griffey Sr. and Jr. first to play together in MLB," *ESPN Classic*, November 19, 2003, espn.go.com/classic/s/moment010831-griffey.
28. Bob Sherwin, "Back-to-Back HRs for Griffeys—Winfield's Shot in 7-5 Angel Win Dulls Pair's Pair," *Seattle Times*, September 15, 1990.
29. Ibid.
30. Art Thiel, 37.
31. Steve Kelley, "Junior: Want to be Good—or Great?" *Seattle Times*, July 8, 1991.
32. Bob Sherwin, "It's Tough to Pick True Stars—Griffey Replies to Critic: 'I'm Still Learning,'" *Seattle Times*, July 9, 1991.
33. Jim Street, "Kid Returns Home True All-Star—'Potential' Now a Forgotten Word," *Seattle Post-Intelligencer*, October 4, 1991.
34. Art Thiel, 37.
35. Hal Bodley, "Griffey's Son the Brightest of Stars," *USA Today*, July 15, 1992.
36. Milton Kent, "Longest Day for Griffey, Gonzalez—Jr. Hits Warehouse, Juan Goes 473 Feet," *Baltimore Sun*, July 13, 1993.
37. Bob Sherwin, "Oh, Baby! Kid Has One of His Own—Son's Birth Makes Junior a Nervous Dad," *Seattle Times*, January 21, 1994.
38. Bill Rabinowitz, "Griffey Raises Hair, Not Hell on Quest," *York Daily Record* (York, Pennsylvania), July 6, 1994.
39. Larry LaRue, "Fleming 'Brilliant,' Junior Hits No. 30," *Tacoma* (Washington) *News Tribune*, June 18, 1994.
40. "Bonds, Williams to Start for All-Stars—Griffey demolishes Carew's record for votes from fans," *San Francisco Chronicle*, July 4, 1994.
41. "Griffey Jr: The Six-Million Vote Man," *Columbus* (Georgia) *Ledger-Enquirer*, July 13, 1994.
42. "Career Timeline With M's," *Kitsap* (Washington) *Sun*, June 2, 2010.
43. Chris Donnelly, *Baseball's Greatest Series: Yankees, Mariners, and the 1995 Matchup That Changed History* (New Brunswick, New Jersey: Rutgers University Press, 2010), 249.
44. "Baby Griffey Evens Score," *Seattle Times*, October 25, 1995.
45. J. Elizabeth Mills, *Sports Families: Ken Griffey Sr. and Ken Griffey Jr.* (New York: The Rosen Publishing Group, 2010), 34.
46. Jim Cour, "The house that Griffey built in Seattle, and the new stadium that will go up in the city, both belong to Junior," *Rocky Mountain News* (Denver), March 30, 1997.
47. "Griffey Leaves No Doubt Mariners Star is Unanimous AL MVP," Associated Press, printed in the *Roanoke* (Virginia) *Times*, November 13, 1997.
48. Rob Parker, "Fans speak, Griffey listens—AL's home run leader changes mind, wins Home Run Derby," *Charleston* (West Virginia) *Daily Mail*, July 7, 1998.
49. Larry Stone, "Fans' Boos are Griffey's Wake-Up Call," *Seattle Times*, July 7, 1998.
50. Hal McCoy, "Junior, Brennaman Have Shouting Match," *Dayton Daily News*, August 24, 2000.
51. Hal McCoy, "ESPN Analysts: Junior Should Sit—Reynolds, Gammons Feel Griffey Shouldn't Risk Further Injury for Last-Place Reds," *Dayton Daily News*, July 18, 2001.
52. Larry Stone, "Griffeys Welcome New Family Member," *Seattle Times*, May 12, 2002.
53. Jon Heyman, "There's a Hard Edge to Griffey this Spring," *Kennebec Journal* (Waterville, Maine), March 18, 2003.
54. John Fay, "Injury Bug Keeps Stinging," *Seattle Times*, July 19, 2003.
55. Kyle Nagel, "Junior's Career in Cincinnati," *Dayton Daily News*, August 1, 2008.
56. Hal McCoy, "Griffey Comeback Winner—Slugger Earned National League Comeback Player of Year Honor," *Middletown* (Ohio) *Journal News*, October 7, 2005.
57. Trent Rosecrans, "Griffey Paying Tribute to Robinson," *Cincinnati Post*, April 5, 2007.
58. Barry M. Bloom, "MLB Ready to Celebrate Jackie Robinson Day," *MLB News*, April 13, 2009, m.mlb.com/news/article/4246882/.
59. Gregg Bell, "Griffey Makes Return to Seattle," *Daily Sentinel* (Scottsboro, Alabama), June 22, 2007.
60. Michael Ko, "Plenty of Cheers to Greet Griffey—Sellout Crowd Celebrates Junior, Ex-Mariner has Many Good Memories," *Seattle Times*, June 23, 2007.
61. Larry Stone, "Mays Says It Was Griffey's Decision," *Seattle Times*, February 20, 2009.
62. Paul White, "Opposite Griffey, Suzuki Click—Stars Bring Glow to '09 Mariners," *USA Today*, September 22, 2009.
63. Larry Larue, "For Griffey & the Mariners, the End is Near," *Tacoma* (Washington) *News Tribune*, May 10, 2010.
64. Tim Booth, "Ken Griffey Jr. Retiring at Age 40," *Seattle Times*, June 2, 2010.
65. Ken Griffey, *Big Red: Baseball, Fatherhood, and My Life in the Big Red Machine* (Chicago: Triumph Books, 2014).

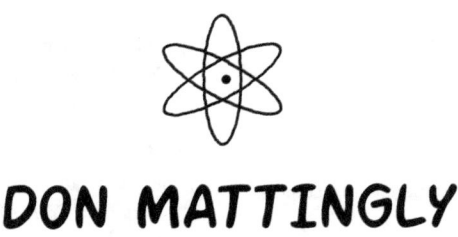

DON MATTINGLY

By James L. Ray

Talk of Don Mattingly's worthiness for enshrinement in the Hall of Fame most often focuses on his offensive statistics. Perhaps not enough is said about his defense. Mattingly has the best career fielding percentage of any player—ever—at any position. His .9959 percentage means that every 1,000 times the ball came his way, he made only four errors. He won nine Gold Glove awards, the second most among first basemen. Not that his offense was to be sneered at: a .307 lifetime batting average, 222 home runs, and three straight seasons of more than 200 hits.

Still, in Mattingly's 15 years on the baseball writers' ballot, he was never favored by more than 28.2 percent of the voters; his percentage on the ballots for the 2014 and 2015 inductions was in the single digits, and he was removed from the baseball writers' ballot. His hopes for election were entrusted to the Hall of Fame's Expansion Era Committee, which votes every three years (including 2016). The debate over Mattingly's merits will continue.

The subject of the debate, Donald Arthur Mattingly, was born on April 20, 1961, in Evansville, Indiana, the youngest of five children of Bill and Mary Mattingly. Bill was a mailman, with a work ethic that would one day rub off on his youngest son. Mary raised the five children: Jerry, the oldest son, who died in a construction accident at 23 years old; Randy, Michael, Judy, and Donnie. Because he was the youngest in the family, his brothers let him tag along to their neighborhood games. Randy Mattingly recalled that even though Don was three or four years younger than most of the guys in the games, he could hold his own in any game with a ball because he was a fierce competitor who was always trying to get better.

Mattingly's introduction to baseball included backyard Wiffle ball. Years later, he recalled those games, saying, "I can't imagine what my parents must have been thinking, with that Wiffle ball banging against the metal door every two minutes."[1]

Wiffle ball helped Don developed his ability to drive the ball the other way. On the backyard field a thickly-leaved tree hung over the field on the first-base side. If you hit the tree, you were out. In left field, however, Mattingly recalled, there was the family garage. A fly ball onto the garage was counted as a home run. Mattingly learned pretty quickly to hit the ball the other way. It was a skill that served him well for many years to come.

Of his childhood, Mattingly described a supportive family that instructed and encouraged their children to work hard and succeed. "I grew up in a family that didn't criticize a lot," he said. "We were told when we did something wrong, but we got a lot of praise. I remember once at a wedding reception, when I was 8 years old, and my father told me he was proud of the way I handled myself. I wasn't sure what I did, but I tried to do it again because of what he said."[2]

At Reitz Memorial High School, Don stood out in three sports. He was the football team's starting quarterback and the basketball squad's star point guard. But it was one American Legion baseball game that convinced Don that he was a baseball player. In a 1976 game against the neighboring town of Owensboro, Kentucky, he faced a pitcher who was the Cincinnati Reds' top draft pick that year. Don, a freshman, hit two doubles off the star. He soon had developed a name for himself. Scouts were occasionally seen at his games, and he began receiving letters offering college scholarships to play baseball. At one point Mattingly helped Reitz Memorial to a 59-game winning streak, with one of those wins coming in the Indiana state championship game in his junior season.

Along with his father, Mattingly said that his biggest influence with respect to his work ethic was his high-school baseball coach, Quentin Merkel, who was always pushing Mattingly to get better.

"Coach would say to me, if you are the best player in the region, you should try to become the best in the state," Mattingly said. "If you are best in the state, then you start thinking about being the best in the country. That ethic, to always get better, helped me in the minor leagues when I was fighting for jobs."[3]

By 1979 Mattingly had become a hot prospect, even earning a brief write-up in *Sports Illustrated* for his exploits. Most teams avoided drafting the high-school star, however, because many expected that he would attend college. Taking a chance, the New York Yankees selected him in the 19th round of the 1979 amateur draft and subsequently signed him to a minor-league deal.

Mattingly enjoyed almost instant success in the minor leagues, hitting .349 with the Oneonta Yankees of the Class-A (short season) New York-Penn League in 53 games in 1979. The next year, he moved up to Greensboro (North Carolina) of the Class-A South Atlantic League, where he led the league with a .358 batting average. After a strong year for Double-A Nashville (Southern League) in 1981 (.315, 98 RBIs), Mattingly was promoted to Triple-A Columbus for 1982. He had another fine season, hitting .315 with 10 home runs and 75 RBIs, and winning accolades for his defensive play.

When major-league clubs expanded their rosters to 40 players in September, the Yankees called up Mattingly Years later, he fondly recalled his first trip to the House That Ruth Built. "I think the time that I really think about the most is just being called up and walking into Yankee Stadium for the first time, walking into the dugout and just seeing the left-field corner and the stands in that corner like the horseshoe there," he said. "And at that point, just realizing the dream to get to the big leagues. So that is a moment that is always one of the freshest and just a great memory for me."[4]

Mattingly made his major-league debut on September 8, 1982, against the Baltimore Orioles in Yankee Stadium, as a ninth-inning defensive replacement for Dave Winfield in left field. Three days later Mattingly had his first major-league at-bat, against reliever Jim Slaton of the Milwaukee Brewers, and popped out to third base on the first pitch. It wasn't until almost three weeks later that he managed his first major-league hit, an 11th-inning single off Boston's Steve Crawford on October 1 in Yankee Stadium. In 12 major-league at-bats in 1982, he had two singles and one RBI.

Mattingly won a roster spot during spring training in 1983, but when the season began, he was used sparingly. Almost two weeks into the season, he had just seven at-bats and two hits, and on April 14, he was sent back down to Columbus. It was his last trip to the minor leagues.

As a player, Mattingly spent his entire career in pinstripes.

In 43 games with Columbus, Mattingly hit better than .340 with 8 home runs and 37 RBIs. And when the Yankees' Bobby Murcer announced his retirement on June 12, a roster spot and a reserve outfield position opened up in the Bronx, and Mattingly was called up to fill it. He spent the balance of the season as a spot starter, pinch-hitter, and defensive replacement in right field, left field, and first base. Mattingly also helped make some baseball history on August 18, 1983, when he played second base (as a left-handed thrower) in the finish of the George Brett "Pine Tar Game," a contest that had begun almost a month earlier.

On July 24, 1983, the day the game began, Brett hit what seemed to be a two-out, two-run home run in the top of the ninth inning off Rich Gossage, putting Kansas City ahead by a run. New York manager Billy Martin protested the home run, claiming that Brett's bat had more than 18 inches of pine tar running up its handle. Home-plate umpire Tim McClelland agreed, called Brett out, and signaled the game over.

But American League President Lee McPhail later reversed the ruling, and Brett was given credit for the home run. When the game was resumed almost a month later, Martin put left-hander Mattingly at second base. He played only one-third of an inning, but became the next to last lefty to play second base in the majors. (As of 2015 Thad Bosley was the last to do it, in 1987.)

For the 1983 season, the 22-year-old Mattingly showed that he was a capable major-league hitter and a very skilled defender, batting .283 with 4 home runs and 32 RBIs in 279 at-bats.

As spring training opened in 1984, new manager Yogi Berra announced that although the team planned to keep Mattingly with the Yankees all season, he would not begin the season as a starter. With Dave Winfield in right field, Steve Kemp in left, and Roy Smalley being groomed for the full-time first-base job, Berra said, Mattingly would best be used as a reserve player and a pinch-hitter because "he has the kind of stroke that enables him to sit for three weeks and still hit."[5]

Mattingly was relieved to have his role defined so early. He was grateful, he said, that "this time, there's no worry about not making the team. Last year, I didn't know and I didn't think I had much chance. I didn't know until the last day of camp, and when I made the team I didn't know how long I'd stay."[6]

But he was less thrilled about being given a reserve role so early in camp, especially since he was batting .474 at the time. "This is kind of hard to swallow without getting any kind of chance at all," Mattingly told the *New York Times* in mid-March, "and there's no way I can accept that. There's no way I can say, OK, sit back, relax and do that. I feel I can change their mind or at least make it a very tough decision to sit me down."[7]

It took only a few weeks of spring training to change Berra's mind. After a March in which Mattingly hit well and continued to show off his slick glove at first base, Berra announced that Mattingly would start the season as the regular first baseman.

Mattingly got off to a hot start in '84, a fact he attributed to having played winter ball in Puerto Rico. By midseason, he was hitting so well that some were beginning to compare him to the other young hitting star in New York City at the time, the Mets' Darryl Strawberry. Among Mattingly's biggest early supporters was Yankees owner George Steinbrenner, who told reporters as early as June 1984 that "Mattingly is the best young talent in baseball. You can talk all you want about Strawberry. I'll take Mattingly."[8] Steinbrenner had plenty of evidence to support his argument; at the time, Mattingly was outhitting Strawberry in every major offensive category.

The biggest surprise in Mattingly's 1984 offensive game was his newly found power stroke. Although he had never hit more than 10 home runs in a season in the minor leagues, he had already hit 12 before the end of June that year. Lou Piniella, then the Yankees' hitting coach, described that summer how he'd worked with Mattingly on his swing all year, urging the young hitter to keep his weight back and hold his body in balance throughout the entire swing.

The slight shift in body weight that Piniella recommended led to more power.

In July Mattingly was named to his first All-Star Game, picked as a reserve by American League manager Joe Altobelli, who couldn't ignore the Yankees first baseman's .339 average and impressive power numbers. Mattingly got into the game with one out in the ninth inning as a pinch-hitter with the American League trailing 3-1. Batting against his former teammate, San Diego Padres closer Rich "Goose" Gossage, Mattingly flied out to left field.

As the second half of the 1984 season rolled on, teammates Mattingly and Winfield got into a heated race for the American League batting crown. Winfield hit like a demon during the first half of the season, and his average climbed to .377 in early July. In August, however, Winfield slipped a little, and Mattingly caught up to him. By the first of September, he was batting .352 to Winfield's .351.

As the month wore on and the Yankees fell out of the divisional race, the competition for the batting title became the best running baseball story in New York City. The back pages of the city's two tabloids, the *Daily News* and the *Post*, wrote about the race or ran full-page pictures of the contestants, almost every day. In a town that was always hungry for baseball success, the batting race took on the role of a surrogate pennant race for Yankees fans. The team's owners loved the competition, because it kept fans coming to Yankee Stadium in droves, despite the fact that the Yankees were 15 games behind the Detroit Tigers. During the last two weeks of the season, the stadium scoreboard constantly displayed each player's batting average, to the ninth digit, right up to the last at-bat. The excitement was justified; after all, no Yankee had won a batting crown since Mickey Mantle in 1956. And no two Yankees had ever finished 1-2 in hitting.

Going into the season's final weekend, Mattingly led Winfield .342 to .341. When asked who he thought would prevail, Piniella predicted that Mattingly would win, but gave him the advantage only because the team was facing three right-handers in a row to close out the season, which favored the left-handed hitter. But Mattingly went just 1-for-7 on Friday and Saturday, and entered the last day of the season trailing Winfield .339 to .342. In the last game of the year, however, he managed four hits in five at-bats, while Winfield was just 1-for-4. After Mattingly got his last hit, Winfield hit a sharp grounder to the shortstop, who forced a sliding Mattingly out at second base. As the new batting champ walked toward the dugout, the fans roared in salute, and after a few moments in the dugout, he re-emerged and walked to first base. Mattingly and Winfield shook hands, and walked off the field together as the crowd cheered. Mattingly had won the race, .343 to .340.

"It was good that we could come off together," Mattingly said. "Dave has been a great person through this whole thing. He handled himself like a gentleman. I have great respect for him. It's good that we're going to be teammates the next few years, at least."[9]

To go along with his batting title, Mattingly topped the American League in hits, with 207, and doubles, with 44. He also finished in the top five in RBIs, total bases, slugging percentage, and extra-base hits, and in November, he finished fifth in voting for the American League Most Valuable Player award. Despite Mattingly's great season, the Yankees finished in third place in the AL East, 17 games behind the eventual World Series champions, the Detroit Tigers.

In the offseason, George Steinbrenner acquired Rickey Henderson from the Oakland A's in exchange for five players and cash. Henderson brought to the Yankees an entirely new level of speed and ability to reach base. He'd stolen at least 100 bases in three of the prior five seasons, and his career on-base percentage was well over .400 at the time. On the Yankees, he'd be a run waiting to score, and one of the top beneficiaries of Henderson's addition would be Don Mattingly. Willie Randolph had been solid as a leadoff hitter in 1984, but his talents were much better suited to the second spot in the order. Randolph was a good contact hitter who walked a lot and rarely

The Hit Man, Donnie Baseball

struck out, a guy who knew how to lay down a bunt. Those talents made him a solid bridge between Henderson, the table-setter, and Mattingly, who was about to become the game's best RBI machine.

The Mattingly-Henderson combination worked just as Steinbrenner had hoped. By the All-Star break, Henderson was batting a league-leading .357, and his on-base percentage stood at .441. He'd stolen 41 bases, which meant that he was on base almost half the time, and when he was on, he usually managed to place himself in scoring position. All told, in 1985 Henderson scored 146 runs, leading the American League by 30 over Cal Ripken's 116.

Mattingly took advantage of Henderson's table-setting skills, picking up a major-league-leading 69 RBIs in his first 83 games. After the break, he was even better, batting .340 with 26 home runs and 76 RBIs in his final 76 games. He finished the season batting .324, third best in the American League, hit 35 home runs, and knocked in 145 runs, the most by a left-handed hitter since Ted Williams drove in 159 in 1949. Mattingly led the major leagues in doubles with 48. He won his first Gold Glove award and in November he easily won the American League MVP award with 23 of 28 first-place votes.

The team, however, had a very disappointing finish to what was an otherwise promising season. The Yankees entered the final weekend of the year three games behind the Toronto Blue Jays, who were heading into Exhibition Stadium for a season-ending three-game series needing a sweep. And then they'd have to beat Toronto in a Monday afternoon playoff game if they expected to go any further. They won the Friday night game, 4-3 and closed the gap to two games with two to play.

But on Saturday afternoon, the Blue Jays finished the Yankees off with a 5-1 win behind a complete-game gem from Doyle Alexander. It was a tough pill to swallow. At one point during the season, the Yankees won 30 out of 36 games, and seemed ready to overtake Toronto, but every time they climbed to within two or three games, they'd fall back again, until the final lost weekend of the season. They finished with 97 wins, two fewer than Toronto.

Despite the fate of the Yankees that season, Mattingly began to draw rave reviews from players, coaches and baseball writers. Lou Piniella called him the perfect blend of Wade Boggs and George Brett. Hall of Famer Stan Musial said, "He reminds me of myself."[10] Musial wasn't the only one to draw the comparison at the time, though he was surely the most credible.

In some respects, Mattingly's 1986 season was even more dominant than his MVP campaign the year before. He hit .352, with 238 hits, 53 doubles, 31 home runs, and 113 RBIs. He finished second to Roger Clemens that year in MVP voting. But once again, the Yankees stumbled. On August 15 they were within three games of the first-place Red Sox, and the Bronx seemed poised for an old-style Yankees-Red Sox pennant race. But the Yankees dropped 13 of their next 20 games, fell behind by 10 games and never made another serious run for the division crown.

They did win a respectable 90 games, but when the playoffs began, the Yankees were once again on the outside looking in.

A conspicuous side note from the 1986 season was the Yankees' trip to Seattle in August of that year. Third baseman Mike Pagliarulo was injured before the first game of a doubleheader on August 30, and the Yankees needed an emergency fill-in. Mattingly volunteered, and manager Lou Piniella gave him the go-ahead, making him the first left-handed-throwing third baseman to play in the majors since Wee Willie Keeler in the early 1900s. In the bottom of the first inning, leadoff batter John Moses hit a grounder to third base, which Mattingly fielded cleanly before making a wide throw to first base that allowed Moses to reach on an error. But he quickly redeemed himself on the next play when he stabbed a sharp grounder from Mickey Brantley and started a 5-4-3 double play. In all, Mattingly played three games at third base, had one putout, 11 assists, one error, and was involved in two double plays.

Mattingly began the 1987 season in a slump. While he had a tendency to start slow, this was worse than usual. After the first 33 games, he was hitting .240 with just three home runs. Then he hit his groove. Between May 14 and June 4, he raised his batting average to .311, and during that 20-game stretch knocked in 15 runs. Just as he was returning to form, however, Mattingly injured his lower back on June 4. The cause of the injury was disputed at the time, with some newspapers saying that it happened while Mattingly and pitcher Bob Shirley were playfully wrestling around in the clubhouse. Mattingly denied the horseplay story and said that it happened while he was fielding groundballs before the game that day.

Although the injury was not devastating, it did require Mattingly to spend five days in traction at NYU hospital. Doctors at the time described the injury as two protruding disks that wouldn't require surgery, but would need a few weeks of rest. While Mattingly was on the shelf, he was replaced by a young up-and-coming left-handed slugger named Dan Pasqua. But Mattingly wouldn't play the role of Wally Pipp to Pasqua's Lou Gehrig, because when he returned three weeks later, he caught fire. In his first 13 games back, Mattingly hit .370 (20-for-54) and knocked home 12 runs. It was a nice prelude for what was to follow.

The streak began on July 8, 1987, in the bottom of the first inning at Yankee Stadium versus the Minnesota Twins, when Mattingly drove a Mike Smithson fastball over the right-field wall for a three-run homer. It continued the next night in a loss to the White Sox that was highlighted only by Mattingly's homer in the sixth inning. The next night Mattingly hit a grand slam in the bottom of the Yankees' seven-run second inning. It was his third bases-loaded round tripper of the season, a notable achievement considering that before 1987 he hadn't hit a single slam in his career. Mattingly hit solo homers in the next two games against the White Sox, extending his streak to five straight games with home runs, one short of the American League record.

Mattingly didn't shrink from the spotlight. At Texas, in the top of the second inning, he cracked his fourth grand slam of the season off knuckleballer Charlie Hough. The streak was now at six games. Mattingly was tied for the American League record held by six players and just two games from the major-league record of eight, set by Dale Long of the Pittsburgh Pirates in 1956.

Between the sixth and seventh games, Mattingly told reporters that he wasn't trying to hit home runs. Rather, he was just trying to hit line drives, and pick up every potential RBI that was out on the bases.

"After sitting out three weeks and missing chances to drive in runs," he said, "I told myself I'm not going to leave anybody on base out there. When we reached the 81-game mark, I told myself I'd like to drive in a run every day for the rest of the year. I don't think that's impossible. I can do it. If someone's on, drive in a run. Or hit a home run. I said that before I got in this streak. I don't know what happened with the home runs. I just got in a groove—bing, bing, bing."[11]

The next night, Mattingly set out to break the American League mark in a swirling Arlington Stadium wind that was keeping the ball from carrying. In the first inning, he hit a bullet to center field that appeared to be headed out, but the wind slowed it up, and the ball slammed against the top of the fence for a double. In the sixth inning, though, he hit one on the screws against lefty reliever Paul Kilgus. The ball ended up in the right-field seats; Mattingly had broken the American League record.

Talking to reporters, Mattingly said "it would be selfish" to try for the major-league record at the expense of the Yankees' ambition to finish in first place. His explanation of his sudden power: "I've found a swing that gets the ball in the air. All of a sudden, without even trying, something has clicked."[12]

The next night against Texas, Mattingly hit a Jose Guzman sinker in the fourth inning that cleared the 11-foot-high fence in left-center field. The ball traveled just beyond the leap of Pete Incaviglia, the left fielder, to tie the major-league mark.

"I didn't think it was going to carry out," Mattingly said after the game, "but the ball carried well to left here. I didn't see the ball go out. I thought he caught it."[13] The capacity crowd of 41,871 at Arlington Stadium, which filled the normally vacant center-field bleachers moments before Mattingly's historic at-bat, stood and cheered until Mattingly reluctantly climbed to the top step of the dugout—after being coaxed by Dave Winfield—and lifted his batting helmet.

"I know I talk about not caring about it," Mattingly said, "but it does feel better after I hit one. I guess it goes on. It's not like I'm worrying about it one way or the other, or I'm going to be disappointed if I don't hit one, or anything like that. It just keeps going on. It's surprising to me."[14]

But it didn't keep going. The next evening he went 2-for-4, with a double and a run scored, but no home runs. The remarkable streak had ended at eight.

Mattingly's offensive statistics during the streak were astounding. In eight games, he hit 10 home runs, two of which were grand slams. He drove in 21 runs and picked up 17 hits in 37 at-bats for a .459 average. He had two doubles and scored 11 runs. He struck out just twice. With 49 total bases in his 37 times at bat, he had a 1.324 slugging average.

Before the 1987 season ended, Mattingly would set another record. On September 29, against Red Sox starter Bruce Hurst, he ripped a grand slam into the right-field upper deck. It was his sixth of the season, surpassing the previous high of five held by Jim Gentile and Ernie Banks.

Mattingly's final numbers for the year were impressive, especially considering that he missed 21 games because of the back injury: a .327 batting average, 30 home runs, 115 RBIs, and a .559 slugging percentage. He finished seventh in MVP voting, but the Yankees dropped to 89-73 and finished fourth in the division. Mattingly was now five full seasons into a splendid Yankees career, but he still hadn't tasted postseason play.

Mattingly continued his All-Star-level play over the next two years. Even though he drove home only 88 runs in 1988, his two-year average for 1988-89 was a .307 average, 21 home runs, and 101 RBIs. Although Mattingly may have slowed down slightly since the mid-'80s, had he been able to maintain even this more modest pace, he looked like a future Hall of Famer. At least that is what a lot of knowledgeable baseball men said about Mattingly during the end of the 1980s.

Sparky Anderson, the first man to manage a World Series champion from each league, said of Mattingly in 1988, "I think he's the greatest single player in our game." George Brett, the Kansas City star and future Hall of Famer who hit .390 in 1980, remarked of Mattingly in the same year, "If he isn't the best, I'd like to know who is."[15] Fireballer Dwight Gooden of the Mets said: "I'm glad I don't have to face that guy every day. Mattingly has that look that few hitters have. I don't know if it's his stance, his eyes or what, but you can tell he means business."[16]

But it wasn't just managers and players who foresaw a plaque in Cooperstown for Mattingly. It was the very writers who held the keys to the Hall that were preparing his table as early as 1989. In a piece headlined "Every Pitcher's Nightmare," *New York Times* writer Murray Chass compared Mattingly favorably to some of the all-time greats after their first five or six seasons. Chass interviewed Piniella for analysis on the first baseman's mechanics:

" 'Mattingly's swing is mechanically unique,' Lou Piniella explains, because of what he calls 'a small take-away.' Every hitter gathers momentum for his swing with an instinctive backward movement of the bat before he brings it forward. Mattingly's backward motion is minuscule. 'We're talking three, four, five inches,' Piniella says. 'When you have a small take-away and when you're as quick as he is, you can look away and handle the ball in. He can still stand on top of the plate and pull.' "[17]

Pitchers at the time felt that the only way to approach Mattingly was with a variety of pitches. "I usually throw my whole repertoire at him,"[18] said Frank Viola, the Minnesota Twins' left-hander, who was the Most Valuable Player in the World Series the previous year. Viola had good success against Mattingly, holding him to nine hits in 50 at-bats over the course of their careers. "You've got to mix it up and hope he's not looking for that certain pitch."[19]

Pitchers especially knew that they couldn't count on striking out Mattingly. Jack Morris, the Detroit Tigers pitcher who won more games than any other pitcher in the 1980s, said that during the course of an at-bat, "if you fool him one time, you're doing a good job. Three times? Forget it."[20]

In the face of all this praise, Mattingly was humble, always preaching the workaday ethic. He described his approach to hitting as more of a mental struggle than a physical feat.

"Each time I go up, I want to get a good pitch to hit and hit it hard," he said. "A lot of guys give away at-bats. They make a mental mistake here, a mental mistake there."[21]

Mattingly felt that lapses in concentration could cost a player a significant number of his 650 or so at-bats per season. He reasoned that if a player could cut down on the number of times he defeated himself by maintaining a high level of concentration, "take 100 of those away, or 50, where you swing at a bad pitch, you'd be so much better off," he said. "It's a challenge, over the course of a season, to stay tuned in. There are times that you're not; it's impossible to be tuned in for 162 games, but you really have to be ready."[22]

During his first six full seasons, Mattingly's career batting average stood at .327, and he averaged 203 hits, 43 doubles, 27 home runs, 114 RBIs, and 97 runs scored. He also won five straight Gold Gloves and made six consecutive All-Star teams. Mattingly made it known that he wanted a new contract, or an extension of his existing deal that concluded at the end of the 1990 season. The Yankees responded by making him the highest-paid player in baseball history at the time.

On April 10, 1990, the first baseman signed a five-year contract that would pay him a total of $19.3 million, an average of $3.86 million per season. The deal was the largest in terms of average dollars, beating out the $3.75 million per year contract signed by Will Clark earlier that year, and well outstripping the $16 million, five-year contract that Mark Langston already had in place.

Yankees owner George Steinbrenner defended the deal by saying: "A superstar is a superstar, so I can justify that salary. A Don Mattingly will attract people to see my club play."[23]

"Don Mattingly is now the best-paid player in baseball," Steinbrenner said. "He will be with the Yankees for five years after this year and hopefully will complete his career here."[24]

Mattingly discussed the deal in his usual understated style. "I'm not going to look at the papers for a few days," he said, "because I don't want to read about it. I'd rather let my playing do all the talking."[25]

The thought of openly discussing his contract was not appealing to Mattingly. He conceded that as a child he had never dreamed about such riches. "It's pretty hard to dream about something you never imagined," he said. "I dreamed about playing baseball more than anything."[26]

But Mattingly's bat didn't do the talking, at least not during the first few months of the 1990 season. Although he typically started the season slowly, it soon became clear that Mattingly's troubles at the plate were not merely the usual April ramp-up to midseason success. By June 1 he was hitting a respectable .278, but his power was simply nonexistent. He had just five homers and 24 RBIs in 45 games. Then things got worse. In 28 games and 116 at-bats in June, Mattingly hit just .216 without a home run. By the middle of July, his average had dropped to .248, and his homerless streak extended beyond 200 at-bats. Something was wrong.

It turned out to be his old nemesis, those two bum disks in his back. On July 2 he told manager Stump Merrill that he'd been suffering from back stiffness and spasms for at least a week, and asked to be taken out of the lineup after making 231 consecutive starts. At the time, a somber Mattingly told reporters that he hoped he would miss only one game. It went on much longer than that.

Although he came back for a pain-filled 10-day stint from July 14 through July 24, the Yankees put Mattingly on the disabled list on July 26. Merrill said the first baseman could be out for the remainder of the season. Although the Yankees reinstated Mattingly from the DL on September 12, it was clear that the chronic back injury, which doctors had described as a congenital disk deformity, severely limited and altered his swing. In the waning days of the 1990 season, Mattingly played sparingly and finished the year with the worst statistics of his career: a .256 average, 5 home runs, and 42 RBIs in almost 400 at-bats.

During the offseason, Mattingly underwent a rigorous physical therapy regimen on his back. He rose at 6:00 A.M. four days a week at his home in Evansville to perform stretches and lifts that he'd learned the summer before while he was on the disabled list. By the time spring training rolled around, the first baseman sounded optimistic that he could regain his old form.

"I have to prove I can stay healthy," Mattingly said. "From there, we'll see what I can do. In the spring, I did the things I wanted to do. Now, I want to get used to doing less hitting and all the extra stuff I did in the past. I wanted to feel comfortable at the plate, and I did."[27]

On March 1, 1991, Mattingly was given even more motivation to get back on top, when he was named the captain of the Yankees. "Once it had a chance to sink in," he said, "it's one of the biggest thrills and biggest honors for me in baseball. I take it seriously."[28]

His teammates were very supportive of the measure. Outfielder Jesse Barfield said, "It's a good move. The guys respect him and the organization respects him." Infielder Randy Velarde put it a little more directly: "Who else could you name captain? When you think of the Yankees, who do you think of? Don Mattingly. It's ideal that Stump did it."[29]

Mattingly said he intended to lead by example, to let his play on the field do the talking. But when the season began, it was clear that he was doing more than just that. During the first few months of the season, he set upon his professional goals with a new fury, writing pep slogans on clubhouse blackboards, setting won-lost quotas for the team on television and, at times, declaring to reporters that an administrative shakeup might be just the ticket.

While he adjusted to the role of captain, Mattingly still struggled at the plate. By midseason he was batting .303, but his power numbers were way down. He managed just 6 home runs, 13 doubles, and 34

RBIs through the team's first 81 games. As Mattingly tried to rediscover his power through the pain, he experimented with different batting stances, grips, and swings. Later in his career, he admitted that this constant jostling of his plate approach may have held him back that year.

He was also growing frustrated with ownership and the direction in which they were guiding the Yankees. The team was 41-40, tied for third place and 8½ games behind the division-leading Toronto Blue Jays. By mid-August, the Yankees had dropped 11 games below .500 and were a dozen games out of first place. Tension in the clubhouse was palpable, and perhaps for the first time in his career, Mattingly became the target of New York tabloid controversy.

No biography about a New York Yankee who played during the Steinbrenner years would be complete without at least one story of a head-to-head faceoff between the player and the Boss. Mattingly had a number of head-butting sessions with Yankees management over the years, and at times he exchanged barbs with Steinbrenner in the New York tabloids. But the most memorable feud began early in the summer of 1991. Frustrated with the team's direction, Mattingly asked to be traded. The Yankees said no, so the slugger kept his mouth shut, and continued struggling to find his perfect swing. Then, on August 15, general manager Gene Michael told the first baseman that he needed to get a haircut. Yes, a haircut. And although Michael and manager Stump Merrill delivered the news, everyone knew whom the request had originated from. George Steinbrenner, who at the time was serving what would turn out to be a three-year suspension for consorting with a gambler, Howie Spira, was watching everything from behind the scenes.

Mattingly refused, even though he knew that he had agreed to the team's well-known "haircut rule" as part of his contract, which required short, trimmed, nicely groomed hair. At the time, Mattingly was in clear violation of the rule, as his hair hung below his shirt collar, his mustache had grown out and, for a short

Don Mattingly compiled a very impressive .996 career fielding percentage at first base.

time, and he looked like a member of the "mustache gang" of the early 1970s Oakland A's.

Although he wasn't drawn and quartered for his refusal to submit to the barber's shears, Mattingly was benched for a game. Nobody was happy. Merrill saw matters in black and white: "If someone from management tells you need a haircut, you get a haircut."[30]

But Mattingly had a different take, seeing the events as proof that he had become expendable and perhaps needed a new place to work. "Maybe I don't belong in the organization anymore," he said. "I talked to Gene Michael about moving me earlier in the year. He said we'll talk at the end of the year. Maybe this is their way of saying, 'We don't need you anymore.'"[31]

The haircut brouhaha eventually died down; Mattingly succumbed to the barber two days later. But the trouble over his disclosure that he was thinking about leaving the Yankees did not subside. As the season drew to a close, things got worse. The Yankees sputtered to a 25-41 record over the last 2½ months of the season and finished in fifth place with a 71-91 record. The team that looked so promising just a few years earlier had dropped to the bottom of the division. Their owner was serving a suspension that was still open-ended. They had gone through four managers in three seasons, and looked poised to hire a fifth for the 1992 season. Their captain, who had been the game's best player just two years earlier, finished what could only be described as a disappointing season, batting a respectable .288 but hitting just nine home runs and collecting only 68 RBIs. Things were looking pretty dire in Yankeeland.

Despite the public-relations problems he'd been forced to endure, and the chronic pain in his back limiting his game on the field, Mattingly entered the 1992 season with a refreshed attitude. His power at the plate might have diminished, but his influence on the players around him only increased. He could no longer spend three hours a day in the batting cage, as he had sometimes done in the '80s, and this gave him more time to talk to younger teammates about handling life on and off the field.

Many credit Mattingly with making the adjustment to major-league life a little bit easier. One story has it that when Bernie Williams first came to the Yankees in 1991, teammate Mel Hall called him "Bambi" because, he said, Bernie's big round eyeglasses made him look like a deer caught in the headlights. What started as fine, good-natured rookie ribbing soon went over the line, with Hall taking advantage of his veteran status to haze Williams mercilessly. For some reason, it was personal for Hall, who may have seen the talented young outfielder as a threat to his own job, and as young and vulnerable as Williams was at the time, it really got to him. Until Mattingly intervened. He was friendly with Hall, and told him to cool it. Then he took Williams under his wing for a while.

"He was real quiet and shy," Mattingly recalled. "I thought he lacked a little confidence. You could see he had the talent, but you could see the insecurities, too. I think confidence was the big key for Bernie. You have to believe you can play here. You can't keep hearing about potential. I think Bernie had to prove that to himself. Once you get that, you can do some things."[32] Williams developed into a five-time All-Star and a four-time World Series champion.

After two years in complete disarray, the Yankees seemed to bond as a team during the 1992 season. They won 76 games, a slight improvement over the prior year, and Mattingly had a resurgence of sorts. He finished with the same .288 batting average he had in '91, but his power came back—not fully, but enough to make a difference. After averaging just 7 homers, 25 doubles, and 55 RBIs during the two previous seasons, he broke through with 14 homers, 40 doubles, and 86 RBIs. He also won his seventh Gold Glove.

In 1993 Mattingly had his best season since the '80s. He hit .291 with 17 home runs and 86 RBIs. He won his eighth Gold Glove and finished 19th in MVP Voting. But more exciting to Mattingly was the development of the team around him. New arrival Paul O'Neill made a big impact, batting .311 with 20 homers and 75 RBIs. Bernie Williams showed promise, and third baseman Wade Boggs, another big offseason signing, hit .302, proving that the rumors of his demise in Boston were premature. Jimmy Key, the crafty left-hander who had helped the Blue Jays win the World Series in 1992, came to the Yankees via free agency and pitched very well, going 18-6 and finishing fourth in the Cy Young Award voting. The Yankees won 86 games and finished in second place for the first time since 1986.

Entering the 1994 season, Mattingly may have begun to feel a sense of urgency. He was now almost 33 years old and entering his 11th full season in the major leagues, and he still had not tasted postseason baseball. At the time he had just over 6,100 at-bats, the most among active major leaguers who had never made it to the playoffs. That weighed on him. But he also must have understood that this year, more than any season in nearly a decade, provided the Yankees with a real shot to win. They were entering their third straight season with Buck Showalter as manager, the longest tenure of any manager to date during the Mattingly era.

The Yankees captured first place in the AL East on May 9, 1994, and they never surrendered their lead. But a dark cloud hung over the season. As the Yankees continued to win, and to extend their lead over the second-place Orioles, news from the labor front was pretty dire. The collective-bargaining agreement between the Players Association and MLB was set to expire at midnight on August 11, 1994, and the parties were making no progress in their negotiations for a new deal. The Yankees knew that the great season they were having might be all for nothing. They would soon be proved right.

On the morning of August 12, 1994, the Players Association went on strike. The Yankees were 70-43 and 6½ games ahead of the second-place Orioles. On the day he left Yankee Stadium for Evansville, Mattingly expressed his disappointment with the strike and even pondered retirement.

"It's kind of weird," Mattingly said as players packed their belongings in the clubhouse. "It could be the last day of the year. It could be the last day of baseball. Who knows what's going to happen? I may never play again. Who knows what's going to happen during the winter?"[53]

Despite some early signs that the owners and players could reach a deal, it soon became clear that the season would be lost when both sides agreed to cancel the remainder of the season and the postseason on September 15, 1994.

It was the first time a World Series had been canceled in 90 years, and the fallout was mostly disgust. Many fans, who were paying a good deal of money to enable players and owners to make millions, felt the players were no longer worth it. Neither the owners, who were handing out money like candy, nor the players, whose average salary was almost $2 million per year, were getting much sympathy.

But because he was such a high-profile and well-liked player, Mattingly drew sympathy from many players, fans and writers, who knew well that his best chance at a postseason, and maybe even a World Series, had been taken away.

Over the winter negotiations were rare and not very promising, and New York columnists continued to discuss Mattingly, and whether he would ever take the field again. A breakthrough in the talks finally occurred in late March of 1995, and on April 3 the strike was settled. The season would open on April 26, and the schedules would be shortened to 144 games. But it was still a season, and now Mattingly had another opportunity to pursue his postseason dream, if he decided to return.

When the Yankees arrived at spring training, Mattingly was there, and told reporters that he had decided to look at the positives from the 1994 experience: "I don't really look at it as our only chance and only golden opportunity," he said. "It happened for us and, with the club we have this year, we have the chance to possibly do it again. If not this year, next year."[34]

In essence, if the Yankees were the elite of the American League in 1994, why couldn't they do it again in 1995? After all, the team did appear to have improved during the tumultuous offseason, trading for 1993 Cy Young Award winner Jack McDowell, to add to a staff that included the 1994 Cy Young runner-up, Jimmy Key. Also new to the Yankees starting rotation was 23-year-old rookie left-hander Andy Pettitte. The Yankees rounded out the rotation by trading for Montreal Expos stopper John Wetteland, who had been one of the top closers in baseball the three previous years.

But Key went down with a torn rotator cuff early on, and the Yankees were without a pitcher who had gone 35-10 over the past two seasons. However, they acquired David Cone, and he proved to be a godsend, posting a 9-2 record for the Yankees down the stretch. Pettitte also proved to be a tough customer, and with McDowell formed a formidable trio in the rotation.

Although they struggled with the injuries and roster shakeups, the Yankees began to jell as August arrived. By the end of the month they were a team on fire, prevailing in 25 out of their final 31 contests to win the wild card by just one game over the Angels on the final day of the season. Down the stretch, Mattingly hit .321 with 8 doubles, 12 RBIs, and 12 runs scored.

After the game in the Yankees clubhouse, the team seemed to be happier for Mattingly than for themselves. Buck Showalter spoke of how much the other players wanted to reach the playoffs for Mattingly. "There is a silent torch that we have all carried for Donnie," he said.[35]

"That kind of guy should be playing in the playoffs and should have the chance to win it all," said Jack McDowell.[36] Said Pat Kelly, whose game-winning homer in the third-to-last game of the season put the Yankees that much closer to a playoff berth: "We might not be telling everybody what's going on. But there is an underlying meaning there." Asked what he meant, Kelly said: "Like, hey, this is big for Donnie. Let's do it."[37]

Even Steinbrenner said, "It's more important for Mattingly than for me, because I've been there. I think the guys rallied for him. I really do."[38]

On the day after the regular season finale, the *New York Times* sports page exclaimed: "Finally! Mattingly Can Become Mr. October!"[39]

In the American League Division Series the Yankees would be facing the Seattle Mariners, who had some of the best hitters in baseball. The Mariners featured Ken Griffey Jr., the superstar center fielder who had missed 90 games with a broken hand, but who was getting hotter as the season rushed to a close. They also had Edgar Martinez, the 1995 American League batting champion; former Yankee Jay Buhner, who had 40 home runs and 121 RBIs that year; and Mattingly's eventual replacement at first base, Tino Martinez, who'd hit 31 homers and knocked in 111 RBIs. They were a force to be reckoned with.

Yankee fans were elated to see their team back in the postseason for the first time in 14 years. The first two games of the new best-of-five ALDS were played at Yankee Stadium.

Talking about that first playoff game, Mattingly later said, "I guess the biggest thrill for me was coming out of the dugout in the first game of the playoffs, in New York, against Seattle. Being pumped about being in the game, in the stadium was a great feeling, and a memory that will never go away. The memory is so fresh, and it was such a cool moment."[40]

In his first playoff game, Mattingly went 2-for-4 with a double and an RBI in the Yankees' 9-6 victory. Game Two pitted the Mariners' Andy Benes against rookie Andy Pettitte, who had had an impressive debut year in New York with a 12-9 record. Seattle took a 2-1 lead after five innings. But in the bottom of the sixth inning, Ruben Sierra tied the game with a solo blast off the upper-deck façade in right field. With the crowd still up in arms after that shot, Mattingly stepped into the box against Benes, and, amid the frenzy of 56,000 screaming New Yorkers, drilled the second pitch of the at-bat over the "385" sign in right-center field. The Stadium exploded. Fans sitting in the upper tiers littered the field with caps, helmets, full cups of beer, Frisbees, and even one grapefruit. An angry Lou Piniella, who was now managing Seattle, pulled the Mariners off the field for five minutes, refusing to send his troops back out on the field until the madness died down.

But the chants of "Don-nie Base-ball, Don-nie Baseball" continued until the captain finally emerged from the dugout and tipped his cap to the crowd. The game continued in seesaw fashion for more than five hours in the cold rainy October night, and didn't end until reserve catcher Jim Leyritz muscled a two-run home run just a few feet over the wall in dead right field in the bottom of the 15th inning.

The shot gave the Yankees a 7-5 win and a commanding 2-0 lead in the series. As the fans stayed in their places and sang along to the PA system blaring Frank Sinatra's "New York, New York," optimistic chants of "Sweep! Sweep!" could be heard throughout the stands.

But a sweep was not in the cards. The Mariners won Game Three behind a brilliant pitching performance from Randy Johnson. In Game Four the Yankees blew an early five-run lead, and eventually succumbed, losing a slugfest, 11-8. It was on to Game Five.

Depending on which team you were rooting for, Game Five may have been a more exciting show than Game Two. With the score tied, 2-2, Mattingly came to the plate in the top of the sixth inning with the bases loaded and one out. He hit a rope, a line drive that skipped over the wall for a ground-rule double to put the Yankees ahead, 4-2. Things stayed that way until Ken Griffey hit a solo homer in the bottom of the eighth. It was Griffey's fifth home run of the ALDS, and it brought Seattle to within one run. A few batters later, reserve player Doug Strange worked a bases-loaded walk off David Cone to tie the contest, 4-4. The game moved into extra innings, and in the top of the 11th, Randy Velarde singled home Pat Kelly to put the Yankees ahead, 5-4.

The lead was fleeting, however. In the bottom of the inning, Jack McDowell gave up back-to-back singles to Joey Cora and Griffey, and up to the plate came the series' most feared hitter, Edgar Martinez. It didn't take long for him to put a nail in the hearts of the Yankees faithful. Martinez drove the third pitch into the left-field corner, scoring Cora easily from third. As left fielder Gerald Williams got a handle on the ball, Griffey kept running, flying around third base and headed for home with Williams' throw trailing him by not more than a foot or two. As he neared home plate, Griffey slid toward the third base side of the plate, and the throw was just a little to the other side. Leyritz caught the ball cleanly and lunged for Griffey, but it was too late. He'd already touched home and ended the game and the series. Don Mattingly's first postseason series was over.

After the game, Mattingly couldn't help but feel a little sullen as he discussed the wonderful plays, wonderful games, and wonderful memories of the prior week. "Everything about it was great, except that we lost. We battled hard for the last 35 or 40 days knowing that we couldn't lose," Mattingly said. "Now, the finality of it is so sudden. Nobody expected to have to go home. We all thought we were going to Cleveland [to face the Indians in the American League Championship Series]. We didn't think we'd be going back to New York yet."[41]

Mattingly made no mention of the fact that in his first-ever October series, he'd gotten 10 hits in 24 at-bats for a .417 batting average, or that he also had four doubles, a home run, and six RBIs. Although he didn't talk about himself, many in baseball noticed Mattingly's performance. Ernie Banks, the legendary Mr. Cub, who himself had never made it to the postseason, had words of encouragement for Mattingly after the loss. Banks told the *New York Times* how much he admired and appreciated Mattingly's style of play, and also knew the pain of never having played in a World Series. "The character of Don Mattingly is just unbelievable," Banks said.[42]

Mattingly announced in the offseason that he wanted to sit out 1996, but did not formally retire, suggesting that he might like to play another year with a team closer to his home in Indiana. His children were growing up, his body needed a rest and the Yankees also had a new first baseman in Tino Martinez. Ironically, the 1996 Yankees won the World Series. It was the team's first championship in 18 years and it marked the beginning of a dynasty that would win five pennants and four World Series crowns between 1996 and 2001.

On January 22, 1997, after his one-year self-imposed rest, Mattingly announced his retirement during a press conference at Yankee Stadium. Seven months later, on August 31, 1997, the team held Don Mattingly Day at Yankee Stadium. During the ceremony, the Yankees retired his number 23 and dedicated a plaque in Monument Park that called Mattingly "a humble man of grace and dignity, a captain who led by example, proud of the Pinstripe tradition and dedicated to the pursuit of excellence, a Yankee forever."[43]

During the ceremony, Mattingly thanked the fans for their years of support, and added: "I wanted the fans to know over the years everything I did was designed to keep everything strictly baseball for me. I tried to stay away from doing too much stuff around town, so when they thought of me, they thought of baseball, not a commercial or something that was going on with you because you became a celebrity."[44]

After the event, Mattingly talked of the pain his back had caused him throughout his career, an issue that he had rarely discussed while he was playing. "I was born with a congenital defect. If I hit too much, I got a pounding soreness. It was like a dead ache in my back. I still get it today when I go out and hit too many golf balls. ... I tried to make the best of it. I didn't want to talk about it. I didn't want any sympathy from people. I didn't want to hear people say, 'How's your back?' Or, 'He's struggling because of his back.' So what? I was able to play for 12 or 13 years, some of those years feeling pretty good, some of those years not feeling so good. I was still able to play in the major leagues, and I was very thankful for that. I didn't feel it was an area that I really wanted any sympathy for."[45]

For the next seven years, Mattingly lived and worked at his horse farm in Evansville. Although he served in various part-time roles as a spring-training instructor and roving minor-league hitting coach over the years, he resisted any attempts to bring him back to full-time baseball. Whenever asked if he would return to the Yankees as a coach, his usual response was, "I'm just a horse farmer from Indiana."[46]

But by 2003, when his oldest son graduated from high school and his two other boys were getting old enough to handle life without having their father home all the time, Mattingly agreed to come back to New York.

On November 4, 2003, the Yankees announced that they had hired Mattingly as the hitting coach. "I've told everyone that, in my mind, if I really wanted to get a job back in baseball, I'd really want to start out as a hitting coach and be able to sit there and watch a great manager work and learn and learn. And then, at some point, be able to manage. So that would be something I would like to do."[47]

The 2004 team tied the White Sox for the major-league lead in home runs, with 242, and finished second in runs with 892. Mattingly earned good reviews from both the players and the pundits. Perhaps his biggest accomplishment was his work with Jason Giambi. The embattled slugger, whose 2004 season had been ruined by revelations of his steroid use and a benign tumor on his pituitary gland, was on the verge of being sent down to the minor leagues in May 2005 because he was hitting just .195. Manager Joe Torre and general manager Brian Cashman met with Giambi and asked that he accept the demotion. The former MVP refused the request, and said that he would be more comfortable working through his prolonged hitting problems with Mattingly rather than with a minor-league coach.

Mattingly tutored Giambi every day for a month. Soon Giambi began to hit again. In June he showed some progress, batting .310 with one home run and nine RBIs. Then, he exploded. In July, Giambi hit .355 with 14 homers and 24 RBIs. He stayed on course through the rest of the season, finishing with a .271 batting average, 32 home runs, and 87 RBIs. In November he won the American League Comeback Player of the Year award and gave credit to Mattingly's mentoring in helping him find his way back.

Mattingly continued as hitting coach through the end of 2006, and was promoted to bench coach in 2007. In each of his four years as a coach, Mattingly reached the postseason, a big change from his days as a player. At the end of the 2007 season, the Yankees and manager Joe Torre parted ways, opening a spot for the team's first new manager in 12 years. Initially, Mattingly was considered by the media as the front-runner for the job, but he lost out to Joe Girardi. A few days after losing the managerial race, Torre was introduced as the new manager of the Los Angeles Dodgers, and his first order of business was to announce that Mattingly would be his hitting coach. A few weeks later, however, Mattingly took a leave of absence from the club because he was going through a difficult divorce. He returned to the club after the All-Star break.

Mattingly continued as the Dodgers' batting coach through the 2010 season. He then succeeded Joe Torre as Dodgers manager. Although his clubs posted winning records during Mattingly's first two years at the helm, the Dodgers did not make the National League playoffs until 2013, when it finished in first place in the NL West. But the Dodgers lost the NLCS in six games to St. Louis. The 2014 season was a virtual repeat. The Dodgers were again the division champs, but lost to St. Louis in the NLDS, 3-1. And the 2015 season nearly mirrored the two prior years. The team won the National League West but lost to the New York Mets in the NLDS in a hard-fought five-game series. A few days after the loss to the Mets, the Dodgers and Mattingly mutually parted ways.[48]

On October 29, 2015, the Miami Marlins hired Mattingly as manager, signing him to a four-year contract.

Mattingly's place in baseball history is an unusual one. For six years he was the game's best player, averaging .327, 203 hits, 43 doubles, 27 home runs, 114 RBIs, and 97 runs scored. But the second half of his career was hampered by his congenitally bad back. Although he won four more Gold Gloves in the 1990s, his batting average dropped. His power numbers also declined to an average of just 10 home runs and 64 RBIs. But if one looks a little deeper into those numbers, it's clear that Mattingly really only had one bad season, 1990. And while 1991 and 1992 were both mediocre, his 162-game averages over the last five years of his career were a .291 batting average, 13 home runs and 83 RBIs.

In his *2001 Historical Baseball Abstract*, statistical guru Bill James ranked Don Mattingly as the 12th-greatest first baseman of all-time. In his comment to the ranking, James described him as "100 percent ballplayer, zero percent bullshit."[49]

In time perhaps Mattingly may find his way into the Hall of Fame. Perhaps not. Either way, Don Mattingly will likely be remembered by baseball fans just as he once wished when he said, "When you think of me, think of me on the baseball field."

And that is where most people will think of Don Mattingly: on the baseball field, his uniform dirty, wearing the eye black, ready to play. Always ready to play. Donnie Baseball.

NOTES

1. *Don Mattingly Yankeeography Video*, June 21, 2002, MLB Productions.
2. Ira Berkow, "The Boss is Confused," *New York Times*, August 25, 1988.
3. *Don Mattingly Yankeeography*.
4. Ibid.
5. Jane Gross, "Yanks Won't Start Mattingly," *New York Times*, March 13, 1984.
6. Ibid.
7. Ibid.
8. Murray Chass, "Mattingly in Good Company," *New York Times*, June 24, 1984.
9. Murray Chass, "Mattingly Wins," *New York Times*, October 1, 1984.
10. Dave Anderson, "I Feel Good for the City," *New York Times*, November 21, 1985.
11. Associated Press, "Mattingly's Numbers Are on the Rise," *New York Times*, July 13, 1987.
12. Dave Anderson, "Mattingly Is a Bargain," *New York Times*, July 20, 1987.
13. Malcolm Moran, "Mattingly Ties Home Run Record," *New York Times*, July 17, 1987.
14. Ibid.
15. Murray Chass. "Every Pitcher's Nightmare," *New York Times*, April 3, 1988.

16 Ibid.

17 Ibid.

18 Ibid.

19 Ibid.

20 Ibid.

21 Ibid.

22 Ibid.

23 Michael Martinez, "Baseball Lead," *New York Times*, April 10, 1990.

24 Associated Press, "Yankees Star Sets Baseball Salary Mark," *Eugene* (Oregon) *Register-Guard*, April 19, 1990.

25 Michael Martinez, "New Salary Won't Affect Mattingly," *New York Times*, April 11, 1990.

26 Ibid.

27 Michael Martinez, "Mattingly Is Named Captain; Will He Go Down With Ship?" *New York Times*, March 1, 1991.

28 Ibid.

29 Ibid.

30 Jack Curry, "Mattingly Chooses Seat on Yank Bench Over Barber's Chair," *New York Times*, August 16, 1991.

31 Ibid.

32 Jack Curry, "Williams Passes Mentor," *New York Times*, April 15, 2002.

33 Jack Curry, "Mattingly Ponders His Future," *New York Times*, August 11, 1994.

34 Jack Curry, "Routine for Mattingly: The Here and the Now," *New York Times*, April 7, 1995.

35 Jack Curry, "Mattingly Can Finally Become Mr. October," *New York Times*, October 2, 1995.

36 Ibid.

37 Ibid.

38 Ibid.

39 Ibid.

40 Don Mattingly Chat on AOL, May 9, 1998.

41 Jack Curry, "The Yankees' Season Runs Aground in the Great Northwest," *New York Times*, October 9, 1995.

42 Harvey Araton, "Mr. Cub's Tribute to a Yankee," *New York Times*, October 10, 1995.

43 Murray Chass, "Mattingly's Monument to Effort," *New York Times*, September 1, 1997.

44 Ibid.

45 Ibid.

46 Murray Chass, "Mattingly In Good Company," *New York Times*, June 24, 1984.

47 Ibid.

48 Dylan Hernandez, "Reason for Mutual Parting of Don Mattingly and Dodgers Is Unclear," *Los Angeles Times*, October 22, 2015.

49 Bill James, *2001 Historical Baseball Abstract* (New York: Free Press, 2001).

STEVE SAX

By Alan Cohen

Sometimes it is by chance. Sometimes it is inevitable. But each time it is accompanied by a certain euphoria. So it was that on August 17, 1981, in San Antonio, Texas, the phone rang. Los Angeles Dodgers second baseman Davey Lopes had been placed on the disabled list with a groin injury. So the call went to Double-A San Antonio for 21-year-old Steve Sax, who was batting .346 for the Texas League team. Manager Don LeJohn told Sax he was to join the Dodgers in Chicago. Sax took a 6:00 A.M. flight the next morning. After his plane landed in Chicago at 10:00 A.M., he went straight to Wrigley Field.[1] And the Dodgers had, in the words of manager Tom Lasorda, "a little breath of fresh air."[2]

Stephen Louis Sax was born on January 29, 1960, in Sacramento, California, the third of five children born to John Thomas and Nancy Jane (Colombani) Sax. Cheryl came first, followed by David, Steve, Tammy, and Dana. The family lived on a small farm and his father drove a truck before a series of heart problems caused him to stay at home. Nancy worked as a secretary to help provide for the family.

As a youngster, Steve was always hustling, and he never stopped. "I just plain loved to run," he once said. "So I ran everywhere. If I was running a race, I would run to the starting line. And yes, I would run to first base after walks."[3] In Little League he was a pitcher, with his older brother, Dave, catching and his father serving as the team's coach. Sax's best memory of those days is the time he pitched a no-hitter.[4]

Baseball was the major passion in young Steve's life, but at age 11 he began playing the drums. He became quite accomplished and twice during his time with the Dodgers played with the Beach Boys.

Sax attended James Marshall High School in West Sacramento. In his junior year he was the league MVP and was named to All-City, All State, and All-American teams, playing shortstop and third base. In his senior year, he batted .357, was selected Golden Empire League MVP, and was named to the All-Northern California baseball team.

Sax was drafted by the Dodgers in the ninth round of the 1978 free-agent draft. He had hoped to be drafted higher, but was still ecstatic when he heard the news. He didn't sign right away as he had one game of Legion ball remaining. His father had just undergone heart surgery and, as Sax told it, was in the hospital when Steve promised to hit a home run for him. In his first at-bat in that American Legion appearance, he fulfilled that promise.[5]

Sax passed up a full scholarship to the University of Arizona and signed with scout Ronnie King of the Dodgers. His brother, Dave, who had not been drafted, was invited to a tryout by King, and also signed with the Dodgers. The brothers played together on four minor-league teams.

That summer they played for Lethbridge (Alberta), the Dodgers' Pioneer League (rookie league) affiliate. Steve batted .328 in 39 games, and was on his way. His next two seasons were at Class A, but finding the right position for him proved problematic. In 1979, with Clinton (Iowa) in the Midwest League, after stints in the outfield and at third base, Sax was put at second base for the first time, playing 34 games there. He batted .290 with 25 stolen bases. In 1980 he played the entire season at second base for Vero Beach in the Florida State League, batting .283, driving in 61 runs, stealing 33 bases, and earning a promotion to Double-A San Antonio the next season.

At San Antonio Sax put up numbers that could not be ignored. His .346 batting average when the call came to join the Dodgers stood up as the league's best. He was named the Texas League's Most Valuable Player.

Resplendent in Dodgers uniform number 52, the 5-foot-11 Sax took the field for the first time on August 18, 1981, at Wrigley Field in Chicago, filling in for Lopes. The players strike that interrupted the season for two months had ended on July 31. So excited was Sax to be in the majors that "even the Bleacher Bums looked good to me," he remembered.[6] Facing the Cubs' Mike Griffin, the right-handed-batting Sax first came to bat in the third inning, hit a slow roller up the middle, and beat out the throw to first base for his first major-league hit. In the field he handled nine chances without an error. The Dodgers won, 5-0.

Five days later, as the Dodgers lost 11-7 to the Cardinals in St. Louis, Sax hit his first major-league home run, off Bob Shirley.

On August 25-26 at Pittsburgh, Sax went on a tear getting, 7 hits in 10 at-bats to raise his average to .364 in his first eight games in Dodger Blue. On August 25, he went 4-for-5 in a 9-7 win and was rewarded with a gold chain with a gold bat, attached to which was a white pearl.[7] The Dodgers won 8 of the first 10 games Sax started.

Sax made his Los Angeles home debut on August 27. It was the season of "Fernando-Mania," but Sax was definitely noticed after his eruption in Pittsburgh. General manager Al Campanis said, "(H)e can hit with power, he's exciting, he's not afraid to get his uniform dirty, he can steal a base, and he can make the pivot."[8] Mark Heisler wrote in the *Los Angeles Times*, "Sax was running out routine grounders [so] ferociously that people feared he was going to wipe himself out at first base." In his second game at Los Angeles, he made an error and holed up in the trainer's room. Pitcher Dave Stewart consoled the youngster, saying, "The thing I like about you, Saxy, is [that] when I'm out there you excite the hell out of me."[9]

Before the strike the Dodgers had compiled the best record in the National League West and, in October, defeated Houston in a division playoff series, then toppled the Montreal Expos in the League Championship Series to advance to the World Series against the New York Yankees.

The trip to the 1981 World Series was the first of two for Sax in his time with the Dodgers. By the time the Series began, Lopes had healed and Sax saw limited action. In Game One, he pinch-hit against Yankee ace Ron Guidry and flied out to center field. He entered Game Two as a pinch-runner in the top of the eighth inning and stayed in the game at second base. The Dodgers lost those first two games but swept the next four games for the world championship.

After the Series the Dodgers broke up their infield of Steve Garvey, Davey Lopes, Bill Russell, and Ron Cey, who had played together since 1973. Lopes was traded to Oakland and Sax took over as the second baseman in 1982. On Opening Day, against San Francisco, the enthusiastic Sax almost missed his debut. While running across the diamond to his position at second base in the first inning, he tripped and almost fell flat on his face. "That was a little embarrassing. If I had fallen down, I would have crawled under second base," he said.[10] He went 2-for-4, was the pivot man on a key sixth-inning double play, and set up the game-winning run with a single in the ninth.

From that auspicious beginning, Sax went on to bat .282, and play a sparkling second base. He was the only rookie named to either All-Star team. In the All-Star Game at Montreal, won by the NL 4-1, he pinch-ran in the fifth inning, stayed in the game at second base, and singled in his only turn at bat. Over the 11 years from 1982 through 1992, Sax was rarely out of the lineup, playing in 150 or more games in eight of those seasons.

Sax's enthusiastic play early on made him a favorite for Rookie of the Year honors. He was often compared to Pete Rose for his style of play. Bob McCoy of *The Sporting News* wrote that Sax "runs out his walks and regards a dirty uniform as a badge of honor."[11] Sax himself said that, "I've patterned myself after (Rose). I'm a very aggressive player, and try to give 100% all the time. I try to force mistakes and make things happen."[12] During August he set a record for hits in a month by a Dodger rookie with 43. The record stood for 31 years. He set a team rookie record for stolen bases with 49. Sax led the Dodgers in runs scored (88), hits (180), and stolen bases (49), and tied with Ken Landreaux for the team lead in triples (7).

In 1983 Dave Sax joined Steve on the Dodgers. On June 3 they were in the starting lineup together for the first time. For a brief interlude Sax became a defensive liability for the Dodgers. All of a sudden, he was unable to make throws to first base on the most routine of groundballs. By the time of the All-Star break, he had committed 24 errors. He said, "I felt myself thinking too much, analyzing my every little mistake. It was like I lost my ability to be spontaneous. I found myself pressing."[13] He remembered when it began: "It was April 6 against the Expos. I took a relay throw from the outfield, and I chucked it home past the catcher. Next day, I made another error. Pretty soon, the monkey was on my back."[14]

Sax's year was made even more trying by his father's health problems. They spoke of his throwing difficulties on the telephone just before his father, only 47 years old, died on June 10. In 1989 Sax remembered, "He told me, 'One day you'll wake up and this whole thing will be gone. I did the same thing when I was in high school.' And he was right. One day I woke up and it was all over." For the last 38 games of the season, Sax played errorless ball. "But about two years later," he said, "I was talking to my mom about it and she said, 'You know, your dad never had that problem. He was just trying to help you get over it.' At the shame of his own pride, he told me that to help me get out of it."[15]

At the plate Sax got off to a slow start and was batting .232 after a Dodger loss to the Pirates on May 2. But then his bat got hot, and he ended the season batting .281. He was third in the league with a career-high 56 stolen bases. There was an extra meaning in those stolen bases. Sax had partnered with the American Diabetes Association and was asking fans to pledge $1 each time he stole a base.[16] Once again he was named to the All-Star team, this time as a starter. In the All-Star Game, played at Chicago's Comiskey Park, he went 1-for-3 with an RBI. His throwing problem resurfaced in the second inning, as he was unable to throw out the American League's Manny Trillo. The AL took a 2-1 lead and went on to a 13-3 win.

The Dodgers finished first in the NL West, but did not advance to the World Series, losing to the Philadelphia Phillies in four games during the best-of-five playoff series. Sax went 4-for-16 in the series with a stolen base.

Before the 1984 Season, Sax was rewarded with a five-year contract extension that kept him in Dodger Blue through 1988. At the beginning of the season the throwing problem re-emerged. Sax was frustrated and said as much: "I don't know. I don't understand it at all. It's aggravating. It's frustrating. My sister can make that throw. Fifty million women in America can do it. I'm just sick and tired of it."[17] But the problem resolved itself during the season. Sax later in his career became a Gold Glove second baseman. Nevertheless, the subject of "The Steve Sax Syndrome" often came up. In 1987, former President Richard Nixon, attending a game at Shea Stadium, told Sax, "Glad to hear you got over your throwing problem."[18]

Sax had an off-year in 1984. His batting average fell to .243, the worst in his time with the Dodgers. The team also fared poorly, finishing in fourth place in the NL West with a 79-83 record. The team and Sax bounced back in 1985. For the third time in five years the Dodgers won the NL West. Sax injured his ankle during a pickoff play in spring training and missed 20 of the Dodgers' first 23 games. At the end of June, he was batting only .229. Then he put things together. He batted .311 over the final 84 games to bring his average to the season to .279, and batted .300 (6-for-20) in the NLCS as the Dodgers lost to the Cardinals in six games.

At the end of spring training in 1986, Sax was looking forward to the coming season. He said, "I'm ready. I'm having my best spring ever. I just feel like it's time for everything to come together for me. ..."[19] He proceeded to put up the best offensive numbers of his career, and embark on a durability path that would see him play in at least 155 games for six consecutive seasons.

Sax also, once and for all, overcame his defensive problems. In June he said, "I'm much more relaxed at the plate and in the field. I never had any Triple-A experience, and had never gone to college. My mental approach (was such that I) didn't handle the bad times very well."[20] He finished second in the league in batting average (.332), hits (210), and doubles (43), and for the first and only time in his years with the Dodgers, he won the Silver Slugger award among the league's second basemen. He played in the All-Star Game after a two-year absence, and, in his only at-bat, singled to drive in a run.

Sax was named National League Player of the Month in September 1986, batting .400 with 11 doubles, 11 stolen bases, and 14 RBIs. He began the month with a 25-game hitting streak and from August 30 through the end of the season reached base safely in each of the 34 games in which he played. His hitting streak was the longest in the National League that season, and it ended with a 0-for-7 performance against the Giants in a 16-inning loss on September 28 at San Francisco. Sax was one of very few bright spots for the Dodgers in 1986, as they finished in fifth place in the NL West.

After the 1986 season it was disclosed that Sax had played much of the season in pain, though he never went on the disabled list. On December 10 he had surgery on a foot to remove a bone spur and reposition a nerve.[21]

Sax's enthusiastic style of play made him a Dodger favorite.

On October 21, 1986, Sax married Debbie Graham. They had met the previous spring. They had two children. Lauren Ashley Sax, born in July 1987, and John Jeremy Sax, born in August 1988. The marriage ended in divorce.

Sax had another solid season in 1987, but the Dodgers again were below .500 (73-89) and finished fourth in the NL West. Sax batted only .198 in April, but came back strong. In September he put together a 19-game hitting streak, and finished the season at .280.

The 1988 season proved to be special for Sax and the Dodgers. In the offseason there had been some thought about moving him to third base and inserting Mariano Duncan at second.[22] But in spring training Pedro Guerrero took over third base, and Sax was back at second by Opening Day. Manager Tommy Lasorda said, "Saxie has become a much more selective hitter. He's one of the best hitters I've ever seen going up the middle. He gets into trouble when he tries to pull everything or tries to hit one out of the ballpark."[23]

Sax batted .277 and had 57 RBIs in 1988, the best during his time with the Dodgers. Always a daredevil on the bases, he had 42 thefts in 54 attempts (77.8 percent), by far his best stolen-base ratio in his time in Los Angeles.

The Dodgers won the NL West and defeated the New York Mets in seven games for the pennant, with Sax getting some key hits during the series. In the World Series the Dodgers, plagued by injuries, went up against the bruising Oakland A's, who featured Jose Canseco, Mark McGwire, and Dave Parker. Sax, after being barreled into by Parker, said he felt he had been run into "by a running condominium."[24] The Dodgers won the Series in five games with Sax batting .300. After it was all done, as Mike Downey noted in *The Sporting News*, "It was a World Series in which the Dodgers reportedly decided to celebrate their championship by pouring bottles of iodine over one another's heads. By the time it ended, Los Angeles manager Tommy Lasorda no longer filled out a lineup card with his nine best players. He just started asking for nine volunteers."[25]

After the season Sax was a free agent and elected to sign with the Yankees. His negotiations with the Dodgers had not gone pleasantly and Dodgers general manager Fred Claire was quoted as saying to Sax, "This is our final offer. If you think you're getting screwed, don't sign it. If you think you can get a better deal, take it." Sax took a three-year, $4 million deal with the Yankees.[26]

His years with the Dodgers were productive and he was definitely a fan favorite. His 290 stolen bases put him fifth on the all-time Dodgers list in that category. But he no longer felt wanted, and it was time to move on. Sax's biggest regret was parting with close friends Mike Marshall and Mike Scioscia, both of whom shared his intensity for the game.

Sax spent three years in the Bronx, but the Yankees were between dynasties. The revolving door to the manager's office was turning rapidly, and Sax played for three managers during his time in New York.

Although the team finished each season well below .500, Sax performed excellently.

In 1989 he was named to the All-Star team and batted a team-leading .315. His 205 hits, 88 runs scored, and 43 stolen bases also led the team. Sax was clearly the most valuable player on a team that won only 74 games. It was the second time in his career that he had more than 200 hits in a season. Defensively he had the best season of his career, leading the league in fielding percentage (.987), making only 10 errors in 782 chances. He led the league in double plays turned at second base (117). A strong contender for the Gold Glove, Sax just lost out to Seattle's Harold Reynolds. Yankees manager Bucky Dent, who had played beside Sax's predecessor, Willie Randolph, said Sax "has done an outstanding job. He plays with super intensity. He's always into the game. I love him."[27]

In 1990 the Yankees hit rock-bottom, finishing last in the AL East with a 67-95 record, Sax stole 43 bases for the second straight year, good for second in the league. He was caught stealing only nine times, and his 82.7 percent stolen base percentage was the best of his career. Once again he was named to the All-Star team and started at second base for the American League. It was Sax's fifth and last All-Star appearance. His batting average, which had been .281 at the end of June, slipped to .260 for the season as he batted only .243 over his last 86 games.

It was a frustrating time for Sax. The intensity was still there despite the disappointing result. As Joel Sherman noted in the *New York Post*, Sax "considers himself a dirty uniform personified, a man who knows how to play only with passion and hustle. Those flying bats and slammed helmets (he broke five helmets in 1989) are not an act, but rather the symbols of his fury, of the rage of a player who plays with his soul as evident as the number six on his uniform."[28]

Before the 1991 season Sax received a four-year contract extension, worth $12.4 million, and he rebounded to have a great season. But it was more of the same for the team, with the squad finishing 71-91 under

Stump Merrill. Sax's batting average of .304 led the Yankees, as did his 38 doubles. He had a career-high 10 home runs. He was the most difficult man in the league to strike out, fanning on average once in every 17.2 at-bats.

On January 10, 1992, after three losing seasons, the pitching-poor Yankees traded Sax to the Chicago White Sox for Domingo Jean, Melido Perez, and Bob Wickman. Although his average dropped to .236 with Chicago, Sax was a key ingredient on a team that during the early part of the season, contended for the AL West lead. On May 17 he drove in five runs as the White Sox defeated Baltimore 14-10 to go into first place by a half-game. However, the team relinquished the lead and finished the season in third place, 10 games behind division champion Oakland.

In 1993 Sax got into only 57 games and batted .235 for the White Sox. By this time, he was no longer playing second base (Joey Cora was the second baseman) and he was used mostly as a left fielder or designated hitter. The White Sox won the AL West, but Sax did not play in the ALCS against the Toronto Blue Jays. His only home run that season came on June 25 against Seattle. It was off his old Dodgers teammate Tim Leary, and was the last of his 54 career home runs.

In April 1994 Sax was placed on the disabled list with a bruised heel. While on rehab with the team's Birmingham Double-A affiliate, he was released by the White Sox. He signed on with the Oakland A's, playing briefly for Tony La Russa. He got into seven games with the A's, batting .250 (6-for-24) and appeared in his last game on May 8, 1994. He underwent surgery, but was unable to return to the playing field, and was released after the season.

For his 14 year major-league career, Sax batted .281 with 1,949 hits and 444 stolen bases.

After retiring as a player Sax contributed commentary on ESPN and was a baseball analyst for Fox Sports' *Prime Time*. He appeared as a characterization of himself on *The Simpsons*. Sax wrote an article on personal responsibility and self-reliance for the *Wall Street Journal*. For a time in 1995, Sax considered running for the California legislature, but withdrew his name from consideration.

During the 2013 season, Sax was the first-base coach for the Arizona Diamondbacks, working with former Dodgers teammate Kirk Gibson, the Diamondbacks manager.

Sax has a Black Belt in Shotokan Karate and is skilled in kick-boxing as well. He has owned a martial arts studio. In 2001 he became a vice president of investments for the Royal Bank of Canada. His clients included several ballplayers. His belief was that the potential for athletes being victimized is very real. In 2005 he said, "I have heard of instances of athletes getting ripped off. It's like giving an 18-year-old the keys to the car with a six-pack in the back-seat. It's a recipe for disaster." He wrote the motivational book *Shift: Change Your Mindset and Change Our World*. In 2014 Sax was on the radio and in media with MLB on Sirius Satellite Radio and MLB Advanced Media.

Sax founded the Steve Sax Foundation, with a goal of helping motivate young people. The program partnered with other organizations, sports teams and corporation, as well as parents, to help aid youngsters.

SOURCES

Book:

Sax, Steve, and Steve Delsohn. *Sax!* (Chicago: Contemporary Books, 1986).

Newspaper Articles:

Boswell, Thomas. "When you call the Hall, Sax certainly has appeal," *Washington Post*, April 20, 1992, C6.

Curry, Jack. "Sax Finds Happiness Being an Ex-Dodger," *New York Times*, March 14, 1991, B-12.

Dilbeck, Steve. "Sax Spurns Dodgers, Signs with Yankees," *San Bernardino County Sun*, November 24, 1988, C-1.

Downey, Mike. "Dodgers Had to Toast Victories with Iodine," *The Sporting News*, October 31, 1988, 4.

Durso, Joseph. "Sax Steps Into Dodger Infield," *New York Times*, March 23, 1982, D25.

Heisler, Mark. "Steve Sax: Chosen One at Second Base for Dodgers," *Los Angeles Times*, April 3, 1982, B11.

Madden, Bill. "Sax Proves Himself a Good Investment," *The Sporting News*, October 9, 1989, 14.

Martinez, Michael. "Sax Combines Comedy and Intensity," *New York Times*, July 10, 1989, C-1.

Oberjuerge, Paul. "Sax Is on Fast Track to Pennant," *San Bernardino County Sun*, August 22, 1988, C-1.

Verrell, Gordon. "No Hypnosis — Not Yet: Sax," *The Sporting News*, August 22, 1983, 17.

_____. "Sax's Throwing Woes Are Back," *The Sporting News*, May 14, 1984, 20.

_____. "Dodgers Can't Blame Sax This Year," *The Sporting News*, June 2, 1986, 25.

Other:

Baseball-Reference.com.

Los Angeles Times.

New York Times.

San Bernardino County Sun.

The Sporting News.

Author interview with Steve Sax, October 28, 2014.

NOTES

1. Mark Heisler, "Is the End at Hand for the Gang of Four?" *Los Angeles Times*, August 19, 1981, E1.
2. Heisler, "Sax Plays a Part as Dodgers Hit High Notes, 6-1," *Los Angeles Times*, August 29, 1981, D1.
3. Steve Sax and Steve Delsohn, *Sax!* (Chicago: Contemporary Books, 1986), 22.
4. *Sax!*, 25.
5. *Sax!*, 29-30.
6. *Sax!*, 37.
7. Megan Morrow, "Everyone but Sax Keeps Tooting His Horn," *The Sporting News*, April 10, 1982, 6.
8. *The Sporting News*, September 12, 1981, 52.
9. Heisler, "Sax Plays a Part."
10. David Leon Moore, "Meet Steve Sax: Dodgers' Mr. Enthusiasm," *San Bernardino County Sun*, April 7, 1982, B-7.
11. Bob McCoy, "Just Call Him Steve Hustle …," *The Sporting News*, July 5, 1982, 13.
12. "Sax Wins NL Rookie Award Over Ray," *Syracuse Post-Standard*, November 23, 1982.
13. *Sax!*, 58.
14. Jon Saraceno, *USA Today*, March 21, 2001. The game actually took place on April 8, the Dodgers' home opener. Sax actually made two errors, the first on a groundball in the first inning and the second on a throw home in the ninth.
15. Michael Martinez, "Sax Combines Comedy and Intensity," *New York Times*, July 10, 1989, C-1.
16. Bud Furillo, "Sax Attacks Diabetes and Throwing Problem," *Dodger Blue*, June 30, 1983.
17. *The Sporting News*, May 14, 1984, 20.
18. *The Sporting News*, September 28, 1987, 6.
19. *The Sporting News*, April 7, 1986, 50.
20. *The Sporting News*, June 2, 1986, 25.
21. *The Sporting News*, January 26, 1987, 39.
22. Gordon Verrell, "Sax Cool to Switching Sacks," *The Sporting News*, January 11, 1988, 46.
23. *The Sporting News*, April 4, 1988, 37.
24. Mike Downey, *The Sporting News*, October 31, 1988, 4.
25. Ibid.
26. Steve Dilbeck, "Sax Spurns Dodgers, Signs With Yankees," *San Bernardino County Sun*, November 24, 1988, C-1.
27. Michael Kay, "Sax's Glove Plays Solid Gold Tune," *New York Daily News*, September 21, 1989, C 29.
28. Joel Sherman, "The Fire Still Burns," *New York Post*, July 27, 1990.

MIKE SCIOSCIA

By Susan Lantz

A 13-year veteran catcher, Mike Scioscia has—through 2015—managed the Los Angeles Angels of Anaheim for 16 seasons, the first major-league manager to reach the playoffs in six of his first 10 seasons. He led the Angels to a world championship in 2002.

Michael Lorri Scioscia was born in Upper Darby, Pennsylvania, on November 27, 1958. He played football, basketball, and baseball at Springfield (Pennsylvania) High School, was named Delaware County baseball player of the year in 1975 and 1976, and was a two-time all-area selection in baseball and football.[1] He was drafted by the Los Angeles Dodgers in the first round (19th pick) of the 1976 amateur draft.[2] He was planning to go to Clemson University, to play baseball there and fulfill his mother's dream. But on the morning of July 6, 1976, the phone at the Scioscia family's home rang: It was Tom Lasorda, the Dodgers' third-base coach, calling to invite Mike to work out with the Dodgers, who were in town to play the Philadelphia Phillies. Scioscia left a note for his parents, hopped in the car when Lasorda and his brother, Eddie, picked him up. "When I got Mike in the car, I told him what it meant to be a Dodger," Lasorda said. "I told him this would be his only opportunity to be a Dodger, and that he had to sign. I told him that our scout saw something in him and talked highly about him, and that we believed in him enough to draft him with our first pick, that I believed in him, and that he needed to believe it, too."[3]

Scioscia went home that night and told his parents he wanted to sign with the Dodgers. His mother, Florence, a grade-school teacher, started crying; she wanted him to go to college. His father was happy, but couldn't show it because his wife was not. The next day Scioscia was on a plane to Walla Walla, Washington, to play pro ball.[4] Scioscia's mother never entirely forgave him for choosing a game over education—and leaving a full-ride scholarship to Clemson unclaimed.[5] His father, Fred, was a salesman for a beer distributor and had been a pitcher on a semipro team in Johnstown, Pennsylvania.[6]

The 17-year-old Scioscia was assigned to Bellingham (Washington) in the Class-A (short-season) Northwest League where, in 46 games, he hit .278, with an on-base percentage of .418.

The following year, 1977, at Clinton (Iowa) of the Class-A Midwest League, Scioscia played in 121 games, five at first base. He improved his defense behind the plate, and continued to be a patient hitter, walking 79 times and achieving a .385 OBP.

Scioscia was named to the Arizona Instructional League's all-star squad, one of only two catchers chosen. (The other was Dale "Pat" Kelly of the California Angels' Double-A El Paso affiliate.)[7]

Scioscia spent 1978 at San Antonio in the Double-A Texas League. He played in 58 games, missing part of the year with an injury, and hit .299, with half of his appearances as a pinch-hitter. He was promoted to the Dodgers' major-league roster after the minor-league season.[8]

With Albuquerque in the Triple-A Pacific Coast League in 1979, Scioscia's batting average was an eye-popping .336, with a .432 OBP and an .861 OPS, and he was selected to the Pacific Coast League All-Star team.[9]

Scioscia played 13 seasons with the Dodgers.

As one of four catchers on the Dodgers' 40-man roster, Scioscia expected to spend much, if not all, of the 1980 season in Albuquerque, but he was called up after Johnny Oates was released and Steve Yeager and Joe Ferguson were injured. Had he not been on the disabled list when the Dodgers ran into catching problems the first week of the season, Scioscia would undoubtedly have made his debut sooner. But he had dislocated the ring finger on his throwing hand in a baserunning mishap during spring training, and he was not eligible until April 20. When he became eligible, he was immediately put into the lineup. In his first major-league at-bat, he doubled and scored a run.[10] It was a good start to his major-league career.

Exclusively a catcher and a left-handed hitter, Scioscia never played any other position in the majors. During his rookie season, he played in 54 games for the Dodgers, starting 44 of them. He allowed two passed balls, made two errors, and threw out 20 of the 68 runners who attempted to steal against him (29 percent). When asked to evaluate his strengths, Scioscia replied: "I'm great at putting on my gear after I make an out. I've been timed in 3.8 seconds."[11]

On July 21 Scioscia was sent back to Albuquerque.[12] By August 4, he had 56 at-bats, 20 hits, and 9 RBIs, and his .357 batting average was second-best in the Pacific Coast League. Called up again in late August, he was 14-for-51 (.275) for the remainder of the season and had his first four-hit game on September 6 against the Phillies.[13]

In 1981 Scioscia left spring training with the Dodgers, and he stayed in Los Angeles for the next 12 seasons. Dodgers manager Tom Lasorda used the same lineup for the first 14 games of the season, except for platooning his catchers: Scioscia played against right-handed pitchers and Yeager against lefties.[14]

Scioscia had a good arm. When he threw out Montreal's Tim Raines trying to steal third on May 2, Raines, who was leading the league with 20 steals in 21 attempts, had to explain how he'd been thrown out. It was that hard to believe.[15] And Scioscia was solid on defense. On May 4 in Montreal, the Expos' Warren Cromartie, trying to score from second on a single, slammed hard into Scioscia at the plate. Scioscia was sent sprawling, but he held the ball. When he regained his feet, he caught Speier in a rundown between first and second as Rowland Office, who had gone from first to third on the play, edged down the line toward the plate. Finally Office broke for home, arriving about the same time as the ball. Again Scioscia was sent flying, only this time the runner was safe. Later in the game, Scioscia was rocked again when the Expos' Andre Dawson was out attempting to score on an infield single.

"I'm sure that's the most collisions I've ever had in one game," Scioscia said, "and I KNOW it's the most times I've been crunched on one play."[16]

Scioscia said the plays at the plate were good, clean plays. "That's the runner's only recourse, to run me over and try to knock the ball loose," he said. "As long as the guy's not trying to hurt you, it's just hard baseball. That's the way I look at it."

Al Campanis, the Dodgers' vice president, said of Scioscia, "He is the best I've ever seen at blocking off the plate." Expos manager Dick Williams praised Scioscia's work: "I really like that kid, and he's got guts back there."

Scioscia had some savvy, too. He was the catcher in five of Fernando Valenzuela's first six wins, four of them shutouts. "I don't think Mike Scioscia is getting enough credit," said former Dodger Don Sutton after Valenzuela had blanked the Houston Astros for the second time. "He called an outstanding game both times against us." (The previous year, Scioscia caught one of Sutton's two shutouts with the Dodgers, after which Sutton rewarded him with a bottle of wine.)[17]

After the players strike began on June 12, young players making at or near the minimum salary sometimes found it difficult to make ends meet. Scioscia said, "I've just got me to feed, but the guys tell me I eat enough for a whole family."[18] The strike came at a bad time for Scioscia, who was batting .299 and was not listed on the All-Star ballot. The time lost to the strike took away any opportunity for write-in votes.[19]

Scioscia, however, had become the Dodgers' number-one catcher, while the veteran Yeager started only 23 of the Dodgers' 110 games.[20] When the strike ended, an extra round of best-of-five-games divisional playoff series between the first-half (pre-strike) and the second-half (post-strike) leaders was devised. The Dodgers won the first half in the National League West Division, and faced the Astros, the second-half winners, for the right to play in the NLCS.

The Dodgers lost the first two games of the Series, then won the next two, and won the decisive fifth game, 4-0, thanks in part to Scioscia singling home a run against Houston's Nolan Ryan.[21] In Game One of the best-of-five NLCS, Pedro Guerrero and Scioscia hit back-to-back home runs off Montreal's Jeff Reardon during a 5-1 Los Angeles triumph. The Dodgers won the series in five games.

The 1981 World Series pitted the Dodgers against the New York Yankees. It was their third World Series meeting in five seasons. The Dodgers won the Series in six games, after losing the first two games on the road. Steve Yeager started five of the six games. In six plate appearances, Scioscia was 1-for-4 with a walk and a sacrifice fly.

Scioscia began the 1982 season as the Dodgers' starting catcher, with Yeager as the backup.[22] The Dodgers won their first two games, then lost eight of the next 10. Scioscia was among those struggling, batting only .222 two weeks into the season.[23]

Scioscia was becoming one of the National League's most formidable plate blockers. When asked how he practiced blocking the plate, he replied: "It's not easy to find guys who will come out early before games and run into you."[24]

Despite his defensive skills, Scioscia continued to struggle at the plate and presented some mixed results in his fielding. He finished the season with a batting average of .219, and he threw out only 40 of 126 runners attempting to steal (32 percent) and allowed 14 passed balls (second most in the league).

At the end of the 1982 season, there were multiple reports that the Dodgers' biggest offseason priority would be a catcher. Good catchers were hard to come by. But Scioscia had not progressed the way the Dodgers hoped he would, and Yeager would turn 34 in 1983.

Realizing his offensive shortcomings, Scioscia set up a batting cage in his garage over the winter and worked at hitting every day. "I admit," he quipped, "it's a little easier hitting a ball off a tee than one thrown by, say, Steve Carlton."[25]

In spring training, the Dodgers planned to re-establish Scioscia as the catcher he had been two years earlier, and they did it one step at a time, beginning with catching the ball. "Mike developed some bad habits last year, so we're going back to the basics," Lasorda explained. "He was in the wrong position to catch the ball, so he had trouble throwing out runners, and he had too many passed balls." Campanis, the Dodgers' vice president, said: "We were disappointed more with his receiving than we were his hitting. He's an excellent signal-caller, he's excellent at tagging runners, but we've got him on a program so he can improve all areas of catching."[26]

Scioscia didn't concern himself with trade rumors. "I can't worry about it because there's nothing I can do about it anyway," he said. "I know I can do the job, I just had an off year. I know this, I'm not going to be a backup. … If they get [Jim] Sundberg [from the Texas Rangers] I'm not going to want to sit around for three or four years until he retires. I want to play."[27]

Five weeks into the 1983 season, Scioscia was hitting .314, but he injured his right shoulder as he threw out San Diego Padres' swifty Alan Wiggins at second base on May 14. The injury healed much more slowly than expected. Scioscia was still on the disabled list at the end of the season.[28] It wasn't until August 1 that the injury was diagnosed as ulceration of the rotator cuff.[29]

Scioscia's progress in spring training in 1984 was notable. Not only was he throwing again, and accurately, but he picked up right where he'd left off with the bat. He damaged ligaments in his left knee on May 5 in Pittsburgh while blocking the plate and was placed on the 15-day disabled list. He returned to the active roster on May 22.[30] But the Dodgers were finding hits and runs hard to come by. At the end of the season Scioscia was hitting .273, and eight of his 38 RBIs were game-winners.[31] He was chosen the Dodgers' most inspirational player.[32]

During the Dodgers' 1985 spring training, Campanis talked about Scioscia in glowing terms. "He's worked hard with his throwing and his hitting, and nobody … I mean, *nobody* … blocks the plate like he does. And he's become a leader on the field. He's like the captain without being named the captain."[33]

In the first inning of a game on July 21, the fearless Scioscia was knocked unconscious in a bone-jarring collision at the plate with the Cardinals' Jack Clark. Scioscia held onto the ball, and Clark was out, but Scioscia was carried off the field on a stretcher. He suffered a mild concussion and was hospitalized overnight, but returned the next night against Pittsburgh, pinch-hitting in the eighth inning and catching the ninth.[34]

When someone suggested that Scioscia, a key to the Dodgers' National League pennant hopes, might benefit from an occasional rest, Lasorda said: "Roy Campanella used to catch every day. So did Yogi Berra, Bill Dickey, Johnny Bench. Why not Scioscia? He's big and strong. Did you ever see an Italian who needed a rest?"[35]

At the end of the season, Scioscia had a .296 batting average, second on the team to outfielder Pedro Guerrero (.320). That was the highest average for a Dodgers catcher since Roy Campanella hit .318 for Brooklyn in 1955. Scioscia was second in the league in on-base percentage (.407; Guerrero was the league leader). The Dodgers won the NL West division by 5½ games over the Cincinnati Reds.

Each of the first four NLCS contests between the Dodgers and the Cardinals was decided by defense—or a decided lack of it. During the second week of October, defensive reputations rose and fell like stock market prices. Scioscia was being rated as the second coming of Mickey Cochrane after throwing out Vince Coleman and Willie McGee back-to-back on first-inning theft attempts in Game Two, but 48 hours later, in Game Three, he was being billed as the reincarnation of Mickey Mouse. In the bottom of the second with one out, Coleman singled and tried to steal but found himself in no-man's land as the Dodgers pitched out. Scioscia ran toward the trapped runner, but fired the ball past first baseman Greg Brock's outstretched glove, allowing Coleman to regroup and race to third.[36] The Cardinals won the series in six games.

During the winter the Dodgers traded Yeager, who had been Scioscia's backup at catcher, to the Seattle Mariners and acquired veteran catcher Alex Trevino from the San Francisco Giants, the defensive insurance they were seeking behind Scioscia.[37] Scioscia was one of eight Dodgers who filed for arbitration. Then he bypassed arbitration and signed a four-year contract for $3.755 million.[38]

In the first week of the 1986 season, Scioscia was involved in five bone-jarring collisions at the plate. Each time, he kept hold of the ball, enhancing his reputation as the best in the game at blocking the plate. "It's unusual to have so many (collisions) in such a short time," said Scioscia. "These plays come in streaks. Really, I don't like collisions. But they're part of the game."[39]

Scioscia's bravery could be a trifle unnerving for his wife, Anne (whom he had met when she delivered cookies to him at Dodger Stadium). Asked if he had some sort of signal to let her know if he was all right after a collision, he replied: "Yeah. She knows if I'm carried off on a stretcher, I'm hurt, and if I stay in the game, I'm OK."[40]

The Dodgers suffered many injuries (Scioscia a June 9 right-ankle injury), and 14 Dodgers in all went on the disabled list, two of them twice. Every regular except Steve Sax was on the DL at least once. The Dodgers ended the season last or nearly so in virtually every category except attendance, and even that suffered a bit. The Dodgers made more errors (181) than any other team in the league; the bullpen floundered; and the team's .251 batting average was 10 points lower than in the previous season. Scioscia, who had quietly become the team's on-the-field leader, hit only .251, 45 points lower than the prior year.[41] Part of the reason was his ankle injury, which severely restricted his pivot in the batter's box.[42]

Scioscia started off 1987 in fine form, but on June 1, broke a bone in the middle finger of his left hand while attempting a drag bunt during batting practice.[43] Still, he was one of six National League catchers named to the 1987 All-Star team.[44] He spotted a mechanical flaw in the delivery of Fernando Valenzuela's fastball and screwball, which, once

Scioscia was named to the All-Star squad twice as a backstop.

corrected, allowed the pitcher to return to his winning ways.[45]

The Dodgers were once again plagued by injury, and finished 73-89, fourth in the National League West. After the season ended, four Dodgers underwent surgery, including Scioscia, who had arthroscopic surgery to remove torn cartilage from his right knee.[46]

After San Francisco lost three of four games in Los Angeles in August 1988, Giants manager Roger Craig called Scioscia "the best all-around catcher in the league."[47] During the series, Scioscia prevented two runs with blocks at the plate, threw out three of the four Giants who tried to steal, collected 5 hits in 16 at-bats, and drove in two runs.[48]

In September Scioscia had trainers cut away part of his left shoe and pad it with foam to ease the pressure on his Achilles tendon, which was tender.[49] He missed five games after a home-plate collision with San Diego's John Kruk on September 21. Scioscia suffered a bruised left hip; Kruk left the game the next evening, and was out for the season with a deep laceration and strained ligaments in his left knee.[50]

The Dodgers won the NL West, then faced the New York Mets in the NLCS. The Mets were favored because they had beaten the Dodgers in 10 of their 11 regular-season meetings. The NLCS was wild and wacky and sometimes controversial, filled with crazy plays. The Dodgers survived the fourth game, winning 5-4 on Kirk Gibson's 12th-inning homer after a two-run bomb by Scioscia off Dwight Gooden tied the score in the ninth. Scioscia, who had hit just three home runs during the regular season, said afterward that he was just trying to hit the ball somewhere. Scioscia's homer stunned the Mets, then Gibson banged out the win, after having gone 1-for-16 in the series.[51]

Game Four was the pivotal point in the playoffs as it evened the NLCS at two games apiece; the Dodgers won it in seven. Scioscia hit .364.

The Dodgers faced the Oakland Athletics in the World Series. Scioscia was caught stealing in Game Four and had to be helped from the field after injuring his right knee. (He had surgery to remove torn cartilage later in the month.[52]) Despite having lost four players to injuries (Gibson, Marshall, Scioscia, and Tudor), the Dodgers finished off Oakland, 5-2, in Game Five.[53]

Beginning his ninth season with the Dodgers in 1989, Scioscia was the senior man on the club.[54] He was named to the All-Star team. Though the Dodgers struggled offensively, they wanted to lock in Scioscia for the future. Rather than let him enter free agency, the Dodgers signed him on August 17 to a three-year, $5.6 million deal, breaking a long-standing club policy by negotiating a contract during the season. The Dodgers did not want to risk losing Scioscia. "I consider Mike to be the best catcher in baseball," Dodgers' executive vice president Fred Claire said. "It was very important for us to sign him."[55]

Scioscia hit .250 for the season, but was rated second among all National League catchers, behind Tony Pena of St. Louis.[56] In a tight race, incumbent Benito Santiago of the Padres edged out Scioscia for the Gold Glove, 29-28.[57] In another contest, Scioscia was selected by the Southern California media as the catcher of the Dodgers' All-Decade team.[58]

The 1990 season started off well. Scioscia was named an All-Star once again and was the National League's starting catcher—the first Dodger catcher to do so since Roy Campanella in 1954. (The Padres' Santiago had been voted in by the fans as the starting NL catcher, but he had suffered a broken arm after being hit by a pitch in mid-June.[59]) Although it was a better season for Scioscia at bat (.264 batting, .348 OBP, a career-best 12 home runs, a career-best 66 RBIs, and 46 runs scored) and a better year for the Dodgers, the team finished second in the National League West, five games behind the Cincinnati Reds.

The Dodgers were seeking a veteran to back up Scioscia, so they invited former Expo, Met, and Giant Gary Carter to spring training in 1991. The Dodgers ended the season 93-69, and finished second in the NL West, one game behind the Atlanta Braves. Scioscia's batting average was the same as the previous year, .264, but he had fewer hits (91) and fewer RBIs (40). His fielding percentage was still excellent (.990). Because Lasorda platooned him and Carter, Scioscia caught 160 fewer innings than in the past two years, falling below 1,000 for the first time in three years.

The 1992 season didn't start well for Scioscia. On April 16 he was hitting just .188 and had thrown out just one of 12 basestealers after Atlanta stole three that evening in Los Angeles. Two nights later Scioscia blocked two runners at the plate, one of them Deion Sanders in a massive collision. "It's the first time I've taken on a football player," said Scioscia. Sanders was the 125th runner Scioscia had stopped at the plate in his career.[60]

In a poll of major-league managers, coaches, and general managers asking which current players were managerial material, Scioscia and the White Sox's Carlton Fisk were the highest rated. Officially, Scioscia denied any managerial thoughts (which may have been politic). "I don't want to think about anything except playing," he said. "I don't rule out managing, but I'm not saying I will or want to. In fact, I never even think about it." When the veracity of his last statement was challenged, he amended: "Well, I don't think about it very often." Third-base coach Joe Amalfitano said, "If I didn't know better, I'd think he lives at the ballpark. He's usually one of the first players to arrive and definitely one of the last to leave. Most of the guys don't hang around the clubhouse to talk baseball anymore. Mike does." Atlanta manager Bobby Cox said, "Scioscia is smarter than hell and is tremendous in his handling of a game. When it comes to leading, he has been as important in the success of the Dodgers' organization as any player they've ever had."[61]

At the end of the season, the Dodgers' record was 63-99, last in the division, and Scioscia's numbers weren't much better. His batting average was .221, with 77 hits, 24 RBIs, and 19 runs scored—all career lows if his injury-shortened 1983 season and 54-game rookie season were not included. He led the league in assists by a catcher (74) and in passed balls (14). By late October, it appeared his days with the Dodgers were over. Scioscia's contract had expired at the end of the season, and he wanted a two-year deal, but the Dodgers were offering only one year. He also wanted assurances that he'd catch 120 to 130 games (he'd caught only 108 that season).[62] Unwilling to accept a one-year deal, Scioscia filed for free agency, but was not offered arbitration.[63] He signed a one-year contract for about $350,000 with the San Diego Padres because they were one of the few teams willing to give him an opportunity to start. "I had more lucrative offers elsewhere," Scioscia said.[64]

Scioscia started the 1993 season on the disabled list after suffering a rotator-cuff injury during spring training. He did not play any regular-season games for the Padres, and was released after the season ended.[65] He attempted a comeback the following year, signing a Triple-A contract with the Texas Rangers, intent on working to become the Rangers' backup catcher,[66] but never played in a regular-season game. Scioscia retired on August 2, 1994.[67] Despite having overcome a similar injury in 1983, when he was 24, and continuing to catch more than 100 games a season and contribute at a high level for the next nine years, at 34 he was unable to do so.

Offensively, Scioscia was generally an above-average player as well as a solid contact hitter, striking out less than once every 14 at-bats over the course of his career. Because of his ability to make contact, he was sometimes used as the second hitter in the batting order—an atypical spot for a player of his stature (6 feet 2 inches, 200-230 pounds) and overall batting average. He was a key player on the Dodgers' 1981 and 1988 World Series teams, and he remains, as of 2015, the Dodgers' leader in games caught (1,395). He played in 1,441 major-league games, had 1,131 hits, 446 RBIs, and 68 home runs. His career batting average was .259.

In October 1994 Scioscia rejoined the Dodgers as a catching instructor. He immediately joined the Dodgers' Arizona Instructional League team. In February 1996 rumors circulated that Lasorda might retire, and speculation ran rampant about who would replace him at the helm if he did. Bill Russell got the nod.

In 1997 and 1998, Scioscia was the Dodgers' bench coach. (Russell was fired in June of '98.) In 1997 Scioscia was rumored to be one of the many candidates to manage the Chicago White Sox.[68] In 1999 Scioscia managed the Dodger's Triple-A team in Albuquerque, guiding them to a 65-74 season, tied for 11th place in the Pacific Coast League.

In November 1999 Scioscia was named manager of the Los Angeles Angels. He said he fell in love with managing while at the helm in the instructional league with the Dodgers in 1997. By the time he was managing Triple-A Albuquerque the following year, he knew he wanted a career as a manager. Turmoil in the ownership and management of the Dodgers, which Scioscia likened to a washing machine, meant his opportunity came 30 miles from where he had played.[69]

Scioscia began his major-league managerial career with the same core group of Angels players who had forced out manager Terry Collins and general manager Bill Basavi. His biggest tasks initially were to unify a team that fought throughout the second half of 1999, restore clubhouse discipline, and squeeze the maximum amount of potential from a shaky starting rotation.[70] The club ended the season in third place, with an 82-80 record. The consensus was that Scioscia "brought harmony to a fractious clubhouse by being even-tempered and even-handed in his dealings with players. His managing style is aggressive but not reckless."[71]

Scioscia's job became more difficult in 2001, when injuries and slumps required him to spend considerably more time juggling his lineup.[72] The club ended the season with a 75-87 record, third in the AL West.

In February 2002 sports reporter Joe Haakenson wrote: "Mike Scioscia has only two years of big-league managerial experience, but he carries himself as though he has been doing the job for a decade. His 13 years playing in the majors earned him instant respect from his players. He further enhanced his standing with an open-door policy and honest approach. … Scioscia maintains an even keel which rubs off on his players."[73]

The Angels started the 2002 season poorly, 6-14, primarily due to a struggling bullpen, although some of the starting pitchers had difficulty, too.[74] By the end of May they'd bounced back and had moved up to second place in the division.[75] They continued playing well, and in early September, their record was 87-54, still second in the AL West. Noted a reporter: "The team reflects manager Mike Scioscia. Players have bought into his hard-nosed, unselfish way of thinking. That's what got them through a rough start this season and what has kept them levelheaded during the good stretches."[76] The club finished with a 99-63 record, having overcome a 10½-game deficit in the division by relying on hitting and running and qualified for the postseason playoffs. The Angels had the best batting average in the American League (.282) and the fewest strikeouts (805, almost 200 fewer than in 2001).

The Angels entered the ALDS as the wild card and won the best-of-five series over the Yankees in four games. Then they won the best-of-seven ALCS over the Minnesota Twins in five games. The Angels faced the San Francisco Giants in the World Series and won in seven games — their first World Series triumph. Scioscia was named AL Manager of the Year, an award his peers believed he deserved for turning the team around after its horrible start.

In 2003 the Angels were 77-85, third in the division. The starting rotation was inconsistent, but the bullpen was one of the team's strengths. In 2004, they won the division with a record of 92-70 — their first division title in 18 years — but they lost the ALDS to the Boston Red Sox in three straight games, and only the final game was close (8-6 loss in 10 innings).

In 2005 the club, now known as the Los Angeles Angels of Anaheim, again won the AL West with a record of 95-67. They won the ALDS against the Yankees in five games. Facing the White Sox in the ALCS, they won the first game, then lost the next four.

The 2006 season was not as good a year, 89-73, but it was good enough for second place in the AL West. For the first time in their franchise history, which dated back to 1961, the Angels had had three consecutive winning seasons.

An improvement in 2007 showed in the Angels' season record of 94-68. They won the division, but were swept in the ALDS by Boston in three games, scoring only four runs in the series. (Boston scored 19.)

In 2008 Scioscia had his first 100-win managerial season, although the club did not lead the league in any offensive category. The Angels won the division, but once again lost to Boston in the ALDS, winning only one game (the third) of the four played.

The team continued its winning ways in 2009. With its 97-65 record, it won the AL West, leading the league in hits (1,604, tied with the Yankees) and batting average (.285). In a welcome change, the Angels won the ALDS over Boston in three games, but lost the ALCS against the Yankees in six games. Scioscia was again named AL Manager of the Year.

In 2010, after six consecutive seasons with records above .500, the club fell to 80-82, third in the division.

During the 45th round of the June 2011 MLB amateur draft, Scioscia's 22-year-old son, Matthew, was drafted by the Angels. Matthew had been selected by the Angels in 2007 but chose to attend Notre Dame on a baseball scholarship, where he played first base and catcher. For the 2011 season, the Angels were 86-76 and second in the division. Their rankings in offensive categories were middle of the pack. On May 8 Scioscia notched his 1,000th victory as a manager.

There was improvement in many areas in 2012, and the Angels were 89-73, third in the division. But in 2013 they again fell below .500, with a 78-84 record. They were third in the division. In a minor-league transaction that made national headlines after the season, the Angels traded Matthew Scioscia to the Chicago Cubs for Trevor Gretzky, son of hockey great Wayne Gretzky. Mike Scioscia claimed that it would be a good opportunity for his son, and brushed off additional questions regarding how the Angels handled communications with him about the trade.[77]

The 2014 season brought marked improvement. The Angels won the division with a record of 98-64, best in the major leagues, and they led the league in runs scored and ranked second in hits. But the ALDS was again their bane; they dropped three straight games to the Kansas City Royals. Scioscia notched managerial career win 1,300 on August 4, becoming the fourth major-league manager to achieve the feat in his first stint at the helm.

In 2015 Scioscia became the longest-tenured manager in the majors, and the Angels' all-time leader in both games managed and wins (1,416 wins, 1,176 losses). But regular-season results on the field held no reward for the Angels. Despite a miraculous ninth-inning rally against the Texas Rangers the afternoon before, the Angels were eliminated from the postseason playoffs on the last day of the season. The team finished third in the division with a record of 85-77, but were last in the division in batting average (.246). Despite an opt-out clause in his contract, Scioscia announced a day after the 2015 season ended that he would return as the Angels' manager in 2016.[78]

But all was not well in Anaheim. The Angels had several incidents in 2015 that tainted the baseball world's perception of the organization and how it was being run.[79] There had been conflicts between Scioscia and general manager Jerry Dipoto—a rift that began when Dipoto fired Scioscia's friend and hitting coach, Mickey Hatcher, in 2012 after 12 seasons. Team owner Arte Moreno refused to choose between the two men, forcing them to patch up their relationship.[80] In late June it was reported that the tension had escalated, extending to the coaches and the players. The latest problem allegedly stemmed from Dipoto's frustration with the coaches' failure to use statistical and scouting information and to convey it to the players. At least one member of the coaching staff and star first baseman Albert Pujols did not react favorably to the general manager's involvement.[81]

Dipoto resigned on July 1, and Scioscia was perceived as the undisputed ruler of the club.[82]

NOTES

1. m.angels.mlb.com/roster/coach/121919/mike-scioscia.
2. SABR's Scouts Committee credits John O'Neil with Scioscia's signing.
3. Colin Gunderson, *Tommy Lasorda: My Way* (Chicago: Triumph Books, 2015), 6-7.
4. Ibid, 8-9.
5. Mark Saxon, "Early Lessons Helped Scioscia Succeed," March 28, 2010, sports.espn.go.com/losangeles/mlb/news/story?id=4962386.
6. "Mike Scioscia," Baseball Player Profiles, baseball.playerprofiles.com/sampleplayerprofile.asp?playerID=685.

7 *The Sporting News*, November 19, 1977: 63.

8 *The Sporting News*, November 18, 1978: 40.

9 "Coast Toasts All-Stars," *The Sporting News*, October 6, 1979: 34.

10 Gordon Verrell, "Dodgers Find Law in Outfield," *The Sporting News*, May 10, 1980: 33.

11 Stan Isle, "Coleman Grieves Over Lack of 'Stengelese,'" *The Sporting News*, May 17, 1980: 17.

12 Gordon Verrell, "Dodgers Finding Their Road Full of Potholes and Hazards," *The Sporting News*, August 9, 1980: 22.

13 Gordon Verrell, "Russell Out—Thomas Vital to Dodgers Bid," *The Sporting News*, September 27, 1980: 8.

14 Gordon Verrell, "Dodgers Roll With Quiet Bats," *The Sporting News*, May 16, 1981: 37.

15 Ian MacDonald, "His Speed Kills," *The Sporting News*, May 23, 1981: 3.

16 Gordon Verrell, "Blocking Plate a Scioscia Specialty," *The Sporting News*, May 23, 1981: 29.

17 Ibid.

18 Gordon Verrell, "Dodgers Will Survive Despite Huge Losses," *The Sporting News*, July 4, 1981: 35.

19 Gordon Verrell, "Dodger Wounds Heal," *The Sporting News*, July 11, 1981: 39.

20 Gordon Verrell, "Dodgers Happy to Have Yeager," *The Sporting News*, November 14, 1981: 52.

21 Gordon Verrell, "Astros Buried in L.A. Graveyard," *The Sporting News*, October 24, 1981: 15.

22 "L.A.'s Only Worry Is Fifth Starter," *The Sporting News*, April 10, 1982: 30.

23 "Six-Game Plunge Shakes Dodgers," *The Sporting News*, May 3, 1982: 21.

24 Bill Conlin, "Haak's Radical View Far Off Mark," *The Sporting News*, May 31, 1982: 19.

25 Ibid.

26 Gordon Verrell, "Scioscia Sent Back to Basic Training," *The Sporting News*, March 7, 1983: 30.

27 Ibid.

28 Gordon Verrell, "Yeager Carries On, Aches and All," *The Sporting News*, June 20, 1983; 28; Stan Isle, "Caught on the Fly," *The Sporting News*, July 4, 1983: 14; Gordon Verrell, "Dodgers Will Seek Bench Strength," *The Sporting News*, December 5, 1983: 48.

29 Gordon Verrell, "Yeager, Scioscia Have Inside Lanes," *The Sporting News*, February 13, 1984: 44.

30 Gordon Verrell, "Guerrero Confident In Wake Of Slump," *The Sporting News*, May 21, 1984: 17; Gordon Verrell "Stubbs Could Be The Next Al Oliver," *The Sporting News*, June 4, 1984: 17.

31 Gordon Verrell, "Fernando May Have Been L.A. MVP," *The Sporting News*, January 7, 1985: 36.

32 Gordon Verrell, "Scioscia Fulfilling Campanis' Prophecy," *The Sporting News*, May 20, 1985: 21.

33 Ibid.

34 Gordon Verrell, "Honeycutt Admits 'Hurting In Head,'" *The Sporting News*, August 5, 1985: 16. He had a number of rough-and-tumble plays. On August 23 in Montreal, Joe Hesketh retired the first six Dodgers he faced, three on strikeouts. In the bottom of the third, U.L Washington beat out a drag bunt and Hesketh walked. Tim Raines hit a sinking liner to center, and the ball skipped out of Candy Maldonado's glove. Right fielder Mike Marshall retrieved the ball, and Washington scored easily. Hesketh headed for home, but Scioscia extended his left leg to cover the plate. Hesketh didn't try to slide and stumbled over Scioscia's leg. Hesketh was out—and out for the season with a broken leg. "I caught the ball and felt him hit me," Scioscia said. "When I reached over to tag him, he kind of flipped over. I didn't really hit him. If he'd slid, I'm sure he would have been safe." Expos manager Buck Rodgers, for eight years a catcher with the Angels, said: "Scioscia did exactly what he had to do. Vance Law (on deck) was signaling for Hesketh to slide. I presume Joe didn't see him." Hesketh didn't blame Scioscia, either. "He was doing his job. I'm not a good baserunner, and I might work on my sliding next spring." See Ian MacDonald, "Expos' Home Stand Marked by Disaster," *The Sporting News*, September 9, 1985: 14.

35 Stan Isle, "The Durable Dodger: Lasorda on Catching Scioscia: 'Ever See an Italian Who Needed a Rest?'," *The Sporting News*, September 30, 1985: 11.

36 Dave Nightingale, "Dodgers and Cards Take Turns Playing Giveaway," *The Sporting News*, October 21, 1985: 22.

37 Bill Conlin, "Trade Winds May Be Brisk," *The Sporting News*, January 6, 1986: 47.

38 "NL West: Dodgers," *The Sporting News*, March 3, 1986: 36.

39 Gordon Verrell, "Scioscia Cracks 'Em Up," *The Sporting News*, April 28, 1986: 17.

40 Ibid.

41 "NL West: Dodgers," *The Sporting News*, April 1, 1987: 31-32.

42 Gordon Verrell, "Healthy Scioscia Carries Quick Bat," *The Sporting News*, May 11, 1987: 24.

43 "N.L. West: Dodgers," *The Sporting News*, June 15, 1987: 21.

44 "Managers Name the All-Stars," *The Sporting News*, July 13, 1987: 14.

45 Gordon Verrell, "Fernando Finds a Flaw," *The Sporting News*, July 13, 1987: 23.

46 Ibid.; "N.L. West: Dodgers," *The Sporting News*, October 19, 1987: 75.

47 "N.L. West: Dodgers," *The Sporting News*, August 29, 1988: 21.

48 Ibid.

49 "Notebook N.L. West: Dodgers," *The Sporting News*, September 19, 1988: 17.

50 "N.L. West: Dodgers," *The Sporting News*, October 10, 1988: 26; "N.L. West: Padres," *The Sporting News*, October 10, 1988: 26.

51 Paul Attner, "N.L. Playoffs: Wild, Wacky War: Craziness and Controversy Mark Showdown Between Dodgers and Mets," *The Sporting News*, October 17, 1988: 16.

52 "Notebook N.L. West: Dodgers," *The Sporting News*, November 7, 1988: 49.

53 "World Series Play-By-Play," *The Sporting News*, October 24, 1988: 43; "World Series Play-By-Play," *The Sporting News*, October 31, 1988: 14.

54 Gordon Verrell, "N.L. West: Dodgers," *The Sporting News*, April 1, 1989: 36.

55 "N.L. West: Dodgers," *The Sporting News*, September 4, 1989: 23.

56 Murray Chass, "Premium Ranking for Clark," *The Sporting News*, November 6, 1989: 42.

57 Ben Henkey, "Davis Turns Fielding Excellence Into Gold," *The Sporting News*, December 11, 1989: 49.

58 "N.L. West: Dodgers," *The Sporting News*, January 8, 1990: 40.

59 Bob Nightingale, "Santiago to Giants: 'I'll Never Forget': Baseball: His season disrupted by a broken arm suffered when he was hit by a pitch, the All-Star catcher says somebody will pay," *Los Angeles Times*, June 24, 1990, articles.latimes.com/1990-06-24/sports/sp-690_1_broken-arm; ———, "Canseco Is Vote Leader As All-Stars Are Listed," *New York Times*, July 5, 1990, nytimes.com/1990/07/05/sports/canseco-is-vote-leader-as-all-stars-are-listed.html.

60 Gordon Verrell, "N.L. West: Dodgers," *The Sporting News*, April 27, 1992: 22.

61 Dave Nightingale, "Managers: The Next Generation," *The Sporting News*, June 29, 1992: 10.

62 Gordon Verrell, "N.L. West: Los Angeles Dodgers," *The Sporting News*, November 2, 1992: 22.

63 Gordon Verrell, "N.L. West: Los Angeles Dodgers," *The Sporting News*, November 21, 1992: 30; Gordon Verrell, "N.L. West: Los Angeles Dodgers," *The Sporting News*, December 21, 1992: 230

64 Chris De Luca, "N.L. West: San Diego Padres," *The Sporting News*, February 22, 1993: 19.

65 Chris De Luca, "N.L. West: San Diego Padres," *The Sporting News*, November 1, 1993: 24.

66 T.R. Sullivan, "A.L.: Texas Rangers," *The Sporting News*, December 27, 1993: 29.

67 Gordon Verrell, "N.L.: Los Angeles Dodgers," *The Sporting News*, October 17, 1994: 47.

68 Scott Gregor, "A.L.: Chicago White Sox," *The Sporting News*, October 13, 1997: 37.

69 Mark Saxon, "Early Lessons Helped Scioscia Succeed," March 28, 2010, sports.espn.go.com/losangeles/mlb/news/story?id=4962386.

70 Mike DiGiovanna, "American League Baseball: Anaheim," *The Sporting News*, January 17, 2000: 64; ——— "American League Baseball: Anaheim," *The Sporting News*, January 31, 2000: 59.

71 Mike DiGiovanna, "American League Baseball: Anaheim," *The Sporting News*, January 29, 2001: 58.

72 Mike DiGiovanna, "American League Baseball: Anaheim," *The Sporting News*, June 25, 2001: 32.

73 Joe Haakenson, "A.L.: Anaheim Angels," *The Sporting News*, February 18, 2002: 51.

74 Joe Haakenson, "American League Baseball: Anaheim Angels," *The Sporting News*, May 6, 2002: 20.

75 Joe Haakenson, "American League Baseball: Anaheim Angels," *The Sporting News*, June 3, 2002: 36.

76 Joe Haakenson, "American League Baseball: Anaheim Angels," *The Sporting News*, September 16, 2002: 65.

77 Ted Berg, "Angels trade manager Mike Scioscia's son for Wayne Gretzky's son," *USA Today*, March 20, 2014, usatoday.com/2014/03/angels-trade-manager-mike-scioscias-son-for-wayne-gretzkys-son; Bill Shaikin, "Angels trade big-name minor leaguers: Matt Scioscia for Trevor Gretzky," *Los Angeles Times*, March 20, 2014, articles.latimes.com/2014/mar/20/sports/la-sp-0321-angels-notes-20140321.

78 D.J. Short, "Mike Scioscia Will Return as Angels Manager in 2016," NBC Sports, October 5, 2015, mlb.nbcsports.com/2015/10/05/mike-scioscia-will-return-as-angels-manager-in-2016/.

79 Ben Perez, "Los Angeles Angels: organization's professionalism questionable," iSports, June 30, 2015, isportsweb.com/2015/06/30/los-angeles-angels-organizations-professionalism-questionable/.

80 Ken Rosenthal, "Tensions return between Angels' front office, manager Scioscia," FoxSports, June 29, 2015, foxsports.com/mlb/story/los-angeles-angels-mike-scioscia-front-office-tensions-jerry-dipoto-ken-rosenthal-062915.

81 Aaron Gleeman. "Angels manager Mike Scioscia and GM Jerry Dipoto are feuding again and it sounds really bad," NBCsports, June 30, 2015, mlb.nbcsports.com/2015/06/30/angels-manager-mike-scioscia-and-gm-jerry-dipoto-are-feuding-again-and-it-sounds-really-bad/; Bob Nightingale. "Mike Scioscia won the battle in Anaheim, but tumult not over for Angels," *USA Today*, July 1, 2015, usatoday.com/story/sports/mlb/2015/07/01/angels-jerry-dipoto-quits-mike-scioscia-power-new-general-manager/29594431/.

82 Jeff Passan, "GM Jerry Dipoto's departure reveals Mike Scioscia to be unquestioned ruler of Angels," Yahoo Sports, July 1, 2015, sports.yahoo.com/news/gm-jerry-dipoto-s-departure-reveals-mike-scioscia-to-be-unquestioned-ruler-of-angels-215115777.html.

OZZIE SMITH

By Charles F. Faber

He was called the Wizard of Oz for his phenomenal fielding feats. A 15-time All-Star, Ozzie Smith won 13 consecutive Gold Gloves and is usually regarded as the greatest defensive shortstop in the history of baseball. Yet he said that his tumble into the Springfield Mystery Spot on *The Simpsons* TV show was one of the highlights of his career.[1]

Osborne Earl Smith was born on December 26, 1954, in Mobile, Alabama, the second of the six children of Marvella and Clovi Smith. When Ozzie was 6 years old, the family moved to the Watts section of Los Angeles. His father drove a delivery truck for Safeway stores, and his mother worked as an aide at a nursing home. During the Watts riots of 1964, the family slept on the floor to avoid stray bullets that might enter their home.[2]

As a child, Ozzie developed quick reflexes by activities such as bouncing a rubber ball off concrete steps and seeing how quickly he could catch it. The lad practiced backflips in sawdust piles at a nearby lumber yard.[3] Smith's first ball glove was reportedly fashioned by wrapping a brown paper bag over his left hand.[4] He played basketball and baseball at Locke High School, but did not excel to the point where he would attract the attention of college recruiters. In 1974 he entered California Polytechnic State University at San Luis Obispo on a partial academic scholarship. He made the baseball team as a walk-on. Cal Poly coach Berdy Harr taught him how to switch-hit. When the college's regular shortstop broke his leg, Smith took over the position and unexpectedly became a star. During June 1976 he was playing semipro ball in Clarinda, Iowa, when he was selected by the Detroit Tigers in the seventh round of the amateur draft. He did not sign with the Tigers, but returned to Cal Poly for his senior year. Upon graduation from college, he was selected by the San Diego Padres in the fourth round of the 1977 draft. He was signed by Bob Fontaine Jr. Jim Weigel was Padres scouting director at the time. The Padres assigned Smith to Walla Walla, Washington, in the Class-A Northwest League, where he hit .303 in 68 games.

In 1978 Smith attended the Padres' spring-training camp at Yuma, Arizona, as a nonroster invitee. His play earned him a roster spot and the 5-foot-11, 150-pound, 23-year-old shortstop made his major-league debut on April 7, 1978, batting eighth in the starting lineup for Opening Day at San Francisco's Candlestick Park. In his first big-league at-bat, facing San Francisco's John Montefusco, he grounded into a force play to end the second inning. The next day he singled off Jim Barr for his first major-league hit. By April 20 he was hitting only .222, but he proved he belonged in the big leagues by making a spectacular fielding play. Jeff Burroughs of the Atlanta Braves was batting. Smith described what happened: "He hit a ball back up the middle that everybody thought was going into center field. I instinctively broke to my left and dove behind second. As I was in the air, the ball took a bad hop and caromed behind me, but I was able to catch it with my bare hand. I hit the ground, bounced up, and threw Burroughs out at first."[5]

In the Padres' last home game of the 1978 season, Smith first performed a backflip for the fans. His backflips, cartwheels, and handsprings later became his trademark. He finished his rookie year batting .258, with an on-base percentage of .311, a slugging average of .312, one home run and 46 RBIs. He was runner-up to Atlanta's Bob Horner in the vote for National League Rookie of the Year, largely because of his superb fielding. Smith was justifiably proud of his fielding prowess: "What I did, I did every day. Anyone can make a great play every now and then on any given day. But what I did, I did every day. … I may not drive in 100 runs each year, but I can prevent 100 runs from scoring against us."[6]

In the 1979 season Smith started out 0-for-32 before going 1-for-4 on April 13 to move his batting average to .029. He did not hit well all season, winding up with a .211 batting average, no home runs, and only 27 RBIs. (Smith did not achieve a .200-level batting mark until August 4. His fielding kept him in the lineup, as he led the league in assists, the first of eight times he led the NL in that category. He also led in putouts twice and in range factor seven times. His 8,375 career assists are the most ever made by any major-league player at any position in the entire history of baseball. Smith won the first of 13 consecutive Gold Gloves in 1980. The next season he was named to the All-Star Game for the first of 15 times.

Smith married Denise Jackson in November 1980. He had met her at the Astrodome in Houston, where she was a part-time usher. The couple had three children: Osborne Earl (called Nikko), Dustin, and Taryn. Nikko, a singer-songwriter, was among the top 10 finalists on *American Idol* in 2005. Ozzie and Denise were divorced in 1996.

On December 10, 1981, Ozzie Smith was part of a six-player swap, with San Diego pitchers Steve Mura and Al Olmsted going to St. Louis for temperamental shortstop Garry Templeton, part-time outfielder Sixto Lezcano, and relief pitcher Luis DeLeon, but the deal was not completed until 62 days had passed. Smith had a no-trade clause in his contract and balked at the trade. "I'm still here in San Diego, and I have no intention of leaving," he said at a press conference on January 26, 1982. "This is my home. I love it here."[7] His wife, Denise, was a producer for a radio talk show in San Diego, which may or may not have had an influence on his reluctance to move to St. Louis. When the shortstop finally agreed to accept the transaction, he credited Cardinals manager Whitey Herzog for his change of heart. "I've always admired Whitey Herzog as a manager," he said. "When he sat down and talked baseball, he was totally different. He was so sincere it was so unreal the way he talked. It took me two weeks to find out that I wanted to play for him. He's a great baseball man."[8]

At the time many observers thought San Diego got the better of the deal. Smith hit .222 the previous season, compared with Templeton's .288. Their lifetime averages to that point were .231 and .305, respectively. What was in Smith's favor, of course, was his fielding. *St. Louis Post-Dispatch* sportswriter Rick Hummel wrote in *The Sporting News* that "the way Smith plays shortstop has been described in ballet-like terms." Smith said that he "tries to play the position a little differently from everybody else. 'I like to add my own little touch. I call it flair. Some people would call it hot-dogging, but I call it flair. It's in a way like an artist.'"[9]

Former New York Mets shortstop Bud Harrelson was quoted as saying, "The thing about Ozzie is, if he misses a ball, you assume it's uncatchable. If any other shortstop misses a ball, your first thought is, 'Would Ozzie have had it?'"[10]

In his first year in St. Louis, Smith helped the Cardinals win the pennant and the World Series. In the NLCS against the Atlanta Braves, he posted some terrific offensive numbers, unusual for him. In 13 plate appearances he drew three walks and collected five hits, for a batting average of .556, a .615 on-base percentage, a .556 slugging average, and an outstanding OPS of 1.171. He batted in three runs and stole one base as St. Louis swept the the best-of-five playoffs in three games. In the World Series victory against the Milwaukee Brewers, Smith came back down to Earth and hit only .208. He followed the same script in 1985, starring in the NLCS and slumping in the World Series. In the best-of-seven playoffs that St. Louis won in six games against the Los Angeles Dodgers Smith went 10-for-23, an average of .435, with an OBP of .500, a .696 slugging average, and an otherworldly 1.196 OPS. He hit a game-winning walk-off solo homer in Game Five, the only postseason home run he ever hit. (The unlikely ninth-inning blast off Tom Niedenfuer was Smith's first-ever round-tripper hit from the left side. Longtime Cardinals radio announcer Jack Buck made an iconic call on the St. Louis airwaves for Cardinal fans to "Go Crazy" while Smith circled the bases. In the World Series the Cardinals lost to the Kansas City Royals, and Smith got only 2 hits in 23 at-bats, for a miserable .087 batting average. During the 1987 postseason he hit .200 as the Cardinals won the NLCS from the San Francisco Giants and .214 as St. Louis lost the World Series to the Minnesota Twins. Smith's final postseason appearances came in 1996. He got one hit against San Diego in the NLDS and was hitless against Atlanta in the NLCS.

The Wizard won 13 consecutive Gold Glove Awards.

In 1992 Smith was involved in an unusual television production.[11] In September 1991 he agreed to be a guest on *The Simpsons* TV show. That is, his voice was to be a guest. Smith himself did not appear in the flesh on the program. Instead, a cartoon figure represented Smith, but Ozzie's actual voice was used. He practiced reading the script ahead of time. "I worked on those lines, even though there wasn't really a whole lot of them," he said. "I just wanted to get the inflections in the right place."[12] His voice was recorded weeks before the program was telecast, as the nine guest ballplayers appearing in the program were never in the same place at the same time. In the show, while standing in line at an Elvis Presley exhibit at Graceland, Smith was recruited to play for the Springfield softball club. However, before the game began he visited the Springfield Mystery Spot and as he stepped inside, he fell to oblivion, never again to be seen.

Early in his career, Smith was the prototypical "no hit, good field" shortstop. It took seven seasons for him to improve on his rookie year batting average of .258. In 1987 Smith finished second to Chicago Cubs slugger Andre Dawson for the NL MVP award when he hit .303, the only time he topped .300 in his long career. But he kept working on his hitting and averaged a respectable .277 over his last 10 years. Many people were surprised to learn that Smith collected 2,460 hits in his career. It took him 19 seasons and a lot of determination, but he did it.

Smith became extremely disenchanted with new manager Tony La Russa's platoon system at shortstop, and announced his retirement on June 19, 1996, effective at the end of the season. On Saturday, September 28, Ozzie Smith Day was celebrated at Busch Stadium II before the game with the Cincinnati Reds. The Cardinals retired Ozzie's number 1, and Smith later singled home a run during a 5-2 victory. He played his final regular-season game on September 29 at the age of 41. He batted leadoff for the Cardinals and went 0-for-2 against Cincinnati's Curt Lyons before being replaced by Royce Clayton in the fourth inning. His career stats were 2,573 games, 1,257 runs scored, 2,460 hits, 28 home runs, 793 RBIs, 580 stolen bases, .262 batting average, .337 OBP, .328 slugging, and .666 OPS. Not the most impressive numbers, but his spectacular fielding was enough to get him elected to the National Baseball Hall of Fame in 2002, his first year of eligibility.

The game of September 29 was not Smith's last major-league game. The Cardinals won the 1996 National League Central and faced the San Diego Padres in the Division Series. Smith started Game Two and collected one hit and two walks, and scored a run. Smith also appeared in Game Three of the NLDS as a pinch-hitter and lined out to left field. He failed to make a hit in nine times at bat in the NLCS versus Atlanta. During his career, Smith appeared in 42 postseason games — two in the NLDS, 19 in the NLCS, and 21 in the World Series.

After retiring as a player, Smith hosted *This Week in Baseball* on national TV in 1997.

From 1997 to 1999 he did color commentary for a St. Louis station, then went to CNN.

In 2012 he rejoined the Cardinals as a special instructor during spring training. He has also been an entrepreneur with several different business interests.

In addition to the National Baseball Hall of Fame, Smith has been inducted into other halls of fame, including the Missouri Sports Hall of Fame, the Alabama Sports Hall of Fame, the St. Louis Walk of Fame, and the St. Louis Cardinals Hall of Fame Museum. He finished third in the voting for shortstops in the Major League Baseball All-Century Team, and appeared on *The Sporting News'* list of the 100 Greatest Ballplayers. A bronze statue of Ozzie Smith stands at the northwest corner of the current Busch Memorial Stadium in St. Louis. The sculpture shows Smith stretched horizontal to the ground while fielding a baseball. At the unveiling of the statue, sculptor Harry Weber told the acrobatic shortstop, "You spent half of your career up in the air. That makes it difficult for a sculptor to do something with it."[13]

SOURCES

In addition to references in the Notes, the author used the following sources:

Spatz, Lyle, ed. *The SABR Baseball List and Record Book* (New York: Scribner, 2007).

baseball-reference.com.

NOTES

1 Erik Malinowski, "The Making of 'Homer at the Bat,' the Episode that Conquered Prime Time 20 Years Ago Tonight," deadspin.com. February 20, 2012.

2 Ozzie Smith and Rob Raines, *Wizard* (Chicago: Contemporary Books, 1998), 4.

3 Smith and Raines, 7.

4 nytimes.com/2002/01/10/sports/on-baseball-wizard-started-with-his-eyes-shut.html

5 Smith and Raines, 21.

6 "Ozzie Smith Biography," IMDb.com, no date.

7 *The Sporting News*, February 13, 1982.

8 *The Sporting News*, March 27, 1982.

9 Ibid.

10 Ron Fimrite, "No. 1 In His Field," *Sports Illustrated*, September 28, 1987.

11 Fox Broadcasting Company, "Homer at the Bat," *The Simpsons*, February 20, 1992.

12 Malinowski.

13 Associated Press, August 11, 2002.

DARRYL STRAWBERRY

By Shawn Morris

For many African American males growing up in poverty-stricken households throughout Los Angeles, sports offered a chance to break away from the cultural and economic restraints imposed on them by their surroundings. This was no different for a young Darryl Eugene Strawberry (born March 12, 1962, in Los Angeles). Darryl was the third boy born to Henry and Ruby Strawberry, and would be followed by two sisters. By 1970 the family was residing in a small house in the Crenshaw neighborhood of South Central Los Angeles. Strawberry recalled his father as being a negative influence early in his life. Henry Strawberry held down a steady job as a postal clerk, but suffered from many of the same vices that would plague Darryl's life. He would often come home in drunken rages and physically assault Ruby, as well as Darryl and his older brother Ronnie. Much of Darryl's younger years were spent in fear of their father until one night when he was about 10 years old. On that night Henry came home intoxicated, and began to verbally and physically assault Ruby. The police showed up and just like that, Henry was gone from his children's lives,[1] only to reappear when it was evident Darryl was a remarkable talent on the baseball field and would be a top pick in the major-league draft.

"It's sad. I never had a real relationship with him. He never sat me down and talked to me kindly, never gave me a word of fatherly advice or counsel, never taught me to tie my shoe or hit a baseball. None of those things a father and son are supposed to do, he either ignored me or beat me, period," Strawberry said in 2009.[2] What Henry did give his youngest son was a love for sports and athletic abilities. Like many of the other children in the Crenshaw neighborhood, Darryl went to the local park to watch his father play on one of the many softball teams in the area. His father could "whip the ball across the plate so fast you wouldn't know where to start your swing. … He'd hit the long ball over and over again, every time he came to bat."[3] After his father disappeared from his life, Darryl felt an absence and turned to sports as a refuge and escape from everything bothering him. "I was very good at every sport I tried," he said. "I'm not bragging. It was just in me. I loved it. It was pure joy for me to play baseball, basketball, and football. While I was playing I could almost forget my anger and my troubles. Almost."[4] Ruby was devoted to her family, held a full-time job at a local telephone company, and supported Darryl playing baseball. She knew how happy it made him, and she was shocked to see that on the field he was not the same, lazy Darryl she knew at home.

After attending numerous junior high schools, Strawberry attended the predominantly African-American Crenshaw High School. Crenshaw was an athletic powerhouse. Scouts came to Crenshaw games; it was Darryl's chance to get noticed, to gain the fame and notoriety so many young athletes from similar circumstances were searching for. Basketball was his first love and his gangly frame gave him an advantage on the court, but baseball came the most natural to him. "Right from the start I could pitch, I could hit home runs, I could steal bases, I could field. I didn't think much about it, I didn't study the game, I just went out there and did it."[5] By the time he reached Crenshaw, Strawberry had earned a reputation throughout the Los Angeles Little League, but none of that mattered to Crenshaw baseball coach Brooks Hurst.

When Darryl entered Crenshaw High for the 10th grade, he was already 6-feet-3. He was long and lean and covered with sinewy muscle, not the type created by hours in a weight room or supplements, but the real thing. "He had the body of a basketball forward and the natural baseball swing, a powerful, looping uppercut, of a historic homerun hitter," a writer said of him.[6] To Brooks Hurst, Darryl was just like many of the young black men he had coached, full of talent and lacking discipline. At Crenshaw, Hurst did his best to instill the qualities his players were lacking to help them succeed on and off the field. Any backtalk or mouthing off to him and he would make them run till they dropped from exhaustion.[7]

For many of his players, Hurst was the only stable male figure in their lives. He was familiar with Darryl and his situation; both older brothers had played for him at Crenshaw. Hurst did his best to watch over Darryl and guide him to make the right choices during his three years at Crenshaw. Strawberry struggled his first year in high school; although there was no denying his talent, he was given no special treatment under Hurst. He tried to drill into Darryl to "beat the ball to the spot" when playing the outfield and to run hard for balls that fell in for base hits, not just glide to them and let singles turn into extra bases. Coach Hurst often found himself annoyed with Darryl and his approach of only giving a half-effort. "I had to sit him down and talk to him a lot. I had him run laps. I would tell him: The scouts come in here with assumptions about inner-city ballplayers. You have to counteract that. Don't give them the ammunition. But finally, I just ran out of patience."[8] Finally, Darryl's first high-school season ended early when he was kicked off the team. "I just said to him, 'This isn't working out. I hope you want to come back next year,'" Hurst recalled. "Darryl took it pretty well. He still came to games. He helped lug the equipment."[9]

Despite his talent, when Strawberry came back for the 1979 season there were some who thought he was not the best talent on the team. He also had to contend with Corrie Dillard and another player who would go on to the major leagues, Chris Brown. Besides those three, the rest of the Crenshaw team was also talented, so much so that many of the second-stringers would end up with professional contracts. On the playing field the 1979 Crenshaw team was in the midst of a spectacular season. Strawberry was having an outstanding year at the plate, in the outfield, and when he took the mound. The team easily defeated many of its inner-city opponents. Early in the season, the *Los Angeles Times* reported, "(A)fter a 15-5 mugging of Hamilton, Crenshaw has now scored 31 runs in its last two games."[10] Many of Darryl's relatives who had been largely absent from his life began to appear at his games as well, including his father. Coach Hurst did his best to shield his players from the circus enveloping them, and keeping their focus on the game itself. Throughout the season the team kept playing at a high level and by the time the regular season was drawing to a close Crenshaw had lost only a handful of games—and in each of those cases Hurst had benched one of his star players for disciplinary reasons.

Strawberry was the first overall draft pick in 1980.

When the regular season finished, the Crenshaw High Cougars entered the Los Angeles Unified School District baseball playoffs. Anchored by senior Chris Brown and junior Darryl Strawberry, it was the first inner-city school in many years that had the talent to compete against those in the San Fernando Valley that benefited from manicured fields, booster clubs, and year-round instruction.[11] Playing the way they had many times during the regular season, the Cougars cruised their way through the first two rounds of the playoffs by a combined score of 23-4. Nothing, it seemed could keep Crenshaw from hitting. In the semifinal round they powered their way over Monroe High by a score of 10-7.[12] In the three playoff games Strawberry hit three triples in addition to a home run, and was the winning pitcher in two of the contests.[13] Next stop for Crenshaw was the championship game at Dodger Stadium.

On June 6, 1979, the Cougars boarded the bus for the short trip to Dodger Stadium. Their opponent was Granada Hills, a team that played with few mistakes and relied on the "small ball" approach, lots of bunting, and good defense. Their third baseman was a high-school football standout, Stanford-bound John Elway. The Crenshaw players had their work cut out for them, and when Granada Hills jumped out to an early 2-0 lead; their task became much more difficult. A strong third inning put Crenshaw back on top by a run and the Granada Hills coach pulled Elway from third base and put him in as pitcher. After his eight warmup pitches, Elway struck out the next batter to end the inning. On the mound Strawberry began to crumble. Unnerved by the Little League tactics of fake bunts, he began to become erratic and after walking several batters he was pulled and sent to the outfield. By the end of the fifth inning, Granada had scored another six runs on three hits because of Crenshaw's bad pitching and sloppy fielding, and the Crenshaw hopes were in rapid decline.[14] Elway shut the Cougars down. "The team that scout George Genovese considered from top to bottom, the most talented assemblage of high-school talent ever, could not win the LA city championship."[15]

When Strawberry returned to Crenshaw for his senior year all of the attention was lavished upon him. Without Brown to share the spotlight, it became the season of Strawberry. Coach Hurst was continuously chasing agents off the baseball field and out of the Crenshaw hallways. Strawberry often found himself surrounded by an entourage and those looking for any piece of stardom that association with him brought. As his ego grew, his attitude only seemed to worsen, according to some teammates. George Cook recalled, "Darryl Strawberry didn't listen to [Coach Hurst]."[16] The press buildup surrounding Strawberry and the coming baseball draft overshadowed anything else he accomplished his senior year. *Sports Illustrated* published a feature on Strawberry late in his senior season, with a picture caption that said, "Darryl, 18, is likened to Ted Williams."[17] "He's got a Williams-type physical makeup — tall, rangy, good leverage," scout Phil Pote told *Sports Illustrated*. "He's got bat quickness, he can drive the ball. The ball just jumps off his bat."[18]

Strawberry had dreamed about being the first overall pick in the draft, and in June of 1980, the New York Mets made that happen. The Mets were hoping he would help turn the franchise around. Not only did he have the potential to help on the field, he could provide them with much-needed box-office revenue as well. The team provided him with a $200,000 signing bonus to forgo college and flew him to New York to show him off to the press. But before Strawberry was able to play in Shea Stadium he had to first prove himself in the minor leagues.

A few days later, Strawberry found himself in a landscape vastly different than that of Manhattan or Los Angeles. Kingsport, Tennessee, was home to the Mets' team in the rookie-level Appalachian League and Strawberry's first step in the Mets farm system. During that 1980 season, in 180 plate appearances he batted .268 with five home runs. His work ethic was still sloppy, according to some and he was often late arriving to the stadium, onetime even missing a game.[19] A player not of Strawberry's status would have had harsh repercussions for missing a game, but not Strawberry; his absence was largely ignored by those in the organization.

The following season Strawberry was assigned to the High-A Lynchburg Mets. He continued to struggle and failed to live up to all the hype that was heaped upon him before the draft. Off the field, the 19-year-old Strawberry was homesick and called his mother every day. On the field he was struggling against many of the pitchers he faced. They easily fooled him with hard fastballs inside and breaking balls. Strawberry possessed the power to put the ball into play, but he struggled to make the contact that had made him a legend at Crenshaw. In 123 games with Lynchburg in 1981, Strawberry managed to hit 13 home runs and bat .255 for the season.

The next spring Strawberry continued to climb the farm-system ladder, and started the season with the Double-A Jackson Mets. It was in Jackson, Mississippi, where he became locked-in at the plate and began to flash the talent the Mets saw in him when they drafted him. He began to see the ball better and figure out opposing pitchers. Although he struck out 145 times, by the end of the season he had driven in 97 runs and hit 34 home runs. Rather than take the winter off, the Mets had Strawberry extend his year by playing winter ball for a team in Caracas, Venezuela. He credited the experience with speeding up his development and better preparing him for the coming season. Strawberry remarked, "I felt confident after my season in South America because I'd been able to hit some of their best pitchers."[20]

To start the 1983 season, the Mets sent Strawberry to their top affiliate, the Triple-A Tidewater Tides. The organization wanted to keep him in the minors for one more season before bringing him up to New York, but many believed he would see the Big Apple before the year was over. Under manager Davey Johnson, Strawberry got off to a great start at Triple A. "My first ten or so games at Tidewater were spectacular. Whether I had improved to the point where I could hit anything any Triple-A pitcher could throw, or whether Triple-A pitching wasn't as good as it was supposed to be, I don't know," he said.[21] At the same time, the Mets were off to a dreadful start and the New York newspaper headlines began to call for Strawberry. In early May Darryl was summoned from Tidewater. Mets general manager Frank Cashen regretted having to call him up ahead of schedule, but Strawberry had the potential to help fill the empty seats and on May 6, 1983, he made his major-league debut.[22]

Strawberry stood an imposing 6-feet-6 with a playing weight of 190 pounds; he batted and threw left, and was a right fielder for most of his career. His debut, against the Cincinnati Reds was less than spectacular, with three strikeouts and a foul popup during six plate appearances in an extra-inning win by the Mets. Strawberry also worked a couple of walks and stole a base late in the game. The Mets' manager, George Bamberger, encouraged the rookie to go out onto the field and have fun. However, Bamberger resigned on June 2 and was replaced by Frank Howard, one of his coaches. Howard began to demand more out of Strawberry and assigned hitting coach Jim Frey to help. Under Frey's tutelage, Strawberry began to blossom and adjust to major-league pitching. His struggles at the plate began to disappear and in September Strawberry found his groove. It was also at this time that Strawberry began to succumb to the New York lifestyle and started experimenting with cocaine. His immaturity and desire to be liked left him vulnerable to negative influences. "Darryl was someone who always wanted to be liked," said his mother, Ruby.[23] During his rookie campaign Strawberry was introduced to cocaine by two Mets veterans who told him, "It was the thing to do in the big leagues."[24] Despite his off-field habits, Strawberry continued to produce quality numbers. His 108 hits, 26 home runs, 74 RBIs, and 19 stolen bases were enough for him to be voted the National League Rookie of the Year. After the season Howard was replaced as manager by Davey Johnson. Under Johnson, Strawberry and the Mets became a powerhouse franchise for the rest of the decade.

Once Johnson was at the helm, the Mets began to turn things around on the field and produce wins with regularity. The attendance at Shea Stadium began to increase, and it was becoming clear throughout the city that the Yankees were not the only show in town anymore. Rookie Dwight Gooden was a stud on the mound, and Strawberry was continuing to rise to stardom in the outfield, being named to the All-Star team in July. He also began to use amphetamines with regularity during the 1984 season.[25] Most members of the hard-partying Mets team already were, as amphetamines allowed the players to go drink and abuse drugs all night, and play the next day with no hangover or ill feelings. By the end of the season, Johnson had guided the Mets from a team that came in last place the previous year to a second-place finish in the NL East.

The 1985 season again saw an increase in the number of Mets victories; the team that won only 68 games in 1983 rang up 98 victories in 1995. Strawberry continued to produce at the plate and help put fans in the seats. Attendance at Shea Stadium was now more than double that of his rookie year: 2.7 million vs. 1.1 million. Strawberry was also married that year to Lisa Andrews, a tumultuous relationship that resulted in court appearances and ultimately divorce. Although he appeared in 37 fewer games than he did in 1984 due to minor health issues and slight injuries, Strawberry still scored 79 runs and hit 29 home runs, both more than his previous year's total. While it was enough to earn Strawberry a trip to his consecutive All-Star Game, his performance was not enough to help power the Mets into the postseason. But that would change the next season.

"We had a sense of destiny in 1986, a belief that it would all come together for us in a great, historic display of baseball power," said Strawberry.[26] The expectations were high for the Mets as early as spring training; they had won 98 games the season before and were in almost every aspect more skilled, more intense, and more arrogant than the Cardinals, Cubs, and the rest of the NL East.[27] After an indifferent start to the season, things began to turn around for the Mets. They went on one of the greatest runs in franchise history, reeling off 11 wins in a row before

Straw's best years were with the New York Mets, for whom he hit 252 home runs.

losing a game, then winning another seven in a row. The Mets were on fire through May. Although he was having a great year on the field, off it Strawberry continued to alienate himself from teammates as his ego grew. His head was as large as the Goodyear Blimp, and with each new magazine cover story and autograph request it only got bigger. His teammates felt he was vicious and selfish, taking a great deal of pride in making others feel inferior.[28] By now Strawberry was routinely abusing drugs and drinking heavily in the clubhouse. Under the MLB drug policy in place in the 1980s, no team could compel a player to take a drug test, and with the Mets winning in amazing fashion on a regular basis, no one was willing to rein in Strawberry and get him under control.

For most of the 1986 season the Mets were the first-place team and the others in the division futilely chased them. The 108-win Mets were heavy favorites to capture the World Series. The National League Championship Series, went six games and included two thrilling extra-inning contests before the Mets emerged victorious over Houston. Strawberry hit a crucial home run in Game Three to help propel the Mets to victory, and finished the NLCS with two home runs and five RBIs. The 1986 World Series, pitting the Mets against the Boston Red Sox, opened at Shea Stadium on October 18. After six games the teams were tied with three victories apiece, and Strawberry was a nonfactor at the plate. But in Game Seven, when it came time to deliver, Strawberry stepped up. Boston had mounted a mini-rally in the top of the eighth inning to pull within one run of the Mets, but when Strawberry led off the bottom of the inning with a solo home run, there was no doubt it was New York's night. The miracle season of 1986, highlighted by so many late-game heroics and the team's never-say-die attitude concluded with the Mets as the world champions.

The Mets' descent from the World Series heights started before the 1987 campaign when ace pitcher Dwight Gooden was admitted into a drug-treatment center a week before the start of the season. Strawberry was able to hide his demons throughout the season and produced at the plate. He had career highs with 108 runs scored, 104 RBIs, 36 stolen bases, and 39 home runs. Despite his increased offensive output, the Mets finished second in the division and missed the playoffs. In 1988 Strawberry again reached the century mark in runs scored and RBIs, smashed a league-leading 39 home runs, and led the National League in slugging and OPS. He was named to his fifth straight All-Star Game and was runner-up to Kirk Gibson for the MVP. The Mets finished in first place in the NL East, winning 100 games. However, they failed to recapture the magic of 1986 and fell to the Los Angeles Dodgers in seven games in the NLCS. In 1989 Strawberry was unable to repeat the success of the two previous seasons. Across the board his numbers fell off dramatically and the turmoil in the Mets clubhouse spilled out in front of the media when Strawberry and teammate Keith Hernandez got into a scuffle during team picture day with the cameras rolling.[29] As Strawberry suffered through his worst year with the Mets statistically (.225 batting average), the team began to falter and failed to make the postseason.

When Davey Johnson was fired early in the 1990 season, Strawberry declared he would leave the Mets at the end of the season as a free agent. He performed well and earned a seventh consecutive All-Star appearance. His last season as a Met concluded with 37 home runs and a career-best 108 runs batted in. That offseason Strawberry was true to his word and left the Mets to return home to Los Angeles, signing a five-year contract for $20.25 million with the Dodgers.

Strawberry's first year in LA, 1991, was his best in Dodger blue, but even though he was named to his eighth All-Star contest in July, he batted just .265 and his other numbers were down. In 1992 Strawberry played in only 43 games before injuring his back. He had back surgery in September. He tried to return far too soon and was off and on the disabled list of much of 1993, getting just 100 at-bats as his batting average tumbled to a disappointing .140.[30] As he fell apart on the baseball field, his personal life was no better. He was going through a messy and public divorce from Lisa, and the ever-present drug- and alcohol-abuse rumors swirled around him despite his claims of sobriety. Eventually Strawberry came clean to the Dodgers about his addiction and they placed him on the disabled list, and sent him off to the Betty Ford Clinic. When he was finally released from treatment, the Dodgers cut ties with the once-hailed hometown hero.

After being away from the game for a little over a year, Strawberry found a team willing to take another chance on him and signed with the San Francisco Giants on June 19, 1994. Strawberry was now 32 and promised the team he was ready to live a drug-free lifestyle. The Giants felt his guarantee of sobriety was genuine and took a chance on the slugger. With Strawberry in the lineup, the Giants flourished and won nine straight to come within 4½ games of the division-leading Dodgers. Despite his less than overwhelming numbers — 4 home runs, 17 RBIs, and a .239 average in 92 at-bats — the Giants were impressed. The players' strike of 1994 interrupted the team's plans to capture the division from the Dodgers, but the Giants were left with a positive impression of Strawberry and his recovery.[31] He had a job waiting for him in 1995 in San Francisco.

But Strawberry would not get the chance to go back to the Bay Area. Troubles with the IRS arose over unreported income from card-show appearances, and, facing the prospect of jail time, Strawberry relapsed into using hard drugs and began to fail drug tests and display erratic behavior. While he was prepared to go to jail for the income-tax charges, Strawberry was let off with probation, community service, and a hefty bill for back taxes. But once again he would get another chance to turn his baseball career around, this time with the New York Yankees.

Yankees owner George Steinbrenner believed he could rehabilitate Strawberry and that the 296-foot porch in right field was no match for his uppercut swing. From 1995 through the 1999 season Strawberry was a member of the Yankees, but the dreams of Strawberry home runs landing in Yankee Stadium's right-field porch with consistent regularity were never realized. He was never able to recapture the glory he had experienced across town at Shea Stadium.

The 1995 season was full of setbacks for Strawberry. His legal troubles resulted in court-ordered restrictions that dictated where he could reside and the hours he was able to be away from his residence. Steinbrenner's determination to help Darryl turn his life around resulted in the Yankees appointing a full-time "guardian" to shadow Strawberry at all times, as well as regular drug testing to ensure that he would not slip up again. After rehabbing at the Yankees' facilities in Tampa, Strawberry was ready to hit the field. In 1995 he played in 31 minor-league games for the Tampa Yankees, Gulf Coast League Yankees, and the Columbus Clippers before rejoining the big-league club for 32 games toward the end of the season.

Strawberry spent 63 games in 1996 with the big-league club and hit 11 home runs. He helped the Yankees defeat the Orioles in the ALCS, hitting three home runs and collecting five RBIs, then went on to win another World Series, over the Atlanta Braves, alongside former Mets teammates David Cone and Dwight Gooden. In 1997 injuries derailed Strawberry and he played in only 16 minor-league games and 11 for the Yankees. For the first time in his career he failed to hit a home run that season. Then 1998 was a bounce-back season for Darryl at the plate, as he played in over 100 games for the first time since the 1991 season. In a part-time role he belted 24 home runs and had 57 RBIs to go along with a .247 average. For the third time in his career he became a World Series winner, but that accomplishment was overshadowed by a diagnosis of colon cancer that kept him from playing in the World Series.

In 1999 after cancer treatments after a 140-day MLB-mandated suspension for possessing cocaine and soliciting an undercover police officer for sex, the 37-year-old Strawberry returned to the Yankees. In limited playing time he managed only three home runs. However he was able to recapture postseason glory once again when he hit a decisive three-run home run that played a critical role in helping the Yankees sweep the Texas Rangers in the Division Series, then hit another homer as then the Yankees knocked off Boston in the ALCS before moving on to another World Series championship, over Atlanta. When the season concluded Strawberry retired from baseball as an eight-time All Star with four World Series rings—not a bad accomplishment for an inner-city kid from an impoverished neighborhood.

After baseball Strawberry continued to struggle with addiction and run-ins with the law. In 2000 his cancer returned and he started chemotherapy. However, this setback was not enough to quench his desire for drugs and he spent much of the next three years in and out of treatment centers and prison on drug-related charges. As of 2015, Strawberry was married to his wife, Tracy, and was an ordained minister. He devoted a great deal of his time to his family, church, and his charity work for those affected by autism. He said he remained remorseful for his past actions and was fully aware of the impact they had on his career. With his natural talent Strawberry could have been one of baseball's greatest hitters if it were not for his naïve nature, immaturity, and ultimately his substance abuse. In a book published in 2009 he admitted, "I made some good choices, and I made some really bad ones."[32]

NOTES

1. Darryl Strawberry with Arthur Rust Jr., *Darryl* (New York: Bantam Books, 1992), 82-88.
2. Darryl Strawberry, *Straw: Finding My Way* (New York: Ecco, 2009), 9.
3. Strawberry, *Darryl*, 76-77.
4. Strawberry, *Straw*, 21.
5. Strawberry, *Straw*, 21-22.
6. Michael Sokolove, *The Ticket Out: Darryl Strawberry & the Boys of Crenshaw* (New York: Simon & Schuster Paperbacks, 2004), 51.
7. Sokolove, 35.
8. Ibid.
9. Sokolove, 54.
10. Sokolove, 75.
11. Sokolove, 80.
12. Sokolove, 82-84.
13. Sokolove, 87.
14. Sokolove, 87-89.
15. Sokolove, 90.
16. Sokolove, 59.
17. Sokolove, 96.
18. Cited in Sokolove, 96.
19. Sokolove, 100.
20. Strawberry, *Darryl*, 128-129.
21. Ibid.
22. Sokolove, 101.
23. Bob Klapisch, *High and Tight: The Rise and Fall of Dwight Gooden and Darryl Strawberry*. (New York: Villard Books, 1996), 26.
24. Ibid.
25. Klapisch, 23-26.
26. Strawberry, *Darryl*, 188.
27. Jeff Pearlman, *The Bad Guys Won* (New York: Harper Collins, 2004), 43.
28. Pearlman, 137-138.
29. Klapisch, 71.
30. Klapisch, 77.
31. Klapisch, 135-138.
32. Strawberry, *Straw: Finding My Way*, 199.

CAP ANSON

By David Fleitz

Cap Anson, baseball's first superstar, was the dominant on-field figure of nineteenth-century baseball. He was a small-town boy from Iowa who earned his fame as the playing manager of the fabled Chicago White Stockings, the National League team now known as the Cubs. A larger-than-life figure of great talents and great faults, Anson managed the White Stockings to five pennants and set all the batting records that men such as Ty Cobb and Babe Ruth later broke. Anson was the second manager (after Harry Wright) to win 1,000 games and the first player to stroke 3,000 hits (though his exact total varies from one source to another). Although he retired from active play in 1897, he is still the all-time leader in hits, runs scored, doubles, and runs batted in for the Chicago franchise.

Adrian Constantine Anson, named after two towns in southern Michigan that his father admired, was born in a log cabin in Marshall (later Marshalltown), Iowa, on April 17, 1852. Adrian was the youngest son of Henry and Jeannette Rice Anson, and was the first pioneer child born in the town that his father had founded. Henry Anson, who was born in New York State and had drifted westward as a young adult, was a surveyor, land agent, and businessman who brought his wife and oldest son Sturgis to Iowa in a covered wagon. He found a promising valley in the center of the state, built a log cabin, and laid out a main street. Henry worked tirelessly to build and promote Marshalltown, and is recognized to this day as the patriarch of the city. Jeannette Anson was a sturdy pioneer housewife who died when Adrian was seven years of age, leaving behind an all-male household.

Adrian, whose family proudly claimed descent from the British naval hero Lord Anson, was a strong, strapping boy with reddish hair and a self-admitted aversion to schoolwork and chores. Not until his teenage years, when baseball fever swept through Marshalltown, did Adrian find an acceptable outlet for his energy and enthusiasm. He practiced diligently and earned a place on the town team, the Marshalltown Stars, at the age of 15. The Stars, with Henry Anson at third base, Adrian's brother Sturgis in center field, and Adrian at second base, won the Iowa state championship in 1868.

Henry Anson enrolled his sons in a preparatory course at the College of Notre Dame for two years beginning in 1865, but Adrian was more interested in baseball and skating than in his studies. A later sojourn at the state college in Iowa City (now the University of Iowa) ended similarly. Young Adrian Anson wanted to play professional ball, and his break came in 1870 when the famous Rockford Forest City club and its star pitcher, Al Spalding, came to Marshalltown for a pair of games. The Forest City team won both matches, but the Anson clan played so impressively that the Rockford management sent contract offers to all three of the Ansons. Henry and Sturgis turned Rockford down, but Adrian accepted and joined the Forest City squad in the spring of 1871.

The 19-year-old Adrian, dubbed "The Marshalltown Infant," batted .325 for Rockford and established himself as one of the stars of the new National Association. The last-place Rockford team disbanded at season's end, but the pennant-winning Philadelphia Athletics quickly signed Adrian to a contract. He rewarded the Athletics with a .415 average in 1872, third best in the Association. He played third base for the Athletics that season, but spent the next three seasons shuttling from first to third base

Anson in 1887, the year he won his third batting title with a .421 average. This is a colorized image from the 1887 Old Judge tobacco card. Courtesy of David Fleitz.

with occasional stops at second, shortstop, catcher, and the outfield. The hard-hitting utility man quickly became one of Philadelphia's most popular athletes.

Boston Red Stockings manager Harry Wright had always dreamed of introducing baseball to England, his home country, and in 1874 Wright and his star pitcher Al Spalding organized a mid-season trip to England. The Red Stockings and the Philadelphia Athletics took a three-week respite from National Association play and sailed to the Old World, where they played both baseball and cricket for British crowds. Adrian Anson led all the players on both teams in batting during the tour, and, more importantly, began a friendship with Spalding. Both were young men from the Midwest, less than two years apart in age, and both had willed themselves to prominence in the baseball profession. Each found reasons to admire the other, and their relationship would play an important role in Anson's life for the next 30 years.

During the 1875 season, Chicago club president William Hulbert signed four of Boston's brightest stars, including pitcher Al Spalding, to play for his White Stockings in the new National League in 1876. Spalding recommended that Hulbert also sign two Philadelphia standouts, Ezra Sutton and Adrian Anson. Sutton and Anson reached agreements with Hulbert, though Sutton later reneged on his deal and returned to the Athletics. Anson moved to Chicago in early 1876, and the White Stockings, managed by Spalding and powered by Anson and batting champ Ross Barnes, won the first National League pennant that year.

On a personal note, Anson began dating Virginia Fiegal, daughter of a saloon owner, during his Philadelphia days. He met Virginia when he was 20 and she only 13 or 14, though this was not considered unusual at the time. Their relationship hit a roadblock after Adrian signed his contract with Chicago, when Virginia strongly objected to Adrian's desire to leave Philadelphia. Anson was no contract-jumper, so he offered William Hulbert $1,000 to buy his way out of the agreement. Hulbert refused, and Anson, unwilling to break his contract and not wanting to lose Virginia, asked Virginia's father for his daughter's hand in marriage. Adrian and Virginia were wed in November 1876 and started a family that eventually produced four daughters, all of whom grew to adulthood, and three sons who died in infancy.

Adrian Anson, powerfully built at 6-feet-2 and over 200 pounds, was the biggest and strongest man in the game during the 1870s. Some reports state that he did not take a full swing at the plate; instead, he pushed his bat at the ball and relied upon his strong arms and wrists to produce line drives. An outstanding place hitter, Anson and the White Stockings worked an early version of the hit-and-run play to perfection. So good was Anson's bat control that he struck out only once during the 1878 season and twice in 1879. He also served as Spalding's assistant on the field, enthusiastically cheering his teammates and arguing with opponents and umpires. Anson had managed the Philadelphia Athletics for the last few weeks of the 1875 season, and looked forward to the day that he would succeed Spalding as leader of the White Stockings.

The Chicago team failed to repeat as champions under Spalding in 1877. Spalding then moved into the club presidency, but passed over Anson and appointed Bob Ferguson as his successor. Ferguson's regime was a failure, and Spalding named Anson as captain and manager for the 1879 season. He was now "Cap" Anson, and in one of his first decisions, the former utility man planted himself at first base and remained there for the rest of his career. His 1879 team challenged for the pennant, but fell apart after Anson was sidelined due to illness in late August. However, Anson's 1880 White Stockings, fortified by newcomers such as catcher Mike Kelly, pitcher Larry Corcoran, and outfielders George Gore and Abner Dalrymple, won the flag with a .798 winning percentage, the highest in league history.

Two more pennants followed in 1881 and 1882 as Anson, who won the batting title in 1881 with a .399 mark, cemented his stature as the hardest hitter and finest field general in the game. He used his foghorn voice and belligerent manner to rile opponents and frighten umpires, and made himself the focus of attention in nearly every game he played. His outbursts against the intimidated umpires earned him the title "King of Kickers." His White Stockings followed Anson's lead and played a hustling, battling brand of ball that won no friends in other league cities, but put Chicago on the top of the baseball world. As baseball grew in popularity, the handsome and highly successful Cap Anson became the sport's first true national celebrity.

Regrettably, Anson used his stature to drive minority players from the game. An 1883 exhibition game in Toledo, Ohio, between the local team and the White Stockings nearly ended before it began when Anson angrily refused to take the field against Toledo's African-American catcher, Moses Fleetwood Walker. Faced with the loss of gate receipts, Anson relented after a loud protest, but his bellicose attitude made Anson, wittingly or not, the acknowledged leader of the segregation forces already at work in the game. Other players and managers followed Anson's lead, and similar incidents occurred with regularity for the rest of the decade. In 1887, Anson made headlines again when he refused to play an exhibition in Newark unless the local club removed its African-American battery, catcher Walker and pitcher George Stovey, from the field. Teams and leagues began to bar minorities from participation, and by the early 1890s, no black players remained in the professional ranks.

Chicago was the highest-scoring team in baseball, and Anson, as its cleanup hitter, was the leading run producer in the game. The *Chicago Tribune* introduced a new statistic, runs batted in, in 1880 and reported that Cap Anson led the league in this category by a healthy margin. The statistic was soon dropped, but later researchers have determined that Anson led the National League in RBIs eight times. He is credited with driving in more than 2,000 runs, behind only Henry Aaron and Babe Ruth on the all-time list despite the fact that National League teams played fewer than 100 games per season for much of Anson's career.

Anson hit more than 12 homers in a season only once. He swatted 21 round-trippers in 1884 by taking advantage of the tiny Chicago ballpark, which featured a left-field fence only 180 feet from home plate (balls hit over the fence had been ruled as doubles in previous seasons). On August 5 and 6, 1884, Anson belted five homers in two games, a record that has been tied (by Stan Musial, among others) but never broken. However, Anson drove in most of his runs with sharp line drives that the barehanded infielders found nearly impossible to stop. Fielding gloves found their way into the National League by the mid-1880s, but Anson's production continued uninterrupted. He batted .300 or better in each of his first 20 professional seasons, and by 1886 he was baseball's all-time leader in games played, runs, hits, RBIs, and several other categories.

He was less successful as a fielder, leading the league in errors several times and setting the all-time career mark for miscues by a first baseman. However, Anson was fearless in stopping hard-thrown balls with his bare hands, and his size made him an excellent target for his infield mates. He was an integral part of the celebrated "Stonewall Infield" with third-baseman Tom Burns, shortstop Ed Williamson, and second-baseman Fred Pfeffer. This unit remained together for seven seasons, from 1883 to 1889, and formed the backbone of the Chicago defense.

Anson had been a teetotaler since his younger days, but his White Stockings were a hard-drinking crew that kept their captain up nights with their behavior. His 1883 and 1884 teams failed to win the pennant, partially due to off-the-field controversies, but in 1885 the White Stockings reclaimed their place at the top of the league. New pitcher John Clarkson posted a 53-16 record and led the team to the pennant after a spirited race against the New York Giants. However, Anson's team played poorly in a postseason "World's Series" against the St. Louis Browns of the American Association. The series ended, officially, in a tie after a disputed Browns victory caused no end of controversy. In 1886 Anson drove in 147 runs in 125 games and led the White Stockings to the pennant once again, but his charges lost the six-game World's Series against the Browns when some of the Chicago players appeared to be inebriated on the field.

Spalding and Anson decided to break up the team, selling Mike Kelly to Boston for a then-record $10,000 and dropping veterans George Gore and Abner Dalrymple, among others. The 1887 squad was a better-behaved bunch, but finished in third place despite Anson's outstanding performance at bat. The 35-year-old captain won the batting title with a career-best .421 in a year in which walks counted as hits (though later researchers removed the 60 walks from his hit totals, leaving his average at .347 and giving the title to Detroit's Sam Thompson). In early 1888 Spalding sold John Clarkson, baseball's best pitcher, to Boston for $10,000. Several new men tried, and failed, to fill Clarkson's shoes, and the White Stockings finished second despite another batting championship by Anson.

After the 1888 season Spalding, owner of the sporting goods company that still bears his name, took the Chicago club and a team of National League all-stars on a ballplaying excursion around the world. Virginia Anson accompanied the party as Anson directed the White Stockings in New Zealand, Australia, Ceylon, Egypt, and the European continent. The trip lost money for its backers, including Anson, but it introduced baseball (and advertised Spalding's business) to countries that had never seen the sport before. The six-month adventure was the high point of Cap Anson's life, and takes up nearly half of Anson's autobiography, published in 1900. At the conclusion of the trip, in April of 1889, Spalding signed Anson to an unprecedented 10-year contract as player and manager of the White Stockings.

By 1890, Anson was a stockholder in the Chicago ballclub, owning 13 percent of the team. A company man through and through, he bitterly criticized the Brotherhood of Professional Ball Players, whose members quit the National League *en masse* in early 1890 and formed the Players League. Anson, one of a handful of stars who refused to jump to the new league, hastily assembled a new group of youngsters (which the newspapers dubbed Anson's Colts) and finished second that year. Spalding worked behind the scenes to undermine the rival circuit, while Anson led the charge in the newspapers, denouncing the jumpers as "traitors" and gleefully predicting the eventual failure of the upstart league. The new circuit collapsed after one season, but Anson's role in the defeat angered many of his former players.

Some reporters called Anson "the man who saved the National League," but many former Players Leaguers hated the Chicago captain for his attitude toward them. Such stars as Hugh Duffy and George Van Haltren refused to return to Chicago after the collapse of the rival circuit, costing Anson much-needed talent. In 1891, Anson's Colts held first place until mid-September, but an 18-game winning streak vaulted Boston into the lead amid rumors that Boston opponents threw games to keep the pennant out of Anson's hands. Chicago finished in second place, and Cap Anson believed for the rest of his life that he lost the championship through the machinations of his former Players League rivals.

Anson, after more than 20 years as a player, began to slow down. His average dipped below .300 for the first time in 1891, though he led the league once again in runs batted in with 120. He had never been a great fielder, but covered so little ground at first base that the pitcher and second baseman had to help out on balls hit to the right side. As stubborn as ever, Anson was the last bare-handed first baseman in the major leagues, finally donning a glove in 1892. At bat, Anson produced one last hurrah with a remarkable .388 average in 1894 at the age of 42, but his slowness on the basepaths bogged down the Chicago offense. As a manager, his increasing strictness and inflexibility angered his charges. He was baseball's biggest celebrity, even enjoying a run as an actor on Broadway in a play called *A Runaway Colt* in December of 1895, but his Colts fell steadily in the standings.

His position as manager was weakened in 1891 when Al Spalding stepped down as team president. Anson might have been willing to retire from the field and accept the position, but Spalding, who retained controlling ownership in the team, appointed former Boston manager Jim Hart to the post. Anson held little regard for Hart, who had served Spalding as business manager of the round-the-world tour four years before, and the two men clashed often over personnel and disciplinary matters during the next several seasons.

Spalding and Hart reorganized the club in 1892, and Anson signed a new contract with the Chicago ballclub. This agreement retained Anson's 13 percent stake in the team, but cut one year off his previous 10-year pact, though Anson claimed that he did not discover the discrepancy until later. At any rate, the new agreement expired on February 1, 1898. Anson, who by 1894 was the oldest player in the league, stubbornly kept himself in the lineup despite his dwindling production and his deteriorating relationships with Hart and the Chicago players. He batted .285 in 1897, a respectable figure today but well below the

Anson as manager of the White Stockings, about 1880. Courtesy of David Fleitz.

league average, and his Colts finished in ninth place. Spalding and Hart declined to renew his contract, and after 27 seasons, Cap Anson's career was over. The 45-year-old Anson retired as baseball's all-time leader in games played, times at bat, runs, hits, doubles, runs batted in, and wins as a manager.

Spalding offered to hold a testimonial benefit for Anson and raise $50,000 as a going-away gift, but Anson proudly turned it down, explaining that accepting such an offer would "stultify my manhood" and smacked of charity. The former Chicago captain then accepted a position as manager of the New York Giants, succeeding Bill Joyce, who had been sharply criticized by the national press for his part in an ugly on-field brawl. Giants owner Andrew Freedman promised Anson full control of the team, but continually interfered with personnel and management issues. He also ignored Anson's request to trade or release Joyce, who remained on the team and retained the allegiance of many of the players. Anson led the Giants to a 9-13 record before Freedman fired him and reinstated Joyce after the controversy over the brawl died down.

After his humiliating exit from the Giants, Anson tried to obtain a Western League franchise and move it to the South Side of Chicago, but Spalding, whose approval for the move was necessary under to rules of the National Agreement, refused permission. This act ended the decades-long friendship between the two men. Anson then served as president of a revived American Association, which attempted to begin play in 1900 but folded due to financial pressures. After this defeat, Anson expressed his bitterness in his autobiography, *A Ball Player's Career*. "Baseball as at present conducted is a gigantic monopoly," stated Anson, "intolerant of opposition, and run on a grab-all-that-there-is-in-sight basis that is alienating its friends and disgusting the very public that has so long and cheerfully given to it the support that it has withheld from other forms of amusement."

Cap Anson was finished with the National League, and although he lived for another two decades, he would never again hold any official position in organized ball. Instead, Anson opened a bowling and billiards emporium in downtown Chicago and served as a vice-president of the new American Bowling Congress. He captained a team that won the ABC five-man national title in 1904, making Anson one of the few men in history to win championships in more than one sport. He then turned his energies to what appeared to be a promising political career. Elected to a term as Chicago city clerk in 1905, Anson soon became embroiled in numerous controversies that he was, by personality and temperament, unable to overcome. He lost a bid for renomination, and his career in public office ended ignominiously. His bowling and billiards business floundered, and in late 1905 the cash-strapped Anson sold his remaining stock in the Chicago ballclub and severed his 29-year connection with the team.

He then devoted himself to semipro ball, investing most of his remaining money in his own team (called Anson's Colts) and building his own ballpark on the South Side. This effort was a money-loser, and in desperation Anson donned a uniform in 1908 and played first base at the age of 56. He could still hit, but was nearly immobile in the field, and his Colts finished in the middle of the City League standings for three seasons. In those years, Anson played many games against the Chicago Leland Giants, the leading African-American team of the era, without apparent complaint. Anson, his finances stretched to the limit, sold his team after the 1909 season and returned to the stage. He created a monologue and performed it in vaudeville houses throughout the Midwest for the next few years.

Anson's later life was filled with disappointment. The National League offered to provide a pension for the ex-ballplayer, but Anson stoutly refused all offers of assistance. He declared bankruptcy in 1910, and by 1913 he had lost his home and moved in with a daughter and son-in-law. Virginia Anson died in 1915 after a long illness, and the widowed ex-ballplayer resumed his stage career in a skit written by his friend Ring Lardner titled "First Aid for Father." The skit starred Anson and his daughters Adele and Dorothy, and the Anson clan crisscrossed the nation, sharing bills with jugglers and animal acts in small town and big city alike. Vaudeville allowed Anson to support himself, but barely, and he retired, penniless, from the stage in 1921. He died on April 14, 1922, three days shy of his 70th birthday, and was buried in Oak Woods Cemetery in Chicago. The National League paid his funeral expenses. Seventeen years later, on May 2, 1939, Anson and his former friend and mentor Al Spalding were named to the Baseball Hall of Fame by a special committee.

SOURCES

Anson, Adrian C. *A Ball Player's Career* (Chicago: Era Publishing, 1900).

Brown, Warren. *The Chicago Cubs* (New York: G. P. Putnam's Sons, 1946).

Levine, Peter. *A. G. Spalding and the Rise of Baseball: The Promise of American Sport* (New York: Oxford University Press, 1985).

Spalding, Albert G. *Base Ball: America's National Game* (New York: American Sports Publishing Company, 1911).

Zang, David W. *Fleet Walker's Divided Heart* (Lincoln: University of Nebraska Press, 1995).

Newspapers and Magazines

Chicago Tribune, *The Sporting News*, *Baseball Magazine*, *Sporting Life*, and *The New York Times* for the 1870-1920 period.

MORDECAI BROWN

By Cindy Thomson

Mordecai Peter Centennial Brown, best known today for his unusual name and his more or less descriptive nickname of "Three Finger," was the ace right-hander of the great Chicago Cub teams of the first decade or so of the Twentieth Century. With Brown leading an extraordinary pitching staff, the Cubs from 1906 through 1910 put together the greatest five-year record of any team in baseball history. His battles with the Giants' Christy Mathewson epitomized the bitter rivalry between two teams that just about matched each other man for man.

Brown was born October 19, 1876, in the farming community of Nyesville, Indiana, to Jane (also known as Louisa) and Peter Brown.

Because the year of his birth was our country's centennial, Mordecai was given an extra middle name. Although it is generally assumed that the quite religious Browns chose their son's names from the Bible, Peter was his father's name, and there was an uncle named Mordecai. The family claimed to be of Welsh and English descent, but genealogical records indicate there may have been some Cherokee Indian heritage as well.

Mordecai had seven brothers and sisters. One of his brothers, John, also played baseball. According to Mordecai's great-nephew, Fred Massey, John was as good as Mordecai though he never played above the semipro level because he didn't apply himself.

In his playing days, Mordecai Brown was 5-feet-10 and weighed 175 pounds. Although not considered a large man by today's standards, he was often referred to as "big" by contemporary baseball commentators. Brown was a switch hitter.

Mordecai's most familiar nickname was Three Finger, although he actually had four and a half fingers on his pitching hand. Because of childhood curiosity, Mordecai lost most of his right index finger in a piece of farming equipment. Not long after, he fell while chasing a rabbit and broke his other fingers. The result was a bent middle finger, a paralyzed little finger, and a stump where the index finger used to be.

Mordecai's other nickname also described him. He was called Miner Brown because he worked in the coal mines when he was a teenager.

In those days the working class found relief from the daily grind by playing baseball. The mining towns near Mordecai's home had their own teams, and Mordecai played for Clinton, Shelburn, and Coxville. While playing third base for Coxville, Mordecai was called on to fill in for Coxville's regular pitcher against the neighboring town of Brazil. The year was 1898, and the pitcher's absence turned into a blessing for Mordecai.

Brown's deformed hand enabled him to throw a bewildering pitch with lots of movement. Although the jumping ball was a problem when Brown was an infielder, it was an advantage when he pitched. Despite having what had seemed like a terrible handicap, Brown's pitching performance that day was daunting. The Brazil manager was impressed, and the team offered Brown more money to play for them, but he didn't jump until he'd completed the season.

In 1901 Mordecai, with the help of 600 fans who threatened to boycott the games if he didn't make the team, secured a spot on the Terre Haute Tots (or Hottentots) in the newly formed Three-I League.

Mordecai led the semiprofessional team to the first-ever Three-I championship, posting a 25-8 record.

Mordecai was picked up by Omaha in the Western League the following year, and reporters started calling him Three Finger. He became the staff workhorse, posting a 27-15 record and finishing every game he started.

After that season in Omaha, Mordecai joined the St. Louis Cardinals in 1903. His major-league debut for St. Louis, against Chicago of the National League, was similar to the outing in Coxville. In both games Brown pitched five innings, and his dominance over hitters was obvious to all observers. While his rookie record was not impressive, 9-13, it should be remembered that St. Louis was the last-place team that year in the National League, 46 1/2 games back. Brown's earned run average was the lowest on the team at 2.60, and his nine wins tied veteran Chappie McFarland for most on the team.

Mordecai and Christy Mathewson began their famous face-offs during Brown's rookie year. The first time they met, on July 9, they dueled through eight innings, not allowing a run. In the ninth inning the Giants got to Mordecai for three runs and beat the Cardinals, 4-2.

After the 1903 season, Brown and pitcher Jack O'Neill were traded to the Chicago Cubs, the team Brown beat in his rookie appearance and the team for which he would set records that have not been broken to date. The Cardinals received veteran pitcher Jack Taylor, who was suspected of throwing games, and rookie catcher Larry McLean. The Cardinals, being the last-place team, were probably desperate for an experienced pitcher, and Brown had not yet proven himself. It was the Cubs, however, who benefited the most by the trade because Brown had his greatest years while pitching for Chicago.

After joining the Cubs in 1904, Brown improved his record to 15-10 and lowered his ERA to 1.86. Brown still holds the Cubs record for most shutouts (since 1900) with 48 and lowest career ERA of 1.80. In addition, Brown is the Cubs record holder for most wins in a season, 29 in 1908, and the lowest ERA in a season, 1.04 in 1906. When Brown joined the club he was already 27 years old, the same age as his manager, Frank Chance, and older than most of his fellow players.

Besides capturing the interest of the Cubs in his rookie year, Brown also caught the eye of Miss Sarah Burgham. They married December 17, 1903, in Rosedale, Indiana, shortly before he joined the Chicago team. The marriage lasted 45 years, until Mordecai's death. Sarah died 10 years later on October 5, 1958. They had no children.

Brown's greatest years were during his tenure with the Cubs, 1904 to 1912, when he won 186 games and had six straight seasons, from 1905 to 1910, posting 20

After jumping to the Federal League in 1914, Mordecai Brown spent a half season as the player/manager for the St. Louis Terriers. Brown spent the remainder of 1914 with the Brooklyn Tip Tops. In 1915 Mordecai was reunited with his old pal and teammate Joe Tinker, as a members of the Chicago Whales, playing their home games at Weeghman Park. Courtesy of the Mordecai Brown Legacy Foundation.

or more wins. During that time he led the Cubs to two World Series championships.

His best year was 1906 when his winning percentage was .813. He pitched nine shutouts that year, and his 1.04 ERA is baseball's third best in a single season. The Cubs won a remarkable 116 games in 1906 but lost the World Series to their cross-town rival White Sox, known as the Hitless Wonders because the team's batting average was a weak .230. Mordecai won one of the World Series games, but one he lost, Game Six, 8-3, lifted his series ERA to 3.66. However, Mordecai could not have been called the Hitless Wonder. At the plate, he went 2-for-6.

The following year was also a good one for Three Finger Brown. In 1907 he posted a 20-6 record and an ERA of 1.39. That year the Cubs did win the World Series, beating the Detroit Tigers in five games. In that series Brown pitched in only Game Five, winning 2-0.

Brown continued his winning ways. In 1908 he posted an ERA of 1.47, second to Christy Mathewson's 1.43.

But if one could ask him when his greatest game was, as many did when he was still living, he'd say October 8, 1908 at New York's Polo Grounds. In John P. Carmichael's *My Greatest Day in Baseball*, Brown said, "I was about as good that day as I ever was in my life." That was the day the Giants and Cubs met for a playoff game to determine the National League championship.

The game was made necessary because of the "Merkle Play." In the ninth inning during the September 23, 1908, game between the Giants and the Cubs, young Fred Merkle failed to touch second base on a play that should have scored the winning run for the Giants. Johnny Evers, remembering a similar play earlier when the call had not gone his way, solicited the ball Al Bridwell had hit. Whether he got that ball or another one is uncertain, but he stood jumping up and down on second base until he captured the umpire's attention. Merkle was called out. Because the field was overrun by fans who thought the game was over, it was decided the game would be declared a tie, only to be replayed at the end of the season if it became necessary. It did. At the end of the season the Chicago Cubs and the New York Giants were deadlocked at the top of the National League standings.

In Brown's *How to Pitch Curves*, an instruction manual written for young boys and published by Chicagoan W.D. Boyce, Brown referred to that playoff game as a time when having nerve served him well in baseball. He had plenty of "pluck," as he put it, to pitch in front of a hostile crowd after receiving death threats. Gambling was commonplace in those days, and many had everything they owned riding on that game.

Jack Pfeister started the game for Chicago, and Christy Mathewson took the hill for New York, a repeat of the Merkle game match-up. Mordecai had started or relieved in 11 of the Cubs' last 14 games so manager Frank Chance decided not to start his ace. The crowd was enormous; some accounts put the total at 250,000 spectators, taking into account the throng outside the gates. While that number is highly unlikely, people did fill every available space inside and outside of the Polo Grounds, lining fence tops, sitting on the elevated train platform, and perching on housetops.

The Giants rocked Pfeister in the first inning, scoring their first run. Not willing to take any chances, Frank Chance called on Mordecai. Pushing through the overflow crowd, Brown made his way in from the outfield bullpen and went on to win his 29th regular season game, securing the Chicago Nationals a third straight pennant and sending them on to play the Detroit Tigers and Ty Cobb in the World Series.

After the game, believing the Cubs had stolen the pennant from their team, New York fans threw hats, bricks, and bottles at the Chicago players. Frank Chance received a blow from a spectator that so injured his throat he couldn't speak for days. The riotous atmosphere required a police escort for the Cubs by paddy wagon.

The following World Series must have seemed anticlimactic. Despite the opener in which Chicago scored five in the ninth to win 10-6—a win Brown received after relieving in the eighth inning—there were no amazing feats to compare with the October 8 playoff. Mordecai also won Game Four, 3-0. Detroit won only Game Three, even with Ty Cobb, American League batting champion, batting .368 in the series. The final game still holds the record for the lowest fan attendance in a World Series game. Only 6,210 Detroit fans showed up to see the Cubs defeat the Tigers.

Ty Cobb once described Brown's lively pitch as the most devastating he'd ever tried to hit. His words are forever enshrined on a marker erected to Mordecai Brown in Nyesville, Indiana. It is high praise from a man who had remarkable success at the plate during the time when the ball had little juice. In his career, Brown won five World Series games for the Cubs and lost four. Cobb hit .273 off Brown during World Series play, but Brown won every World Series game he pitched against Cobb and the Tigers.

During the Deadball Era defense was king. The ball didn't travel far, unlike today, and low scoring games were common. Teams couldn't afford costly errors. Brown was an excellent fielder. In 1908 he handled the ball without error in 108 chances.

The rivalry continued between Brown and Christy Mathewson throughout their careers. Brown lost to Mathewson on June 13, 1905, a no-hitter for Matty, but after that he beat the Giants star nine consecutive times. The ninth game was the October 8 replay of the Merkle game.

The Cubs in those days were a rowdy bunch. Fights in the clubhouse were common, sometimes landing players in the hospital. But Brown was well respected. A search in Brown's file at the National Baseball Hall of Fame produced a quote from teammate, Johnny Evers. Evers described Brown as having "plenty of nerve, ability, and willingness to work under any conditions. He was charitable and friendly to his foes."

By 1912 Brown had lost his previous form. By that time he was 35 and only appeared in 15 games, posting a 5-6 record. After the 1912 season, ailing from a knee injury, he was traded to the Cincinnati Reds, where he went 11-12.

In 1914 Brown joined with other big leaguers and jumped to the short-lived Federal League. There he was player/manager for the St. Louis team before going to Brooklyn. Between the two teams he was 14-11 with a swelling ERA of 3.52. When he joined the Chicago Federals in 1915, he improved to 17-8 with an ERA of 2.09, and his team won a championship.

When the Federal League folded, Brown returned to the Cubs. His records indicate that major league dominance was behind him. At age 39 he made only 12 appearances, winning two games and losing three. His ERA was his highest ever at 3.91. Brown's final game in the majors was September 4, 1916, the final face-off against rival Christy Mathewson, now pitcher and manager for the Cincinnati Reds. The Labor Day event was highly promoted and turned out to be the last big-league performance for both pitchers. Although Mathewson won that day, Brown slightly bested him over all, going 12-11 with one no-decision in their 24 matchups.

With his big-league years behind him, Brown accepted an invitation from his old Cubs teammate, Joe Tinker, now manager of the Columbus Senators of the American Association, to pitch in Ohio's capital. Brown was 40 years old by then and posted a 10-12 record. Mordecai filled in as manager whenever Tinker was out scouting players. An article in the July 11, 1918, *Columbus Citizen*, notes that while playing in Louisville, Brown received more applause than the home team did. His popularity may in part explain the large fan attendance Columbus enjoyed while he played there. In 1917 the Senators drew just under 105,000—in a city with a population not much larger than that. In 1918 he appeared in only 13 games, but that was a year shortened by war and the flu outbreak.

In 1919 Brown went back to Terre Haute, Indiana to manage his former semipro team. Later that year, after Terre Haute's season was completed, he joined Indianapolis of the American Association, but made little contribution to their pennant aspirations. His last year pitching was 1920, but after that he kept his hand in the game by managing oil company teams and buying an interest in the Terre Haute team.

Later in life Brown owned and operated a gas station in Terre Haute. He remained popular, occasionally showing up in newspaper reports about old-timer games or columns about players' lives after baseball.

In his 14 years in the majors, Brown won 239 games and lost only 130. He led the league in wins once, in 1909, and led the league with most shutouts in 1906 and 1910. He had a lifetime ERA of 2.06 and from 1905 to 1910 he posted 20 or more wins—numbers sparking the attention of the Hall of Fame Committee on Baseball Veterans. He was elected in 1949. He may have known he was being considered for election, but he didn't live to see it because he died on February 14, 1948 in Terre Haute, Indiana at the age of 71.

Forty-six years after Mordecai Brown died, his relatives, led by great-nephews Joe and Fred Massey, erected a three-foot-high granite stone to mark the birthplace of Nyesville's famous son. On July 9, 1994, on land donated by farmer David Grindley, family and friends of the legendary three-fingered pitcher gathered to remember him. The author of this biography, cousin to Mordecai Brown, was in attendance.

In *How to Pitch Curves*, Mordecai leaves a farewell, "I would like to meet every one of you personally if such a thing were possible. But as it isn't possible, I want you to believe right now that Mordecai Brown's hand is reaching out to you in the distance and he is wishing you—good luck."

Mordecai "Three Finger" Brown, always the sports reporter's friend, poses for a press photo during the 1909 season. Courtesy of the Mordecai Brown Legacy Foundation.

SOURCES

Anderson, David W., *More Than Merkle* (Lincoln: University of Nebraska Press, 2000).

www.baseball-almanac.com

Brown, Scott, personal family collection

Brown, Mordecai, *How to Pitch Curves* (Chicago: W.D. Boyce Company, 1913).

Carmichael, John P., *My Greatest Day in Baseball: Forty-seven Dramatic Stories by Forty-seven Stars* (Lincoln: University of Nebraska Press, 1996), c.1945.

National Baseball Hall of Fame Research Library, Mordecai Brown file.

JIM CREIGHTON

By John Thorn

James Creighton was the greatest pitcher of his day. Famous principally for his exploits on behalf of the champion Excelsiors of Brooklyn in the years 1860 to 1862, he possessed an unprecedented combination of speed, spin, and command that virtually defined the position for all those who followed. Prior to Creighton, pitchers had been constrained by the rule that "the ball must be pitched, not thrown, for the bat." This meant that (a) the ball had to be delivered underhand, in the stiff-armed, stiff-wristed manner borrowed from cricket's early days and (b), in the absence of called strikes, an innovation of 1858, or called balls, which came into the game six years later, the ball had to be placed at the batter's pleasure: the infant game of baseball was designed to display and reward its most difficult skill, which was neither pitching nor batting, but fielding.

The 1850s did produce some pitchers who tried to deceive batters with "headwork"- which meant changing arcs and speeds, and sometimes bowling wide ones until the frustrated batter lunged at a pitch. (The latter tactic produced such incredible, documented pitch totals as that in the second Atlantic-Excelsior game of 1860, when the Atlantics' Matty O'Brien threw 325 pitches in nine innings, Creighton 280 in seven.) On balance, however, the pioneer pitcher and batter were collaborators in putting the ball in play rather than the mortal adversaries they have been ever since Creighton added an illegal but imperceptible wrist snap to his swooping low release.

Known to few fans today and an unlikely, if deserving, candidate for the Baseball Hall of Fame, Jim Creighton was a remarkable embodiment of transecting trends in America and in baseball: cricket vs. baseball, amateur vs. professional, North vs. South, playing by the rules or playing with them. The legion of baseball players followed along the path that Creighton blazed. In life he was a star performer, but it was his startling death that transformed his life into legend.

Born to James and Jane Creighton on April 15, 1841, in Manhattan, Jim moved to Brooklyn with his widowed father in February 1858, when he was age 17. Indeed, his baseball precocity may have secured for him and his father a fine income.[1] By the age of 16, his abilities in cricket and baseball had become evident, particularly with the bat. He and some neighborhood youths started a junior baseball club, which they called Young America. It played a handful of games in 1857, and then disbanded. Jim then joined the fledgling Niagaras of Brooklyn, for whom he claimed second base. Playing shortstop was George Flanley, another accomplished young player.

In 1859 the Niagaras challenged the Star Club, then the crack junior team. In the fifth inning of the game, with the Niagaras trailing badly, their regular pitcher, Shields, was replaced by Creighton. Peter O'Brien, captain of the Atlantics, witnessed this game, and "when Creighton got to work," he observed, "something new was seen in base ball—a low, swift delivery, the ball rising from the ground past the shoulder to the catcher. The Stars soon saw that they would not be able to cope with such pitching. Their captain, after consulting other base ball players present, sent in his wildest pitcher. They, by these tactics, were enabled to win the game, which resulted in the breaking up of the Niagara Club, and Creighton and Flanley at once joined the Stars. The next year he with Flanley joined the Excelsior Club."[2]

How to explain all this movement? That old snake in the garden: money. In the 1860s such restlessness came to be termed revolving; today it would be called free agency. According to the sporting press, Creighton was a high-principled, unassuming youth whose gentlemanly manner and temperate habits were ideal attributes for the amateur age of baseball; all the same, he became (at the same time as Flanley) baseball's first professional, through under-the-table "emoluments" from the Excelsiors, who were hungry to surpass the rival Atlantics. Just as he changed the game forever more by breaking the rule against the wrist snap, so did he assure that skilled baseball players could never again be content with field exercise followed by groaning banquets.

In 1860 the Excelsiors embarked on the first tour by any baseball club, with stops in Albany, Buffalo, Canada, Philadelphia, Washington, and Baltimore, among others. That year, in 20 match games, Creighton scored 47 runs while being retired only 56 times. Not once did he strike out. He also started baseball's first recorded triple play, on September 22, and threw baseball's first recorded shutout, on November 8.

But the best was to be saved for last. After another championship campaign in 1861, Creighton went through the 1862 season as not only the game's peerless pitcher but also its top batsman, being retired only four times, either in plate appearances or on the basepaths.

At the same time that Creighton was extending the frontier in baseball he was also a prominent member of the cricketing fraternity. The national sport of England and its boyish variants like wicket had been played in America since the Colonial period, and the first formal American cricket club had taken shape in Boston in 1809 (the Union Club of Philadelphia followed in 1832, and the St. George of New York in 1838). When the all-England team crossed the Atlantic to play against (and drub) selected American clubs at the Elysian Fields and elsewhere, Creighton took part in the contests. In a match of 11 Englishmen against 16 Americans, Creighton clean bowled five wickets out of six successive balls. English Cricketer John Lillywhite, on seeing Creighton pitch a baseball, instantly saw the dilemma that overmatched American batsmen faced: "Why, that man is not bowling, he is throwing underhand. It is the best disguised underhand throwing I ever saw, and might readily be taken for a fair delivery."[3]

Cricket continued to be a source of pleasure and profit for Creighton through the next two years, during which he and the Excelsiors were proving themselves to be the top baseball team in the land. Coincidentally, several other Excelsiors were good enough at cricket to play for established clubs - John Whiting, A. T. Pearsall, John Holder, and Asa Brainard, later to become famous as Creighton's successor with the Excelsiors and as the pitcher for the undefeated Cincinnati Red Stockings of 1869. Creighton performed for the American Cricket Club in both 1861 and 1862, joined by Brainard in both years but with John "Death to Flying Things" Chapman of the Atlantics taking the place of the Virginian Pearsall in 1862; he had returned to Richmond when hostilities broke out to enlist in the Confederacy.

In 1861 Brainard and Creighton had jumped the gentlemanly Excelsiors for the working-class Atlantics, no doubt lured once again by covert lucre. After three weeks, without having played a game in the hated rivals' uniforms, the pair sheepishly returned to the fold.

On October 14, 1862, in a match against the tough Unions of Morrisania, Creighton played the field while Brainard pitched the first five innings. In four trips to the plate, he hit four doubles. In the sixth he came in to pitch, and then in the next inning something happened. John Chapman later wrote: "I was present at the game between the Excelsiors and the Unions of Morrisania at which Jim Creighton injured himself. He did it in hitting out a home run. When he had crossed the [plate] he turned to George Flanley and said, 'I must have snapped my belt,' and George said, 'I guess not.' It turned out that he had suffered a fatal injury. Nothing could be done for him, and baseball met with a severe loss. He had wonderful speed, and, with it, splendid command. He was fairly unhittable."4

Creighton had swung so mighty a blow - in the manner of the day, with hands separated on the bat, little or no turn of the wrists, and incredible torque applied by the twisting motion of the upper body - that it was reported he ruptured his bladder. (Later review of the circumstances, aided by modern medical understanding, pointed to a ruptured inguinal hernia.) After four days of hemorrhaging and agony at his home at 307 Henry Street, Jim Creighton passed away on October 18, at the age of 21 years and 6 months, having given his all to baseball in a final epic blast that Roy Hobbs (the cinematic one, that is) might have envied.

But is that the way it really happened? Creighton's last run home instantly ascended to the realm of myth, giving baseball its martyred saint. Obsequies included such syrupy statements as: "He was very modest, and never severe in his criticisms of the play of others. He did not care to talk about his own playing, was gentlemanly in his deportment, and very correct in his habits, and to sum up all, was a model player in our National Games [understood here not as a typo, but signifying baseball and cricket]. His death was a loss not only to his club but to the whole base ball community, which needed such as he as a standard of honorable play and ability."5 Rule-breaking, revolving, sub rosa professionalism, all were now to be dismissed. Icon-making was in full production.

Creighton's Excelsior teammates mourned his loss at their black-draped clubhouse at 133 Clinton Street and subscribed toward a fine monument over his remains, in Brooklyn's Greenwood Cemetery. (Both the clubhouse and the monument are still standing, and represent two of baseball's oldest and greatest shrines; if you go to Greenwood to pay homage to Creighton, as I did, stop at Henry Chadwick's gravesite, too. I signed baseballs to each and placed them on top of their tombs; you'll know what to do.) But the Excelsiors were not at all sure that it was a good thing for baseball to take the blame for Creighton's death; this might not promote the healthful properties of the new game. What if his injury had been sustained a day or two earlier, say, at a cricket match?

According to a contemporary account, at the National Association convention of 1862, the Excelsior president, Dr. Jones, "briefly made allusion to the death of Creighton, and paid high tribute to his memory; in doing which he availed himself of the opportunity to correct a mis-statement that has found its way into print in reference to his death being caused by injuries sustained in a baseball match. This, he said, was not so; the injury he received in a cricket match."6

The battle for the nation's sporting allegiance was at a crucial point. Cricket had been the favored sport until only recently, when the Excelsior tour and Creighton's exploits had created a mania for baseball and had elevated it into parity. Now, with Creighton gone and the Excelsiors falling back into the pack, might the British import be restored to primacy? These fears may have been running through the minds of some in the baseball community, already

Jim Creighton, from baseball's earliest days.

concerned with the new game's incipient professionalism, and thus may have moved them to propagandize for baseball's spotlessness, as well as Creighton's. Jim had carried the game to new heights; in death he would prove even more useful.

Smart lad, to slip betimes away
From fields where glory does not stay
And early though the laurel grows
It withers quicker than the rose.
— A. E. Housman

Creighton preserved, even enhanced, his purity by dying young. Celebrated though he was, at the time of his demise he was not the game's greatest player - by general acclamation the laurels went to his catcher, Joseph B. Leggett. Who hears of him today? (I know, who hears of Creighton - well, at least a thousand for every one that recognizes Leggett's name.) Creighton died when he was all potential - no possibility of loss through aging, change, even growth. He became a plaster saint onto whom one could project whatever social or moral values one wished to promote in the population at large. Cut off in his prime, he joined other such deified national figures - mostly martial ones like Nathan Hale or Davy Crockett. Those golden boys who die young, from Arthur Rimbaud to Harry Agganis, from Charlie Ferguson to Buddy Holly, from Ernie Davis to Lyman Bostock, are forever young in the land of might have been, safe.

A Johnny Appleseed of baseball through his role in the grand tour of 1860, Creighton won far-flung fame. His death, coming as it did "in action" and at a time when the nation was preoccupied with the destruction of a generation, became emblematic of the losses of the Civil War. At the end of all the carnage, the lamented pitcher even became a symbol of national reconciliation.

On July 5, 1866, the Nationals of Washington visited the Excelsiors, reciprocating the favor of their visit six years earlier. The Brooklyn team gave them a warm reception, capped by a visit to Creighton's monument (according to the *New York Times* report, "a silent tear was dropped to the memory of the lamented James Creighton, whose beautiful monument is a prominent feature of the city of the dead.")[7] Two years later, a team in Norfolk, Virginia took the name "Creightons." And in 1872 a Creighton club was formed in Washington, D.C. Oddly, on this team named in homage to the fallen hero - whose appetite for money had given rise to professionalism and, even in his lifetime, gambling - was a young player named Albert Nichols who in 1877 would be one of the four Louisville players expelled from baseball for game-fixing.

In death Creighton's real accomplishments rapidly took on an accretion of myth, much as his death itself may have. Baseball, today universally recognized as a vibrant anachronism, was not always a backward-looking game in which the plays and players of yore set unsurpassable standards of excellence. In the 1850s and '60s, baseball was new, and strictly a "go ahead" business, in the watchword of the day. Creighton's death implanted the game with nostalgia. More than 20 years after his passing, veteran observers might say without fear of challenge that Keefe and Radbourn were fine pitchers, sure, but they *"warn't no Creighton."*

SOURCES

Most of my research into the exploits of baseball's first great pitcher was conducted at the New York Public Library, where I found news clippings among the Chadwick and Spalding scrapbooks. Odd bits -*Clipper* and *Mercury* notes, as well as Will Rankin columns from the Charles Mears Collection at the Cleveland Public Library were also helpful. Retrospective notes about the late lamented Creighton were plentiful in the decade after his death, and beyond. *The National Chronicle*, *The Ball Players' Chronicle*, and the *Beadle Guides* supplied good material, as did *The Spirit of the Times* and the *Baltimore Sun*

Secondary sources provided some additional data, but these are potential land mines for the researcher, as even the basic facts of Creighton's death were in dispute before the body was laid to rest. Tom Shieber's excellent reconstruction of the medical facts underlying Creighton's fatal injury was valuable.

In 1983, if memory serves correctly, Mark Rucker and I were scouring the photo archives of the Northeast, public and private, looking for images of nineteenth century baseball to fill our upcoming "special issue" of *The National Pastime*. At the Culver Studio in New York City, we came upon several great finds, one of them a unique carte de visite of Jim Creighton posed in the backswing of his pitching motion. Glued to the back of the card was a tattered and torn biographical note, likely issued three or four years after his death and as such a testament to his already legendary status.

Here is the text of that note, transcribed as the fragments permitted; gaps are noted with an ellipsis:

"It would be useless to attempt to do justice to the many qualities that rendered James Creighton so popular a member of the baseball and cricket fraternity. His is a record that […] may well be proud of, and although he was taken away … age of … in his brief career, made such a clear […] has a […] dear to every base ball player in …. [*other gaps in paragraph indecipherable*].

"James Creighton was born in New York city … a child his parents removed him to Brooklyn, where they […] resided. When base ball was first introduced in this [*city?*] Creighton took a great interest in the game, and with the assistance of several others, started a little club which was known as the Young America, which, however, lasted but a brief season. He next assisted in starting the Niagara Club, for whom he played second base. George Flanley, now captain of the Excelsior club (18__) [*1864?*] playing short stop.

"They played many matches in which they were successful, which gave them such a confidence in their prowess that they resolved to play the Star Club, then the crack Junior Club, and it was in this match that Creighton gave evidence of those qualities that afterwards made him so renouned [*sic*]. On the fifth inning of this game, when the Stars were a number of runs ahead of the Niagara the pitcher of the latter was changed, Jimmy taking that position. Peter O'Brien witnessed this game, and when Creighton got to work something news [*sic*] was seen in base ball - a low, swift delivery, the ball rising from the ground past the shoulder to the catcher. The Stars soon saw that they would not be able to cope with such pitching. Their captain, after consulting [*other?*] base ball players present, sent in his wildest pitcher. They, by these tactics, were enabled to win the game, which resulted in the breaking up of the Niagara Club,

and Creighton and Flanley at once joined the Stars. The next year he with Flanley joined the Excelsior Club. He was very modest, and never severe in his criticisms of the play of others. He did not care to talk about his own playing, was gentlemanly in his deportment, and very correct in his habits, and to sum up all, was a model player in our national Games. His death was a loss not only to his club but to the whole base ball community, which needed such as he as a standard of honorable play and ability. The Excelsior Club erected a fine monument over his remains, in Greenwood. Members of other clubs attended his funeral, and at times even [*wept over?*] the grave where poor "Jim" lies. His age at the time of [*his death?*] was twenty-one years and six months."

NOTES

1 Outstanding research on Jim's father, his recruitment by Brooklyn baseball clubs, and his likely *sub rosa* payments, appears here: Tom Gilbert, "Searching for James Creighton," *Base Ball*, 2014: 17-35.

2 Creighton posed for a photographer in the backswing of his underhand motion; the image is preserved as the front of a *carte de visite* issued after his death. Glued to the back of the card was a tattered and torn biographical note, the source of the Pete O'Brien quotation cited. Mark Rucker and I found his card in the archives of Culver Pictures in 1983.}

3 *New York Clipper*, August 5, 1911: 12.

4 Alfred Henry Spink, *National Game*, 128. Spink credits the Chapman quote to "a recent article in the *Boston Magazine*."

5 Creighton *carte de visite*, op. cit.

6 Albert Spalding Baseball Collections, Chadwick Scrapbooks, vol. 5 (*Clipper*, 1862, undated: 293).

7 "Out-Door Sports," *New York Times*, July 7, 1866: 8.

HONUS WAGNER

By Jan Finkel

"There ain't much to being a ballplayer, if you're a ballplayer," said the greatest player of his time, or most any other time—Honus Wagner. He may be the greatest player in National League history.

One of five sons and four daughters of the former Katrina Wolf and Peter Wagner, Honus (a diminutive of Johann or Johannes, the German equivalents of John) was born Johannes Peter Wagner in the coal country of western Pennsylvania on February 24, 1874. The Wagners lived in the tiny borough of Chartiers, about six miles southwest of downtown Pittsburgh.

Albert, an older brother considered the best ballplayer in the family, began playing the game professionally, and in 1895 when his Steubenville, Ohio, (Inter-State League) team needed help, he suggested Honus. Honus's first year was an odyssey covering five teams, three leagues, and 80 games. He hit wherever he played (between .365 and .386) and showed his versatility by playing every position except catcher.

Edward Barrow, wearing several hats with the Wheeling, West Virginia, team (Iron and Oil League), liked what he saw and in 1896 took Honus with him to his next team, in Paterson, New Jersey (Atlantic League). Honus rewarded Barrow's faith by playing wherever he was needed –first, third, the outfield, or second—and hitting .313 with power and speed. He followed up by hitting .375 in 74 games for Paterson in 1897.

Recognizing that Wagner should be playing at the highest level, Barrow contacted the Louisville Colonels, who had finished last in the National League in 1896 with a record of 38-93. They were doing better in 1897 when Barrow persuaded club president Barney Dreyfuss, club secretary Harry Pulliam, and outfielder-manager Fred Clarke to go to Paterson to see Wagner play. Dreyfuss and Clarke weren't impressed with the awkward-looking man, not surprising, as Wagner was oddly built—5-feet-11, 200 pounds, with a barrel chest, massive shoulders, heavily muscled arms, huge hands, and incredibly bowed legs that deprived him of any grace and several inches of height. Pulliam, though, persuaded Dreyfuss and Clarke to take a chance on him. Wagner debuted with Louisville on July 19, and hit .338 in 61 games.

Pulliam was right. The awkward-looking Honus would become the best pure athlete in the game. Seeing Wagner at bat, standing straight up waiting for the pitch, was to witness raw power. He held his heavy bat (well over 40 ounces) with his hands several inches apart, a grip that allowed him to slap an outside pitch to right at the last moment or slide his hands together and pull an inside pitch down the left-field line. Now obsolete, the split-handed grip was relatively popular in the early part of the twentieth century. Wagner and Ty Cobb used it, winning 20 batting titles and accumulating about 7,600 hits between them.

Honus was deceptive on the bases, too. He didn't look fast, but he stole over 700 bases and legged out almost 900 doubles and triples. His speed got him the nickname "The Flying Dutchman." In baseball, as in the worlds of myth and legend, titles and nicknames are earned. (The direct albeit coincidental allusion to the myth and Richard Wagner's opera of the same name didn't hurt, either.) Wagner's form as seen in early film was distinctive as he tore around the bases with his arms whirling like a berserk freestyle

Honus Wagner, circa 1911. Courtesy Library of Congress.

swimmer. Honus thought the arm motion gave him speed, and he got results.

Wagner was a sight in the field as well. His huge hands made it difficult to tell whether he was wearing a glove. The glove that seemed too small for his hand was made even smaller by cutting a hole in the palm and pulling out much of the stuffing. Doing so, he thought, gave him better feel and hand mobility, reasonable given the pancake-shaped glove he used. Quick of foot and reflex, he covered the left side of the infield, knocking down balls (making errors on balls that other shortstops wouldn't have reached) as necessary and throwing out runners with his powerful arm. He would irritate Clarke by taking his time making the throw on close plays at first. Wagner told Clarke he'd change when he quit throwing runners out. His one weakness in the field stemmed from his oversized feet, which sometimes got in the way.

At bat, on the bases, and in the field, Wagner wasn't pretty, just effective.

Wagner played in 151 games in 1898, handling first, second, and third, and hitting .299. He wouldn't see the south side of .300 again until 1914. Louisville improved to 75-77 in 1899, helped by Honus's hitting. That winter things would change drastically for all concerned.

National League officials reduced league membership from 12 teams to eight. The Louisville club was dissolved. Dreyfuss bought stock in the Pittsburgh Pirates and through clever maneuvering became president of the club. Replacing unproductive Pirates with top players from Louisville, including Wagner, Dreyfuss pushed the Pirates to second behind the Brooklyn Superbas in 1900. Wagner thanked Dreyfuss for bringing him home, hitting and slugging career-bests .381 and .573.

The decade spanning 1900 to 1909 belonged to Wagner. He led in every significant category except triples (second behind Sam Crawford of the Cincinnati Reds and Detroit Tigers) and home runs, (tied for fifth). A summary of Wagner's year-by-year hitting titles shows the following: batting average (7 times); on-base percentage (4); slugging (6); runs scored (2); hits (1); total bases (6); doubles (7); triples (3); RBIs (4); and stolen bases (5). Furthermore, he led the league in various categories up to 1912 and stayed among the leaders a few years after that.

The rise of the American League in 1901 triggered bidding wars and player raids that decimated most National League teams. Wagner showed his loyalty to Dreyfuss, the Pirates, and Pittsburgh by refusing an offer of $20,000 up front from Chicago White Stockings pitcher-manager Clark Griffith. The tale, perhaps apocryphal, doesn't hurt Wagner's legacy.

Pittsburgh survived the war between the leagues relatively unscathed, capturing the pennant from 1901 to 1903 and the World Series in 1909, and remaining strong throughout the decade. The team's won-lost record of 938-538 and winning percentage of .636 are the best of the period.

Led by Wagner, the 1901 Pirates began a three-year stranglehold over the National League. Their 90-49 record was 7½ games better than the Philadelphia Phillies, with Wagner's 126 RBIs the major-league best for the decade. The 1902 unit went 103-36, storming to a major-league record 27½-game margin over runner-up Brooklyn. Honus contributed by leading the league in slugging, doubles, steals, runs, and RBIs. The Pirates couldn't decide where to play him, though. He had played every position except catcher at least adequately, often brilliantly. In two stints on the mound he gave up no earned runs (but several unearned ones), giving him the lowest ERA of anyone in the Hall of Fame — 0.00. His roaming around the diamond would change in 1903, as he finally found his permanent home at shortstop.

Wagner had primarily played shortstop in 1901, especially after the Pirates' longtime shortstop Bones Ely jumped to the American League. Wid Conroy took over the position for the 1902 season, moving Wagner to right field, but he turned out to be a spy for the American League and was released. Clarke then put Tommy Leach at short and Wagner at third, instructing Leach to persuade Honus to swap positions. The con game worked, as Honus grudgingly took the position for good.

Position notwithstanding, Wagner led the league at .355. The Pirates were weakened by the defection of their top pitcher, Jack Chesbro, to the New York Highlanders (now the Yankees) but still took the pennant, going 91-49. During the season Dreyfuss challenged the American League to a championship playoff at the end of the season. Henry Killilea, president of the league champion Boston Americans (now the Red Sox), accepted the challenge. The World Series was born.

Though plagued with injuries — Wagner's right leg, pitcher Sam Leever's sore arm, and pitcher Ed Doheny's emotional collapse — the Pirates went into the best-of-nine Series as the favorites. Deacon Phillippe, the only healthy Pirate pitcher, threw complete games to take the first, third, and fourth games. Wagner went 5-for-14 and drove in three runs. Phillippe's arm gave out, and Boston won four straight behind pitchers Cy Young and Bill Dineen and third baseman-manager Jimmy Collins to take the Series. The last four games were a nightmare for Wagner: 1-for-14, no RBIs, and the humiliation of making the final out of the Series on a called third strike. Worse, the acknowledged greatest player in the National League had led in only one category — errors, with six. Several Boston writers, noting Wagner's miserable performance, implied that he might be "yellow," a slap that would haunt him for years.

From 1904 to 1907, the Pirates moved back and forth between second and fourth place, occasionally challenging the New York Giants and the Chicago Cubs on their runs to glory. Wagner was still Wagner, always among the league leaders. He won the first of four consecutive batting titles in 1906 and led the league in doubles and runs.

Honus's offseasons had been matters of routine. Tending to gain weight, he stayed in shape by fishing, hunting, and taking up the new sport of basketball, playing on several local teams. The horseless buggy allowed him to indulge in "automobiling," as it was called. More enthusiastic than able, Honus had several mishaps while driving. He opened a garage to repair cars and sell the Regal; no salesman, he loved tinkering with engines. He raised chickens. He hated spring training and held out on principle or did anything he could to avoid or at least delay it. There were plenty of friends to lift a glass with. And with simple tastes and frugal (but not miserly) living, not to mention Dreyfuss's wise investment help and some good real-estate properties, he was on solid financial ground. He retired.

How genuine Wagner's retirement was is debatable. He said he was tired, had suffered his share of injuries, and wanted to take at least a year off. Dreyfuss refused to panic at losing his star, in public anyway. It's possible, even likely, that Wagner was using his "retirement" to get a hefty raise. In any case, Dreyfuss doubled Honus' salary to $10,000 (the figure he maintained until his last season), making him the highest-paid player in the game for several years.

Wagner put together his greatest season in 1908. Both leagues hit just .239, but Honus didn't notice. His .354 batting average led the league comfortably. Settling for second in homers and runs scored, he led in everything else. It added up to an offensive winning percentage of .878 in Lee Sinins' *Sabermetric Baseball Encyclopedia* — the greatest single season in National League history until Barry Bonds' astounding 2001 through 2004 seasons.

And it wasn't enough. In the closest National League pennant race ever, the Pirates could have forced a three-way tie with the Cubs and Giants by winning their finale against the Cubs. Instead, they lost, 5-2, Wagner's two errors not helping. The ghosts of 1903 were alive and well.

A winter of frustration, brooding, and anger brought the Pirates back with a vengeance in 1909. They went 110-42 for the greatest season in club history, six games better than the Cubs. The Cubs got one measure of satisfaction, with Ed Reulbach beating Vic Willis, 3-2, on June 30 to spoil the opening of the new Pirates home, Forbes Field. Otherwise, it was the Pirates' year, and Wagner carried them with league-leading figures in hitting, slugging, on-base percentage, doubles, RBIs, total bases, and extra-base hits. The stage was set for the best-of-seven World Series with the Detroit Tigers, coming off their third straight American League title and their nominee for baseball's top player, Ty Cobb.

The Series didn't disappoint, as the Pirates won in seven games behind the pitching of Babe Adams and the hitting of ageless wonders Wagner, Clarke, and Leach. Wagner outplayed Cobb, hitting .333 to .231 for Cobb, stealing six bases to Cobb's two, and getting six RBIs to five. Honus's six steals stood as the Series record until Lou Brock stole seven in both 1967 and 1968. The Series victory was particularly sweet for Wagner, who had vindicated himself.

The Series provided one of the most noted (probably) non-events in the October madness. The Cobb-Wagner confrontation has been hashed over countless times. This much is certain: In the fifth inning of the first game Cobb reached first. The rest is folklore that has become a morality play.

Cobb called Wagner "Krauthead," warning him that he intended to steal second on the next pitch. Wagner told "Rebel" he'd be waiting. Then Wagner laid a tag on Cobb's mouth that — depending on the version — knocked out or loosened teeth, or opened a multi-stitch cut on Cobb's lip. There are several holes in the story. First, "kraut" and "krauthead" as slurs for people of German descent didn't arise until the World Wars. Second, catcher George Gibson's throw was low and late, forcing Wagner to try a swipe tag, so he couldn't tag Cobb hard. Third is Cobb's categorical denial of the incident, noting that angering Wagner would have been foolhardy. (However, Cobb also suggested to Wagner that they go into vaudeville to re-enact the play, reasoning that they might as well make a few dollars from it.) A final objection to the tale is that a month after the Series Wagner accepted Cobb's invitation to Georgia for some hunting. Honus didn't exactly say it happened, didn't exactly say it didn't — winking and never discouraging those who "saw the whole thing."

On paper Wagner's 1910 season looks decent. Although his .320 average was his lowest since 1898, he tied teammate Bobby Byrne for the league lead in hits with 178. The season was in fact a disaster. The Pirates fell to third behind the Cubs and Giants and were never in the pennant race, finishing a distant 17½ games behind league-leading Chicago. Wagner struggled, hitting well below .300 while fielding lackadaisically, and only a late-season surge got him to acceptable territory. The Pirates attributed his subpar performance to an injury, then a lingering cold, or maybe just a slump, but the real cause was an open secret — his out-of-control drinking. Honus had more than his share of run-ins with umpires, receiving several ejections and suspensions, and some ugly confrontations with teammates. The situation was serious enough for Clarke to have a long talk with Wagner after the season.

The only good thing to come out of 1910 was the now-famous T-206 card, one of which commanded over $1 million at auction in 2000. Pirates secretary John Gruber, making $10 on the deal, sold the American Tobacco Company a picture of Wagner to reproduce in card form to be inserted in Piedmont cigarettes. Wagner, who smoked cigars and chewed but didn't like cigarettes, stopped the deal, sending Gruber a check for $10. Wagner didn't want kids buying cigarettes and didn't think they should have to pay for his picture. The few cards that got out before the print run could be stopped were snapped up and held, making the Wagner T-206 card the most prized sports card on record.

Honus had his last big seasons in 1911 and 1912, winning his final batting title in 1911 and leading the league in RBIs the next year. He hit exactly .300 in 1913, the last time he would reach that level.

Wagner and the Pirates declined together. The team fell to seventh in 1914 as Wagner hit .252. On June 9 he got his 3,000th hit, doubling against Philadelphia's Erskine Mayer to become the first player to achieve that milestone in the twentieth century. The team improved to fifth in 1915 with Honus having something of a last hurrah. Playing all 156 games, he had enough left in his battery to leg out 32 doubles and 17 triples and drive in 78 runs. The season had one highlight, as he hit a grand slam off Brooklyn's Jeff Pfeffer on July 29. Forty-one years old at the time, he was thought to be the oldest player to hit a grand slam.[1]

Clarke retired after the 1915 season. Dreyfuss brought in Jimmy Callahan, but the Pirates fell to sixth. Wagner's modest .287 was good enough for eighth in the league. Honus ended 1916 on a bright note, though, on December 31 marrying Bessie Baine Smith, whom he'd been seeing for several years.

Wagner was dubious about playing another year. Bessie's cooking was having its effect on his waistline, and he wasn't working out or hunting much. He started the season fairly well, but he and the Pirates were finished, the team dropping to the cellar while he hit .265 in just 74 games. Callahan was fired, and Honus, who had served as acting manager when Clarke was unavailable, agreed to take over, but after winning his first game and losing the next four, he told Dreyfuss the job wasn't for him. He played his last game on September 17, three innings at second base.

Wagner's final résumé included major-league records (at the time) for games, at-bats, extra-base hits, and total bases. In addition, he held National League records for doubles, triples, and batting titles (8, later tied by Tony Gwynn). He's second behind Cap Anson in hits (3,435 to 3,420), RBIs (2,075 to 1,733), and runs scored (1,999 to 1,739). His 733 stolen bases rank third behind Billy Hamilton's 914 and Arlie Latham's 742.[2]

The Wagners awaited the birth of their first child. Tragically, Elva Katrina was stillborn on January 9, 1918. Honus threw himself into war work, making speeches urging Americans to buy Liberty Bonds and becoming an entertaining speaker. Betty Baine

Wagner swung a heavy war club. Courtesy Library of Congress.

Wagner was born on December 5, 1919, followed by Virginia (Ginny) Mae on May 3, 1922. A doting father, Honus took the girls everywhere, taught them to play ball, and called them "my boys." Betty married Harry Blair in 1948 and two years later presented Bessie and Honus with Leslie Ann, their only grandchild and descendant. Answering to "Buck Jay" from an adoring Leslie, Honus read to his little sweetheart and slipped her the occasional Hershey bar.

Wagner's life after he finished playing was a mix of highs and lows. He had political jobs: state fish commissioner and sergeant-at-arms of the Pennsylvania legislature. He bought properties around Carnegie, building on them and making a decent rental income. He coached the Carnegie High School football team and the Carnegie Institute of Technology (now Carnegie Mellon University) basketball and baseball teams. Most prominent of his ventures was the sporting-goods store bearing his name. The business went through several weak phases, as Wagner lacked business sense and had some less than ideal partners. Honus and Pie Traynor, an honest man as well as a great third baseman, tried to make a go of it, but the Depression finished it off.

The Wagners were hit fairly hard by the Depression. William Benswanger, taking over the Pirates' leadership after the death of his father-in-law, Barney Dreyfuss, heard of Wagner's situation in 1933 and gave him a coaching job. Honus's first task was to make a big-league shortstop out of the hard-hitting Arky Vaughan, who went on to a Hall of Fame career. He primarily coached and encouraged the rookies, becoming a substitute father to them, and chatted with the fans. He spun yarns, like the time he scooped up a grounder in his steam-shovel hands along with grass, pebbles, and a rabbit that had run onto the field and heaved the whole mess to first, nailing a fast runner—by a "hare." Once shy, he became a fine after-dinner speaker and barroom raconteur. Age and injuries catching up with him, he retired in 1951.

Beyond Bessie and the "boys," the grandest moment of Honus's life was his election in 1936 —with Cobb, Babe Ruth, Christy Mathewson, and Walter Johnson—as one of the five charter members of the Baseball Hall of Fame. He starred at the induction ceremonies on June 12, 1939, reminiscing with the giants of a bygone era.

Honus lived out the remainder of his years at home in Carnegie, making his customary journeys to the Elks Club and the various watering holes that Pittsburgh offered. He made his last public appearance on April 30, 1955, at the unveiling of the Frank Vittor statue of him that would stand in Schenley Park outside Forbes Field. Too weak to leave the car, he waved to the crowd and left before the ceremonies ended. The 10-foot-high bronze statue atop a granite base shows Wagner following through on his swing and watching the flight of the ball. The monument later graced the entrance to Three Rivers Stadium and now greets visitors to PNC Park, the Pirates' current home.

Beset by injuries, illness, and age, Honus Wagner died in his Carnegie home at 12:56 A.M. on December 6, 1955, less than an hour after Betty's birthday. He was buried on December 9 in Jefferson Memorial Cemetery in Pleasant Hills, south of Pittsburgh.

Honus Wagner was no angel or saint. Some opponents thought him a fine fellow off the diamond but overly rough on it. Most umpires thought he "kicked" too much. He affected to dislike formal affairs, but he really hated the next morning. Yet he also embodied the American dream as the son of immigrants who rose from humble roots to greatness. Frailties aside, he was one of baseball's first heroes, a basically gentle, hard-working man, a loyal friend and teammate who treated young players kindly, dealt with adversity, inspired millions, and was devoted to Bessie, the "boys," and Leslie. Bill James in *The Historical Baseball Abstract* put it best: "[T]here is no one who has ever played this game that I would be more anxious to have on a baseball team."

Note: A slightly different version of this biography appeared in Tom Simon, ed., *Deadball Stars of the National League* (Washington, DC: Brassey's Inc., 2004).

Acknowledgments: I am grateful to Jay Brinton for helping me correct my description of Frank Vittor's statue of Wagner. Special thanks go to David Jones, Tom Simon, Russ Lake, Len Levin, and Bill Nowlin, whose editing, fact-checking, and encouragement have made this a better piece.

SOURCES

Unless noted otherwise, all statistics are from Baseball-Reference.com and Retrosheet.org.

Anderson, David W. *More Than Merkle: A History of the Most Exciting Baseball Season in Human History* (Lincoln and London: University of Nebraska Press, 2000).

DeValeria, Dennis, and Jeanne Burke DeValeria. *Honus Wagner: A Biography* (New York: Henry Holt and Company, 1995).

Fleming, G.H. *The Unforgettable Season: The Most Exciting & Calamitous Pennant Race of All Time* (New York: Holt, Rinehart and Winston, 1981).

Hageman, William. *Honus: The Life and Times of a Baseball Hero* (Champaign, Illinois: Sagamore Publishing, 1996).

Hittner, Arthur D. *Honus Wagner: The Life of Baseball's "Flying Dutchman"* (Jefferson, North Carolina, and London: McFarland, 1996).

Hoie, Bob, Carlos Bauer, et al, eds. L. Robert Davids, *The Historical Register: The Complete Major & Minor League Record of Baseball's Greatest Players* (San Diego and San Marino: Baseball Press Books, 1998).

Honig, Donald. *The Greatest Shortstops of All Time* (Dubuque, Iowa: Elysian Fields Press, 1992).

Honus Wagner Files at the Carnegie Library (Main Branch) in Pittsburgh.

Honus Wagner Files at the National Baseball Hall of Fame and Museum in Cooperstown, New York.

James, Bill. *The Bill James Historical Baseball Abstract* (New York: Villard Books, 1986).

Lieb, Frederick G. *The Pittsburgh Pirates: An Informal History* (New York: Putnam, 1948).

Meany, Tom. *Baseball's Greatest Hitters* (New York: A.S. Barnes, 1950).

_____. *Baseball's Greatest Teams* (New York: A.S. Barnes, 1949).

Ritter, Lawrence S. *The Glory of Their Times: The Story of the Early Days of Baseball Told by the Men Who Played It* (New York: Macmillan, 1966).

Thorn, John, Pete Palmer, and Michael Gershman, eds. *Total Baseball*. 7th ed. (Kingston, New York: Total Sports Publishing, 2001).

Because of the huge amount of material on Wagner, this list is necessarily selective. For an exhaustive listing, see The Baseball Index (TBI), accessible at the Society for American Baseball Research website at sabr.org.

NOTES

1 L. Robert Davids noted that Cap Anson was 42 on August 1, 1894, when he hit a grand slam (the only one of his long career) off the St. Louis Browns' Ernie Mason. For discussion see L. Robert Davids, "Young and Old Home Run Hitters" at http://research.sabr.org/journals/young-and-old-home-run-hitters. In addition, Julio Franco likely put the old-age grand slam record out of reach on June 27, 2005, when as a 46-year-old pinch-hitter he victimized the Florida Marlins and Victor De Los Santos.

2 Anson's numbers include his five years in the National Association. The figures comply with those available in November 2014. However, since research into statistics is a continually ongoing process, we must take our numbers with a grain of allowance. As Alan Schwarz admonishes us in Chapter 8 of *The Numbers Game: Baseball's Lifelong Fascination With Statistics*, "All the Record Books Are Wrong."

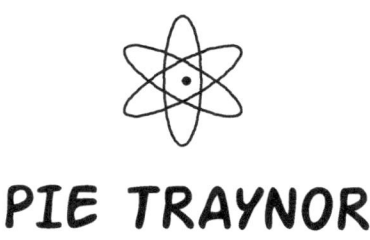

PIE TRAYNOR

By James Forr

For one generation of Pittsburghers, Pie Traynor was that tanned, silver-haired old man on *Studio Wrestling*. For another generation, he was the monotone voice that came out of the radio every evening to talk about sports. But for an older generation—and for most baseball fans outside the Pittsburgh area—he was the greatest third baseman of their time.

Harold Joseph Traynor was born on November 11, 1898, in Framingham, Massachusetts, about 22 miles west of Boston. He was the second child of 23-year-old James and 18-year-old Lydia Traynor. The Traynor family immigrated to the United States from Canada very shortly before Harold's birth, although it is unclear exactly when. Their names appear to be absent from official immigration records and later census documents are inconsistent. The border between the Maritime region and New England was quite porous at the time so it is possible they entered the country illegally.

James and Lydia would have seven children. When Harold was 5 years old, the family relocated to Somerville, three miles northwest of downtown Boston, and soon he was nagging the older boys in his neighborhood to let him join their baseball games. When they finally gave in, they put 6-year-old Harold behind the plate—without a mask. In his first game, a pitch smacked him in the mouth and knocked out two teeth.

Undeterred by that rough initiation, Harold became a fixture at the neighborhood games, where he met the man who tagged him with his memorable nickname. Reporters told several different stories about where "Pie" came from and Traynor himself told different tales depending on the day. The truth seems to be that Traynor and the other kids in his neighborhood befriended a slightly older boy named Ben Nangle, whose family owned a popular corner store. "The kids, in fact nearly everybody in town, used to gather at [the] store in the afternoon or evening," according to Traynor.[1]

Nangle sometimes would umpire the younger children's games and then parade them back to the store. When they arrived, Nangle would ask them what they wanted. Without fail, Traynor would request a slice of pie. Nangle took to calling him "Pie Face," which his buddies later shortened to "Pie." Nangle later entered the clergy but he remained a baseball fan and kept in touch with Traynor for years, occasionally giving him a heads-up on a promising young player. "Only the other day I received a note from him, asking to find a job for a kid he believes is a good prospect," said Traynor shortly after taking over as Pirates manager in 1934.[2]

James Traynor made a decent living working as a typesetter for the *Boston Transcript*, but with such a large family to feed, young Pie had to pull his weight. Starting at the age of 12, he worked after school as a messenger boy and office hand, adding a few extra dollars to the family war chest. When he wasn't at school or work, Pie played pickup baseball games on Boston Common and for his high-school team in Somerville. In 1917 the United States entered World War I. Pie, charged up with patriotism and anxious to follow his brother Edward into the military, was turned down for enlistment. Instead, he left home for the first time and ventured to Nitro, West Virginia, where he took a job as a railroad "car checker." His duties put him on horseback 12 hours a day checking the arrival and departure of railroad freight cars loaded with explosives. It was a somewhat dangerous job, and not just because of the dynamite. Traynor ended one shift covered in blood after being thrown from his horse, an accident that left a small but noticeable scar on his forehead. After a short time, Traynor returned home, taking a similar wartime job at the Boston Navy Yard.

After the war, Traynor managed to secure a tryout with the Boston Braves. "I wanted to play for the Braves ever since I was a little boy in Framingham," he said. But the tryout was a disaster. He started out by taking some groundballs during batting practice. "Then the bell rang for fielding practice and I stayed in the infield," he remembered. "I didn't even know what the bell meant. I soon found out. [Braves manager] George Stallings ran me out of there in a hurry and I was so scared I never came back."[3] Instead, he spent the summer of 1919 playing for Falmouth in the Cape League (later known as the Cape Cod League). The next spring, though, *Boston Record* sportswriter Eddie Hurley arranged for Traynor to work out with the Boston Red Sox. Veteran pitcher Joe Bush watched Traynor pick groundball after groundball during batting practice. "I grabbed a fungo stick one day and yelled to him, 'Hey, Sonny, let's see you get the ones I'm going to hit you.' The kid was amazing."[4] But veteran Red Sox shortstop Everett Scott, perhaps with an eye toward protecting his own job, told manager Ed Barrow that he wasn't all that impressed. So instead of signing Traynor, Barrow recommended him to Portsmouth of the Class-B Virginia League, a team with which the Red Sox had an unofficial but not legally binding working relationship. Traynor signed with Portsmouth for $200 a month on May 11, 1920. According to Barrow, "I made it plain [to Portsmouth owner H.P. Dawson] he belonged to Boston, even though I hadn't signed him to a Red Sox contract."[5]

Batting leadoff and playing shortstop, Traynor batted .270 in 104 games. Although his glove work was suspect (31 errors), major-league teams took notice. So Dawson, who obviously looked at Portsmouth's relationship with the Red Sox a little differently than

Pittsburgh's Pie Traynor. Courtesy Library of Congress.

Barrow did, sat back and dangled Traynor before one suitor after another. The New York Giants wanted Traynor, but refused to pay more than $7,500, an offer Dawson dismissed. Washington Senators owner Calvin Griffith, still annoyed more than a quarter-century later, claimed that Traynor should have been his. "They owed me the pick of their club in exchange for three ballplayers I sent them the summer before," Griffith griped to *Washington Post* columnist Shirley Povich in 1947. "So I picked Traynor and thought he belonged to me. Then the owner weaseled out of it. He told me I'd have to give him $5,000 extra. … If we'd have had Traynor for third base and [Ossie] Bluege for shortstop we would have won four straight pennants instead of two."[6] On September 11, 1920, it was the Pittsburgh Pirates who, on the recommendation of scout Tom McNamara, finally met Dawson's asking price, shelling out $10,000 for Traynor; up to that point it was the largest amount ever paid for a Virginia League player. Like Griffith, Barrow thought he'd been had. "I hit the ceiling. I grabbed the phone and called Dawson and called him everything I could think of."[7] He even appealed to American League President Ban Johnson, but there was nothing Johnson could do. The Red Sox had just let one of the best players of his generation slip through their fingers. "I never stopped giving Barrow the needle about his mistake," said Bush.[8]

Traynor signed a contract for $2,200 in August and joined the Pirates on September 13. Two days later, in his hometown, Traynor played in his first major-league game. When shortstop Bill McKechnie hurt his leg in the seventh inning of the second game of a doubleheader against the Boston Braves, manager George Gibson summoned Traynor. He went 1-for-2 against Braves right-hander Dana Fillingim, doubling home the Pirates' lone run in the ninth inning of a 4-1 defeat. Clearly, though, Traynor needed more seasoning. He played in 17 games with the Pirates in 1920, batting just .212. His defense was even worse; he committed 12 errors at shortstop, many on wild throws, for a ghastly fielding percentage of .860.

Traynor spent most of 1921 with the Birmingham Barons of the Class-A Southern Association, where he hit .336 and stole 47 bases. Manager Carlton Molesworth called him the best prospect he had seen in 20 years. Defensively he remained a mess, making 64 errors at shortstop. But in late August, clinging to a slim lead over the New York Giants in the standings, Pittsburgh called up the 21-year-old Traynor and thrust him right into the middle of the pennant race. The Bucs had been barely making do with rookie Clyde Barnhart at third base. Although Barnhart was a decent player who would have his moments over the years, 1921 was one of his worst seasons. Traynor almost immediately replaced Barnhart in the lineup, starting three consecutive games at third base in early September. On September 5 his throwing error in the top of the 13th inning allowed the game-winning run to score as the Pirates dropped the first game of a doubleheader to Cincinnati. Gibson benched Traynor for the second game that afternoon—and for the rest of the season. He appeared in only two more games and was an innocent bystander as the Pirates wilted down the stretch and finished four games behind the Giants. Teammate Max Carey believed Gibson gave up on Traynor way too soon: "He could play rings around Barnhart and he didn't get into any of our critical games."[9]

Gibson's loss of confidence in Traynor was especially puzzling in light of the lavish praise he heaped upon the young man a few months later. Speaking in New York in January, the Pirates manager called Traynor the only man on his roster whom he absolutely would not trade. "This boy has ability sticking out all over him," raved Gibson. "By that I mean that I can put him anywhere on my team except in the box or behind that bat."[10] Actually, Gibson really never did figure out what to do with him. No way was Traynor going to displace Rabbit Maranville at shortstop. He began spring training 1922 at second base, but he was unfamiliar with the position and played poorly. So after a couple of weeks Gibson moved him to third base. Early in the season, he played a little bit of third and a little bit of shortstop, with Maranville shifting over to play second. At the end of June, with the club struggling to play .500 ball, Pittsburgh replaced Gibson with McKechnie, who planted Traynor at third base for good. That's where he would stay for the next 13 years.

For once, Traynor's defense was not a liability. He made strides at third base as the year went along, thanks to tutoring from Maranville and McKechnie. "The hardest thing in going from shortstop to third base was learning to play that much closer to the hitter. It was important to know your hitters and station yourself correctly," said Traynor.[11] It was also around this time that he received a hitting tip from the Cardinals' Rogers Hornsby, who suggested to Traynor that he use a heavier bat. Traynor said the switch to a 42-ounce bat meant he was no longer just a pull hitter. "I began to hit line drives to right field and right center."[12] Traynor wrapped up his rookie season hitting .282—nothing special in a league where the average was .292. But he finished in the top 10 in both triples and stolen bases.

From 1923 until injuries started to take their toll around 1929, Traynor probably was the best defensive third baseman in baseball. He was 6 feet tall, which was large for a third baseman of his era, but very agile. He was brilliant at charging bunts and weakly hit groundballs, and had a knack for moving quickly to his right and making backhanded stops. "Pie had the quickest hands, the quickest arm of any third baseman," said former teammate Charlie Grimm. "And from any angle he threw strikes."[13] The Cubs' Billy Herman agreed. "Most marvelous pair of hands you'd ever want to see."[14] To columnist Red Smith, watching Traynor play third was "like looking over daVinci's shoulder."[15] Traynor led National League third basemen in assists three times, putouts seven times, and double plays four times. His biggest defensive flaw was his arm—extremely strong, but often wild; but he learned how to compensate, according to Herman. "You'd hit a shot at him, a play that he could take his time on, and he'd catch it and throw it right quick, so that if his peg was wild, the first baseman had time to get off the bag, take the throw, and get back on again. It was the only way Traynor could throw; if he took his time, he was *really* wild."[16]

Dick Bartell, who broke into the majors as a shortstop and second baseman for the Pirates from 1927 to 1930, waspishly referred to those years playing alongside Traynor as "a learning experience." Bartell didn't like Traynor much; he thought he was selfish and a bit of a phony. But his critique of Traynor's defense might have some validity. He said Traynor's quick throws on even the most routine plays caused some problems that most people wouldn't recognize. "The first baseman had to play close enough to the bag so he'd be there when the throw arrived; as soon as Pie got the ball he'd be throwing it. That forced the first baseman to play closer to first, cutting down his range. Things like that don't show up in the fielding stats." Bartell also noted that Traynor's great range sometimes caused problems for a shortstop. "A ball would be hit to me at short. As I came in to field it, Pie would cut across in front of me, trying to get it. Usually he would miss it, but as he crossed in front of me I'd lose sight of it. I was charged with plenty of errors that way. … Those were routine plays for me and most of the time he couldn't come close to making them." Bartell was a feisty guy, even as a young player; he went to Traynor and told him to back off. "Don't you call me off," Traynor supposedly snapped back. "I'll tell you what to do. I'm going to take everything I can." Bartell kept his mouth shut after that. "He wasn't my idea of a great team player. But I never called him off again."[17]

Traynor established himself as an offensive force in 1923, putting together what might have been his best overall season at the plate. He hit .338 with a career-high 12 home runs and 101 RBIs. His 19 triples tied teammate Max Carey for tops in the major leagues, and his 28 stolen bases were also a career best. Traynor, Carey, Honus Wagner, and future Pirates stars like Paul and Lloyd Waner, Roberto Clemente, and Matty Alou had lots of similarities as hitters. Not a lot of home run power, didn't necessarily walk much (although Carey and Paul Waner did), but they could drive the ball into the gaps and fly around the bases. Those kinds of hitters could thrive at a place like Forbes Field, with its cavernous outfield.

Over the winter of 1923-24, Traynor began thinking more about his post-baseball life. He turned down an offer of $700 to go on a 20-game barnstorming tour (perhaps he was insulted because Hornsby reportedly received $10,000 to play on the same team) and instead enrolled at a business school in Boston to try to earn enough credits to qualify for admission to Boston University. But when his eyes began bothering him a doctor suggested that he was studying too hard; he was advised to either drop out of school or get glasses. Traynor, so fanatical about his eyes that he avoided movie theaters, ditched school, and went to work as a traveling salesman for a couple of months.

The 1924 season was a bit of a letdown. Traynor's offensive numbers dropped off almost all the way across the board. McKechnie even benched him for a time in June. Then in the fall, he found himself in the middle of a minor controversy. Prior to the 1924 World Series, Commissioner Kenesaw Mountain Landis banned Giants outfielder Jimmy O'Connell and coach Cozy Dolan for trying to pay off Phillies shortstop Heinie Sand to "go easy" in a late-season game. Pirates owner Barney Dreyfuss piled on, accusing Dolan—and, indirectly, John McGraw—of tampering with Traynor near the end of the '23 season. Dreyfuss believed Dolan, at the behest of McGraw, had asked Traynor to hold out for a $15,000 salary in hopes that Dreyfuss would refuse and trade his third baseman to the Giants.[18] Dolan told Landis he was paying Traynor an innocent compliment, just suggesting that he deserved more money. Nothing official ever came of Dreyfuss's allegations.[19]

The Giants set the pace in the National League early in 1925, but by mid-June the Pirates were charging hard. After the Pirates beat the Giants 13-11 in 10 innings on June 16 to complete a four-game sweep), Harry Cross of the *New York Times* wrote of the Giants, "Their temperature is far above normal, respiration is alarming, blood pressure is kiting, and they are suffering from housemaid's knee and their appetites have gone blooey."[20] The rumors of the Giants' death were greatly exaggerated, though; they went back and forth with the Pirates until August. But from August 26 through September 23 Pittsburgh won 22 of 30 games, including a pair of nine-game winning streaks, and took the pennant by 8½ games. Traynor was marvelous, batting .320 with 106 RBIs, and leading third basemen in fielding percentage and total chances. His 41 double plays set a National League record for third basemen that stood for 25 years; four of those double plays came in one game, which set a major-league record later tied by Johnny Vergez in 1935. Traynor was an easy choice for *The Sporting News*' all-star team, and finished eighth in the Baseball Writers Association of America MVP voting. Just 25 years old, Traynor already was starting to receive acclaim as one of the all-time greats. In September, McGraw called him "one of the best third baseman I have ever seen."[21] McGraw's right-hand man, Hugh Jennings, agreed, calling Traynor, "the best third basemen I have seen since the days of Jimmy Collins and Bill Bradley."[22]

After having an abscess on his hip lanced in late September, Traynor was fully healthy for the World Series matchup against defending champion Washington. In Game One, Traynor homered off Walter Johnson and made a spectacular diving grab of a Muddy Ruel smash, but the Senators won, 4-1. Down three games to one, the Bucs rallied to force a classic Game Seven. In the rain and muck of Forbes Field, the Senators touched Vic Aldridge for four runs in the first inning. But Pittsburgh chipped away; in the seventh inning, Traynor rocketed an RBI triple deep into the fog to tie the game, 6-6. He was tagged out trying to stretch it into a home run. Then with the score tied 7-7 in the bottom of the eighth, Kiki Cuyler lashed a bases-loaded two-run double off a worn-out Johnson to give the Pirates their second World Series championship. Jennings called Traynor "the real hero of the series."[23] He batted .346 and gave a virtuoso performance in the field.

At spring training in Paso Robles, California, in 1926, Traynor was joined in camp by his brother Art, four years Pie's junior. Art was an infielder who had bounced around the minor leagues for a few years. His chances of making Pittsburgh's major-league roster were slim—and were reduced even further

Pittsburgh Pirates manager Harold "Pie" Traynor looking out towards the field from the dugout at Braves Field. 1938. Courtesy Leslie Jones Collection, Boston Public Library.

by injuries and immaturity. Early in the spring he sprained his ankle. Then just when his ankle had healed, he smacked his face off a bedpost while horsing around with a teammate. Another time he reported to a game stiff and sore after taking a long, jarring horseback ride through the woods. Just before the Pirates went east, they farmed him out to Columbia (South Carolina) of the Class-B South Atlantic League. Within a couple of years, Art's life had taken a sad turn. He washed out of baseball, moved to Hoboken, New Jersey, and started drinking a little too much. In May 1929 he was arrested while trying to rob a jewelry store in New York City. He pleaded guilty and was sentenced to 7½ to 15 years in Sing Sing prison.

Almost everyone from the Pirates' championship club returned in 1926, and they added the great Paul Waner to the outfield mix. But internal dissension ripped the team apart. Pirates vice president (and former player and manager) Fred Clarke was a major problem. Dreyfuss let Clarke sit in full uniform on the bench, where he forced his advice on McKechnie and delivered withering critiques of the men on the field. Some of the players couldn't stand him. In August Carey, Carson Bigbee, and Babe Adams called a meeting to try to get the players to vote to remove Clarke from the dugout. Dreyfuss got wind of the so-called player revolt, immediately released Adams and Bigbee, and sold the struggling Carey to Brooklyn. The Pirates had a two-game lead at the time, but they ended up in third place, five games behind pennant-winning St. Louis. Traynor, appointed team captain after the Carey trade, felt that the controversy drained the team. "We lost our spirit. We had no zip. We slopped around and finished third when we had the best team in the league. The players started to slump off. You never saw a great club melt away so fast."[24] Dreyfuss fired McKechnie at the end of the season and replaced him with Donie Bush.

In desperate need of rejuvenation and solitude after a frustrating year, Traynor retreated to the woods of Wisconsin to do some fishing and bird hunting. Upon returning to Boston, he found himself caught up in a whirlwind of public appearances and speaking engagements. Traynor was a gregarious, jovial man who usually enjoyed shaking hands and talking baseball. But enough was enough. "For one solid week I never went to bed before two in the morning, and never in my life did I see so much cold roast beef and potato salad."[25] So in January he left home early and fled back to Wisconsin for some more peace and quiet. Those winter treks to Wisconsin became an annual ritual; Traynor would camp there for weeks at a time, often accompanied by baseball friends like Burleigh Grimes, Dave Bancroft, and Fred Lindstrom.

The 1927 Pirates added little Lloyd Waner to the lineup. Traynor took one look at the 132-pound Waner and deemed him "too small, too thin, and too scrawny."[26] But his .355 batting average helped propel the Pirates to another National League pennant, as they edged out St. Louis and the Giants in a spirited race. Traynor batted .342, drove in 106 runs, finished seventh in the National League MVP voting, and was *The Sporting News'* all-star third baseman for the third straight season. He and Paul Waner shared a bat during the '27 season; it was one they had salvaged in the spring from Tim Hendryx, a former major leaguer playing out the string with San Francisco of the Pacific Coast League. It lasted them the entire season and then some. "We had taped it and nailed it together as long as we could," said Traynor. "I guess Paul and I must have made more than 600 hits with it."[27] Traynor was a proud bat scavenger. "I'd find one that suited me in the Giants' rack, for instance, and I'd tell Bill Terry I was taking it. What could he say but, 'Sure, go ahead, Pie."[28] In a 1931 interview, Traynor boasted that the Pirates hadn't needed to buy him a bat since he was a rookie.

In the World Series, Pittsburgh was merely fresh meat for the '27 Yankees, perhaps the greatest team ever. "We had just gone through as tough a pennant race as you could image ... and we were worn to a bone," recalled Traynor. He claimed that he was down to 150 pounds (from his normal playing weight of 170), while Paul and Lloyd Waner had shriveled to

125 and 127 pounds, respectively. "We were whipped before we took the field," Traynor remarked. Legend has it that prior to Game One the young Pirates stood in front of their dugout mesmerized as Babe Ruth and Lou Gehrig sent one towering drive after another out of the park. Traynor always asserted that was bunk. "It's just not true. We finished our batting practice and immediately went in for a clubhouse meeting."[29] There is no disputing what happened once the games began, however. The Yankees ripped through the Pirates in four straight, winning the deciding game on a wild pitch by Johnny Miljus in the bottom of the ninth. Traynor was a nonfactor in the series, going 3-for-15 with one extra-base hit, although his eighth-inning single in Game Three ended Herb Pennock's bid for a no-hitter.

The Pirates won 85 games in 1928 but fell to fourth place. Despite hitting only three home runs, Traynor piled up a career-best 124 RBIs. He also bunted a lot, leading the National League with 42 sacrifice hits (defined, until 1953, as sacrifice bunts plus sacrifice flies). Only a handful of players have ever driven in 100 runs and led their league in sacrifice hits in the same season; Traynor is the only player to do so twice, in 1927 and '28. He ended up sixth in the baseball writers' MVP voting in 1928. Traynor finished in the top 10 in the voting six times during his career, but 1928 was the closest he came to winning the award.

The next winter Pittsburgh traded shortstop Glenn Wright to Brooklyn; Bush planned to fill the hole by moving Traynor back to his original shortstop position and turning over third base to promising rookie Jim Stroner. Dreyfuss was skeptical, but Traynor was willing to give it a try. He hadn't completely forgotten how to play the position; even after becoming a full-time third baseman in 1922, he had filled in at short for a game or two here and there over the years. Stroner, though, was slow to recover from an appendectomy, and Traynor was struggling with a mysterious back ailment ("One of the couplings in his vertebrae dropped out or something," recalled Dick Bartell. "I'm not sure what it was; probably nobody else was sure either.")[30] So Traynor stayed at third in 1929, and the Pirates plugged in Bartell at shortstop. It worked out well for everyone except Stroner, who played in just six games, then vanished from the majors for good. Bartell batted .302, while Traynor came through with a mark of .356, striking out just seven times in 540 at-bats. Traynor had to cope with that sore back all season; he missed 23 games and his defense slipped a little, but he was still good enough to be named baseball's best third baseman by the baseball writers and *The Sporting News*. After the season Dreyfuss wanted him to stick around Pittsburgh for more treatment on his back—at least one doctor wanted to put him in a body cast, while another suggested eight weeks of bed rest. But Traynor said no and instead made his annual winter sojourn to Wisconsin.

A nasty eye infection had Traynor on the sidelines for several weeks during the spring of 1930. It was so bad that he could hardly see out of his left eye. Thinking that the infection stemmed from another infection in his teeth, doctors resorted to pulling two teeth in hopes of clearing the bacteria from his system; even after his vision returned to full strength, Traynor still had to wear smoked glasses to protect his eye from the sunlight. He didn't return to the lineup full time until late May, but he compiled the highest batting average (.366) and on-base percentage (.423) of his career. His most memorable day came in Philadelphia on July 23, when he hit a ninth-inning home run to win the first game of a doubleheader and then, for an encore, walloped a three-run homer in the 13th inning to win the nightcap.

As he entered his 30s, Traynor had come to assume that he would be a lifelong bachelor. Even though he was usually glib and personable, he was kind of a klutz around women; a writer for *The Sporting News* described him as "girl shy."[31] But during the summer of 1930, the 31-year-old Traynor announced his engagement to a tall, slender 25-year-old named Eve Helmer, who worked as a telephone operator at the Hotel Havlin, where the Pirates stayed on their trips to Cincinnati. Traynor had a couple of things working in his favor. First, unlike at many hotels, the switchboard at the Havlin was located in the lobby area, so it was easy for him to casually sidle over toward Eve and pass the time of day. Second, Eve was a baseball fan even before meeting Pie, so they had something to talk about. They married on January 3, 1931, honeymooned in California, and then moved on to Paso Robles for the start of spring training.

The Pirates struggled to a fifth-place finish in 1931 and Traynor was a big reason why. His defense was well below its usual standard, due in large part to a sore throwing arm that he nursed all season. It was a bit of an ordeal at the plate for him, too; for the first time in seven seasons, Traynor fell short of the .300 mark, at .298. Nonetheless, he drove in over 100 runs (103, to be precise) for the fifth straight year; among third baseman, only Traynor and the Atlanta Braves' Chipper Jones would be able to make that claim. The offseason was a challenging one for the organization, full of changes. The Pirates fired manager Jewel Ens and although Traynor was reported to be one of the front-runners for the job, the Bucs surprised most observers by rehiring George Gibson. They sold veteran infielder George Grantham and brought in 20-year-old Arky Vaughan to play shortstop. Then in February, Dreyfuss died of complications following surgery. Traynor spend much of the winter in Los Angeles, reporting to Wrigley Field regularly to let Angels trainer Frankie Jacobs work his arm back into shape.

Traynor and the Pirates both enjoyed nice recoveries in 1932. Although a sore shoulder in late May snapped his streak of 317 consecutive games played, Traynor boosted his average back up to .329, tightened up his defense a bit, and finished third (behind Chuck Klein and Lefty O'Doul) in the balloting for *The Sporting News*' National League MVP. Against the Boston Braves on August 30, he recorded his 2,000th career hit. The Pirates entered August leading the National League by 5½ games, but a 10-20 record that month doomed them to second place, four games behind Chicago. The Cincinnati Reds wanted Traynor as their player-manager for 1933, but Traynor said he wasn't interested — and even if he were, Pirates management wasn't about to let him go. In '33, the Pirates again came home in second place, this time five games behind the Giants. Traynor hit .304 and was named to his seventh and final *Sporting News* all-star team. On July 6 he appeared as a pinch-hitter in the inaugural major-league All-Star Game at Comiskey Park, doubling off Lefty Grove in the seventh inning.

The Pirates started strong in 1934. On May 24 they moved into first place, thanks in part to a reinvigorated Traynor, who was batting .469 (Traynor had played in only 13 games by this point thanks to a shoulder that sometimes hurt so much that he could hardly sleep). By June, though, the Pirates were in a tailspin and the fans, frustrated by the near misses of '32 and '33, had turned on Gibson. At a June 17 game, which the Pirates lost, 9-3, a crowd of 16,000 booed Gibson lustily every time he stuck his head out of the dugout. Two days later, with the Pirates 27-24 but losers of seven of their last eight games, Pirates president Bill Benswanger released Gibson and asked a stunned Traynor to take over as player-manager. (Officially, the Pirates said Gibson had resigned, but he admitted to friends that he had been fired.) The transition of power was unusually amicable. Traynor, Gibson, and Benswanger emerged from their meeting and addressed the team together. Gibson shook Traynor's hand and asked permission to stop by and hang around the clubhouse from time to time, which Traynor said was fine. "I accept [the job] gladly … when I realize there is no hard feeling between me and George Gibson, for whom I have always had great respect," said Traynor.[32] He named first baseman Gus Suhr the new captain, spent 30 minutes posing for photographers in the dugout, then went 2-for-5 as the Pirates lost their first game for their new skipper, 5-3 to the Giants, and tumbled into fifth place.

Traynor promised a more aggressive style of baseball: "We have a fast team and we must take advantage of our speed if we're going to get anywhere." *The Sporting News*, however, noted an even more pressing need: "Something must be done about that Buc pitching staff pronto."[33] Traynor didn't disagree. "We're going to spend our time hunting for a couple of fellows who can throw that ball past hitters with plenty of smoke on it."[34]

Pittsburgh fans were excited about their new manager. "The man with the smile always wins," declared one man, "and that's Pie Traynor for you all over."[35] Traynor's wife, Eve, wasn't quite so sanguine. "I'll worry more than ever now, because Pie is a worrier. He worried so much as a player, think what he'll do as a manager."[36] Traynor did give the team a short-term boost. Inserting veteran Waite Hoyt into the rotation proved to be a wise move. He also pulled aside the notoriously free-swinging Lloyd Waner and asked him to be more selective at the plate; Waner took the advice to heart and walked 12 times over his next 18 games. The Bucs won 10 of their first 16 games under Traynor; however, much of that record was built up against second-division punching bags Cincinnati and Philadelphia. During one of those games in Philadelphia he suffered an injury from which he would never fully recover. Traynor overslid the plate on a close play at home, and as he reached back to touch it, catcher Jimmie Wilson fell on his arm. "I felt something snap and was certain I had a broken arm," said Traynor. "I didn't, but I couldn't throw well anymore."[37]

Just when it appeared Pittsburgh was crawling back into the race, the Pirates lost nine straight in July and freefell out of contention, eventually finishing in fifth place. Traynor ended the year with a .309 batting average, down from .320 when he assumed managerial duties. He appeared in his last All-Star Game that summer, playing all nine innings and carving out a place in the record books. His steal of home in the fifth inning (part of a double steal with Mel Ott) remains the only steal of home in All-Star Game history.

Through it all, Traynor appeared to be teetering on the edge of nervous breakdown. As it turned out, Eve really knew her man. Traynor was, in many ways, psychologically unsuited for the role of major-league manager. By August he had lost 10 pounds in two months, appeared remarkably gaunt, and had all but stopped sleeping. "I can't help it," said a desperate Traynor. "I go to bed at night and can't get to sleep. Often I awaken more tired than when I crawled between the sheets. I'm of a nervous temperament at all times and piloting a team which isn't going anywhere has taken its toll."[38] When the season was over he admitted, "I often wished I was just a player again with no other worries."[39]

Another of Traynor's shortcomings as a manager was that he was just too nice a guy; players walked all over him. According to Al Abrams of the *Pittsburgh Post-Gazette*, "Pie's tactics would have gone over great with a high school or college athlete where he would have been looked up to as a hero and leader, but with a gang of thoroughly hardened, grown-up men, driving leadership is sometimes required."[40] Traynor's teams were notorious carousers and troublemakers. They also earned a reputation, fair or not, for underachieving. "His players didn't respect him," said Bartell. "When one got into a brawl and wound up in the police station, Pie would bail him out and keep it quiet. No fines. No suspensions. No leadership."[41] Traynor defended himself against charges that he didn't yell at his players enough. "I won't do it and ruin some of my men. I tell them when they're wrong but I'm not going to browbeat them."[42]

Traynor hired former Pirates manager Jewel Ens as a coach for the 1935 season. Ens would prove to be an invaluable sounding board for Traynor. On the road they would rehash every game as they walked together from the ballpark back to the hotel. Traynor played in 57 games in 1935, but the Pirates likely would have been better off if he hadn't. He batted around .230 for much of the year. A late surge got him up to .279, but that was still the lowest mark of his career for a full season. Worse, his arm was completely gone. He made 18 errors in just 49 games at third base. By July the pitching staff had imploded, the fans were booing, and Traynor's weight was plummeting. The Bucs got hot in late August, winning 10 straight and moving to within six games of first; but ultimately they finished in fourth place, in line with most preseason predictions, at 86-67.

Over the winter Traynor made a regrettable trade, sending rookie right-hander Claude Passeau, catcher Earl Grace, and $25,000 to the Phillies for 33-year-old catcher Al Todd. Traynor spent every offseason as a manager looking for a staff ace; he had one in Passeau (who won 162 games in a 13-year major-league career), didn't recognize it, and never found anyone else as good. Reporters constantly got Pirate fans in a tizzy with rumors of one big-name pitcher or another coming to Pittsburgh, but it never worked out. In November 1934 Traynor blundered when he turned down the Giants' offer of All-Star left-hander Carl Hubbell for pitcher Larry French and outfielder Fred Lindstrom. Hubbell went on to win 71 games for New York over the next three seasons. Two years later the Bucs made a play for brilliant right-hander Dizzy Dean, but the Cardinals' demand of Arky Vaughan, six other players, and $175,000 proved too much. Traynor's bids for other star pitchers like Paul Derringer, Van Lingle Mungo, and Hal Schumacher also fell short. Nor were the Pirates able to develop any great young arms in-house. Traynor was good at squeezing an extra year or two out of retreads like Hoyt, Red Lucas, and Jim Weaver; but he never found a long-term solution to his mound problems. In 1937, *New York Times* columnist John Kieran noted that the Pirates needed to find more pitching to contend, but remarked that Traynor had "a better chance of finding 12 oil wells in his cellar."[43]

Traynor's playing days quietly melted away. He spent the 1935-36 offseason working with doctors in Cincinnati and California trying to get his arm in shape. He came to spring training with plans to play if he had to, but Cookie Lavagetto and perennial prospect Bill Brubaker showed enough promise at third base that Traynor decided not to take the field at all in 1936, although he kept himself on the active roster. In July 1937 injuries forced Traynor back into the lineup for a series against the Dodgers. He hadn't taken infield or batting practice in weeks and admitted before his first game back, "I'm nervous as a bride. I'm really a little scared."[44] Batting eighth, he went 2-for-12 in the series and made a couple of nice defensive plays in the finale, but he hurt his finger fielding a line drive late in that game and was back on the bench the next day. On August 14 he entered a game in St. Louis as a pinch-runner, scored the game-winning run on a Paul Waner single, and that was it. The Pirates didn't need him to play anymore that season, and as he prepared to sign his contract for 1938, he specified that it was to be a managerial contract only. With no fanfare, Traynor the player was done. His career totals over 17 seasons included 2,416 hits, a batting average of .320, and 1,863 games played at third base, a major-league record that would stand until 1960. At the time, his 1,273 RBIs were second only to Honus Wagner in Pirates history.

After fourth- and third-place finishes in 1936 and 1937, Traynor was feeling the pressure even more than usual. Pittsburgh fans were tired of teams that were good, but not good enough, and Traynor supposedly admitted to friends he thought he needed to win a pennant in 1938 to keep his job. The season didn't start well. Pittsburgh's most dependable starter, Cy Blanton, reported to spring training overweight. Russ Bauers, a talented but goofy right-hander who Traynor thought had "as much stuff as Dizzy Dean," burned his hand while lighting a match. A few weeks later Bauers got liquored up with some teammates on a train, got into a friendly wrestling match, and hurt his knee. The Pirates, as they had the year before, got off to a fast start; they won their first seven games. By late May, though, they had slipped below .500 and a frazzled Traynor, who had been ejected from only two games in the previous 16 years, was thrown out twice in a span of four days. But the Pirates caught fire in June and July, going 40-14 over those months, including a 13-game winning streak. They entered September with a comfortable seven-game lead over the Chicago Cubs.

Chicago player-manager Gabby Hartnett returned from a broken thumb in September, and the Cubs immediately started playing their best baseball of the year. But still, seven games seemed a lot to overcome.

Giants manager Bill Terry joked that the Pirates ought to quit baseball if they blew the lead. Traynor was irate when he read that, but a lot people agreed with Terry. On September 21, with the lead down to 3½ games, Shirley Povich wrote in the *Washington Post* that the World Series was coming to Pittsburgh "unless the Pirates suffer a complete collapse." The next day Roscoe McGowen of the *New York Times* predicted that nothing short of "the greatest flop in history" would keep the Pirates from the pennant. A *Chicago Tribune* headline blared "Cubs Must Work Miracle." The Pirates moved ahead with the sale of World Series tickets (they sold $1.5 million worth) and the construction of special bleachers at Forbes Field. But the Cubs didn't care. They just kept on winning.

Traynor was showing a bold front. "We have the edge and will continue to have it as long as we're in first place," Traynor bragged. "You can call it confidence or spirit, we have both."[45] Privately, though, the team was a basket case. Benswanger was taking two different anti-anxiety medications. Traynor had dropped almost 20 pounds and was smoking like a fiend. With Al Todd wearing down, coach Johnny Gooch begged Traynor to activate him and let him catch instead of Todd, and some of the players agreed with him. The Pirates' lead was down to 1½ games going into a late-September series in Wrigley Field, and even rookie pitcher Rip Sewell could see the team was in trouble. According to Sewell, "I pleaded with Pie to use me in that series, but I could understand when he told me he simply had to go with his regular starters."[46] On September 27 the Cubs won the first game of the series, 2-1, to close to within a half-game. Then the next day, with darkness approaching, Hartnett smacked a Mace Brown pitch over the wall in the bottom of the ninth to give the Cubs a 6-5 victory. The home run became known in Cubs lore as "The Homer in the Gloamin'." Although Pittsburgh still had five games remaining, that blow by Hartnett shattered their spirit. The Cubs won the next day, 10-1, and officially clinched the pennant on October 1.

Reflecting on the pennant race 22 years later, Traynor was philosophical. "We really didn't rate being up there. We were scrappy, but not a sound team in personnel."[47] But at the time he was devastated. "No one knows what starts such a thing like that, and after it starts there's not a thing in the world you can do about it except just sit and suffer."[48] Traynor ran into Detroit pitcher Bobo Newsom in the offseason and told him, "I wish I had a complete-game pitcher like you last September. We wouldn't have lost that National League pennant."[49] Traynor also blamed Todd for questionable pitch-calling down the stretch, and traded his catcher to the Boston Bees over the winter. "Traynor had to put the rap on somebody and he made me the goat," Todd fired back. "It's a funny thing to me why he let me catch [more games] than any other catcher in the league the last two seasons if I was so lousy behind the plate."[50]

In light of the supposed weakness of the 1938 Pirates' pitchers and catchers, it is worthy to note an incident that happened before the season ever began. Over the winter, Chester Washington of the black newspaper the *Pittsburgh Courier* sent Traynor the following telegram:

"KNOW YOUR CLUB NEEDS PLAYERS STOP HAVE ANSWER TO YOUR PRAYERS RIGHT HERE IN PITTSBURGH STOP JOSH GIBSON CATCHER FIRST BASE B. LEONARD AND RAY BROWN PITCHER OF HOMESTEAD GRAYS AND S. PAIGE PITCHER COOL PAPA BELL OF PITTSBURGH CRAWFORDS ALL AVAILABLE AT REASONABLE FIGURES STOP WOULD MAKE PIRATES FORMIDABLE PENNANT CONTENDERS STOP WHAT IS YOUR ATTITUDE? STOP WIRE ANSWER"

Traynor never responded, which earned him a rebuke from noted Negro League historian John Holway. In fairness, the decision to integrate the major leagues is not one Traynor could have made independently. The next summer he told the *Pittsburgh Courier*, "It is a known fact that there are plenty of Negroes capable of playing in the big leagues" and that he would sign them if only he could.[51] Not quite a decade later, when Traynor was working as a sportscaster, he used his radio pulpit to urge the Pirates to follow the lead of the Brooklyn Dodgers and integrate their organization by signing a pair of local black players, Maurice Peatros and Joe Atkins. In his later years Traynor enjoyed a good relationship with minority players like Roberto Clemente and Willie Stargell. Maybe he could have pushed harder for the Pirates to integrate in 1938; at the very least he should have afforded Washington the courtesy of a response. But by no means was he a virulent racist. Nevertheless, with Josh Gibson catching instead of Al Todd and with Satchel Paige in the rotation instead of, say, Cy Blanton or Jim Tobin, the 1938 pennant race could have turned out much differently.

Benswanger stood by his manager after the Pirates' implosion, saying "We … do not blame him in the slightest for the loss of the pennant."[52] Reportedly, the Pirates even raised Traynor's salary from $16,500 to $18,000. In spring training, Traynor tried to set a new tone for his club, releasing veteran pitcher Ed Brandt for violating curfew. "I'm sick and tired of these playboys and I'm going to have discipline if I have to run one or two more players off the squad," Traynor vowed.[53] But he couldn't wipe the slate clean; after the 1938 collapse he seemed to have lost confidence in his team and perhaps himself: "Even if we're out in front by ten games next September 1, we'll keep looking back over our shoulders."[54] First baseman Elbie Fletcher, who came over from the Bees in June, observed, "That's all they talked about on that Pirate club that year: Hartnett's home run. I knew they weren't going to win it. That home run was still on everybody's mind, haunting them like a ghost."[55] The Bucs hung around the periphery of the pennant race for a while, but a 12-game losing streak in August doomed the Pirates to their worst finish in 22 years.

By late September Traynor was a dead man walking. As Bob Considine of the *Washington Post* so delicately put it, "Even the dear lady fans, who possess a persevering kind of baseball dumbness, knew that Pie was getting the old brass-knuckle sandwich."[56] On September 28, exactly one year removed from Hartnett's crushing homer, Traynor went to Benswanger, tendered his resignation, and accepted a job within the organization as a scout. The *Pittsburgh Post-Gazette* reported that Traynor, gracious to the end, knew he was done and chose to quit to make it easier on his old friend Benswanger. Traynor issued a statement assuring everyone that "a change in managers will put the club up where it belongs and give the fans of the Pittsburgh district a better brand of baseball."[57] Privately, he was miserable. "Some fellows can say, 'Oh, what the heck.' But for me, something died down here (pointing to his heart). I'm like a kid. It really hurt."[58]

Traynor probably didn't relish the thought of being out of uniform for the first time in 20 years. He met with Leo Durocher about a job on the Brooklyn Dodgers coaching staff. Durocher offered him the position, but Traynor turned it down. Over the next couple of years his name was mentioned in conjunction with minor-league managerial openings in Seattle, Buffalo, and Albany, but ultimately he remained with the Pirates. He mostly was responsible for scouting within a 100-mile radius of Pittsburgh, but he spent a good deal of time at his home near Cincinnati. After a couple of years of scouting, he seemed restless to move on. In October 1942, with the United States engaged in World War II, Traynor tried to enlist in the Army but he was rejected because of his age. Then in 1943, he and the Pirates parted ways. According to Pirates vice president Sam Watters, "[In December] he told us he had a couple of offers. We told him to go ahead and take one of them if he wished."[59] Millions of young men were overseas, and minor-league teams were folding; there just weren't enough players to fill the rosters. With fewer minor leaguers, teams needed fewer scouts, so the Pirates weren't unhappy to see Traynor go. In November 1943, he took a job in Cincinnati at the United States Playing Card Company, whose plant had been converted to the production of airplane parts. He vowed to return to baseball after the war.

For Traynor, World War II was a time of transition. Soon, he would come back to Pittsburgh and embark on his second career—broadcasting. In 1944 one of Traynor's old friends, former Pittsburgh sportswriter Jimmy Murray, took over as manager of KQV Radio and contacted Traynor about an opening for a sports director. Traynor came to Pittsburgh, auditioned, and reached a handshake agreement. In January 1945 KQV announced that Traynor would begin broadcasting six days a week on KQV. He had a 15-minute sports broadcast every weeknight at 6:30 and a 30-minute show on Saturday morning in the spring and summer called *The Pie Traynor Club*, during which he talked baseball with local kids. The job came at an opportune moment; Traynor needed the money. His salary had always been modest by major-league standards, he had absorbed a big hit during the stock market collapse, and the sporting-goods store he owned with Honus Wagner had gone under in just two years. Pittsburgh embraced Traynor again. About 100 people—including two judges, a state senator, Pittsburgh Steelers owner Art Rooney, and some of his friends from baseball—welcomed him home with a raucous celebratory dinner that lasted into the wee hours of the morning. He made his on-air debut the following evening, and remained at KQV for the next 21 years.

Pittsburghers loved to listen to Traynor, and his ratings usually were very good. But he was never a smooth, golden voice. Frankly, his style was a little rough. His spoke in a monotone and never used a script, contending, "I think the fans like it better when you speak straight from the heart."[60] That would have been fine, except he admitted that he always got nervous when it was time to go on the air, which sometimes made for some awkward-sounding radio. One day Traynor was interviewing a boxer who was absolutely petrified; Traynor's first question was met with absolute silence. So was the second. And the third. But Traynor kept plowing forward, bombarding the poor guy with one question after another. "We got calls from people thinking something had gone wrong with their radio because they could only hear one side of the conversation," said former KQV news director Alan Boal.[61] In 1964 KQV's new program director, John Rook, arrived in Pittsburgh from Denver. As he drove into the city for the first time he tuned to his new station, which spent most of the day playing hit records; he couldn't believe what was coming out of his radio. "I strained to hear the voice of a hesitant old man announcing the day's sporting news. A pause that seemed like an eternity was broken only by the shuffle of his script, as he began to voice a commercial for a local steakhouse," wrote Rook. "Clearly, the announcer didn't do much for the tempo of the station. ... I made a note to inquire first thing the following morning to find out who this man was and why was he on KQV." Rook met Traynor for lunch the next day, and as they walked to the restaurant he learned why the station had kept this "hesitant old man" on the air for so long. "Folks along the way offered their greeting to Pie; even the corner traffic cop tipped his hat as he stopped traffic for us during the noontime rush."[62]

Actually, anyone who lived in Pittsburgh during the 1950s or 1960s probably saw Traynor walking at one time or another. He never learned how to drive. "I was afraid I'd find an excuse not to walk, which I always found so enjoyable, so relaxing and healthful."[63] He lived about five miles from the KQV studios and, for a while, sometimes took public transportation to work. But during a transit strike in the mid '50s he started walking to work and never stopped. His endurance was legendary and sometimes pushed the limits of sanity. Once when he was in New York City to file reports from the World Series, he walked 127 blocks from his hotel on 34th Street to Yankee Stadium on 161st. It took him 3½ hours. "Sure, I was tired when I got there, but I was loosened up and relaxed."[64] Even as a player and manager he occasionally hoofed it from Ebbets Field in Brooklyn to the Alamac Hotel in uptown Manhattan. St. Louis sportswriter Bob Broeg suspected Traynor was "part mountain goat."[65] A chance encounter on the sidewalk with Pie Traynor was part of life in Pittsburgh. The *Pittsburgh Post-Gazette*'s Roy McHugh strolled alongside one day as Traynor roamed the streets like a pied piper, surrounded by a kaleidoscopic gaggle of friends and fans. "Wherever he may be," McHugh wrote, "Traynor has chain conversations, the other participants coming and going, new faces joining in the dialogue or making way for another."66

In February 1948 Traynor received baseball's highest honor — induction into the Hall of Fame. He received 93 of 121 votes, just over the required 75 percent, to become the first third baseman elected to the Hall by the writers. (Jimmy Collins got the nod from the Veterans Committee in 1945.) Traynor's induction ceremony did not occur until June 13, 1949, when he and the late Herb Pennock were officially enshrined along with the Hall of Fame class of 1949 (Three-Finger Brown, Kid Nichols, and Charlie Gehringer). Traynor got the biggest ovation of the day and made a 40-word acceptance speech that was over in seconds.

During the late '40s, Traynor was comfortably settling into the role of "Mr. Pittsburgh." The man was everywhere. He became a sort of professional raconteur, traveling all over western Pennsylvania, often several nights a week, speaking to clubs and fraternal organizations. In 1946 he was appointed Allegheny County's recreation supervisor for county parks, which paid him about $3,300 a year to set up baseball schools for area kids, modeled after those that Rogers Hornsby ran in Chicago. He remained in that post for about 18 months, until general manager Roy Hamey welcomed him back into the Pirates family as a scout and goodwill ambassador. Traynor's responsibilities were light; he ran tryout camps and baseball schools, and represented the team at public events. Traynor had a chance to get back into uniform at least once, when the Cincinnati Reds offered him a coaching position in 1948; but between the radio gig and his work with the Pirates, Traynor was content.

In the early '50s, Traynor helped found the Pittsburgh Professional Baseball Association, a group dedicated to raising money for a statue of Honus Wagner, which was unveiled outside Forbes Field on April 30, 1955, seven months before Wagner's death; it remain standing in 2015 outside PNC Park in Pittsburgh. In the spring of 1957 Traynor joined the Pirates as a special instructor at their training camp in Fort Myers, Florida. It was his first trip to spring training in nearly 20 years. Traynor's first assignment was to work with Frank Thomas and Gene Freese on their defense at third base. That particular project wasn't too successful; but until his death, Traynor came back to Florida for a couple of weeks every spring, putting on the uniform, riding the team bus on road trips, umpiring intrasquad games, and for many years taping interviews and reports for KQV. Unlike a lot of old-timers, Traynor refused to mire himself in the past. "The ballplayers have changed but the talent is always there," he observed. "I guess I have a soft spot for the old timers but I respect the kids playing today."67 They respected him, too. On June 19, 1972, Roberto Clemente passed Traynor for second place on the Pirates' all-time RBI list, but refused to acknowledge the standing ovation. "The man whose record I broke was a great ballplayer, a great fellow. And he just died here a few months ago. That's why I didn't even tip my cap."68

Traynor lost his radio job in 1966. ABC, which owned KQV, preferred Howard Cosell and his syndicated sports show. According to Rook, "They argued that Pie was limited to mostly Pirate and/or baseball information; and Cosell covered the full gamut of sports, especially Muhammad Ali and football, that Pie ignored." On top of that, Rook noted that Traynor, by then in his mid-60s, was having a tougher time getting around. "During some cold and snowy days, Pie found it difficult to make the walk from his home to the studios, and a daily 5:55 P.M. five-minute program became less than reliable."69

But by the time of his departure from KQV, Traynor's broadcast career had already taken a new, bizarre turn — into the world of professional wrestling. Every Saturday night, Pittsburgh television station WIIC broadcast *Studio Wrestling* to homes throughout western Pennsylvania. The great Bruno Sammartino was the show's big star, with "bad guys" like Killer Kowalski and George "The Animal" Steele as his foils. Traynor announced the matches alongside local TV legend Bill Cardille. "He liked nothing more than to stop and chat with little old ladies about pro wrestling," *Pittsburgh Post-Gazette* sports editor Al Abrams said of Traynor.[70] To baseball people who sniffed at the thought of Traynor getting involved with such a shady venture, he would wink and say, "Wrestling. That's the only honest game left." Traynor also turned into a popular local TV pitchman. His spots for American Heating Company were particularly memorable and unavoidable; Traynor's tagline—"Who can? Ameri-can!"—became part of Pittsburghers' lexicon.

In 1969 Traynor received what he once called his highest honor when he was named the third baseman on Major League Baseball's all-time team. Two years later he threw out the first pitch of Game Three of the 1971 World Series at Three Rivers Stadium. Then on November 20 of that year, Pittsburgh sportswriters held a "Night for Pie," which brought 16 Hall of Famers to town to pay tribute to their old friend. The writers sent Traynor a check from the profits of that evening, but Traynor sent it back, insisting, "The night alone was a whole lot more than any person could have expected."[71]

By this time years of smoking were catching up with Traynor. The first sign of trouble came in 1958, when he was hospitalized with what was termed an "asthmatic condition." Although outwardly Traynor appeared to be in wonderful physical condition, his breathing continued to deteriorate; eventually he was diagnosed with emphysema. A few days after the writers' dinner, he was put in intensive care. Newspapers said he was suffering from a "respiratory ailment," but that didn't do justice to the gravity of his condition; physicians had to perform a heart massage to keep him alive. Nevertheless, Traynor headed to Bradenton, Florida, for spring training in 1972 as though everything was OK; as usual, he worked with the infielders and mingled with fans, signing autographs. A discussion he had with writer Bob Broeg gives some insight into Traynor's perspective on his health at that time. Traynor emceed a banquet honoring living Hall of Famers. He was on top of his game that night, spicing up their affair with jokes and colorful memories. After the dinner Broeg congratulated Traynor on an admirable performance, especially given Traynor's advanced emphysema. "I don't have emphysema," replied Traynor.[72] Traynor returned to Pittsburgh on March 11 to be inducted into the Fraternal Order of Eagles' Hall of Fame. Five days later he was visiting a friend when he collapsed onto a couch. His host discovered him unconscious and called police, who administered oxygen as they rushed him to Shadyside Hospital. Traynor never regained consciousness and was pronounced dead at 5:34 P.M. He was survived by his wife, Eve (who died in 1977), and three brothers. He had no children.

Down in Bradenton, the Pirates were stunned by Traynor's death. "I just couldn't believe it when I heard that Pie died. I just couldn't believe it," said Willie Stargell.[73] Third baseman Richie Hebner took Traynor's passing especially hard. "I guess Pie took a liking to me because I came from Massachusetts and so did he. I used to enjoy listening to his stories."[74] Not only did Hebner and Traynor share the same home state and the same position, but Hebner also wore Traynor's uniform number 20. "I told Pie they should have retired his number. ... The guy would have gotten a kick out of that ... but he seemed to want me to wear it. Pie never wanted to make a big thing out of it."[75] (The Pirates posthumously retired Traynor's number at the 1972 home opener). Former teammates were stunned, too. "It's a big shock," remarked Max Carey. "Pie Traynor was not only a great ballplayer, he was a great human being. He was a superstar before anybody knew what a superstar was."[76] "When I heard tonight that he had died it kinda made me feel like crying," admitted Lloyd Waner.[77] At the funeral, Rabbi Solomon Freehof, a friend of Traynor's who delivered the eulogy, noted, "It was surprising that the newspaper articles printed since his death dealt mostly with the inner man and his friendliness."[78] At the conclusion of the service, Eve carefully removed three roses from a floral arrangement: "For third base. And we were married on the third."[79]

Traynor's reputation as a third baseman has taken a bit of a beating in recent years. Although people once called Traynor the best third baseman in history, Bill James ranks him just 15th. A discussion on the Baseball Think Factory website indicates there are some very knowledgeable fans who think Traynor is grossly overrated, some who don't even consider him a worthy Hall of Famer. There are several explanations for this. For one, almost everyone who saw Traynor play is dead; there are no World Series highlight films or former teammates to remind us of how good he was. For another, although he was unquestionably a brilliant third baseman during his peak years, his career defensive stats aren't anything special. At the end of his career his arm was dead, his reflexes had slowed, and his fielding percentage and range factor were below the league average for several years. But most importantly, third basemen ain't what they used to be. During Traynor's career, third base was primarily a defensive position; anything a third baseman could do at the plate usually was considered a bonus. That changed during the second half of the 20th century, when third base became a sluggers' position. It is interesting to note that on James's list, the only pre-1930 player listed ahead of Traynor is Frank Baker. Baker probably was better, but not by much. So for a long time those who called Traynor the greatest third baseman in history could make a very legitimate case. But not now. Traynor's numbers pale against those of modern third basemen like Eddie Mathews, George Brett, Mike Schmidt, and Chipper Jones.

If the Beatles had released "Please Please Me" or "She Loves You" in 2015 instead of 1963, we never would have heard of them. Those songs sound terribly dated today; people don't make music that sounds like that anymore. Times change. But that doesn't diminish the Beatles' legacy or the historic significance of those early recordings; in the context of their time, they were amazing. Similarly, in the context of his time, Pie Traynor was an amazing third baseman. Although history might have overrated Traynor for a while, today the pendulum seems to have swung a little too far in the other direction. No discussion of great third basemen should exclude him.

SOURCES

Alexander, Charles. *John McGraw* (New York, London: Viking, 1988).

Barrow, Edward Grant. *My Fifty Years in Baseball* (New York: Coward-McCann, Inc., 1951).

Bartell, Dick, and Norman Macht. *Rowdy Richard* (Berkeley, California: North Atlantic Books, 1987).

baseballlibrary.com

baseball-reference.com

baseballthinkfactory.org/files/primer/discussion/24808/teams/phi.html

Boal, Alan. Telephone interview with author, February 18, 2006.

Boston Globe

Chicago Tribune

DeValeria, Dennis and Jeanne. *Honus Wagner* (New York: Henry Holt & Company, 1995).

Holway, John B. *Josh and Satch* (Westport, Connecticut, and London: Meckler Publishing, 1991).

Honig, Donald. *Baseball When the Grass was Real* (New York: Coward, McCann, and Geoghegan, 1975).

James, Bill. *The New Bill James Historical Baseball Abstract* (New York: The Free Press, 2001).

johnrook.com

Kelley, Brent. *The Negro Leagues Revisited* (Jefferson, North Carolina: McFarland & Company, 2000).

Lanctot, Neil. *Negro League Baseball* (Philadelphia: University of Pennsylvania Press, 2004).

Los Angeles Times

Markusen, Bruce. *Roberto Clemente: The Great One* (Sports Publishing, LLC, 2001).

New York Times

Parker, Clifton Blue. *Big and Little Poison* (Jefferson, North Carolina: McFarland & Company, 2003).

Pie Traynor player file at the National Baseball Hall of Fame and Museum, Cooperstown, New York.

Pittsburgh Post-Gazette

Pittsburgh Press

Pittsburgh Tribune Review

Rook, John; email correspondence, April 23, 2005.

The Sporting News

United States Census, 1910 and 1920.

Washington Post

NOTES

1. *Pittsburgh Press*, June 21, 1934.
2. Ibid.
3. *New York Times*, July 12, 1934.
4. *The Sporting News*, January 28, 1967.
5. Ed Barrow and James Kahn, *My Fifty Years in Baseball* (New York: Coward-McCann, 1951), 113.
6. *Washington Post*, March 1, 1939.
7. Barrow, 113
8. *The Sporting News*, January 28, 1967.
9. Greene, Lee, "At Third Base, Pie Traynor," *Sport*, July 1962.
10. *The Sporting News*, January 5, 1922.
11. *The Sporting News*, August 2, 1969.
12. Bob Broeg, *Super Stars of Baseball* (St. Louis: Sporting News, 1971), 255.
13. Ibid.
14. Donald Honig, *Baseball When the Grass was Real* (New York: Berkley Publishing, 1974), 129.
15. *Washington Post*, August 31, 1971.
16. Clifton Blue Parker, *Big and Little Poison* (Jefferson, North Carolina: McFarland, 2003), 163.
17. Dick Bartell and Norman Macht, *Rowdy Richard: The Story of Dick Bartell* (Berkeley California: North Atlantic Books, 1993), 70.
18. *Washington Post*, October 3, 1924.
19. *The Sporting News*, October 16, 1924.
20. *New York Times*, June 17, 1925.
21. *Los Angeles Times*, September 13, 1925.
22. *New York Times*, October 17, 1925.
23. Ibid.
24. Bartell and Macht, 43.
25. *Los Angeles Times*, October 20, 1927.
26. Parker, 66.
27. *Los Angeles Times*, December 16, 1931.
28. Harry Keck, "Stolen Bats Sweetest: Traynor," *Baseball Digest*, July 1945.
29. *New York Times*, October 5, 1960.
30. Bartell and Macht, 69.
31. *The Sporting News*, January 8, 1931.
32. *Washington Post*, June 20, 1934.
33. *The Sporting News*, June 21, 1934.
34. *Pittsburgh Press*, June 20, 1934.
35. *Pittsburgh Post-Gazette*, June 20, 1934.
36. *Pittsburgh Post-Gazette*, March 17, 1936.
37. *The Sporting News*, August 2, 1969.
38. *The Sporting News*, August 9, 1934.
39. *The Sporting News*, November 15, 1934.
40. *Pittsburgh Post-Gazette*, October 2, 1939.
41. Bartell and Macht, 55.
42. *The Sporting News*, July 23, 1936.
43. *New York Times*, March 14, 1937.
44. *Pittsburgh Press*, July 21, 1937.
45. *Chicago Tribune*, September 28, 1938.
46. *The Sporting News*, November 30, 1949.
47. *The Sporting News*, October 5, 1960.
48. *Chicago Tribune*, September 20, 1938.
49. *Washington Post*, January 7, 1939.
50. *Los Angeles Times*, March 26, 1939.
51. Neil Lanctot, *Negro League Baseball* (Philadelphia: University of Pennsylvania Press, 2004), 223.
52. *Pittsburgh Press*, October 18, 1938.
53. *The Sporting News*, March 20, 1939.
54. *Los Angeles Times*, March 9, 1939.
55. Honig, 51.
56. *Washington Post*, September 30, 1939.
57. *Washington Post*, September 29, 1939.
58. *Washington Post*, February 22, 1940.
59. Pie Traynor file at National Baseball Hall of Fame Library, Cooperstown, New York.
60. Ibid.
61. *Pittsburgh Tribune Review*, August 8, 1999.
62. johnrook.com/johnrook.pie.htm (accessed March 20, 2015).
63. *The Sporting News*, August 2, 1969.
64. Ibid.
65. Pie Traynor Hall of Fame file.
66. *Pittsburgh Press*, November 19, 1971.
67. *Pittsburgh Post-Gazette*, March 17, 1972.
68. Bruce Markusen, *The Great One* (Champaign, Illinois: Sports Publishing, 2001), 293-294.
69. John Rook, email correspondence, April 23, 2005.
70. *Pittsburgh Post-Gazette*, March 18, 1972.
71. *Pittsburgh Press*, March 22, 1972.
72. *The Sporting News*, April 1, 1972.

73 *Pittsburgh Post-Gazette*, March 21, 1972.
74 Ibid.
75 Ibid.
76 *Pittsburgh Post-Gazette*, March 17, 1972.
77 Ibid.
78 *Pittsburgh Post-Gazette*, March 21, 1972.
79 Ibid.

HARRY HOOPER

By Paul Zingg and E. A. (Betsy) Reed

One of the best defensive right-fielders in baseball history and one of the top leadoff hitters of the Deadball Era, Harry Hooper was also a team leader, superb practitioner of the inside game, and clutch hitter who played a key role in four Boston Red Sox world championships. As a product of rural California, but a college man who earned a degree in engineering, Hooper also symbolized baseball's transition, ongoing during the Deadball Era, from a game rooted in the eastern cities and played by professionals who were largely uneducated and illiterate, to a game that broadened its geographical horizons and expanded its social appeal through players like Hooper.

Although his play at times achieved the spectacular, Hooper eschewed flamboyance for simplicity, exaggeration for modesty. Possessing neither the crafted appeal of Christy Mathewson nor the raw excitement of Babe Ruth, Hooper practiced his profession quietly, skillfully, and confidently. More Everyman than Superman, he is a mirror of the game and its human touches in ways that his myth-encrusted contemporaries never can be. Though he never led the American League in any major statistical category, Hooper crafted a solid statistical resume that included 2,466 hits, 1,429 runs, and 1,136 career walks, good for a lifetime .281 batting average and .368 on-base percentage. In 92 career World Series at-bats, Hooper batted a solid .293; in the 1915 Fall Classic he batted .350 with two home runs.

Harry Bartholomew Hooper was born on August 24, 1887 in California's Santa Clara Valley, the fourth and youngest child of Joseph and Mary Katherine Keller Hooper. In 1876, Joseph had left Canada's Prince Edward Island, slowly working his way westward through a series of jobs before landing in California, where he met Mary Keller, a German immigrant working as a housekeeper, and married her in 1878. Growing up on the family ranch, Harry first honed his athletic skills by tossing fresh eggs against the side of the family's barn. This merited little reaction from his parents, and Harry spent more time throwing various objects, challenging himself in distance and accuracy.

His first formal exposure to nine-man-a-side baseball came during a trip East with his mother. While visiting her family in Central Pennsylvania, Harry watched with great interest the Lock Haven team play. He capped the trip with a visit to relatives living in New York City, and a chance to see his first Major League game. The Brooklyn Bridegrooms played the Louisville Colonels, and although the home team lost, Hooper's dedication and love of the game solidified. Just before he and his mother began the long journey back to California, he received from his uncle something he later called "the best of all" his boyhood treasures: a bat, ball, and well-worn fielder's glove.

Harry Hooper's formal baseball career began when he left the family's farm in August, 1902, for the high school attached to Saint Mary's College of California, then located in Oakland. Although Hooper originally arrived for a two-year secondary program, the Christian Brothers who ran the school quickly recognized his mathematical aptitude, and encouraged his parents to consider allowing him to complete the full baccalaureate program, which would stretch his time at the school from two years to five. Consistent with the emerging sense of education as a means to economic opportunity, Harry's parents agreed to the school's request. At roughly the same time, he earned a place on the secondary school's new baseball team.

Working his way up through the four teams at the school, Hooper earned a place as a starting pitcher on the junior varsity as a collegiate sophomore, but his stature—he stood slightly over five feet tall at the time—and pitching velocity limited his chance to earn a spot on the varsity squad. The top team's head coach suggested a switch to an outfield position, which Hooper accepted. It assured him the starting left-field spot on the College's varsity nine at the start of the 1907 season, a team regarded by many as one of collegiate baseball's finest in the pre-World War I era. With a roster that contained five future big leaguers, Hooper played alongside catcher Eddie Burns, infielder Ed Hallinan, pitcher Harry Krause, and outfielder Charlie Enwright, on a team that completed a 27-game season with a record of 26 wins and one tie.

Among that year's victims were Stanford University, the University of California, a Pacific Coast League all-star team, and the Chicago White Sox who the Phoenix faced in an exhibition game prior to the start of the major-league season.

Hitting for a .371 average during his senior season, Hooper drew the attention of several organized ball representatives, and signed his first contract—for 10 days—to play with the Alameda Grays club of the independent California League, where he teamed with outfielder Duffy Lewis for the first time; the two had been schoolmates but not teammates at St. Mary's. Ironically, the short length of the contract was Hooper's idea. Focused primarily on his engineering career, he agreed to play only for the time between the end of the Phoenix's season and his graduation date. His strong play during the short stretch earned Hooper a 1908 contract with the Sacramento Senators, also of the California League, which he agreed to accept with the proviso that Sacramento's owner arrange a surveying position for him, which was done.

Late in the 1908 season, after hitting .347, scoring 39 runs, and stealing 34 bases in 68 games, Hooper earned the tag, "Ty Cobb of the State League," and an offer from his manager, Charlie Graham, who also served as a scout for the Boston Red Sox. Initially when approached about the possibility Hooper recalled saying he thought baseball "was a sideline to engineering to make enough money for a living." Graham persisted and Hooper agreed to meet with Red Sox owner John Taylor, who soon would be in the area to observe several prospects for his team. At their meeting at a Sacramento saloon, the two agreed to a contract that would pay the 21-year-old Hooper $2,800 for the 1909 season, approximately $1,000 more than he would have made combined through his California baseball play and his job with the Western Pacific Railroad.

Hooper's career with the Boston Red Sox began on March 4, 1909 when he arrived in Hot Springs, Arkansas for the team's training camp. The Red Sox of 1909 represented a team in transition. Following the demise of the championship clubs of 1903 and 1904, owner Taylor aspired to build a pennant contender with young pitchers, power hitting, and speed on the bases. The rotation included Smoky Joe Wood, Eddie Cicotte, and Frank Arellanes. Other than Heinie Wagner (shortstop), no member of the squad had two complete seasons with the team.

Hooper's major-league debut came on April 16, in Washington, D.C., during the team's second series of the season. Called upon to start in left field and bat seventh, Hooper lined a single in his first at-bat that also notched his first RBI. That day he went 2-for-3 at the plate, with "a clever steal in the ninth," three flies caught including "a superb running back catch" that saved a triple, and one assist when he threw out Gabby Street at home. During the first month of the season, he played occasionally, always fielding well.

A natural right-handed hitter and fielder while at St. Mary's, the 5-feet-10, 168-pound Hooper experimented with switch hitting. Playing in an era when manufacturing runs one at a time mattered more than sheer power, Hooper decided to take advantage

Harry Hooper remains the only man to have played for four World Championship Red Sox teams.

of his abilities and reduce one step from the batter's box to first base by making the move to full-time left-handed hitting. His hard work and dependable play, especially in the field, made personnel decisions easier for the club's management. By the season's midpoint, Hooper firmly held the fourth outfield position, and often entered games in the late innings because of his defensive skills. The squad finished the year in third place, 9½ games behind the Detroit Tigers, but also 25 games over .500. Hooper recorded a .282 average in 81 games, while completing the transition from one side of the plate to the other.

The Red Sox that assembled in Hot Springs, Arkansas in March, 1910 had reason to be optimistic about the coming season. Most of the lineup returned, with Hooper virtually assured one outfield spot. With Tris Speaker secure in center, the only question was whether it would be right or left on a day-to-day basis. The arrival of another veteran of the St. Mary's Phoenix in camp, George "Duffy" Lewis, largely settled the issue. The outfield trio of Tris Speaker, Harry Hooper in right, and Duffy Lewis in left made its debut on April 27. Through the course of that season—when they hit a combined .296—and the next five, the "Million Dollar Outfield" played more than 90 percent of Boston's games. After batting .267 in 1910, Hooper improved to an impressive .311 average in 1911, scored 93 runs, and posted a .399 on-base percentage. The club, however, failed to finish better than fourth in either season.

Despite his .242 batting average, Hooper was an integral piece of the 1912 pennant-winners, ranking second on the team with 98 runs scored, 66 walks, 29 stolen bases, and 12 triples (tied with Speaker). In that year's World Series against the New York Giants, Hooper elevated his play, batting .290 for the Series and making several crucial plays at bat and in the field. In Game One, Hooper rapped a game-tying double in the seventh inning to secure a 4-3 Boston victory. After taking a three-games-to-one lead in the Series, the Red Sox saw the Giants even things at three games each. There was one tie game.

Despite numerous baserunners for both teams, the Giants held a slim 1-0 lead in the seventh inning of the deciding Game Eight at Fenway Park, which would have been greater if not for Hooper's catch of Larry Doyle's fifth-inning drive to the right-field fence, robbing him of a home run. The game was tied 1-1 after nine and the Giants scored a run in the top of the 10th. In the bottom half, after pinch-hitter Clyde Engle reached second when Fred Snodgrass muffed a fly ball, Hooper followed with "a sure triple" that Snodgrass caught, but it advanced Engle to third. After a walk to Yerkes, Speaker, after receiving new life when his foul pop-up near first base was allowed to drop, singled in Engle with the tying run. Yerkes took third on the play, Speaker took second on the throw home. After an intentional walk to Lewis, Larry Gardner's sacrifice fly won the World Series for the Red Sox.

Hooper's "paralyzing catch" in the final game earned him accolades in the press, but John McGraw paid an even higher compliment when he labeled the Californian, "one of the most dangerous hitters in a pinch the game has ever known." In the next day's *Boston Globe*, Speaker called Hooper's catch "the greatest, I believe, that I ever saw."

Coming off the championship year, Hooper married Esther Henchy, a 20-year-old banker's daughter from nearby Capitola, California, but remained dedicated to his offseason training. Although the Red Sox struggled as a team in 1913 and finished second in 1914, Hooper personally improved his offensive output, hitting .288 in 1913 and scoring 100 runs, and batting .258 with 85 runs scored in 1914. On May 30, 1913, Hooper hit home runs to lead off both games of a double-header, a feat not equaled until Rickey Henderson did it 80 years later.

In 1915 the Red Sox returned to championship form and began a stretch of success where the team played the best, and most consistent, baseball in the major leagues. Between 1914 and 1917, the team won at least 90 games each season, and likely would have done so again in 1918 if World War I had not shortened the season to end in early September. The successes came through the team's effective use of the strategies of the era. Rather than power hitting and home runs, the Red Sox won by manufacturing runs, playing strong defense, and, most of all, getting solid pitching. In fact, during the four-year stretch, the team never featured more than one hitter with an average of .300 or higher. As Hooper wrote, "With the best pitching staff and the best defensive outfield…we played for one run—tried to get on the scoreboard first and then increase our lead."

In 1915, Hooper's average dipped to .235, but he compensated by collecting 89 walks, fifth best in the league, and posting a respectable .342 on-base percentage. Once again, he saved his best work for the World Series, when he helped Boston finish off the Philadelphia Phillies in five games with a .350 batting average and two home runs, both of which came in the final game of the Series, making Hooper only the second player in World Series history to homer twice in the same game. (Both homers bounced into Baker Bowl's temporary stands; today they would be considered ground-rule doubles.)

After another world championship in 1916, and a disappointing second-place finish nine games behind the Chicago White Sox the following year, Hooper's Red Sox entered the 1918 season in a tenuous position. Although Boston's roster suffered fewer losses to the military and war-related industries than other teams, the lineup managed a woeful team average of .249, the third-worst in the American League; Hooper posted a .289 batting average and a .405 slugging percentage (second on the team to Babe Ruth in both categories). He also helped the team to another pennant in a war-shortened season (126 games) that ended with a dramatic labor challenge during the World Series.

During the Fall Classic against the Chicago Cubs, Hooper demonstrated his clear thinking and effective leadership, representing his fellow players' concerns in a manner that preserved the integrity of baseball, while also exposing some of the inherent weaknesses of baseball's ruling system. Due to wartime travel restrictions, the teams played the Series in a 3-4 format, with the first games in Chicago (ironically at Comiskey Park). The rest of the games took place at Fenway Park. The Red Sox returned home enjoying a 2-1 lead, but all was not well. For several war-related reasons, attendance and gate receipts during the regular season and World Series in 1918 fell well below pre-war levels. However, at this time the players' postseason bonuses came from gate receipts and the owners would not guarantee a minimum payment. The two teams, traveling on the same train, appointed four representatives, including Hooper, to speak to the governing National Commission and press their case. Specifically, the teams sought a guarantee of $2,600 each for the winners and $1,400 for the losers, with 10% going as a donation to the Red Cross. The National Commission begrudgingly listened, and agreed to consider the matter, but made no promises.

With Boston leading three games to one, the players delayed the start of the fifth game by more than one hour in an attempt to secure concessions from the Commission. Although Hooper negotiated an end to the strike, and secured a verbal promise from Ban Johnson of no reprisals, he forever regretted not securing the guarantee in writing. After Boston won the Series 4-2, its last for 86 years, the players received the smallest financial awards in World Series history ($1,108.45 for each Red Sox player and $574.62 for each Cub). In December the Boston players all received letters from John A. Heydler, acting president of the National League and a Commission member. It informed them that, "Owing to the disgraceful conduct of the players in the strike during the Series…(the players) would be fined the World Series emblems that were traditionally awarded to the winners." Although a modest symbol, the emblems—really lapel pins—became a symbol of the lack of respect accorded the players in the years before a strong players union and free agency.

After a .312 season in 1920, Harry Hooper's career with the Boston Red Sox ended on March 4, 1921, when Boston owner Harry Frazee thwarted a holdout by trading him to the Chicago White Sox for outfielder//first-baseman Shano Collins and outfielder Nemo Liebold. Hooper posted some of the best offensive seasons of his career during his five years with the White Sox. In 1921 he batted .327; the following year he notched career highs in runs scored (111), home runs (11) and RBIs (80). In 1924, he posted a career-best .328 batting average and .413 on-base percentage. In 1925, his last major-league season, Hooper batted .265. Playing in his final major league game on October 4, 1925, Hooper went 1-for-4 with a double.

Upon his retirement, Hooper returned to California and worked in real estate for one year before accepting a job as player-manager with Mission (San Francisco) Bells in the Class-AA Pacific Coast League. Hooper lasted one year with the club, batting .282 in 81 games and guiding the Missions to a disappointing 86-110 record. Let go after the season, Hooper returned to the real estate business for a few years while also playing minor league baseball in nearby Marysville and Santa Cruz, then became coach of the Princeton baseball team in September, 1930. Hooper stayed at the post for two years, posting a 21-30-1 record before Depression-era finances forced the college to cut back on Hooper's salary, leading to his resignation. He once again returned to the real estate business in California, survived the Depression, and became wealthy in his old age. He also served as postmaster of Capitola for over 20 years. His greatest honor came in 1971, when the Veteran's Committee elected him to the Baseball Hall of Fame. Hooper was also one of the inaugural inductees when the St. Mary's College Athletic Hall of Fame was established in 1973; his son John, a center fielder during the 1940s, was inducted four years later. Harry Hooper died at the age of 87 on December 18, 1974, following a stroke. He was laid to rest in an above-ground crypt in the center of in Aptos, California. He was survived by two sons and a daughter.

SOURCES

This biography is drawn from Paul Zingg's book *Harry Hooper: An American Baseball Life* (Urbana: University of Illinois Press, 1993).

Harry slides into third against Harry Lord of the Chicago White Sox during the official opening of Fenway Park, May 17, 1912. Umpire Silk O'Loughlin makes the call.

NAP LAJOIE

By David Jones and Stephen Constantelos

The first superstar in American League history, Napoleon Lajoie combined graceful, effortless fielding with powerful, fearsome hitting to become one of the greatest all-around players of the Deadball Era, and one of the best second basemen of all time. At 6-feet-1 and 200 pounds, Lajoie possessed an unusually large physique for his time, yet when manning the keystone sack he was wonderfully quick on his feet, threw like chain lightning, and went over the ground like a deer. "Lajoie glides toward the ball," noted the *New York Press*, "[and] gathers it in nonchalantly, as if picking fruit...."[1] During his 21-year career, Lajoie led the league in putouts five times, assists three times, double plays five times, and fielding percentage four times.

But he was even more memorable in the batter's box, where the right-hander captured four (or five) batting titles, including a modern-era record .426 mark for the Philadelphia Athletics in 1901, won the first Triple Crown in American League history, and finished with a lifetime .338 batting average. An expert bunter who was capable of hitting the ball to all fields, Lajoie was nonetheless completely undisciplined at the plate, regularly swinging at pitches down at his ankles or up at his eyebrows, and occasionally thwarting attempts to intentionally walk him by reaching out for those pitches, too. For years the conventional wisdom among American League pitchers was to try to upset Lajoie's timing with off-speed stuff, but Francis Richter thought this strategy ineffective, noting that no pitch could fool Lajoie for long. "Good Old Ed Delahanty could clout the horsehide some," Hugh Duffy once observed, "but [Lajoie] seemed to be just as powerful, if not more so."[2] Indeed, Lajoie swung so hard and met the ball with such force, that on three separate occasions in 1899 he managed to literally tear the cover off the ball.

Napoleon Lajoie (typically pronounced LAJ-way, though Nap himself is supposed to have preferred the French pronunciation, Lah-ZHWA) was born on September 5, 1874, in Woonsocket, Rhode Island, the youngest of eight surviving children of Jean Baptiste and Celina Guertin Lajoie. The Lajoie clan traced its origins to Auxerres, France, though Jean Baptiste was born in Canada, and emigrated with his family to the United States in 1866, initially settling in Rutland, Vermont before moving to Woonsocket. During Napoleon's early years, Jean worked as a teamster and a laborer, but his premature death in 1881 forced his children to find employment as soon as they were physically able. After attending school for only eight months, Napoleon was obliged to forsake his formal education in 1885, when he found work as a cardroom sweeper in a local textile mill.

About the same time the young lad was seized by the baseball craze sweeping the country. His mother did not approve of his ball playing and so his teammates gave the dark-haired Lajoie the nickname Sandy to hide his presence on the diamond. By 1894 Lajoie was clerking for an auctioneer named C.F. Hixon and playing part time with the semipro Woonsockets. As word of his ability spread, Lajoie discovered that other semipro teams wanted him to play for them in critical games. He obliged them all and his rate of pay ranged from $2 to $5 per game, plus round-trip carfare. Off the diamond, Nap followed in his father's footsteps and became a teamster. He drove a hack out of the Consolidated Livery Stable, providing him with the nickname The Slugging Cabby. In 1896 Lajoie joined the Fall River (Massachusetts) club in the Class B New England League, which offered him $500 for the five-month-long season. Lajoie was making $7.50 per week as a cabby and his words of acceptance served as his slogan for his entire career: "I'm out for the stuff."³

Lajoie's career with Fall River lasted only until August 9, when he and teammate Phil Geier were purchased by the Philadelphia Phillies. With his .429 batting average and .726 slugging percentage, Fall River had no trouble soliciting offers for Lajoie, but Philadelphia was the only franchise that agreed to the asking price of $1,500. During his abbreviated minor-league career, Lajoie had played mostly center field, but when he joined the Phillies, manager Billy Nash installed the rookie at first base, which had been manned on an emergency basis by Ed Delahanty. This allowed Del to return to his best position, left field. In 1898 Phils manager George Stallings made several sweeping defensive changes. The most important was shifting Lajoie to second base, where he would achieve his enduring fame. Stallings later explained this move by saying, "He'd have made good no matter where I positioned him."⁴

Over his final three seasons with Philadelphia, Lajoie matured into one of the game's best second basemen, using his excellent speed, quick reflexes, and soft hands to adeptly handle all the position's tasks. "He plays so naturally and so easily it looks like lack of effort," Connie Mack would later observe. "Larry's reach is so long and he's fast as lightning, and to throw to at second base he is ideal. All the catchers who've played with him say he is the easiest man to throw to in the game today. High, low, wide — he is sure of everything."⁵ Unlike his contemporaries, Lajoie preferred to break in a new fielding mitt each season, and he also parted from accepted practice by cutting the wrist strap off his glove, providing his large hands with added flexibility and control.

At the plate, Lajoie wasted little time demonstrating that his gaudy minor-league numbers had been no fluke. From 1896 to 1900 he never batted lower than .324, and he led the league in slugging percentage in 1897 and doubles and RBIs in 1898. He posted a .378 batting average in 1899, though an injury following a collision with Harry Steinfeldt limited him to just 77 games played. It was the first of several seasons in which Nap would miss significant playing time, though the causes of his absences from the starting lineup were rarely typical. In 1900 Lajoie lost five weeks after breaking his thumb in a fistfight with teammate Elmer Flick. Two years later, legal squabbles between the American and National Leagues cut into his playing time, and in 1905, Nap's leg nearly had to be amputated after the blue dye in his socks poisoned a spike wound. The leg recovered, but the incident led to a new rule requiring teams to use sanitary white socks.

During his career, Lajoie also had some famous run-ins with umpires. In 1904 he was suspended for throwing chewing tobacco into umpire Frank Dwyer's eye. After one ejection, Lajoie, who stubbornly refused to leave the bench, had to be escorted from the park by police. And in 1903, Nap became so infuriated by an umpire's decision to use a blackened ball that he picked up the sphere and threw it over the grandstand, resulting in a forfeit.

But Lajoie's most famous battle came off the field, when he jumped his contract with the Phillies to join the insurgent American League in 1901. Prior to the 1900 season, Lajoie had been assured by Philadelphia owner John Rogers that he and teammate Ed Delahanty would receive equal pay. After the season began, however, Lajoie discovered that his salary of $2,600 was actually $400 less than Delahanty's pay. As Lajoie later explained, "I saw the checks."⁶ Incensed, Lajoie exacted his revenge on Rogers in the offseason, when he jumped to Connie Mack's Philadelphia Athletics of the upstart American League.

When he abandoned the National League in favor of the new organization, Lajoie almost single-handedly legitimatized the AL's claim to major-league status. Rogers, however, immediately moved to block the deal, suing for the return of his "property." While the case worked its way to the Pennsylvania Supreme Court, Lajoie, a major star at the peak of his powers, capitalized on the golden opportunity of playing in a newly formed league with a diluted talent pool by putting together one of the most impressive seasons in major-league history. Nap punished the American League's overmatched pitchers in 1901, becoming just the third Triple Crown winner in baseball history with a .426 batting average (the highest posted by any player in the 20th century), 14 home runs, and 125 RBIs. Lajoie also led the league in hits (232), doubles (48), runs scored (145), on-base percentage (.463), and slugging percentage (.643). Despite those figures, the Athletics could only finish in fourth place.

Ironically, Connie Mack's team would win the pennant the following year, but they would do so without Lajoie, who moved to the Cleveland franchise after Rogers succeeded in getting an injunction from the Pennsylvania Supreme Court which prevented Nap from playing ball in the state for any team other than the Phillies. Lajoie was able to circumvent the ruling by signing with Cleveland, and skipping all of the club's games in Philadelphia. (The fact that the A's never had to face the league's best hitter in their home park undoubtedly helped them capture the pennant; indeed, the .339 difference between Philadelphia's home and road winning percentages in 1902 remains the second-highest differential in baseball history.) In the peace agreement brokered between the two leagues following the 1902 season, Rogers dropped his claim on Lajoie, and Nap remained with Cleveland through the 1914 season. During his 13 years with the club, Lajoie became such a powerful symbol of the franchise that the press soon took to calling the team the Naps, thus making Lajoie the only active player in baseball history to have his team named after him.

With his legal status secured, in 1903 and 1904 Lajoie solidified his reputation as the league's best hitter, winning his third and fourth consecutive batting titles. In 1904 he batted .376, led the league in on-base percentage (.413), slugging percentage (.552), hits (208), and RBIs (102). Despite that performance, and despite the considerable offensive contributions of teammates Bill Bradley and Elmer Flick, the Naps finished a disappointing fourth, and in September

Ward McDowell, outfield prospect, watches Larry "Nap" Lajoie demonstrate fielding. Bain News Service. Library of Congress.

manager Bill Armour tendered his resignation. After the end of the season, Lajoie formally accepted the position as field manager.

Though he finished his managerial career with a .550 winning percentage, Lajoie was not a successful manager. When he assumed control of the team in late 1904, Lajoie inherited one of the league's most talented rosters. In addition to himself, the Naps featured several promising players under the age of 30: Bradley, Flick, shortstop Terry Turner, and center-fielder Harry Bay. Their pitching rotation was anchored by a trio of young pitchers, none of whom were older than 25: Addie Joss, Earl Moore (who had won 52 games in his first three seasons), and Bob Rhoads, who posted a record of 38-19 for the Naps in 1905 and 1906.

Despite this assortment of talent, under Lajoie's leadership the Naps only twice challenged for the American League pennant, losing out to the White Sox by five games in 1906 and the Detroit Tigers by .004 in 1908. Lajoie blamed himself for the team's second-place finish in 1908, as he batted just .289 for the season and failed in the clutch in two critical games down the stretch. In fact, there is much evidence to suggest that Lajoie's managerial responsibilities detracted from his on-field performance. After winning four consecutive batting titles from 1901 to 1904, Lajoie put together only one comparable season during his managerial career, posting a

.355 batting average in 1906. In both 1907 and 1908, Lajoie failed to clear the .300 barrier.

As manager, Lajoie was criticized for his rudimentary method of relaying signals to the outfielders. He had a way of wiggling his finger behind his back as notice to his outfield when his pitcher was going to throw a fastball, and wiggling two fingers for a curve. Enemy pitchers in the bullpen often could read Nap's signals, and they were never a mystery to Connie Mack. One contemporary observed of Lajoie, "The great player-artist rather disdained the subtleties of the game and responsibility sat heavily upon him. He failed to lift up lesser players to the batting and fielding heights that he had attained so easily. He knew how to do a thing, but to impart to another how it should be done eluded him."[7]

Midway through the 1909 season, with the team once again languishing in the standings, Lajoie resigned as manager. Free to once again focus exclusively on his on-field performance, Nap batted over .300 every year from 1909 to 1913. From 1910 to 1912 he batted better than .360 every season, with his .384 mark in 1910 finishing second—or first, depending on your point of view—in the American League batting race.

In one of the most famous episodes of the Deadball Era, Lajoie and Ty Cobb entered the closing days of the season neck-and-neck for the American League batting crown, with the winner set to receive a brand new Chalmers automobile, one of the finest makes of the day in a time when automobiles were still rare commodities. On the season's final day, the Naps faced the St. Louis Browns in a doubleheader, with Lajoie trailing Cobb and needing a base hit in virtually every at-bat to secure the batting crown. The Browns manager, Jack O'Connor, no fan of the ill-tempered Georgia Peach, ordered rookie third-baseman Red Corriden to play deep, well behind the bag throughout both games. Seizing the opportunity, Lajoie dropped seven straight bunts down the third base line for hits, though an eighth bunt was recorded as a sacrifice. His eighth and final hit was a triple belted over the center-fielder's head. O'Connor was fired for his actions, and Lajoie received a congratulatory telegram from eight of Cobb's teammates, but one week later American League president Ban Johnson declared Cobb the batting title winner, by a margin of .000860. (Subsequent research would determine that Cobb had been erroneously credited with two extra hits, and when this clerical error was corrected, Cobb's average dropped to .383, giving Lajoie the higher batting average. Nonetheless, in 1981 Commissioner Bowie Kuhn rejected an appeal to declare Lajoie the true 1910 batting champion.) The Chalmers company reacted to the controversy by giving both players free automobiles, but according to Lajoie's nephew, Nap "didn't want to accept it," though his wife insisted that he do so. "He just thought that he, not Cobb, had won that championship and was angry that Cobb had been ruled the winner."[8]

In 1914 Lajoie struggled to a .258 batting average, as bad eyesight gradually diminished his effectiveness. Following the 1914 season, Lajoie's contract was purchased by the Philadelphia Athletics, and Nap was reunited with his old friend and manager, Connie Mack. Unfortunately, Nap arrived one year too late to get his first shot at winning a pennant. In 1915 and 1916, Lajoie played out the string as Eddie Collins's replacement at second base, posting batting averages of .280 and .246, respectively, while the A's plummeted into the American League cellar.

Lajoie with Cleveland, 1913. Harris & Ewing, photographer. Library of Congress

Following Philadelphia's dismal 36-117 performance in 1916, Lajoie announced his retirement from the majors. On January 15, 1917, he signed as playing manager of the International League's Toronto Maple Leafs. Toronto won the pennant and Lajoie captured the batting title with a resounding .380 mark. The following year he signed as player-manager for Indianapolis of the American Association, batting .282 and leading the Indians to a third-place finish in the war-shortened campaign. One month away from his 44th birthday, Lajoie offered his services to his draft board. They declined, with thanks.

Lajoie had married the former Myrtle I. Smith, a divorcée, on October 11, 1906. They purchased a small farm of about 20 acres in the Cleveland suburb of South Euclid and this remained their residence until they moved to a smaller home in Mentor, Ohio in 1939. Long popular in Cleveland, Lajoie was put up as the Republican candidate for sheriff of Cuyahoga County. Failing election, he was named commissioner of the old Ohio and Pennsylvania League. He also dabbled around in a rubber company, sold truck tires, and finally set up a small brass manufacturing company. These businesses were merely diversions to occupy his time. Lajoie had been careful with his money and he and Myrtle lived a comfortable life.

In 1943 the Lajoies made a permanent move to Florida and finally settled in the Daytona Beach area. Myrtle passed away of cancer in 1954. Nap died on February 7, 1959, of pneumonia. The couple had no children.

Note: This biography originally appeared in David Jones, ed., *Deadball Stars of the American League* (Washington, D.C.: Potomac Books, Inc., 2006).

SOURCES

For this biography, the authors used a number of contemporary sources, especially those found in the subject's file at the National Baseball Hall of Fame Library.

NOTES

1. J. M. Murphy, "Napoleon Lajoie: Modern Baseball's First Superstar," *The National Pastime: A Review of Baseball History* 7, No. 1 (Spring 1988: 72).
2. Alfred Henry Spink, *The National Game* (The National Game Publishing Company, 1910), 200.
3. J. M. Murphy, 12.
4. David Jones and Stephen Constantelos, "Napoleon Lajoie," biography on the SABR BioProject website (http://bioproj.sabr.org)
5. J. M. Murphy, 72.
6. Nap Lajoie as told to Lee Allen, *The Sporting News*, November 4, 1953: 14.
7. Tom Meany, *Baseball's Greatest Hitters* (New York, A.S. Barnes, 1950), 115.
8. J. M. Murphy, 35.

GABBY STREET

By Joseph Wancho

Gabby Street may not have been much of a batsman in his career. His high mark for batting average was .238 in 1905, a season he split between Cincinnati and the Boston Beaneaters. Perhaps he was aided by only 105 at-bats, the second lowest total of his career. There may have been a slight decrease in that .238 average had he made more trips to the plate. His strength as a big-league catcher was how he handled his position, worked the pitching staff. During his time in Washington, Street was a favorite backstop of Walter Johnson. "You don't see Gabby's kind of a catcher anymore. He never hit much, but what a receiver he was—big fellow, a perfect target, great arm, slow afoot, but spry as a cat on his feet behind the plate, always talking, always hustling, full of pep and fight," said Johnson. "Gabby was always jabberin', and he never let a pitcher take his mind off the game. When we got in a tight spot, Gabby was right out there to talk it over with me. He never let me forget a batter's weakness."[1]

As a catcher, Street honed his ability to take charge. It was his capability as a leader that served him well in World War I, and as a pennant-winning manager for the St. Louis Cardinals in 1930 and 1931. Gabby led the Cards to their second world championship in 1931. He was proclaimed a "Miracle Man" for delivering a title to the Mound City. "Miracle Man? Who? Me? Hell no! I'm just an old ballplayer with a bunch of fighting cocks on my roster that woulda won the pennant with Butch the Batboy directing them. Forget the 'Miracle Man' stuff, woncha?" said the self-deprecating Street.[2]

But what was it that makes fans remember Gabby Street? Ironically, it was for something outside the lines of a baseball diamond. No, it was not his appearance on the Simpsons episode "Homer at the Bat," which aired on February 20, 1992. D'oh! Gabby had passed away 41 years earlier and he was appearing in pop culture.

No sir, Gabby Street was perhaps known for catching a ball dropped from atop the Washington Monument on August 21, 1908. Senators fans Preston Gibson and John Biddle had made a wager of $500 on whether the feat could be done. After all, the ball would travel 555 feet, and at a high rate of speed. Gabby was never one to be deterred from a challenge and set his place at the foot of the monument. Gibson and Biddle climbed to the top with a basket full of baseballs, and constructed a wooden chute so the ball would slide to arc away and clear the wide base of the enormous structure. The first 10 baseballs caromed off the base of the monument, so the chute was discarded and the pair of fans took turns throwing the ball from their perch. Gabby, dressed in street clothes, with arms outstretched over his head as if to corral a pop fly, made the successful catch on the 15th attempt. It was calculated that the baseball had picked up 300 pounds of force by the time it landed in Street's mitt, which almost hit the ground from the impact. "I didn't see the ball until it was halfway down," said Gabby. "It was slanting in the wind and I knew it would be a hard catch."[3]

As for Gabby, he went on his way to work. He caught Walter Johnson that day as the Nats defeated the Detroit Tigers, 3-1.

Charles Evard Street was born on September 30, 1882, in Huntsville, Alabama, one of seven children of Williams and Sis Street. "I played ball on the grammar and high-school teams there, and then at South

Kentucky College at Hopkinsville," Street said. "In 1900, a small Class-D league was formed, the 'KIT' League, the right name of which was the Kentucky, Illinois, and Tennessee League (also known as the KITTY League). I was offered $60 a month to catch for the Hopkinsville team (1903), and accepted. That was big money."[4]

Street was sold the next season to Terre Haute (Indiana) of the Class-B Central League. His contract was then purchased by the Cincinnati Reds, and Street made his major-league debut on September 13, 1904. He appeared in 11 games, backing up starting catcher Admiral Schlej. The Reds had called up another catcher in 1904, Branch Rickey from Dallas of the Class-C Texas League. But when Rickey refused to play baseball on Sundays he was returned to Dallas, thus clearing the way for Street to join the team.

In 1905 Street began the season with Cincinnati but was "loaned to the Boston Beaneaters" on June 5. Both of Boston's catchers had been injured in the June 3 game and so the National Commission facilitated a loan of Street to the Beaneaters.[5] He hadn't gotten off to a good start for Boston, committing four errors in the June 7 game against the Cubs, two of them on throws which effectively cost Boston the game.[6] The very next day he himself was hurt, his index finger hit by a pitch that broke it, but with no other catcher available he had it bandaged and continued.[7] The 1905 Boston team was one of special note, as four different starters totaled 20 or more losses on the year. The feat was repeated again in 1906. By the time Boston passed through Cincinnati, Street had been returned to the Reds, on June 15.[8]

Back with the Queen City, remaining in the role of a backup catcher, Street caught in 31 games in all for the Reds. His contract was again purchased, this time by San Francisco of the Class-A Pacific Coast League in February 1906. He spent the next two seasons in the City by the Bay, although on April 18, 1906, he almost got dumped into the Bay. "I was living in the Golden Gate Hotel, patronized largely by baseball players and members of the theatrical profession and during the wee hours of April 18 of that year, I was thrown from my bed," said Street. "Out in San Francisco they still refer to the Act of God which tossed me from my bed as 'The Fire,' but the force that removed me from my mattress to the floor was an earthquake. Aroused, I rubbed my eyes, looked out the window and saw buildings crumbling, and having heard whispers of quakes, I headed for the street. If I live to be a hundred I shall always remember that scene. As we hit the street, en masse, the rear of the hotel collapsed and the water tank on the roof, halved by the second shock, washed everyone of us. I walked through showers of brick and mortar to the Golden Gate Park where I spent the night."[9]

Street was ready to jump the Seals and head to an "outlaw" league and play in Williamsport, Pennsylvania. Although his exit from San Francisco was delayed, he eventually made it to the Keystone State, playing in 102 games for the Millionaires club of the Independent Tri-State League. However, he returned to the Seals for the 1907 season, appearing in 159 games and registering a .231 batting average in 523 at-bats. It was the most playing time Street had received since Terre Haute.

Persistence paid off for Street, and his contract was sold to the Washington Senators. Of the 504 games Street played in the major leagues, 429 were over the next four years (1908-11) with Washington. His calling card was his defense, as he led the league in putouts and double plays in both 1908 and 1909. In 1910 he was atop his peers with a fielding percentage of .978. In today's vernacular Street's batting average would be characterized as worthy of the "Mendoza Line," as his average with the Senators was a meek .210. Catchers of the day were never expected to hit that well, and in any event Washington was not fielding a championship team in those years, finishing no better than seventh place in the American League and no closer than 22½ games back of the pennant winner.

Importantly, Walter Johnson favored Street, acknowledging him as a first-rate catcher. "He always kept the pitcher in good spirits with his continual chatter

Gabby Street, 1910. Bain News Service. Library of Congress

of sense and nonsense," said the Big Train. " 'Ease up on this fellow, Walter, he has a wife and two kids,' he would call jokingly when some batter was hugging the plate and getting a toehold for a crack at one of my fast ones. 'This fellow hasn't had a hit off you since you joined the league,' might be his next remark and so on throughout the game."[10]

On April 14, 1911, Cleveland pitcher Addie Joss died at 31 of tubercular meningitis. Joss, who was one of the great pitchers of the Deadball Era, or any era for that matter, was also well-respected and well-liked by his peers. His Cleveland teammates began to canvass other American League players to play in a game to raise funds for Joss's widow, Lillian, and her two children. The game was played on July 24, 1911, at Cleveland's League Park. It was an unofficial "All-Star Game" that predated Arch Ward's concept by 22 years. It was also one of the greatest collections of baseball talent as the Cleveland Naps took on the American League stars. The Naps were led by Joe Jackson, Napoleon Lajoie, and Jack Graney. The All-Stars were rightly named; they included Ty Cobb, Tris Speaker, Sam Crawford, Frank Baker, Eddie Collins, Hal Chase, and Walter Johnson. Street volunteered to participate. "As far as I am concerned, that outfit can stand as the all-star team of all time, outside of the backstop of course," He said. "I didn't need to be good with that bunch. Cy Young started on the mound for Cleveland as I recall it and he was still pretty good for an old fellow, but these fellows just blasted him."[11] Attendance for the game was reported to be 15,270, and $12,914 was raised for Lillian Joss.[12]

On February 17, 1912, Street was dealt to the New York Highlanders (now the Yankees) for utility players John Knight and Rip Williams. But Street was suffering from inflammatory rheumatism, and his playing time was limited to 29 games. He was sold to Providence of the Double-A International League. From 1913 to 1917, Street played in the Class-A Southern Association with both Chattanooga and Nashville.

Gabby Street became known as Sergeant Street when he enlisted in the Army in March 1918. As Street put it, he was going off to fight in the "real" World Series.

"I was sent to Fort Slocum, N.Y., and everybody interested in baseball thought it was great that I should be on hand to catch the army team. I finally convinced my lieutenant that I joined the army to fight, pointing out that I could have continued playing baseball for a salary. I was one of the first 50,000 to get over and took part in three major engagements: Chateau Thierry, St. Mihiel and the Argonne. That St. Louis regiment, the 138th, was as fine as an outfit as I ever saw, and I was proud to be attached to it," said Sergeant Street.[13]

Street was assigned to the 1st Gas Regiment, Chemical Warfare Division. He and his men joined the 138th in the Battle of the Argonne. Street's men held down a smoke screen for the 138th Infantry on September 26, 1918. A machine-gun bullet from a German airplane punctured his right leg on October 2, 1918. He was awarded the Purple Heart, and his fighting days were at an end.

Street returned to Nashville after his discharge, but at the age of 36 his playing days were coming to an end. Street's goal was to return to the major leagues as a coach or manager. And he paid his dues, serving as a player-manager for the next nine seasons for six teams in three leagues. While managing Joplin (Missouri) of the Class-C Western Association in

1922-23, he met Lucinda Rona Chandler of Joplin. They were wed in 1923 and had two children, Charles Jr. and Sally.

The St. Louis Cardinals were building a juggernaut under the direction of general manager Branch Rickey. The Redbirds topped the Yankees in 1926, winning the franchise's first world championship in 1926, but were swept by New York in 1928. Sandwiched between the two pennant-winning seasons was a second-place finish by 1½ games to Pittsburgh. Gabby Street was added to new St. Louis manager Billy Southworth's coaching staff in 1929, but the Cardinals fell on hard times, finishing in fourth place, 20 games back. Southworth was replaced by Bill McKechnie just after midseason. St. Louis owner Sam Breadon had a penchant for making changes, especially managers. For the 1930 season, he replaced McKechnie with Street. Street was Breadon's sixth new manager to start a season in six years. Breadon said he had hired Street "because I believe he is just the man to give us a winner. He knows baseball through and through, is smart, a hustler, and the game is his main interest in life. The players like him and respect him. He was glad to get the job. It was unanimous."[14]

The team Street took the reins of was by no means a rebuilding project. Jim Bottomley, Frankie Frisch, George Watkins, Jimmie Wilson, and Chick Hafey anchored a formidable lineup in which each starter hit over .300 and the team scored 1,004 runs. The pitching staff was led by Jesse Haines, Bill Hallahan, and spitball hurler Burleigh Grimes. Street did not have the burden of developing players as he had in the minor leagues. Indeed it was a smart manager who recognized the talent on his club and did not tinker with it too much. "The difference is I don't have to show these fellows how to play ball," said Street. "Most of them have had long experience. They do the work and make my job easy for me."[15]

On July 31 the Cardinals were tied with Pittsburgh for fourth place, 11 games behind front-runner Brooklyn. But St. Louis went on an incredible streak in the final two months of the season, going 23-9 in August and posting a 21-4 record in September, clinching their third pennant with two games to play. On the last day, a young hurler named Dizzy Dean toed the rubber in his first major-league start. The brash youngster came as advertised, beating the Pirates 3-1 on a three-hitter. Street could add "miracle worker" to his other monikers, Gabby and Ol Sarge.

The Cardinals were matched up with the Philadelphia Athletics in the World Series. Frisch came down with a case of lumbago. He played, but his back was covered in bandages and plaster. He hit .208 for the Series. Only one Cardinal batted over .300 for the Series, shortstop Charlie Gelbert, who hit .353 while playing on a sore leg that was heavily wrapped each game. Lefty Grove and George Earnshaw each won two games as the A's took the Series in six games.

Frustration overcame Street as he dealt with Dean and his antics during spring training in 1931. Dean would often be late or just miss workouts and meetings altogether. "Let some of the other clucks work out for the staff. Nobody can beat me"[16] was a line Dean often fed to Street. The veteran players and Street had a respectful relationship and although Street might talk tough, he was extremely well-liked. There was no denying Dean's ability, but he drove Street and later Frankie Frisch crazy with his clowning around. Dean was eventually sent down to Houston of the Texas League, where he spent the bulk of the 1931 season. Prophetically, Street remarked, "I think he's going to be a great one. But I'm afraid we'll never know from one minute to the next what he's going to do or say."[17]

The 1931 season would prove that no miracle was needed. The Cards held a slim lead over the rest of the pack on May 30, then built on it and coasted to their second straight pennant with a record of 101-53. The 48-year-old Street put on the catching gear for one last time on September 20, 1931, starting a game against the Brooklyn Dodgers and playing long enough to get one at-bat. That wrapped up a career in which he batted .208 in 504 major-league games, hit two home runs, and drove in 105 runs. A relatively new face in the Cardinal lineup was center fielder

Pepper Martin. In his first full season with the Cards, Martin hit .300 and drove in 75 runs. Except for Mike Gonzalez and Frisch, the rest of the team were products of Rickey's farm system. Their opponent in the World Series was again the Athletics. Before the Series, Connie Mack said of the Cardinals, "I don't worry about their big hitters — Frisch, Bottomley, Hafey — but they've got a young man named Martin who bothers me. He's the kind of aggressive, unpredictable who could be the hero or the goat."[18]

Pepper Martin certainly was no goat, batting .500 with four doubles, one homer, five RBIs, and five stolen bases. Grimes and Hallahan each won two games. Grimes won the all-important Game Seven, 4-2, while Hallahan had what today would be recorded as a save. St. Louis scored two runs in the first inning, one on a wild pitch by Earnshaw, and one on an error by first baseman Jimmie Foxx. George Watkins hit a two-run homer in the third inning off Earnshaw to make the score 4-0, and the lead held up. The Cardinals had their second world championship. "I've seen a lot of great ballclubs in my day, but for pitching, hitting, spirit, and all-around balance, I would back my 1931 Cardinal team against any of them," Street said.[19] Frisch agreed with his skipper: "There's no question in my mind that the best club that I ever played with was the happily efficient Cardinal team of 1931."[20]

It may have been surprising that the Cardinals dropped to sixth place in 1932 with a 72-82-2 record. It did not get much better in 1933. Street was not around to see the end of the latter season, resigning on July 23 with a 46-45 record. Gabby's undoing began in spring training, when the sportswriters began to write about his "board of strategy." In essence, Street allowed some of the veteran players to assist him in the decisions he made on the field. The result was a cooperative team and two pennants. When the Cards started losing, Street's way naturally began to take a hit in the press. Suddenly Street felt he was not getting the credit he deserved for the two pennants.

In a spring-training meeting in 1933, Street blew up at his team, telling them that he and he alone would be making every decision in the dugout. "Gabby didn't like those stories about the Cardinal 'board of strategy' on the ballclub," said Frisch. "There wasn't going to be any board of strategy from there on. He'd crack the whip, he'd make all the decisions, he'd take all the responsibility, and maybe after the next pennant the Old Sergeant would get just a little bit of credit as manager of this club.

"Spoken or not, the sentiment was: 'We'll let him manage the ballclub, we'll let him crack the whip, and we'll let him get all the credit, and we'll just keep our damned mouths shut.' It hurt me to see the absolute divorce between manager and squad. I got him alone one day and asked him why in the world he had lost his temper and popped off like that to a club that thought so much of him. 'Frank,' he said, 'I just got so damned sick of that junk in the newspaper that I couldn't stand it any longer.'"[21]

Street returned to the minor leagues, managing the Mission (San Francisco) Reds of the Pacific Coast League (1934-35) and the St. Paul Pioneers of the American Association (1936-1937). He returned to St. Louis to manage the Browns in 1938. He was fired with 10 games left in the season and a record of 53-90. The Browns finished in seventh place, 44 games behind the New York Yankees. Street's career record managing in the big leagues was 365-332, a winning percentage of .524.

Street, an avid golfer and quail hunter, did not stay away from baseball for long. With a nickname like Gabby, he was a natural for a color commentator on radio broadcasts. He started his second career in 1940, providing his unique insight to Browns games, and was eventually paired with a young Harry Caray to broadcast Cardinals games from 1945 to 1950.

Charles Evard Street died of pancreatic cancer at the age of 67 on February 6, 1951, in Joplin, Missouri. In 1966 he was inducted into the Missouri Sports Hall of Fame. His former broadcast partner Caray served as the host. "Gabby could talk because he lived through so much," Caray said. "To be able to have this man as my friend was the greatest thing that could happen to me."[22]

And just how did Street get his nickname? "Down south, if you see a black boy, and want him, and don't know his name, you yell 'Hey Gabby.' It works in St. Louis too. And if you don't believe me, try it. To me, all black boys have been 'Gabby' and I got my nickname from the use of that word, and not, as is commonly believed, because I am a chatterbox."[23]

SOURCES

In addition to the sources mentioned in the notes, the author also consulted:

sabr.org/

stlouis.cardinals.mlb.com/index.jsp?c_id=stl&tcid=mm_cle_sitelist

baseball-reference.com/

baseball-almanac.com/

National Baseball Hall of Fame-Player File

NOTES

1. Alan Gould, Associated Press, "Gabby Street, Ace of the Cards," September 20, 1931.
2. *The Sporting News*, October 2, 1930, 5.
3. Unidentified clipping from Street's player file at the National Baseball Hall of Fame.
4. Ibid. The Street parents' occupation is unknown.
5. *Chicago Tribune*, June 6, 1905.
6. *Boston Globe*, June 8, 1905. Street's four errors in 18 chances in his three games with Boston saddled him with a .778 fielding percentage in the short stay, from which he also returned with a broken finger.
7. *Boston Globe*, June 10, 1905.
8. *Washington Post*, June 16, 1905.
9. Ibid.
10. Henry W. Thomas, *Walter Johnson: Baseball's Big Train* (Lincoln: University of Nebraska Press, 1995), 55.
11. Gould.
12. Baseball-almanac.com
13. *The Sporting News*, October 2, 1930, 5.
14. Gould.
15. Ibid.
16. John Heidenry, *The Gashouse Gang* (New York: Public Affairs, 2007), 51.
17. Lee Lowenfish, *Branch Rickey: Baseball's Ferocious Gentleman* (Lincoln: University of Nebraska Press, 2007), 199.
18. Norman Macht, *Connie Mack: The Turbulent and Triumphant Years—1915-1931* (Lincoln: University of Nebraska Press, 2012), 616.
19. Peter Golenbock, *The Spirit of St. Louis: A History of the St. Louis Cardinals and Browns* (New York: HarperCollins, 2000), 144.
20. Ibid.
21. Ibid. 163-164.
22. Street player file at the National Baseball Hall of Fame.
23. *The Sporting News*, October 2, 1930, 5.

American Tobacco Company T206 baseball card. Library of Congress.

SHOELESS JOE JACKSON

By David Fleitz

Shoeless Joe Jackson was a country boy from South Carolina who never learned to read or write much ("It don't take school stuff to help a fella play ball," he once said[1]) but is widely hailed as the greatest natural hitter in the history of the game. A left-handed batter and right-handed thrower, Jackson stood 6-feet-1 and weighed 178 well-built pounds. He belted sharp line drives to all corners of the ballpark, and was fast enough to lead the American League in triples three times. He never won a batting title, but his average of .408 in 1911 still stands as a Cleveland team record and a major-league rookie record.

Unfortunately, after Cleveland traded him to the Chicago White Sox, Jackson's career ended ignominiously because of his involvement in the infamous Black Sox Scandal of 1919. He was expelled from the game in his prime, and for that reason he has never received a plaque in the Baseball Hall of Fame at Cooperstown.

Joseph Jefferson Wofford Jackson was born on July 16, 1888, in rural Pickens County, South Carolina.[2] His father, George, was a laborer who settled in nearby Greenville soon after Joe's birth and found employment at Brandon Mill, a textile factory that paid $1.25 a day. Brandon Mill stood on the west side of Greenville, and there George Jackson and his wife, Martha, set up a household in one of the small, company-owned houses. Joe, the oldest of eight children, began working at the mill at age 6 or 7. He never attended school, but he did learn to play baseball. Brandon Mill sponsored a team that faced squads from other mills and factories, and Joe earned a spot in the lineup when he was 13 years old. He had his father's unusually long arms and he excelled at throwing and hitting a ball. He soon became renowned throughout the Carolinas as an outfielder, pitcher, and home-run hitter, which were known throughout the mill league as "Saturday Specials."

A local fan named Charlie Ferguson made bats in his spare time, and he chose a four-by-four beam from the north side of a particularly strong hickory tree to make one for young Joe Jackson. It measured 36 inches long and weighed about 48 ounces. Ferguson darkened the bat with tobacco juice; Joe called it "Black Betsy" and eventually took it to the major leagues.

Joe played for factory teams and semipro clubs until 1908, when Greenville obtained a franchise in the Carolina Association, a new Class D league on the lowest level of Organized Baseball. He signed a contract with the Greenville Spinners for $75 a month. Jackson, who was making about $45 a month between working at the mill and playing ball, reportedly told manager Tom Stouch, "I'll play my head off for $75 a month."[3] Although Jackson later learned to trace his own name, he signed his first professional contract with an "X."

The strong, agile 19-year-old quickly became the biggest star in the Carolina Association, leading the league with a .346 average, making phenomenal throws and catches in center field, and serving as mop-up pitcher. A reporter for the *Greenville News* tagged him with his nickname that season, when Joe played a game in his stocking feet because his new baseball shoes were not yet broken in. For the rest of his life he was known as Shoeless Joe Jackson. He didn't like his nickname and later told Atlanta reporter Furman Bisher, "I've read and heard every kind of yarn imaginable on how I got the name.... I never played the outfield barefoot, and that was the only day I ever played in my stockinged feet, but it stuck with me."[4]

He also gained a wife that year, marrying 15-year-old Katie Wynn on July 19, 1908. She had brown hair and brown eyes, and some education, since she could read and white. She remained married to Joe for 43 years, and until the day Joe died she wrote his letters, managed his money, and read his contracts in and out of baseball.

In August 1908 Philadelphia Athletics manager Connie Mack bought Jackson's contract for a reported $900.[5] Joe was reluctant to go north, and Greenville manager Stouch accompanied him on the train ride to Philadelphia. Joe made his first major-league appearance on August 25, and singled in his first trip to the plate. However, Joe was homesick, and three days later he boarded a train back to Greenville. He returned in early September, but Philadelphia, a city of 2 million people, was frightening to the illiterate country boy. Jackson jumped the team once more before the 1908 season ended, finishing his first major-league stint with three hits in 23 at-bats.

Jackson bounced between Philadelphia and the minors for the next two years. He won batting titles at Savannah in 1909 and at New Orleans in 1910, but did not hit well in Philadelphia in a 1909 late-season call-up. Joe admired manager Connie Mack ("a mighty fine man [who] taught me more baseball than any other manager I had"[6]) but he did not get along with his A's teammates, many of whom teased him mercilessly about his illiteracy, which he tried to hide, and lack of polish. Mack reluctantly decided that Joe would never succeed in Philadelphia, and traded him to the Cleveland Naps for outfielder Bris Lord and $6,000 in July 1910. In mid-September, at the conclusion of New Orleans' season, Joe reported to Cleveland.

Cleveland was a smaller city than Philadelphia. Many of Jackson's new teammates were either Southerners or had played in the South, so Joe fit in well. Playing in right field and center field, Joe batted .387 in the final month of the 1910 season and claimed a permanent place in the Cleveland lineup.

In 1911 he made a major leap to stardom, battering American League pitching for 233 hits, 45 doubles, 19 triples, and a .408 batting average. He did not win the batting title (Detroit's Ty Cobb batted .420), but he set Cleveland team records for hits, average, and outfield assists (32) that still stand (as of 2014). His torrid hitting helped lift the Naps to a third-place finish. Cobb paid tribute to Jackson as the season ended. "Joe is a grand ball player, and one who will get better and better. There is no denying that he is a better ball player his first year in the big league than anyone ever was."[7]

Jackson swung the bat harder than most of his contemporaries, and players swore that his line drives sounded different from anyone else's. Many other players held their hands apart on the bat and punched at the ball, but Joe put his hands together near the bottom of the handle and took a full swing. "I used to draw a line three inches from the plate every time I came to bat," Jackson said many years later. "I drew a right angle line at the end of it, right next to the catcher, and put my left foot on it exactly three inches from home plate."[8] He stood in the box, feet close together, then took one long step into the pitch and ripped at it with his left-handed swing. "I copied my swing after Joe Jackson's," Babe Ruth told Grantland Rice in 1919. "His is the perfectest."[9]

Though the Naps fell from third place to fifth in 1912, Jackson batted .395, with 121 runs scored, 226 hits, and 30 outfield assists. He also set a new American League record with 26 triples, a mark that was tied by Sam Crawford in 1914 but has never been surpassed. However, Joe once again finished second in the batting race to Cobb, who batted .409 for the Tigers. "What a hell of a league this is," Jackson wailed to a reporter. "I hit .387, .408, and .395 the last three years and I ain't won nothing yet!"[10]

Jackson displayed his power on June 4, 1913, when he belted a fastball from the Yankees' Russ Ford; the hit bounced off the roof of the right-field grandstand at

A posed photo of Joe Jackson, possibly 1920. Courtesy of David Fleitz.

the Polo Grounds and into the street beyond. The newspapers claimed that the blast traveled more than 500 feet. Jackson's .373 average that year trailed Cobb once again, but he led the league in hits with 197 and doubles with 39, finishing second in the Chalmers Award balloting. His total of walks also increased sharply.

Joe turned down offers from the new Federal League in early 1914, though two Cleveland pitchers joined the new circuit and left the Naps shorthanded on the mound. Federal League raids and the sudden decline of Nap Lajoie caused the Naps to drop from contention, and injuries to Jackson and shortstop Ray Chapman doomed them to last place for the first time in their history. Forced by a broken leg to miss 35 games, Joe saw his average dip to .338 with only 61 runs scored and 53 runs batted in, and he posted new career lows in the speed-dependent categories of triples and stolen bases.

Controversy swirled around Jackson during the 1915 season. He had spent the winter months headlining a vaudeville show that drew curious crowds throughout the South. Joe enjoyed the theatrical life so much that he refused to report for spring training, threatening to quit baseball and begin a new career on the stage. Katie Jackson reacted poorly to that idea, and filed for divorce that March (though she and Joe soon reconciled). In May, team owner Charles Somers ordered manager Joe Birmingham to move Jackson to first base to make room for rookie Elmer Smith in the outfield. Joe played 30 games at first, but the experiment ended when Joe left the lineup with a sore arm. Somers became incensed when Birmingham blamed the position switch for Jackson's injury, and the team owner soon fired Birmingham, appointing coach Lee Fohl to succeed him.

In 1915 Somers, teetering on the edge of bankruptcy, decided that he could not afford to keep his two best players, Jackson and Chapman. He needed to trade one and rebuild the ballclub (which was renamed the Indians after the team sold Lajoie to Philadelphia that spring) around the other. Somers' mind was made up when the newspapers reported that the Federal League had offered Jackson a multiple-year contract at a salary of $10,000 per year. Somers feared that Jackson would bolt for the new circuit, leaving the Indians with nothing in exchange, so the Cleveland owner solicited offers for his cleanup hitter.

Jackson, who at the time was in the second season of a three-year contract for $6,000 a year, was not opposed to a trade. "I think I am in a rut here in Cleveland," he told local sportswriter Henry Edwards, "and would play better somewhere else."[11] Indeed, Jackson's batting average had now declined for four consecutive years. The Washington Senators offered a package of players for Jackson, but Somers rejected the bid to await a better one, which soon came from the Chicago White Sox. Owner Charles Comiskey coveted Jackson, and sent his secretary, Harry Grabiner, to Cleveland with a blank check. "Go to Cleveland," Comiskey ordered, "watch the bidding for Jackson, [and] raise the highest one made by any club until they all drop out."[12]

On August 21, 1915, Grabiner and Somers reached an agreement. Somers signed Joe to a three-year contract extension at his previous salary, then sent him to Chicago for $31,500 in cash and three players (outfielders Bobby Roth and Larry Chappell and pitcher Ed Klepfer) who collectively had cost the White Sox $34,000 to acquire. In terms of the total value of cash and players, this $65,500 transaction was the most expensive deal ever made in baseball up to that time.

Joe's five-year stay in Cleveland ended with some sniping from the sports pages. Henry Edwards of the *Plain Dealer* criticized Jackson on his way out of town. "While he does not admit it, he was becoming … a purely individual player who sacrificed team work for Joe Jackson. … If he were still the Jackson of 1911, 1912, and 1913, the team would not have let him get away."[13]

Jackson joined a contending team, one that featured four future Hall of Famers (second baseman Eddie Collins, catcher Ray Schalk, and pitchers Red Faber and Ed Walsh). Jackson hit poorly (for him) in the last six weeks of the 1915 season, and some observers believed that Joe's career was on the downslide. However, he rebounded in 1916, batting .341 with a league-leading 21 triples as the White Sox challenged Boston for the league lead. Chicago finished second that season, but roared to the pennant with a 100-win season in 1917 despite a subpar performance by Jackson, who was hobbled all year after he sprained an ankle in spring training. Joe's average dipped to .277 in early September, but he finished with a flurry of hits that lifted his final mark to .301.

With the pennant safely clinched, the White Sox sent Jackson and Buck Weaver to Boston for an all-star game to benefit the family of the popular player-turned-sportswriter Tim Murnane, who had died in February. Before the game, Jackson won a distance-throwing competition by heaving a ball 396 feet, 8 inches, which was said to be a modern record for a big leaguer.[14] The all-stars, with an outfield of Ty Cobb, Tris Speaker, and Jackson, and Walter Johnson on the mound, lost 2-0 to Babe Ruth and the Red Sox.

Glove in hip pocket, Joe Jackson takes batting practice, 1919. Courtesy of David Fleitz.

During the World Series New York Giants manager John McGraw used left-handed starting pitchers in four of the six games in a bid to neutralize the hitting of Collins and Jackson, but Joe batted .304 and saved the first game with a circus catch in left field. Red Faber won three decisions as the White Sox defeated the Giants four games to two for their second World Series championship, and the last one they would win for more than eight decades. Joe celebrated the victory, and the $3,669.32 winning share that went along with it, by purchasing a new Oldsmobile Pacemaker from a dealership in his new home of Savannah, Georgia, where he and Katie had moved to after his trade to the White Sox.

The White Sox were rocked by the entry of the United States into World War I. Several Chicago players enlisted in the military, while others were drafted in the early months of 1918. Joe, as a married man, was granted a deferment by his hometown draft board in Greenville, but after he played 17 games with the White Sox the board reversed its decision and ordered him to report for induction.[15] Instead, Jackson found employment at a Delaware shipyard, where he helped build battleships and played ball in a hastily assembled factory circuit, the Bethlehem Steel League. Jackson was the first prominent player to avoid the draft by opting for war work, for which he was severely criticized in the sporting press, especially in Chicago.

When two of Jackson's close friends, pitcher Lefty Williams and reserve catcher Byrd Lynn, followed him into the shipyards, owner Charles Comiskey swore he would not let any of them return to his team. "There is no room on my club for players who wish to evade the army draft by entering the employ of ship concerns!" he fumed.[16] But after a sixth-place finish and the war's end, he changed his tune. Jackson won the factory league batting title with a .393 average and helped lead the Harlan & Hollingsworth team to the championship among shipyards on the Atlantic coast, but the controversy permanently damaged his relationships with the Chicago sportswriters.

With little leverage, Jackson signed a new one-year contract for $6,000—the same salary he had been receiving since 1914—and returned to the White Sox. He was healthy again, and led the club in batting as the White Sox grabbed first place and held it for most of the 1919 season. Joe finished fourth in the league in batting with a .351 mark, his best average since 1913, with 181 hits and 96 runs batted in. Faber, Chicago's leading pitcher, was sidelined late in the season with a sore arm, but Eddie Cicotte (29-7) and Lefty Williams (23-11) picked up the slack and pitched the White Sox into a comfortable lead in the standings. On September 24 Jackson drove home the winning run in the pennant-clinching game against the St. Louis Browns.

The White Sox were considered the most talented team in baseball, but they were also one of the unhappiest. The biggest problem facing the team was the same one that had been festering for several years. Eddie Collins, Red Faber, and Ray Schalk made up one clique, while Chick Gandil, Fred McMullin, Swede Risberg, and Buck Weaver made up an opposing faction. The two groups sniped at each other all season long. "The wonderful (Philadelphia) Athletic teams I played for believed in teamwork and cooperation," Collins said many years later. "I always thought you couldn't win without those virtues until I joined the White Sox."[17] A third group, including Jackson, Happy Felsch, and Lefty Williams, rarely spoke to the college-educated Collins and Faber, less out of animosity than out of a lack of common interests.

Late in the season, first baseman Chick Gandil, the leader of the first group, concocted a plan to fix the coming World Series against the Cincinnati Reds. Jackson, according to his own later admissions, rebuffed Gandil's first offer to throw the Series for $10,000 but he later agreed to participate after Gandil upped the offer to $20,000—an amount more than three times his annual salary.[18] Jackson had nothing to do with the planning of the fix; unlike Gandil, he had no contacts in the netherworld of gambling and nightlife. Joe's participation consisted solely of trusting Gandil, a stunning amount of faith in a man whom he didn't know very well. It was an incredible lapse of judgment, as well as a failure of character, on Jackson's part.

Jackson, who ultimately received only $5,000, batted .375 against the Reds but failed to drive in a run in the first five games, four of which the White Sox lost (it was a best-of-nine Series that year). Chicago won the sixth and seventh games, but fell behind quickly in the eighth contest. Jackson belted a homer, the only one of the Series, and drove in three runs in Game Eight, but his production came too late. Cincinnati defeated the favored White Sox by a 10-5 score and won its first World Series title. Jackson tied a record with his 12 hits in the Series, but eight of the 12 came during the four games the White Sox tried to win. In Chicago's first four losses, Jackson went 4-for-16.

Before going home for the winter, Jackson went to Comiskey's office in the ballpark and waited to see the Old Roman. Jackson wanted to tell Comiskey about the fix and possibly to return the money he had received. He stayed for several hours, but Comiskey holed up in his office and Jackson eventually left without talking to the White Sox owner.

In February 1920 team secretary Harry Grabiner traveled to Jackson's home in Savannah and signed him to a substantial raise, a three-year deal for $8,000 per year. Jackson operated a successful poolroom there and a dry-cleaning business that employed more than 20 people. He and Katie used the money he had received for fixing the World Series to pay for his ill sister Gertrude's hospital bills.

Despite the cloud of suspicion that hovered over him and several of his teammates, Jackson gave one of his finest performances in 1920, with a .382 average, a career-best 121 runs batted in, and a league-leading 20 triples. However, amid growing rumors that the White Sox were continuing to throw games in the 1920 season, Jackson felt alienated from most of the other Series conspirators. His evenings on the road

Jackson poses in front of the dugout, 1920. Courtesy of David Fleitz.

consisted of going to the movies or bars with Lefty Williams, his best friend on the team.

With the White Sox fighting for a pennant entering the season's final week, Jackson's season ended abruptly on September 28, a day after a Philadelphia newspaper published allegations by gambler Billy Maharg claiming that eight members of the White Sox had helped him and other gamblers fix the World Series. Later that day, on the advice of White Sox team counsel Alfred Austrian, Cicotte, Jackson, and Williams appeared before a Cook County grand jury investigating the matter and testified about their involvement. Comiskey immediately suspended Jackson and the six other accused players who were still with the team.

Jackson's appearance before the grand jury on September 28 was responsible for one of the most enduring legends in sports. As reported by Charley Owens of the *Chicago Daily News*, a small child is said to have looked at Jackson exiting the court building and begged, "Say it ain't so, Joe." Jackson and many others denied that the incident ever happened. "There wasn't a bit of truth in it," Jackson told reporter Furman Bisher in 1949. "When I came out of the building, this deputy asked me where I was going, and I told him to the South Side. ... There was a big crowd hanging around the front of the building, but nobody else said anything to me. It just didn't happen, that's all. Charley Owens just made up a good story and wrote it."[19]

Despite being acquitted by a trial jury, all eight accused players, including the retired Gandil, were eventually expelled from baseball for life by new Commissioner Kenesaw Mountain Landis. The scandal brought a sad and untimely end to Joe Jackson's brilliant baseball career.

Jackson, whose lifetime batting average of .356 is the third highest in the game's history, played semipro and "unorganized" ball, mostly in the South, for many years thereafter. Wherever he went, his cannon arm and effortless swing drew attention. In 1923 he signed with a team from Americus, Georgia, in the outlaw South Georgia League, and helped lead them to a championship. There was some controversy because the league did not want its younger players to be penalized or banned from Organized Baseball for playing with him. However, he batted well over .400, made incredible catches and throws, and drew large crowds throughout the season.

In 1923 Jackson hired a Milwaukee-based attorney, Ray Cannon, and sued the White Sox for back pay he felt was owed to him after his acquittal in the Black Sox trial. Joe believed that Harry Grabiner had taken advantage of his illiteracy in obtaining his signature on a contract that included the hated "reserve clause," which effectively allowed teams to control their players in perpetuity. A jury sided with Jackson and awarded him more than $16,000 in back pay, but Jackson's deposition about his involvement in the World Series scandal clashed so much with his 1920 grand jury testimony that the judge threw out the verdict and charged Jackson with perjury. Jackson settled with Comiskey for an undisclosed amount and went back home to Georgia.[20]

For the next several years, Jackson played ball in the South, where folks regarded him with kindness and still stood in awe of his ability. He sported a sizable paunch around his midsection, but he could still knock the stuffing out of a baseball until he was nearly 50 years old. He gave a few newspaper interviews in which he made his case for reinstatement, but mostly stayed out the public eye during the last three decades of his life.

"All the big sportswriters seemed to enjoy writing about me as an ignorant cotton-mill boy with nothing but lint where my brains ought to be," Jackson said in 1949. "That was all right with me. I was able to fool a lot of pitchers and managers and club owners I wouldn't have been able to fool if they'd thought I was smarter."[21]

Jackson eventually moved back to his old neighborhood in Greenville, near the Brandon Mill textile factory, where he operated a successful restaurant and a liquor store for many years. He spent a great deal of time teaching baseball to the local youngsters and organizing impromptu games, even as he suffered from diabetes and liver and heart problems in his later years. In September 1951 Cleveland Indians fans honored him by voting him into the team's Hall of Fame and, in the ensuing publicity blitz, Jackson agreed to travel to New York to appear on Ed Sullivan's "Toast of the Town" television show. However, just two weeks before his scheduled appearance, Jackson suffered a heart attack and he died at home, at the age of 63, on December 5, 1951. He was buried in Woodlawn Memorial Park in Greenville.

Note: A version of this biography originally appeared in David Jones, ed., *Deadball Stars of the American League* (Washington, D.C.: Potomac Books, Inc., 2006).

NOTES

1 Paul Dickson, *Baseball's Greatest Quotations* (New York: Harper Perennial, 1992), 204.

2 Jackson's date of birth has been recorded as 1887, 1888, and 1889 in different places. The family Bible was lost in a fire many years ago, but although Joe's official birth certificate lists his birth year as 1889, his tombstone lists his year of birth as 1888.

3 F.C. Lane, "The Man Who Might Have Been the Greatest Player in the Game," *Baseball Magazine*, March 1916, 59.

4 Furman Bisher, "This Is the Truth," *Sport Magazine*, October 1949.

5 *Greenville News*, August 17, 1908. Mack paid $1,500 for Jackson and outfielder/pitcher Scotty Barr. The Greenville newspaper reported that Jackson's value was $900, though other sources differ on the breakdown.

6 Bisher, "This Is the Truth."

7 *Cleveland Plain Dealer*, October 4, 1911.

8 Bisher, "This Is the Truth."

9 Peter Golenbock, *Fenway: An Unexpurgated History of the Boston Red Sox* (New York: Putnam Publishing, 1992), 56.

10 Harvey Frommer, *Shoeless Joe and Ragtime Baseball* (Dallas: Taylor Publishing, 1992), 41.

11 *Cleveland Plain Dealer*, August 21, 1915.

12 *The Sporting News*, August 26, 1915.

13 *Cleveland Plain Dealer*, August 21, 1915.

14 However, several minor leaguers had cleared 400 feet in earlier distance-throwing competitions. And in 1881, pitcher Tony Mullane had thrown a ball nearly 417 feet.

15 *Chicago Daily News*, May 3, 1918.

16 *The Sporting News*, June 20, 1918.

17 Bob Broeg, *Superstars of Baseball* (St. Louis: The Sporting News, 1971), 38.

18 This is the explanation Joe Jackson gave in his testimony to the Cook County Grand Jury on September 28, 1920.

19 Bisher, "This Is the Truth."

20 *Chicago Herald-Examiner*, February 16, 1924.

21 Bisher, "This Is the Truth."

HOMER SIMPSON

By Bill Nowlin

Homer Simpson may live forever in baseball history as the man who pinch hit for Darryl Strawberry—who had already hit nine home runs (four-base hits often dubbed "homers")—in the 1992 City Championship game between Springfield and Shelbyville. It was Simpson who knocked in the winning run, being knocked *out* in the process, and gave victory to Springfield.

Patrick Henry once uttered "Give me liberty or give me death!" Numerous other public figures have been immortalized for short or snappy sayings. No one tops Homer Simpson. Simpson's most-noted and most-quoted words (actually, it's just one word) are (is), "D'oh!" which may now be found in the *Oxford English Dictionary*, albeit without the apostrophe.

Like many baseball players of yesteryear, Homer Jay Simpson's precise birthday may never be known. It's commonly understood that he was born in March of 1956, though some accounts have him being born a year earlier. The latter date may have been his "baseball age," designed to make him look younger for baseball scouts on the look for fresh prospects.

Homer's parents were Abraham Jay-Jedediah and Mona Penelope (Olsen) Simpson. Abraham claimed that he came to America as boy from the "old country," but has never been able to remember which old country that had been. Young Abe was raised in New York City by his parents, Orville J. Simpson and Yuma Hickman, since deceased. Abe Simpson's occupation remains unknown, along with his true place of birth, both ripe subjects for research by genealogists. He is known to have served his country as a sergeant with the Flying Hellfish during the Second World War and to have a love for the show *Matlock* (1986- 1995), a television series starring Andy Griffith. Abe Simpson also had a bit of a wandering eye, and had two illegitimate children, one named Herbert Powell, the other being a daughter named Abbie who was conceived while he was stationed in England during WWII. Even less is known about his brothers Cyrus and Chet. Abe Simpson was briefly married to his son Homer's short-term wife Amber (Homer married her on a short visit to Vegas with neighbor Ned Flanders and Abe was later tricked into marrying her when she visited Springfield)—this may have been more confusing to the parties involved than to the reader. Abe Simpson was also married for a very short time to Homer's sister-in-law Selma Bouvier.[1]

A born storyteller, Abe's stories sometimes seem to get lost in the telling, and his loving son Homer ultimately had to consign him to the care of the Springfield Retirement Castle.[2]

Mona Simpson became estranged from Abe; she was forced to abandon her family after seeing Joe Namath's long hair during Super Bowl III and consequently (quite understandably) becoming caught up in the hippie movement. She joined a commune with fellow hippies Seth and Munchie, and in time hippiedom led to yippiedom and she became politically active. At one point, protesting germ research, she was part of a group which broke into C. Montgomery Burns's laboratory and destroyed all the biological warfare experiments in progress. She served no time for the offense but was later tried in court on another matter, a carjacking. She was acquitted, after an impassioned speech by son Homer, though the long arm of the law finally caught up with her and she was imprisoned for signing into a national park under a false name. Mona Simpson later died (well after doing her time), as documented in the episode "Mona Leaves-a," and was cremated, her ashes thrown to the wind (where they disrupt a missile launch.)[3]

Homer Simpson's wife is Marjorie (née Bouvier, and perhaps related to Jacqueline Kennedy.) Her own mother was indeed named Jacqueline, and her father named Clancy. He was a former flight attendant. Marge was either older or younger than Homer; her birthday was on October 1, 1954 — or 1956. With her twin older sisters Patty and Selma, the bevy of Bouviers attended Springfield High School, where she met Homer in their senior year. Marge never held as many jobs as Homer, who could be said to be something of a workaholic[4], but in addition to her prime responsibility as homemaker, she had also held positions as a nuclear technician at Springfield's nuclear power plant, selling real estate, running a pretzel business, working at an erotic bakery, and as a police officer for a little less than one episode. She appeared on the cover of the November 2008 issue of *Playboy* magazine. Not six months later, Homer Simpson became the first living former baseball player to appear on a postage stamp issued by the United States Postal Service.[5]

The couple had three children (Bartholomew JoJo "Bart" Simpson, born on April Fool's Day, 1979; Lisa Marie Simpson, born on September 28, 1981; and Margaret "Maggie" Simpson, born in November 1986 on a date not fully pinned-down.) There have been inconstant rumors ("impersistent" is not a valid word in Scrabble) that Bart Simpson was named in part with a thought to Commissioner of Major League Baseball A. Bartlett Giammati, though if so it was in honor of his presidency of Yale University, since Giammati was only named Commissioner well after his namesake was born.[6] The Simpson's family respect for higher education is long-established, dating back at least to Grandpa Simpson's noted reverence for Harvard-educated attorney Benjamin Leighton "Ben" Matlock.

One wonders, of course, if Homer's parents had baseball in mind when they named their son.

How many baseball scouts tracked Homer Simpson in his developmental years is unknown; the answer could well be: none.[7]

It seems evident that Simpson did not benefit from consultation with a team nutritionist at any stage of his career, nor did he spend much (if any) time at Mark Verstegen's EXOS in Phoenix (formerly Athletes' Performance Institute - API).

Just three (or four) years younger than Scott Boras (born 1952), young Homer came of age just too late to truly benefit from agent representation. It was only on March 16, 1976 that Andy Messersmith was granted free agency and signed with the Atlanta Braves. Homer was available to sign as an amateur free agent but remained undrafted, beginning his career playing industrial league ball or town ball with the Springfield Nuclear Plant team.

Truth be told, the first time Simpson was seen in public was on April 19, 1987, when he and his whole family — even Maggie — appeared on *The Tracey Ullman Show*. None of his baseball skills were exhibited during that appearance; he was not what any scout would term a "five-tool player" — though he did gave eight other attributes that have been amply evident from the start: he was "crude, bald, overweight, incompetent, clumsy, lazy, a heavy drinker, and ignorant."[8] He ranked a solid 20 on most scouts' 20-to-80 skills scale.

Simpson's baseball career came in the midst of his duties as a Nuclear Safety Inspector in section 7G for the Springfield Nuclear Power Plant.

If a lengthy resume is any sign of hard work, Simpson was a hard worker indeed. Some might counter that it was proof he was hardly working. It has been calculated that he has held 188 jobs.[9] "Well, those are side jobs — he's worked at the nuclear plant forever," one of his creators, James L. Brooks once said. "That's his steady gig — let's call it one job and 187 part-time jobs."[10]

Indeed, before settling in for the position he was seemingly destined to perform — that of Nuclear

Safety Inspector—Simpson did have quite a number of other jobs. A partial alphabetical list of his work history is appended.[11]

A right-hander, he signed up for a company softball team that had come off a tough 2-28 season in 1991. It had been their best season to date. Standing in at 5-foot-9 7/10, Simpson is listed with a weight that usually fluctuates around 239-241 pounds.[12] That puts him perhaps a little under Rich Garces and a full 40-plus pounds less than Adam Dunn.

His principal claim to fame in the National Pastime came during the 1992 season when he hit home run after home run with the Wonderbat, his custom-crafted home-made bat. It was Simpson who inspired and led Springfield's Nuclear Power Plant team to a worst-to-first season that year. As indicated, the prior season had been their best year ever, but they still had finished in the cellar. In 1992, with Homer hammering homers in game after game, the team rose in the standings, right up to the point when the city championship was on the line.

With expanded rosters, and new field manager C. (for Charles) Montgomery Burns taking charge, a number of very recently-hired Nuclear Power Plant employees were penciled in for postseason play. Some of the names were well-known former ballplayers from other leagues, and two of them—Wade Boggs and Ozzie Smith—are members of the National Baseball Hall of Fame.

When Roger Clemens, pitching b.p., fired an underarm fastball that shattered Simpson's bat during warmups for the 1992 City Championship game, the evidence was clear: the Wonderbat was a legitimate one. This was no corked bat, nor was it stuffed with superballs.[13] It was indeed a smooth, round stick not more than 2 ¾ inches in diameter at the thickest part and was one piece of solid wood. Carved by Homer himself from a limb struck by lightning in his own backyard, he had perhaps not secured approval from MLB's Rules Committee prior to use. The Commissioner of Major League Baseball declined to acknowledge a request for data on the Wonderbat.[14]

Just prior to the game itself, what could be described as "a series of unfortunate events" befell all but one of the new members of the Springfield team. The only remaining one of the new men was Darryl Strawberry, who already had eight seasons with the New York Mets under his belt and, following a November 1990 free agent signing with the Los Angeles Dodgers, had continued to play right field on the West Coast. Burns assigned Strawberry to play right for Springfield, leaving Simpson on the bench for the critical title game against the Shelbyville Nuclear Power Plant nine. The 1992 City Championship was on the line.

Needless to say, Simpson was not pleased by having Strawberry supplant him. As the leader of the team, he was now the only one on the team no longer in the starting lineup. He gripes that Strawberry is "bigger than me, faster than me, stronger than me, and he already has more friends around the plant than I do." Simpson grabbed some bench; his moment was yet to come.

The story is told elsewhere, but the score stood 43-43 in the bottom of the ninth. There were two outs and the bases were loaded, with Strawberry striding to the plate. He already had nine home runs in the game (the major-league record is a trifling four, a record shared by 16 players.) Strawberry is a left-handed hitter who later wrapped up his career in the big leagues with 335 homers and exactly 1,000 runs batted in.

The wily Mr. Burns told Strawberry to hit the showers so he could put in a right-handed batter against Shelbyville's southpaw. "It's called playing the percentages," he explained. "It's what smart managers do to win ballgames." Burns called on Homer Simpson. But Simpson was without the Wonderbat. Burns reminded Simpson of the signals, but Simpson became confused and was clearly distracted watching Burns in the third-base coaching box. The pitch came in high and hard—and hit Homer in the head. He fell down, knocked out cold, across home plate. The runner on third moved his unconscious body aside and stepped on the plate, forced in thanks to the hit-by-pitch with the tie-breaking run. Simpson had won the game for Springfield, 44-43.

Questions regarding Simpson's use of androstenedione during the regular season were deflected by Simpson's agents, as the supplement was not banned by the International Olympic Committee until 1997, and later Major League Baseball. Credentialed sportswriters who regularly covered Springfield Nuclear Plant games…actually don't exist, but it was observed that Simpson's locker often contained empty cartons of doughnuts and empty cans of Duff Beer. Neither are subject to testing under the Dangerous Contaminated Supplements list agreed to in collective bargaining by MLB and the Players' Association. Despite his athletic accomplishments during both the 1992 regular season and the championship game, a study commissioned by London's *Daily Mail* concluded that 59% of parents in the United Kingdom felt that Homer promoted an unhealthy lifestyle.[15]

It appears that Simpson was content to go out on top and declined to pursue a career in the game. Strawberry reverted to the major leagues.

Despite having played on the same team as Darryl Strawberry and the rest of the ringers, and driven in the winning run, an exhaustive search of the records of *The Sporting News* and databases Retrosheet.org and Baseball-Reference.com turn up no player of the name Homer Simpson in Organized Baseball.

SABR's Minor League Database also lacks a player of the name. There were eight major-league ballplayers with the surname Simpson, including two All-Stars (Harry "Suitcase" Simpson and Wayne Simpson), and 117 minor leaguers named Simpson, 21 of which have no known first names. Those with unknown first names played in years ranging between 1887 and 1946, so there is the possibility of a baseball pedigree there, but this will require further research by SABR's dedicated Minor Leagues Committee members. There was one player intriguingly listed as "H. Simpson" but he played in 1910 in the Class D Southwest Texas League (61 games, batting .210 for the Bay City Rice Eaters.) Clearly, this couldn't have been the Homer Simpson born in the mid-1950s, but might perhaps have been a progenitor should Abe Simpson's notion of coming to America from the Old Country been confused.

There have been 13 with the first name Homer, but that's probably neither here nor there. There are none at all with the first name of Single, Double, or Triple, and none with names such as Sacrifice Fly.

Simpson has continued to work for Springfield's nuclear plant at 100 Industrial Way. Not once during his tenure has the plant experienced a complete meltdown.

Being the safety inspector at a nuclear power plant is a job requiring dedication and diligence. One has to be on one's toes at all times, and run a shipshape shop. The only surprise inspection during his tenure turned up some minor violations, as any unannounced visit is wont to do: the emergency exits signs were actually just painted on walls that really went nowhere. There were only 340 violations on the visit, things such as luminous rats and mutant three-eyed fish and the like, perhaps due to some of the pipes and drums leaking radioactive waste. Some of the waste was dumped a little out of the way in a children's playground. Possibly the plutonium paperweight was not proper. All in all, though, Simpson had held his trusted position for more than 25 years so things couldn't have been too bad.

In any particular stressful day monitoring plant safety, he can always look back on the day he made Springfield proud, being carried off with the trophy after the 1992 championship game.

SOURCES

In addition to the sources noted in this biography, the author did not consult any player files or player questionnaires from the National Baseball Hall of Fame, and his consultation of the *Encyclopedia of Minor League Baseball*, Retrosheet.org, Baseball-Reference.com, or the SABR Minor Leagues Database, accessed online at Baseball-Reference.com, was all in vain. Efforts by SABR's Oral History Committee to reach Simpson proved fruitless, apparently due to his lifelong aversion to modern dentistry.

NOTES

1. Much of the painstaking work documenting Abraham Simpson's genealogy is available on the blog located at http://thesimpsonsrocks.wordpress.com/abraham-simpson/

2. Members of SABR's Oral History Committee are urged to contact Simpson there to take down his life story, but are cautioned to bring backup batteries for their digital recorders.

3. http://thesimpsonsrocks.wordpress.com/mona-simpson/

4. This depends, of course, on who's doing the saying.

5. First day covers are dated May 7, 2009.

6. The rumors are traceable to suppositional remarks made by the author during SABR's annual convention in Houston, Texas on August 1, 2014, but have never gained traction anywhere.

7. A thorough search of the Hall of Fame's Diamond Minds exhibit turned up nothing, and consultation with SABR's Scouts Committee database was equally unproductive.

8. The characterization was succinctly supplied by an anonymous contributor to the noted website known as Wikipedia where — truth be told (or something often approaching truth) — a great deal of Simpsons' lore may be mined. One of SABR's standard BioProject biographies goes through a rigorous series of peer reviewers and fact-checkers. That seemed a little pointless in the current case, given that almost everything regarding the subject is fictional — whether factual or not. Credit is due, however, to various anonymous contributors to the internets. We would accord them individual credit by name if we knew their names, though we're not sure all of them would want to acknowledge they actually took the time and trouble to know the things they post.

9. Larry Carroll, "'Simpsons' Trivia, From Swearing Lisa To 'Burns-Sexual' Smithers" MTV, July 20, 2007. Retrieved September 21, 2008.

10. The author came across this quotation somewhere.

11. Simpson's job history, as of a certain date, is summarized below, in an unconventional alphabetical listing. Most of the jobs he seems to have held for less than 30 minutes, or fleeting mention is made of them. Presumably, these were not all paid positions, and it is safe to assume he is not drawing unemployment benefits from more than a dozen or two of them.

    - Army private ("G.I. (Annoyed Grunt)")
    - Agent (3 times)
        - Lurleen Lumpkin ("Colonel Homer")
        - Lisa and Cameron, Aka Johnny Rainbow ("A Star Is Torn")
    - Ambulance driver ("Diatribe of a Mad Housewife")
    - Amateur-Division Professional Arm Wrestler ("Marge's Son Poisoning")
    - Astronaut for NASA[2] ("Deep Space Homer")
    - Attack-dog trainer for the Pitiless Pup Attack Dog School ("I Married Marge")
    - Baby Proofer for his own baby proofing company "Wee Care" ("Bye Bye Nerdie")
    - Bartender for Moe's Tavern and Homer's Hunting Club ("Homer the Moe")
    - Blackjack dealer of Monty's Casino ("$pringfield")
    - Bodyguard of Mayor Joe Quimby ("Mayored to the Mob")
    - Bootlegger
        - Of beer as the "Beer Baron" ("Homer vs. The Eighteenth Amendment")
    - Bowling alley employee, or "Pin Monkey", of Barney's Bowl-o-rama ("And Maggie Makes Three")
    - His dream job, but held only briefly.
        - Boxer ("The Homer They Fall")
        - Butler ("The Frying Game")
    - Candle maker of Ye Olde Candlemaker, Olde Springfield Towne ("I Married Marge")
    - Car designer for Powell Motors ("Oh Brother, Where Art Thou?")
    - Carny ("Bart Carny")
    - CEO of nuclear power plant ("C.E. D'oh")
    - Chauffeur for Classy Joe's ("Homer vs. Patty & Selma")
    - Springfield Chief of Police ("Papa's Got a Brand New Badge")
    - Child Caretaker of Uncle Homer's Daycare ("Children of a Lesser Clod")
    - Choreographer for the Super Bowl Halftime Show ("Homer and Ned's Hail Mary Pass")
    - Chiropractor ("Pokey Mom")
    - Clown - Krusty Impersonator ("Homie the Clown")
    - Coach for Bart's Little League American football team ("Bart Star")
    - Cook at a diner when fleeing from a Florida sheriff ("Kill the Alligator and Run")
    - Con artist/Grifter with son Bart ("The Great Money Caper")
    - Conceptual artist ("Mom and Pop Art")
    - Convenience store night-clerk for the Kwik-E-Mart ("Lisa's Pony")
    - Detective ("King-Size Homer" not shown, but mentioned by Marge)
    - Door-to-door knife salesman for Slash-Co. ("I Married Marge")
    - Door-to-door sugar salesman ("Lisa's Rival")
    - Door-to-door spring salesman ("The Old Man and the "C" Student")
    - Employee at Gulp 'n' Blow Drive-through ("I Married Marge")
    - Executive of Globex Corp., Cypress Creek ("You Only Move Twice")
    - Executive Vice President of Power Plant ("Weekend at Burnsie's")
    - Farmer ("E-I-E-I-(Annoyed Grunt)")
    - Film critic ("A Star Is Burns")
    - Film producer ("Beyond Blunderdome")
    - Fireman (volunteer) ("Crook and Ladder")

NUCLEAR-POWERED BASEBALL

- Fish gutter ("Thirty Minutes over Tokyo")
- Fisherman ("The Wife Aquatic")
- Food critic for the *Springfield Shopper* ("Guess Who's Coming to Criticize Dinner?")
- Foot Locker employee ("Marge Gamer")
- Fortune cookie writer ("A Hunka Hunka Burns in Love")
- Founder and Junior Vice President Compu-Global-Hyper-Mega-Net ("Das Bus")
- Garbage Commissioner - see Sanitation Commissioner ("Trash of the Titans")
- Grease collector ("Lard of the Dance")
- Guard of Springfield Juvenile Correctional Facility ("The Wandering Juvie")
- Ice Cream Truck Driver ("Ice Cream of Margie (With the Light Blue Hair)"): He takes the Ice cream truck from an ice cream truck driver who dies.
- Impotency Spokesman for Viagrogaine ("Barting Over")
- Informant for the F.B.I. ("The Trouble with Trillions")
- Internet service provider ("Das Bus"): Sets up his own small business, "compuglobalhypermeganet" in which he gives himself the title "Junior Vice President."
- Inventor ("The Wizard of Evergreen Terrace, Flaming Moe's, The Old Man and the "C" Student)
- Mall Santa Claus ("Simpsons Roasting on an Open Fire")
- Manager of Country Music performer Lurleen Lumpkin (See Agent)
- Marriage Counselor ("Marge and Homer Turn a Couple Play")
- Mascot, known as "Dancing Homer" ("Dancin' Homer")
- Mattress Salesman ("The Boys of Bummer")
- Mayor of New Springfield ("A Tale of Two Springfields")
- Mayoral candidate ("See Homer Run")
- Mexican wrestler ("Jazzy and the Pussycats")
- Mini-golf assistant for Sir Putts-A-Lot ("I Married Marge")
- Missionary ("Missionary: Impossible")
- Monorail conductor ("Marge vs. the Monorail")
- Mountain climber ("King of the Hill")
- Musician
  - Member/Songwriter/Frontman of the Be Sharps, winning a Grammy Award[2] ("Homer's Barbershop Quartet")
  - Composer of "Everybody Hates Ned Flanders" single with David Byrne ("Dude, Where's My Ranch?")
  - Composed songs for Lisa Simpson's music career ("A Star Is Torn")
  - Member/Songwriter/Frontman of the grunge band Sadgasm ("That 90's Show")
- Night school teacher (See Teacher)
- Nuclear Power Plant manager ("Kiss Kiss, Bang Bangalore")
- Oil-rig worker ("Half-Decent Proposal")
- One Man Band ("Bart Gets Famous")
- Opera singer ("The Homer of Seville.")
- Ordained Minister ("There's Something About Marrying")
- Outsider Artist ("Mom and Pop Art")
- Owner
  - ZiffCorp ("The Ziff Who Came to Dinner") *Majority Stock Holder*
  - SpringShield ("Papa's Got a Brand New Badge")
  - the Denver Broncos ("You Only Move Twice")
  - CompuGlobalHyperMegaNet - Internet based company - ("Das Bus")
  - the Springfield Power Plant ("C.E. D'oh")
  - Mr. Plow ("Mr. Plow")
- Paparazzo ("Homerazzi").
- Performance artist -Getting hit with a cannonball ("Homerpalooza")
- Personal assistant
  - Briefly becomes the assistant and friend of Alec Baldwin and Kim Basinger. ("When You Dish upon a Star")
  - Briefly taking Smithers' place as Mr. Burns' right-hand man. ("Homer the Smithers")
- *Prank monkey* for Mr. Burns ("Homer vs. Dignity")
- Public speaker ("HOMR")
- Roadie ("How I Spent My Strummer Vacation")
- Railroad Engineer (implied) ("Maximum Homerdrive")
- Rollercoaster Rebuilder ("Please Homer, Don't Hammer 'Em...")
- Referee ("Marge Gamer")
- Safety inspector Homer's main job.
- Safety Salamander ("See Homer Run")
- Sailor in the Naval Reserve ("Simpson Tide")
- Salesman (see Used Car salesman and Matress salesman)
- Sanitation Commissioner ("Trash of the Titans")
- Security Officer ("Papa's Got a Brand New Badge")
- Silhouette Model ("Midnight Towboy")
- Singer ("Homer's Barbershop Quartet")
- Smithers (Assistant) (see personal assistant)
- Smuggler
  - of beer ("Homer vs. The Eighteenth Amendment")
  - of prescription drugs ("Midnight Rx")
  - of vegetables ("Itchy & Scratchy Land")
  - of Sugar ("Sweets and Sour Marge")
- Snowplow proprietor and driver ("Mr. Plow")
- Soccer referee ("Marge Gamer")
- Street musician ("Bart Gets Famous")
- Superhero ("Simple Simpson")
- Spokesperson/Walking Billboard, ("My Fair Laddy")
- Sprawl-Mart greeter ("On a Clear Day I Can't See My Sister")
- Talk Show Host ("Today I Am a Clown")
- Teacher ("Secrets of a Successful Marriage")
- Television Producer
- Telemarketer ("Lisa's Date with Density")
- Tomacco Creator/Farmer/Salesman (see Farmer) ("E-I-E-I-(Annoyed Grunt)")
- Tow Truck Driver ("Midnight Towboy")
- Town crier ("Lisa the Iconoclast")

- Traveling salesman of Simpson & Son, Revitalizing Tonic ("Grampa vs. Sexual Inadequacyts")
- Trucker ("Maximum Homerdrive")
- Union leader ("Last Exit to Springfield")
- Used Car salesman ("Diatribe of a Mad Housewife")
- Voice actor ("The Itchy & Scratchy & Poochie Show") - playing "Poochie the Dog"
- Webmaster ("The Computer Wore Menace Shoes")

12 How-tall.com puts his height at 177 cm. See http://how-tall.com/homer%20simpson but competing site howtallis sees him at 183 cm, or 6 foot even. See http://howtallis.info/homer-simpson.html. The unassailable HIPpomanguyperson wrote, "In one episode he weighed 239 lb, and another much later episode he weighed 241 lb. However he weighed 260 lb in Season 2 episode 18 entitled "A brush with greatness." He was trying to lose the weight by dieting. The most he has ever weighted was 315 lb in the episode entitled "King Sized Homer" (Season 7 episode 7). The least he has weighted was probably 140 lb-150 lb….in the episode entitled "Hungry, Hungry Homer." See http://wiki.answers.com/Q/How_much_does_Homer_Simpson_weigh

13 Graig Nettles of the New York Yankees' bat was found to contain six superballs when it broke on September 7, 1974, and when home run hitter Sammy Sosa's bat shattered on June 3, 2003, it was found to have been corked.

14 Author letters to Acting Commissioner Allan H. Selig dated December 8, 1992, with followups on the same date in 2002 and 2012. The UMass-Lowell Baseball Research Center declined to offer a comment for publication.

15 What do they know about baseball, you might ask? See the article "The influence Homer Simpson has on children," *Daily Mail*, August 13, 2005. This from the country which brought us Reggie and Ronnie Kray, and Jimmy Savile. Harrumph.

HOMER AT THE BAT

By Bill Nowlin

The episode begins with Bart writing 10 times on the blackboard "I WILL NOT AIM FOR THE HEAD."

When the signup sheet for softball is posted in the nuclear plant break room, Homer is the fourth employee to sign up. The other employees remind him that the team was 2-28 the previous season. "I know it wasn't our best season," he says. "Actually, it was," reminds a fellow worker. Homer says it will be different this year, that he has a secret weapon. He made his own bat, the Wonderbat, from a tree limb felled in his yard during a thunderstorm.[1]

Opening Day 1992 pitted the Nuclear Plant vs. the Springfield Police. Homer presented the lineup card for his team, and Chief Ralph Wiggum for the police team. The Plant wasn't doing too poorly, but still was down by three runs, 5-2, in the bottom of the ninth. With two outs and the bases loaded, Homer was due up. A right-handed hitter, and the team's right fielder, he pulled out the Wonderbat for the first time and stepped into the batter's box. On the first pitch, he swung and connected and hit the ball high over the left-field fence (and off the head of a picnic-ing father who was outside the field with his family.) The Nuclear Plant won its first game, and in the spirit of good sportsmanship, Homer taunted the losers with a singsong, "Ha, ha! Cops can't wi-in!"

He connected again in the game against East Springfield, after calling his shot to right field. Again, the ball cleared the fence in left, prompting him to revise the called shot by pointing to left.

Some serious slugging followed. His fourth-inning home run in the night game against Fort Springfield built on an already overwhelming 33-7 lead. There was no mercy rule in Springfield softball.

Before the game against Springfield Heights, the other members of the Nuclear Plant team all bring out special bats of their own, including a piano leg, a borrowed wooden leg, etc.[2]

Springfield itself later had a minor-league team named the Isotopes.[3] Homer served as a mascot for the team.

Waylon Smithers notifies C. Montgomery Burns that Springfield has won again and that if they beat Shelbyville in the upcoming contest, they will have won the pennant. Burns bets on baseball — to the tune of a million dollars — against the owner of Shelbyville's nuclear power plant, fellow magnate Aristotle Amadopoulos.

Assured by the loyal Smithers that it is OK for him to cheat to win a million-dollar bet, he declares, "I've decided to bring in a few ringers. Professional baseballs. We'll give them token jobs at the plant. He names them: Honus Wagner, Cap Anson, Mordecai Three-Finger Brown…."

Smithers interrupts to let Burns know, "I'm afraid all those players have retired and…passed on. In fact, your right fielder has been dead for 130 years."[4]

Burns instructs Smithers to find some living players from the American League, the National League, and the Negro League. He has 24 hours.

The first person he approaches is Jose Canseco, who is signing memorabilia at a show. He's offered $50,000 to play one game. "It's a paycut," he says.

"But what the heck? It sounds like fun." He recruits Mike Scioscia, who is out hunting. Ozzie Smith is taking a tour of Graceland, when Smithers catches up with him. He finds Don Mattingly at home, washing dishes. Steve Sax is playing in a small jazz combo –playing string bass. The team is rounded up, within the appointed time.

Mr. Burns then announces the new employees to a gathering at the plant. They are the new additions to "our happy power plant family…our new security guard, Roger Clemens; our new janitor, Wade Boggs; our new lunchroom cashier, Ken Griffey Jr.; our new…well, uh…we'll make up jobs for these fellas later. Say hello to Steve Sax, Don Mattingly, Darryl Strawberry, Ozzie Smith, Mike Scioscia, and Jose Canseco.

The team is down. They worked so hard to get to the championship and now they realize they'll be consigned to the bench.

The expanded team dons uniforms and only the replacement players have names and numbers on the backs of their jerseys. Burns—wearing a Zephyrs jersey, the only jersey that has a team name on the front, instructs them all that they will be drinking a special Brain & Nerve Tonic. There is a quick workout with medicine balls and other equipment. Burns brings in a hypnotist as well to give them extra confidence.

During practice, Homer calls for a ball but Strawberry leaps high and grabs it. When he complains that he called for it, Burns says, "There's no 'I' in team" and Strawberry responds obsequiously, "Some of these guys have a bad attitude, Skip."

Scioscia decides not to play ball, that he'd rather work handling radioactive waste where the pressure isn't as great as it is in major-league ball. You make a mistake there, and the press is all over, he allows—then he spills a wheelbarrow full of radioactive material.

During batting practice, Homer steps to the plate, but a Roger Clemens fastball shatters Wonderbat.

Homer failed to make the team.

Misfortunes begin to afflict Burns' team of ringers. The Springfield police arrest Sax for suspicion of various unsolved murders in New York. Scioscia is in the hospital, unable to raise his arm, with acute radiation poisoning. Ken Griffey Jr. drank too much of the tonic and developed a greatly-enlarged head, a case of gigantism. Canseco saves a baby from a burning house, then the owner's cat, and then goes back in to save her player piano and is kept busy saving various other objects. Barney punches out Wade Boggs in an encounter at Moe's Tavern arguing over who was England's greatest prime minister; Boggs claimed it was Pitt the Elder and Barney asserting it was Lord Palmerston. The hypnotist seems to have inadvertently turned Clemens into a clucking, strutting chicken.[5]

Burns constantly berates Mattingly to cut his sideburns—which he conspicuously doesn't have—and fires him. "I still like him better than Steinbrenner," says Mattingly under his breath as he departs.

Burns is forced to address the original team, and starts out telling them he knows they hate him but that he hates them even more. The one ringer who remains is Darryl Strawberry and it's he who takes right field, leaving Homer on the bench. "You stink, Strawberry! We want Home Run Homer!" comes a voice from the crowd—Lisa Simpson's. Bart and Lisa start up a taunting "Darr-yl, Darr-yl" chant.

Somehow the score is a tidy 43-43 in the bottom of the ninth (Retrosheet play-by-play has not yet been compiled as of this writing). There are two outs and the bases are loaded again, with Strawberry coming to the plate. He's a left-handed hitter—who's already got nine home runs in the game - and the crafty Burns, managing to the max, tells him to hit the showers so he can put in a right-handed batter against Shelbyville's southpaw. "It's called playing the percentages," he explains. "It's what smart managers do to win ballgames." Burns calls on Homer Simpson. He reminds him of the signals but Homer's mind wanders to a big bag of potato chips waiting for him at home.

Homer is so distracted watching Burns run through the signals from the third-base coaching box that the pitch hits him in the head. He falls down, unconscious, on home plate. He's won the game for Springfield. RBI—Simpson. A still-knocked-out Simpson is borne aloft by the celebrating Springfield team, celebrating the City Championship win.

Terry Cashman sang a special song, "Talkin' Softball," as the closing credits scrolled.[6]

Lead writer on the episode was John Swartzwelder. Simpsons creator Matt Groening told *Sports Illustrated*, "Virtually all the writers on the staff are rotisserie league junkies."[7]

NOTE: This episode of *The Simpsons* is directly credited with saving two lives. Early in the show, there is a scene where Homer starts to choke on a donut and there is a poster in the workroom which shows the Heimlich maneuver. In the first part of May 1992, 10-year-old Chris Bencze of Auburn, Washington saved the life of his 8-year-old brother Alex, who was choking on an orange. He used the Heimlich and the offending fruit popped out of Alex's throat. Their mother Karen Bencze said that Chris had learned the maneuver watching *Homer at the Bat*.[8]

NOTES

[1] In one of those amazing coincidences that often populate the history of baseball, Simpsons scholars later unearthed the information that a popular motion picture entitled *The Natural* also featured a homemade bat hewn from a fallen limb of a tree struck by lightning, though that particular bat was dubbed "Wonderboy."

[2] The wooden leg by the character Carl is purportedly an allusion to the July 15, 1973 game when Norm Cash of the Detroit Tigers came to the plate with a table leg instead of a bat. He'd already struck out three times and Nolan Ryan was in the process of pitching a no-hitter. When told he couldn't use the non-regulation bat, he is said to have replied, "Why not? I won't hit him anyway." See http://blog.detroitathletic.com/2011/11/01/when-norm-cash-took-a-table-leg-to-the-plate-for-the-detroit-tigers/. One can also see video of the incident at: http://m.mlb.com/video/v10183417/mlb-network-remembers-nolan-ryans-second-nohitter.

[3] In another astounding real-life coincidence, the Albuquerque Dukes Triple-A minor-league team were replaced by a franchise moving south from Calgary. There had been an episode of *The Simpsons* ("Hungry, Hungry Homer" in 2001) in which "the mayor of Albuquerque tries to steal the Springfield Isotopes away, and Homer goes on a hunger strike to save the team." [Dennis Latta, "Team President Throws Isotopes Name Into Play," *Albuquerque Journal*, September 5, 2002.] The online *Albuquerque Tribune* conducted a local poll for a new name and "Isotopes" received two-third of the 120,000 votes. The Albuquerque Isotopes began play in 2003.

[4] Jim Creighton did indeed die on October 18, 1862. He was a little more than 21 years old at the time.

[5] It was Clemens' erstwhile teammate Boggs who had a baseball ritual of eating chicken on the day of every baseball game. He is listed as the author of *Fowl tips: My favorite chicken recipes* (Narragansett Graphics, 1984.)

[6] Lyrics: Now Mr. Burns had done it / the power plant had won it/ with Roger Clemens clucking all the while / Mike Scioscia's tragic illness made us smile /while Wade Boggs lay unconscious on the barroom tile/ We're talkin' softball / from Maine to San Diego / talkin' softball / Mattingly and Canseco / Ken Griffey's grotesquely swollen jaw / Steve Sax and his run-in with the law / we're talking Homer / Ozzie and the Straw

[7] *Sports Illustrated*, January 27, 1992.

[8] *Aberdeen Daily News* (and numerous other newspapers running an Associated Press story), May 21, 1992. Fox publicist Antonia Coffman told the media that the studio had already heard of one other such instance. In December 2007, reportedly Aiden Bateman saved his friend Alex Hardy's life, armed with the same information from the show. See Paul Jeeves, "Boy saves pal's life…by listening to Homer," *The Express*, December 15, 2007.

RYAN TOSSES NO-HITTER; CASH WIELDS TABLE LEG

JULY 15, 1973: CALIFORNIA ANGELS 6, DETROIT TIGERS 0 AT TIGER STADIUM

By Gregory H. Wolf

As Detroit Tigers first baseman Norm Cash prepared to dig in against California Angels right-hander Nolan Ryan, who was just one out away from a no-hitter, he looked at home-plate umpire Ron Luciano and asked with all seriousness, "Aren't you going to check my bat?"[1] Known for his unusual humor, Cash had sauntered to the batter's box in the tense situation wielding a table leg. When Luciano, unamused by the prank, calmly informed the slugger he couldn't use the ersatz bat, Cash supposedly replied, "Why not, I won't hit him anyway."[2] Cash was right: he popped up and Ryan recorded his second no-hitter in two months. Ryan's 17-strikeout performance, wrote Angels beat reporter Ron Rapoport, "left friend and foe groping for superlatives."[3] Jim Hawkins of the *Detroit Free Press* called it "one of the most impressive one-man shows in baseball history."[4]

When Detroit and California headed to Tiger Stadium on Sunday, July 15, 1973, to play the final contest of a four-game series, they appeared to be going in opposite directions. Manager Billy Martin's Tigers had pennant aspirations. They had captured the AL East crown the previous year, and were playing their best ball of the season. A five-game winning streak pushed them into fourth place, at 48-42, but only 1½ games behind the division-leading New York Yankees. As for the Angels, skipper Bobby Winkles had gotten the team off to a promising start and briefly occupied first place, but the club had lost its previous four games and 11 of the last 17 games to fall to fourth place at 45-43.

The pitching matchup was a contrast in styles. The Tigers' 37-year-old righty, Jim Perry, faced off against the 26-year-old Ryan. While Perry relied on pinpoint control and ball movement, Ryan overpowered the opposition. Perry, a 15-year veteran and a former Cy Young Award winner with a record of 189-147, was winding his career down. Ryan, who had battled control problems since his debut with the New York Mets in 1966, emerged as baseball's most feared strikeout artist the previous season, his first with the Angels. Expectations in 1973 were high for Ryan, coming off a league-leading 329 strikeouts and nine shutouts. On May 15 Ryan joined Bo Belinsky and Clyde Wright as the only Angels hurlers to toss no-hitters by blanking the Kansas City Royals and fanning 12, but had since then won just five of 13 decisions. "I don't feel like I've done as much for the club as I could be doing," a modest Ryan told the *Los Angeles Times*, pointing to his disappointing 10-11 record and ignoring his 203 punchouts in 180 innings.[5]

On a beautiful summer afternoon, with temperatures in the mid-70s, Tiger Stadium was filled with a large crowd of 41,411 spectators on Cap Day to witness one of the most dominant pitching performances in baseball history. Ryan's first pitch to leadoff batter Jim Northrup was a knee-buckling curveball that ricocheted off catcher Art Kusnyer's shin guard and hit Luciano's right knee. After Northrup flied out, the "Ryan Express" went into overdrive. The 6-foot-2 Texan registered 12 of the next 13 outs by strikeout and also walked three before light-hitting Ed Brinkman grounded to short to end the fifth inning. "I've never seen anyone throw that good before," said Dick McAuliffe, who whiffed in each of his three plate appearances.[6]

The weak-hitting Angels, who ranked 11th of 12 teams in runs scored and batting average and last in slugging percentage that season, scored the game's first run in the third inning. After consecutive one-out singles by Kusnyer and Sandy Alomar, Vada Pinson hit a sacrifice fly to right field to give the Angels the lead. Through the top of the sixth, Perry kept the pressure on Ryan by limiting California to just four hits.

Northrup led off the sixth inning with the Tigers' one "reasonably hard-hit ball," but center fielder Ken Berry traced its arc and snared it in front of the warning track for an easy out.[7] A tough-nosed competitor, Ryan looked for any psychological edge in his battle with hitters. When Cash came to bat in the sixth, Ryan asked Luciano to examine his bat for cork filler. A quick worker on the mound, Ryan kept rolling while his heater and curveball inspired awe. "The curve was really outstanding," said Kusnyer, a little-used backup catcher who was a game-time replacement for the injured Jeff Torborg. "It was really going down. You could tell the hitters were chopping down on the ball."[8] According to Tigers reliever Ed Farmer, Billy Martin ordered his players on the bench to pay $5 early in the game and pull a number out of a hat predicting how many strikeouts Ryan would have.[9] In the seventh, Ryan struck out the side for the third time in the game, and pushed his strikeout total to 16, just three shy of the major-league record of 19 (in a nine-inning game) set by Steve Carlton (1969) and Tom Seaver (1970).

The Angels blew the game open in the eighth inning when Winston Llenas, Bob Oliver, and Al Gallagher each connected for two-out singles off relievers Bob Miller and Farmer to give the Angels a commanding 6-0 lead. But the offensive fireworks had an unintended effect on Ryan. "My arm stiffened up," he said after the game about the long delay. "I was kind of anxious to get going. I knew personally that I didn't have the same stuff. They were hitting my pitches."[10]

In an attempt to jinx Ryan, Martin remained on the dugout steps for the final two innings, reminding the pitcher of his no-hitter. Ryan ignored the taunts and sent down the final six batters in order, but whiffed just one. The final two outs were arguably the most dramatic of the game. Gates Brown hit a line drive to the shortstop, Rudy Meoli. "If it was not right at somebody, it was a hit," wrote Rapoport.[11] In fact, Ryan thought it was a hit, reported Jim Hawkins, but Meoli had shaded Brown slightly to the right and caught the ball on his toes about a foot above his head.[12] After Cash's escapade with the table, he popped up to Meoli in shallow left field. "Ryan didn't require any super plays," wrote Dick Miller in *The Sporting News*, to preserve his gem.[13]

Both squads seemed genuinely impressed with Ryan's dominant performance. Frank Robinson, the Angels' prized offseason acquisition, offered some historical perspective: "I've never seen anyone throw harder and that includes Sandy Koufax."[14] Ryan threw so hard that Kusnyer's left hand was dangerously swollen and had turned purple. "It's a bone bruise," said the catcher proudly in the clubhouse after the game.[15]

"I was more excited about this one," responded Ryan when asked to compare his two no-hitters. "You know what the pressure is and you know you don't want to lose it." He threw 126 pitches (86 for strikes) and completed the game in 2 hours and 21 minutes. As of 2014, Ryan, Johnny Vander Meer (1938), Allie Reynolds (1951), Virgil Trucks (1952), and Roy Halladay (2010) are the only big-league hurlers to toss two no-hitters in the same season (although Halladay's second no-no was in the National League Division Series). Ryan's gem was also the last no-hitter thrown in Tiger Stadium.

Nolan Ryan went on to throw seven no-hitters and win 324 games in his 27-year Hall of Fame career, yet this game has entered baseball lore because of Norm Cash's practical joke. When Cash came to the plate in the ninth inning, Tigers announcer Ernie Harwell described the bat erroneously as a piano leg.[16] Initially, Cash's escapade did not attract much media attention, and many contemporary game reports, such as in the *Detroit Free Press*, did not mention it. But over time, the story gathered traction as Ryan's stature grew. Whether involving a piano leg or table leg, the anecdote came to epitomize the impossible task of hitting a pitch. Cash's antics moved into the realm of pop culture in 1992 when Carl, a cartoon character in *The Simpsons*, went to the plate with a piano leg in a special episode entitled "Homer at the Bat."

SOURCES

In addition to the sources cited in the notes, the author consulted:

BaseballReference.com

Retrosheet.org

SABR.org

NOTES

1. Ron Rapoport, "Encore! Ryan Hurls Second No-Hitter," *Los Angeles Times*, July 16, 1973, III, 2.
2. Ibid.
3. Ibid.
4. Jim Hawkins, "Ryan No-Hits Tigers . . . Strikes Out 17 To Boot," *Detroit Free Press*, July 16, 1973, 1-D
5. " . . . Feels He Hasn't Done Enough For Angels," *Los Angeles Times*, July 16, 1973, III, 2.
6. Rapoport.
7. Ibid.
8. Ibid.
9. Rob Goldman, *Nolan Ryan: The Making of a Pitcher* (Chicago: Triumph Books, 2014).
10. Rapoport
11. Ibid.
12. Hawkins.
13. Dick Miller, "Ryan's Smoke Sends Tigers Into No-Hit Blind," *The Sporting News*, July 28, 1973, 15.
14. Ibid.
15. Miller.
16. "Bat tales: our favorite stories of all-time," *Detroit Free Press*, March 30, 2008. freep.com/article/20080330/SPORTS02/80330021/Bat-tales-Our-favorite-stories-all-time.

THE NEW SPRINGFIELD NINE

By Jonah Keri

The baseball analytics revolution has helped us answer many questions that might have seemed unknowable before. We can now measure not only a pitcher's velocity but also the exact horizontal and vertical break on his pitches, the precise coordinates of his arm slot, and dozens of other variables. We can calculate the worth of catchers who excel at framing pitches. We can even take the sum of a player's contributions and find a reasonable estimate of his overall value.

Lovely pursuits, all. But mere trivialities next to the most pressing baseball question the world has ever had to face: If Mr. Burns had to re-staff the Springfield Nuclear Power Plant softball team with a lineup full of present-day players, who should he choose?

To answer the question, we spent hours considering a wide array of variables. Like the original Springfield Nine, this new team needed to have plenty of star power. It would take a carefully crafted blend of youth and experience, one that would foster a harmonious clubhouse. On the strategy front, you'd want power with a touch of speed, hitters and ace defenders, World Series experience, and a few players hungry to win it all for the first time. Finally, we wanted a group of players who'd blend well into the Simpsons universe, meshing their own personalities and backstories with those of the show's characters. Our new lineup needed to suffer misfortunes that stack up to Ken Griffey Jr.'s gigantism, while also matching up with their own personality quirks.

Here then is the new Springfield Nine, and the calamities that would conspire to get Lenny, Carl, and the rest back on the field for Homer's climactic plunking in this 2.0 version of events.

Pitcher: Felix Hernandez

Flush with cash after signing a seven-year, $175 million contract but fearing a correction in the high-flying stock market, Hernandez meets with German investors Hans and Fritz. Intrigued by the Germans' plans to buy the Cleveland Browns, Hernandez signs over his entire 2013 salary, only to discover that Hans and Fritz are secretly bankrolling an Uterbraten plant in Dusseldorf. Racked by guilt and shame, Felix abruptly leaves Springfield, returns to the big leagues, and fires 12 more perfect games.

Runner-up: Jose Valverde

Trying to find his way back to the Show after all 30 teams failed to sign him this offseason, Valverde goes shopping for new eyewear. Finding a pair of specs in the discount bin at the Try-N-Save, Valverde drops $9.99 in hopes of improving his vision, ratcheting up his command, and attracting an interested buyer. Back on the mound, he runs into even more trouble finding the plate before realizing the terrible truth: The goggles do nothing.

Catcher: Buster Posey

Shopping for a mode of transportation while in town for the big game, Posey decides to splurge for a new car. Unable to find any respectable dealers in town, Posey stumbles onto Crazy Vaclav's. He finds a sub-sub-sub compact he likes, pays cash, and drives off the lot. But despite following Vaclav's instructions that he put it in "H," the car stalls, leaving Posey stranded miles from the stadium with the game about to start.

NUCLEAR-POWERED BASEBALL

Runner-up: Yadier Molina

In search of volunteer work in the community, Molina finds a gig volunteering at the Springfield Retirement Castle. Finding someone willing to talk to him for the first time since wearing an onion on one's belt was in style, Grampa begins bombarding Molina with long, pointless stories until both men fall asleep. When Molina finally wakes up, the game is over, and Grampa's firing epithets at the St. Louis catcher, since it will be a cold day in hell before he recognizes Missour-ah.

First Base: Prince Fielder

The Tigers slugger flies in for the game, only to realize he has nowhere to stay. Disco Stu graciously agrees to put Prince up for as long as he needs. It's an offer born of generosity but also a smattering of self-interest: Fielder could make an excellent wingman, and, with the proper guidance, could become an ambassador for Stu's master plan to usher in a new golden age of disco. Fielder's skeptical at first, telling Stu he should probably take it easy with the game coming up. But Stu wears Prince down, persuading him to come out and see Springfield's best (and only) disco act, Earth, Wind & Tire Fire. The night goes smoothly until Fielder, donning a three-sizes-too-small leisure suit that Stu lent him, develops a severe allergic reaction to the polyester, costing the team its starting first baseman.

Runner-up: Joey Votto

The brilliant Votto joins Springfield's Mensa group. Caught up in the fast-paced, glamorous nerd world fostered by Professor Frink, Comic Book Guy, and company, Votto falls into a wormhole of quantum physics and Confucianism, abandoning baseball to begin a search for the meaning of life that remains unsolved to this day.

Second Base: Brandon Phillips

Hoping to leverage his bubbly personality and big Twitter presence into a media career, Phillips begins shadowing newscaster Kent Brockman. Summoned to cover a 50th-anniversary celebration for Lard Lad Donuts, Brockman invites Phillips along to learn the intricacies of doing a remote broadcast. Tragedy strikes as the giant metal donut, never fully refastened after Lard Lad's murderous Halloween rampage, plummets to the ground, crushing four bystanders. Brockman and Phillips narrowly escape a direct hit, but Phillips breaks his ankle diving out of the way of the glazed nightmare.

Runner-up: Dustin Pedroia

Seeking to acquire a handheld laser gun to spruce up his self-proclaimed Laser Show, Pedroia seeks the help of Rigel 7's orneriest brother-sister pair, Kang and Kodos. The decision backfires when Springfield's oppressed residents revolt against the tyrannical duo, leaving Pedroia caught in the crossfire. Pedroia gets his leg impaled by a bigger board with a bigger nail but avoids serious injury, requiring only a tetanus shot to cure his wound. Unfortunately, Homer had just received Dr. Hibbert's last available tetanus shot a day earlier, forcing Pedroia to turn to Dr. Nick for help. It does not go well.

Shortstop: Derek Jeter

Shunned by New York's bachelorette population after handing out one too many gift baskets, Jeter loses his confidence with the fairer sex and retreats to Springfield a broken man. There he finds a kindred spirit in Moe, the only man on Earth lonelier than the heartbroken Captain. Moe teaches Jeter how to cope with being alone, telling tales of Birthday Fries offers gone awry and the Flaming Moe's fortune that vanished overnight. The two leave Springfield to start a holistic living clinic in North Haverbrook and are never heard from again.

Runner-up: Jimmy Rollins

Rollins joins the Springfield Police Department as a volunteer deputy. After he earns the trust of his fellow officers, Lou and Eddie invite him to participate in their weekly squirrel-wagering game. Untrained at the art of stuffing squirrels down his pants for the purposes of gambling, Rollins is bitten by one of the squirrels, which turns out to be rabid. Although Mr. Burns is initially impressed with Rollins appearing so motivated to play that he's frothing at the mouth, Springfield's manager quickly realizes this is not actually a good thing.

Third Base: Adrian Beltre

Beltre's legendary aversion to having his head touched becomes such a burden on himself and his teammates that he seeks therapy to correct the problem. After years of counseling, he finally overcomes his fear, just as Burns invites Beltre to play for Springfield. On the night before the big game, Beltre meets up with Homer, who invites him to watch Stan "The Boy" Taylor Jr. and the rest of the Springfield Atoms take on their archrivals, the Shelbyville Sharks. In a rare display of generosity, Homer buys a nacho hat and invites Beltre to wear it. But seconds later, unable to control his primal urges, Homer begins frantically pawing at the newly indoctrinated Nacho Man's head. Just as the cheese begins to dribble through a gaping hole in the top of the hat, Beltre comes unhinged, lunging at Homer and strangling him. Realizing the gravity of the situation, Beltre flees the scene, never to return to Springfield, or have anyone touch his head ever again.

Runner-up: Alex Rodriguez

His life and career derailed by injuries and new accusations of PED use, A-Rod decides he must reconcile with the one person who understands him best: Madonna. To do so, he enlists the help of Rabbi Hyman Krustofsky. Under the rabbi's tutelage, Rodriguez's knowledge of kabbalah grows until it matches that of the Material Girl's. A-Rod is last seen on Madonna's world tour in Zurich, performing as a backup dancer during a spirited rendition of "La Isla Bonita."

Left Field: Josh Hamilton

Clean, sober, and born again after years of battling substance abuse, Hamilton happily accepts Burns's invitation to play for Springfield, earmarking his appearance fee for various charities. Upon arriving in town, Hamilton heads to church to watch Reverend Lovejoy's sermon. There, he's approached by Ned Flanders, who warns that baseball is a game rife with sin, complete with steroids, excessive drinking, and Baseball Annies who can cloud even the most devout man's judgment. Hamilton politely thanks Flanders for his concern, then gets up to leave. As soon as he steps outside, Rod and Todd jump him and throw him in a van emblazoned with the slogan "If this van is a'rockin', it probably means we're reading from Deuteronomy." Hamilton disappears forever.

Runner-up: Ichiro Suzuki

Seeking a new image for its brand of dishwasher detergent, the joint venture of Matsumura Fishworks and Tamaribuchi Heavy Manufacturing Concern fires Homer and hires Ichiro to be the new face of Mr. Sparkle. Seeking revenge, Homer invites Ichiro out for sushi, then has Akira serve his new friend a plate of compromised fugu. And that's the end of that chapter.

Center Field: Bryce Harper

Reacting to Harper's famous retort to an overzealous reporter, Krusty sues the Nationals star for copyright infringement, arguing that the phrase "Klown Kwestion" is his own intellectual property. Seeking damages totaling $100 million, Krusty hires the most ruthless lawyer in town. With Lionel Hutz no longer around to work on contingency (RIP), Harper decides to defend himself. The case gets tied up for more than a year, forcing Harper to miss the game.

Runner-up: Andrew McCutchen

Aiming to get his trademark dreadlocks camera-ready, McCutchen heads to the local salon for a touch-up. Finding the nearest dryer, he turns it on, only to learn that the dial's been turned to Maximum Marge setting. Already skeptical of even the slightest deviations from traditional hairstyles and grooming trends, the conservative Burns bristles at McCutchen's new 7-foot 'fro and kicks him off the team.

Right Field: Giancarlo Stanton

Afraid he might follow Jose Reyes's lead and get traded soon after buying a new home in south Florida, Stanton starts looking for real estate opportunities in Springfield instead. But when he wanders onto the west side of town, Cookie Kwan mistakes him for a competing real estate agent, and violence erupts. Stanton still makes it back to the game in time, starting in right field and hitting nine home runs while his backup, Homer, gathers splinters on the bench. In the ninth inning, with the score tied, the bases loaded, and Stanton due up, Burns calls on Homer to pinch-hit. Though both Stanton and Homer are right-handed hitters, Burns cites Homer's higher ground-ball rate and Shelbyville's weak infield defense as the reason for the switch … proving yet again that he's the greatest strategist the game has ever known.

This article originally ran at Grantland.com on March 6, 2013.

In October 2010, Joe Posnanski watched Episode 3 in Season 22 of *The Simpsons*, the episode named "MoneyBART." The next day he posted the following article to his blog:

THE SIMPSONS BASEBALL EDITION

By Joe Posnanski

Got to do something fun Sunday night: Went to Bill James' house to watch *The Simpsons*. I do realize that under normal circumstances this might not sound especially riveting. But Sunday night, the Simpsons episode was called "Moneybart," and the plot revolved around the ongoing fight between statistics and tradition in the game. And Bill had a line.

If you have not seen the episode, you should probably be warned that there are all sorts of spoilers below. In fact, this whole thing is kind of a spoiler. Proceed at your own peril.*

I assume everyone here as either seen The Simpsons or at least knows the basics … but, as pointless as it feels, I'll put some very quick basics here: Marge and Homer are Mom and Dad. Homer is one of the great television characters ever. Bart, Lisa and Maggie are brother, sister and baby sister, Moe is bartender, Flanders is fussy neighbor and so on.

***

One thing many things I love about The Simpsons is that, often, the main implausible plot is sparked by an even more unlikely mini-plot at the start. In this case, we need to get to the point where Lisa is managing Bart's baseball team. To get to this point, they bring in a former student who has gone on to attend an Ivy League school. And when Lisa expresses her own desire to go to an Ivy, the woman says that Lisa better get involved in more extra-curricular activities.

Marge: "Don't worry, you can still attend McGill University, the Harvard of Canada."

Lisa: "Anything that is the something of the something isn't really the anything of the anything."

At this point, Flanders, the fussy neighbor, comes by to say that he can no longer coach Bart's Little League baseball team because he cannot live with his conscience after not complaining when an umpire calls his shortstop's foul ball a home run (Flanders: "Call me Walter Matthau because I'm a Bad News Bearer").

After Homer refuses to take over the team (Homer: "Sorry Marge, last time I stepped on a baseball field I got tazed"), Lisa becomes the team manager.*

There's a small moment here I love: Bart is walking by the baseball field when he happens to notice his teammates are practicing joyfully. He goes to the field to find out what's going on. But in order to express the joyfulness of practice, you can hear the players shouting baseball things, including this shout from Nelson (the school bully): "Look at me, I'm Whitey Ford!" I just love that. It might be my second-favorite line in the show.

Bart, of course, expresses doubt that her sister—knowing nothing about baseball—can handle the job. Lisa has anticipated this bit of doubt:

Lisa: There have been plenty of female managers in baseball: Connie Mack, Sandy Alomar*, Terry Francona, Pinky Higgins.

NUCLEAR-POWERED BASEBALL

Nelson: Those are dudes!

I feel sure that, more than once, the brilliant writers of The Simpsons put in something wrong just to get baseball goofballs like myself to notice. This is one of those. Sandy Alomar never managed in the big leagues.

But Lena Blackburne did. So did Jewel Ens, Blondie Purcell and Jo-Jo White. And if you think that those writers didn't do this just to get people like me to look up some managers who had women's first names, you don't know the evil powers of The Simpsons.

Yes, now, we have reached the crux of the episode. Lisa must learn baseball. For this she goes to Moe's to seek the counsel of her father and men watching the game on television.

Moe: "The only thing I know about strategy is that whatever the manager does, it's wrong. Unless it works in which case he's a button pusher."

Moe then points her to the corner ... where a mini-SABR convention has broken out. There are four nerdy guys with computers and stat books discussing the game.

Nerdy stat guy 1: As a pitcher Cliff Lee is CLEARLY superior to Zack Greinke.

Nerdy stat guy 2: Yes I completely agree with the following COLOSSAL exception: Before the fourth inning, after a road loss, in a domed stadium. Then it's great to be Greinke!*

I would love to believe that I played a small part, just a tiny part, in inspiring this scene. But I think it's more likely that the word "Greinke" is funnier than, say, "Roy Halladay."

Lisa is impressed by their knowledge, and here she is told that the key to understanding baseball is sabermetrics: "The field was developed by statistician Bill James," Nerdy Stat Guy 2 says.

At this point, he shows Lisa his computer, where there's a picture of Bill. And Bill utters his one line: "I made baseball as much fun as doing your taxes!"

It was quite the moment at the James household. Everybody applauded and, during a commercial break. Bill did the line again for us with some Shakespearean zeal. There have been many achievements for Bill James. The man was named one of Time's 100 most influential people, for crying out loud. But playing himself on The Simpsons? I'm not sure it gets a whole lot bigger than that*.

Though I should say that there are plans in the works — I don't want to jinx it, but there are plans in the works — for me to be a guest DJ on E-Street Radio. More on that as details firm up.

Lisa — armed with her newfound statistics — turns around Bart's team. She moves the fielders around so that they are always perfectly situated*, which absolutely will NOT inspire me to make a Brooks Conrad joke.

At one point, Lisa moves her first baseman into the crowd, and sure enough a foul ball is hit right to him. A good gag, but once again they did something for goofballs like me to notice: The first baseman was left-handed when he was put in the crowd. But he turned into the right-handed Ralph when the foul ball was hit to him. I wonder how much fun they have over there putting in these little details they know 99.999% of the people won't notice, but will drive the other .001% mad.

Lisa's maneuvers are making the team a winner, but Bart cannot help but feel that the joy of the game is being drained. When Lisa tells him to not swing — the pitcher is wild — he is furious.

Bart: "But I'm on a hot-streak.

Lisa: "Hot streaks are a statistical illusion."

Bart: "I wish YOU were a statistical illusion."

Lisa: "Well, there's a 97% chance I'm not, so do what I say."

He disobeys her and hits a walk-off home run. His teammates pick him up and chant his name ("Bart! Bart! Bart!") and while they're doing it, she throws him off the team leading to a new chant ("Conflicted! Conflicted! Conflicted!").

Now, of course we have family strife. Marge and Homer take sides:

Marge: Flyballs and fungoes come and go. But families are forever.

Homer: Sorry Marge, I've got to call bullcrap on that. The '69 Mets will live on forever. But you think anyone cares about Ron Swoboda's wife and kids? Not me. And I assume not Ron Swoboda."

Marge: Think of Bart's feelings!

Homer: Boys don't have feelings. They have muscles.

That night, Marge reads to Bart a slightly altered version of the three little bears. Homer reads to Lisa the story of Pete Rose running over Ray Fosse in the All-Star Game.

The baseball season goes on without Bart (Lisa: "He thought he was better than the laws of probability. Anyone else here think he's better than the laws of probability?"). Lisa moves Nelson into the leadoff spot because of his on-base percentage*. The team wins again and earns a spot in the Little League Championship (Announcer who sounds quite a bit like Vin Scully: "It's a triumph of number-crunching over the human spirit, and it's about time.")

*OK, this has little to do with The Simpsons … but I have watched just about every inning of every postseason game so far. This means two things:

1. I have now seen so many "Glory Daze" promos that it is now beginning to invade my own personal memories. I find myself thinking about that time I agreed to have myself branded. Also, I would love to strangle that guy who goes on that emergency run for the doughnuts in that car commercials. I do not believe in hate. But I hate every single thing about that guy.

2. I have noticed that national announcers, in general, still call games almost EXACTLY like they did 25 years ago. I mean exactly — with batting average, home runs, RBIs, pitcher wins, the idea that pitching is 75% of baseball, the same cliches about bunts and intentional walks, like there's no other side.

I'm actually OK with this for the most part. I think baseball games are to be enjoyed, not to be infused with a lot of statistical analysis. And I know most fans want what is familiar to them, I get it, I really do. It might drive me nuts, but I'm not a typical viewer.

Just one thing: I really wish that they could at least mention on-base percentage. Just that. I get that many people are never going to like advanced stats, never going to appreciate the Dewan plus/minus or WAR or xFIP or whatever. I get that. I know that people don't necessarily want a discussion of BABIP in the sixth inning of a 2-2 game.

But if I could have any impact on the game at all, any impact, I would love for it to be helping to making OBP more mainstream. Just that.

In The Simpsons, there's a funny little moment where Lisa is looking at her stats book and there's a confusing looking formula for OBP. It looked like so:

$H + W + HBP / AB + W + HBP + SF$

That does indeed look confusing, doesn't it. Probably would not look as confusing if you did this:

Times on Base / Plate Appearances (minus sac hits).

Yeah, that looks a bit simpler doesn't it? Frankly I don't even like the sac hit adjustment. Personally, I would just do times on base over plate appearances, simple as it gets. But even so, it's still pretty simple. OBP tells you as simply as possible how often you get on base, and how often you make an out.

Now, let's look at batting average. Most people think the system is simply "Hits / At-bats) and it is. But let's look at it in a different way.

$TOB - W - HBP / PA - W - HBP - SF - SH$.

There's your simple, not-advanced batting average statistic. At-bats are a completely invented number that removes a bunch of pretty important things — especially *walks, but also illogical things like sacrifice hits. You already know that if you BUNT a runner over from second to third it's a sacrifice and doesn't count in your batting average. But if you give yourself up by hitting a ball to the right side, and move the runner from second to third, it DOES count against your batting average. And so on.*

And don't even get me started on the hit/error conundrum.

Batting average as calculated IS a complicated thing and an advanced stat. It's just an advanced stat that we grew up with so it seems simpler than it really is, not unlike the plot for the Star Wars movies. On-base percentage is a much simpler statistic, I have no doubt in my mind about this. It is NOT an advanced stat, not compared to batting average. OBP is also a much more telling statistic.

And I just wish these national baseball announcers would mention it every so often. Just mention it. Instead of wondering why Carlos Pena with his .196 batting average is even in the lineup ("Well, he hits with power"), you could at least mention that he walked 87 times, and while his .325 on-base percentage is not good, it's not tragically bad either.

The last few minutes of the Simpsons include a fine performance from Mike Scioscia (when he loses a World Series ring while riding on a roller coaster, he says: "That's OK, I'll win another one"), the obligatory steroid mention (Ralph is juiced — he is surrounded by juice boxes and is saying, "I didn't know what I was putting into my body!) and a classic shot, best line of the show, from the radio/television announcer:

Announcer: "That's why anyone who invested with Lenny Dykstra really should call that number, lawyers are standing by."

And it ends with Bart trying to steal home, which leads to two plot breakthroughs. (1) It allows Lisa to finally see the excitement of the game beyond the numbers; (2) Cost his team the championship because of course he is out at the plate. That sounds about right.

"You made me love baseball," Lisa told Bart afterward, "not as a collection of numbers, but as an unpredictable passionate game beaten in excitement only by every other sport."

* * *

UPDATE: I did not mention the opening, because it was not baseball. But I suspect for Simpsons fans, it will be what it remembered from this show. It was done by the guy the Internet calls "Infamous graffiti artist Banksy." It's a brilliantly dark portrait of laborers making Simpsons merchandise — including the making of DVDs using a worn-down unicorn.

There was a followup post on November 13, 2010:

It Had To Be Done (Simpsons Follow)

Nerdy stat guy 1: As a pitcher Cliff Lee is CLEARLY superior to Zack Greinke.

Nerdy stat guy 2: Yes I completely agree with the following colossal exception: Before the fourth inning, after a road loss, in a domed stadium. Then it's great to be Greinke!

— Moneybart episode, *The Simpsons*

If you saw this Simpsons episode, you probably remember the scene — Lisa went to the back of Moe's Tavern to find a little SABR convention going on. They were having this talk, where one was saying that Lee was better, and the other said it was true except, well, you see it above — before the fourth, after a road loss, in a dome.

Well, you knew that at some point I was going to look it up, right? I mean … it had to be done. Cliff Lee? Zack Greinke? A nerdy stat like that? OF COURSE I'm going to look it up. The only surprise is that it took this long.

I went back to 2008. I did not have to go back any more. It turns out that Zack Greinke pitched six games in domes after road losses (I counted retractable roof stadiums like Toronto and Seattle). And, by pure coincidence, Cliff Lee ALSO pitched six games after road losses.

I was praying for The Simpsons' statistic to be right. I figured they had 50-50 shot at it, and I figured that maybe, just maybe, some geek on the staff looked it up just to be sure.

Unfortunately …

Zack Greinke in domes before the fourth inning after road losses: 18 innings, 12 earned runs, 6.00 ERA.

Cliff Lee in domes before the fourth inning after road losses: 18 innings 0 earned runs, 0.00 ERA.

Sigh.

This article first appeared on Joe Posnanski's blog on October 11, 2010 and is reprinted here with permission. His blog may be visited at: www.joeposnanski.com/joeblog/

BALLPLAYERS MENTIONED IN THE SIMPSONS

Shown in each instance are the episode number in which the player appears or is referenced, the episode title, and its original airdate.

A

Sandy Alomar—episode 467, "MoneyBART," October 10, 2010

Cap Anson—episode 52, "Homer at the Bat," February 20, 1992

B

Sal Bando (character)—episode 376, "Regarding Margie," May 7, 2006

Johnny Bench—episode 301, "Pray Anything," February 9, 2003

Wade Boggs (character)—episode 52, "Homer at the Bat," February 20, 1992

Barry Bonds—episode 443, "Bart Gets A 'Z'," October 4, 2009

Mordecai Brown—episode 52, "Homer at the Bat," February 20, 1992

Bill Buckner—episode 228, "Brother's Little Helper," October 3, 1999

Brett Butler—episode 228, "Brother's Little Helper," October 3, 1999

C

José Canseco (character)—episode 52, "Homer at the Bat," February 20, 1992

Roger Clemens (character)—episode 52, "Homer at the Bat," February 20, 1992

Ty Cobb—episode 43, "Bart the Fink," February 11, 1996

Jim Creighton—episode 52, "Homer at the Bat," February 20, 1992

D

Dom DiMaggio—episode 372, "Million-Dollar Abie." April 2, 2006

Joe DiMaggio—episode 320, "'Tis the Fifteenth Season," December 14, 2003, and episode 343, "Homer and Ned's Hail Mary Pass," February 6, 2005

Dick Drago—episode 467, "MoneyBART," October 10, 2010

F

Rollie Fingers—episode 514, "A Tree Grows in Springfield," November 25, 2012

Whitey Ford—episode 164, "The Twisted World of Marge Simpson," January 19, 1997

Ray Fosse—episode 467, "MoneyBART," October 10, 2010

Terry Francona—episode 467, "MoneyBART," October 10, 2010

G

Eddie Gaedel—episode 466, "Loan-A Lisa," October 3, 2010

Oscar Gamble — episode 467, "MoneyBART," October 10, 2010

Lou Gehrig — episode 211, "Kidney Trouble," December 6, 1998, and episode 378, "Marge and Homer Turn A Couple Play," May 21, 2006

Kirk Gibson — episode 440, "Four Great Women and a Manicure," May 10, 2009

Zack Greinke — episode 467, "MoneyBART," October 10, 2010

Ken Griffey, Jr. (character) — episode 52, "Homer at the Bat," February 20, 1992

H

Tommy Henrich — episode 396, "The Boys of Bummer," April 29, 2007

Pinky Higgins — episode 467, "MoneyBART," October 10, 2010

Harry Hooper — episode 52, "Homer at the Bat," February 20, 1992

Steve Howe — mentioned in the book *Flanders' Book of Faith* published in 2008

Carl Hubbell — mentioned in the book *Flanders' Book of Faith* published in 2008

J

Reggie Jackson — episode 81, "Krusty Gets Kancelled," May 13, 1993, and episode 222, "Mom and Pop Art," April 11, 1999

Shoeless Joe Jackson — episode 52, "Homer at the Bat," February 20, 1992

Derek Jeter — episode 422, "Lost Verizon," October 5, 2008, and episode 427, "MyPods and Broomsticks," November 30, 2008

Randy Johnson (character) — episode 370, "Bart Has Two Mommies," March 19, 2006

Chipper Jones — episode 343, "Homer and Ned's Hail Mary Pass," February 6, 2005

Wally Joyner — mentioned in the book *Flanders' Book of Faith* published in 2008

K

Sandy Koufax — episode 184, "Bart Star," November 9, 1997

L

John Lackey — mentioned in the book *C. Montgomery Burns' Handbook of World Domination*

Napoleon Lajoie — episode 52, "Homer at the Bat," February 20, 1992

Cliff Lee — episode 467, "MoneyBART," October 10, 2010

M

Connie Mack — episode 18, "Dancin' Homer," November 8, 1990, and episode 467, "MoneyBART," October 10, 2010

Don Mattingly (character) — episode 52, "Homer at the Bat," February 20, 1992

Willie Mays — episode 520, "Love Is A Many-Splintered Thing," February 20, 2013

Mark McGwire (character) — episode 228, "Brother's Little Helper," October 3, 1999

O

Tomokazu Ohka — episode 306, "C. E. D'oh," March 16, 2003

Mel Ott — mentioned in the book *Flanders' Book of Faith* published in 2008

P

Mike Piazza — appears in the April 2008 comic book, *Bart Simpson's Comics* #41, page 7.

R

Jackie Robinson — episode 547, "Luca$," April 6, 2014

Pete Rose — episode 467, "MoneyBART," October 10, 2010

Babe Ruth — episode 165, "Mountain of Madness," February 2, 1997, and episode 242, "Pygmoelian," February 27, 2000

S

Ron Santo — episode 324, "Margical History Tour," Feburary 8, 2004

Steve Sax (character) — episode 52, "Homer at the Bat," February 20, 1992

Mike Scioscia (character) — episode 52, "Homer at the Bat," February 20, 1992, and episode 467, "MoneyBART," October 10, 2010

Ozzie Smith (character) — episode 52, "Homer at the Bat," February 20, 1992

Warren Spahn — mentioned in the book *Flanders' Book of Faith* published in 2008

Darryl Strawberry (character) — episode 52, "Homer at the Bat," February 20, 1992

Gabby Street — episode 52, "Homer at the Bat," February 20, 1992

Ron Swoboda — episode 467, "MoneyBART," October 10, 2010

T

Gene Tenace (character) — episode 376, "Regarding Margie," May 7, 2006

Joe Torre — episode 343, "Homer and Ned's Hail Mary Pass," February 6, 2005

Pie Traynor — episode 18, "Dancin' Homer," November 8, 1990, and episode 52, "Homer at the Bat," February 20, 1992

V

Fernando Valenzuela — mentioned in the book *Flanders' Book of Faith* published in 2008

Omar Vizquel — episode 58, "Bart's Friend Falls in Love," May 7, 1992

W

Honus Wagner — episode 52, "Homer at the Bat," February 20, 1992

Ted Williams — mentioned in the book *Flanders' Book of Faith* published in 2008

Y

Esteban Yan — episode 306, "C. E. D'oh," March 16, 2003

Carl Yastrzemski — episode 34, "Three Men and a Comic Book," May 9, 1991, and episode 58, "Bart's Friend Falls in Love," May 7, 1992

Thanks to simpsonswiki.com for providing all the data from which this list was compiled. Some of the characters who were mentioned in TV episode also appear in, for instance, *Flanders' Book of Faith*, and *Bart Simpson Comics*.

CONTRIBUTORS

FREDERICK C. (RICK) BUSH, his wife Michelle, and their three sons Michael, Andrew, and Daniel live in northwest Houston. He has taught both English and German and is currently an English professor at Wharton County Junior College in Sugar Land. Though he is an avid fan of the hometown Astros, his youth has left him with an abiding affinity for the Texas Rangers and Pittsburgh Pirates as well. He has contributed articles to SABR's BioProject and Games Project sites and has written contributions for upcoming SABR books about the 1986 Boston Red Sox, 1979 Pittsburgh Pirates, 1972 Texas Rangers, Milwaukee's County Stadium, the Montreal Expos, and baseball's winter meetings. Currently he is serving as an associate editor, photo editor, and contributing writer for a SABR book about the Houston Astrodome.

ALAN COHEN has been a member of SABR since 2011, and is active in the Connecticut Smoky Joe Wood Chapter. He has written more than 25 biographies for SABR's bio-project, and has contributed to several SABR books. His first game story about Baseball's Longest Day—May 31, 1964 has been followed by several other game stories. His research into the *Hearst Sandlot Classic (1946-1965)*, an annual youth All-Star game which launched the careers of 88 major-league players, first appeared in the Fall 2013 edition of the *Baseball Research Journal*, and has been followed with a poster presentation at the SABR Convention in Chicago. He is currently expanding his research and is looking forward to having a book published. He serves as the datacaster (stringer) for the Hartford Yard Goats, the Colorado Rockies affiliate in the Class-AA Eastern League. A native of Long Island, he now resides in West Hartford, Connecticut with his wife Frances, two cats, and two dogs.

In addition to Nap Lajoie, **STEPHEN CONSTANTELOS** has written BioProject biographies of Jim Bagby, Sr., Bob Bescher, Bill Bradley, and George Stovall.

GEOFFREY DUNN is an award-winning documentary filmmaker and investigative journalist. His films include *Dollar a Day, Ten Cents a Dance*; *Miss... or Myth?*; and *Calypso Dreams*. His books include *Santa Cruz Is in the Heart*, *Chinatown Dreams*, *The Lies of Sarah Palin*, and *Images of America: Sports of Santa Cruz County*. A former semipro infielder and captain of his high school baseball team, Dunn is a lifelong fan of the San Francisco Giants.

CHARLES F. FABER is a native of Iowa, currently living in Lexington, Kentucky. He holds degrees from Coe College, Columbia University, and the University of Chicago. A retired public school and university teacher and administrator, he has contributed to numerous SABR projects, including editing *The 1934 St.Louis Cardinals*. Among his publications are dozens of professional journal articles, encyclopedia entries, and research reports in fields such as school administration, education law, and country music. In addition to textbooks, he has written 10 books (mostly on baseball) published by McFarland. His most recent work, co-authored with Zachariah Webb, is *The Hunt for a Reds October*, published by McFarland in 2015.

A retired English professor and a member of SABR since 1994, **JAN FINKEL** has contributed to *Deadball Stars of the National League*, *Deadball Stars of the American League*, the *Baseball Research Journal*, *NINE*, and the SABR Biography Project. He served as chief editor of the Biography Project from 2002 to 2015.

DAVID FLEITZ is a writer, baseball historian, and computer systems analyst from Pleasant Ridge, Michigan. A former teacher, David wrote numerous articles for magazines and newspapers on a freelance basis before turning his attention to writing books. Since 2001, he has written eight books on baseball history, including biographies of Shoeless Joe Jackson, Louis Sockalexis (the first Native American major leaguer), and Cap Anson. His latest work, *Napoleon Lajoie: King of Ballplayers*, was published by McFarland in 2013. David is a member of SABR, and is a four-time winner of SABR's annual national baseball trivia championship.

JAMES FORR is a past winner of the McFarland-SABR Baseball Research Award, and co-author (with David Proctor) of *Pie Traynor: A Baseball Biography*. He lives in Columbia, Missouri and is one of the leaders of SABR's Games Project.

EMILY HAWKS has been a SABR member since 2008 and has served on the SABR Board of Directors since 2013. She also serves as a Vice Chair on the SABR Bioproject committee, with a focus on players of the 1980s, 1990s and 2000s. Emily holds a Bachelor of Science in Mathematics and Business from the University of Puget Sound as well as a Master of Science in Computational Finance and Risk Management from the University of Washington. She works in the field of financial and risk analysis, and is based in Seattle, Washington. Thanks to TBS, Emily spent her childhood years in Idaho as a spoiled fan of the 1990s Atlanta Braves, but has since countered those bountiful years by suffering as a Seattle Mariners fan since relocating to the Pacific Northwest.

DAVID JONES edited the book *Deadball Stars of the American League* for SABR, which was published in 2006. He has written an even dozen biographies for SABR's BioProject, ranging from Home Run Baker to Heinie Zimmerman.

JONAH KERI is a staff writer for Grantland. His book *The Extra 2%: How Wall Street Strategies Took a Major League Baseball Team From Worst to First* was a *New York Times* bestseller. His new book, *Up, Up, and Away*, on the history of the Montreal Expos, is a #1 Canadian bestseller.

RUSS LAKE lives in Champaign, Illinois, and is a retired Professor Emeritus. He was born in Belleville, Illinois, on the "other side of the river" from downtown St. Louis. The 1964 Cardinals remain his favorite team, and he was grateful to go to 28 games at Sportsman's Park (aka Busch Stadium I) before it was demolished in late 1966. His wife, Carol, deserves an MVP award for watching all of a 14-inning ballgame in Cincinnati with Russ in 1971—during their honeymoon. He joined SABR in 1994 and, later in that same year, was an editor for David Halberstam's *October 1964*.

SUSAN A. LANTZ, Ph.D., a forensic mechanical, biomechanical, and biomedical engineer, and former college professor, attended her first baseball game at the ripe old age of 26 and was immediately and forever hooked on baseball, Wrigley Field, and the Cubs. She began her professorial career in Detroit, in the days when cable TV was limited to a few channels, and since Cubs games were few and far between, she began following the Detroit Tigers, watching their games every evening while writing lecture notes for Thermodynamics. Much to her husband's dismay, she will watch any baseball game, but she prefers to see her beloved Cubs or Tigers play.

LEN LEVIN has been the copyeditor for most of SABR's recent books. He retired as an editor at the Providence Journal, currently has a part-time job editing the decisions of the Rhode Island Supreme Court, and follows the Red Sox through thick and thin.

ERIK MALINOWSKI is a freelance journalist based near San Francisco. He is a frequent contributor to Rolling Stone, Sports on Earth, and Uproxx Sports. His work has also appeared in Wired, Slate, Atlas Obscura, The New Republic, Fox Sports, BuzzFeed, and Deadspin. Erik's feature story on "Homer at the Bat" was published in the

Best American Sports Writing 2013 anthology, and he has had stories recognized as Notable in the 2014 and 2015 books. A graduate of Boston University, Erik lives in San Mateo, California, with his wife and 2-year-old son. He can be reached at erikmalinowski@gmail.com.

SHAWN MORRIS is a newer member to SABR. He is an avid fan of *The Simpsons* and still never misses an episode. During the baseball season, he can be regularly found at Canal Park in Akron, Ohio where he is a RubberDucks season ticket holder. As a doctoral candidate in the history program at Kent State University, he aims to focus his dissertation upon how sports has, and continues to, successfully break down social and cultural barriers. He has also authored articles regarding the historiography of Negro League Baseball in Cleveland, and the city's first professional black baseball team, the Tate Stars. Currently, he is working on a couple of encyclopedia entries regarding sports in Colonial America.

BILL NOWLIN can still remember when his parents got only the second TV first in his Lexington, Massachusetts neighborhood and lots of the kids would come over to watch *The Howdy Doody Show* in the late afternoons. He also can remember when, before it became its own show, "The Simpsons" was a segment on the *Tracey Ullman Show*. He still watches close to 81 away baseball games each season, and MSNBC, but tries to keep from getting drawn into too many serials so he can work on researching, writing, and editing material on baseball.

JOE POSNANSKI is national columnist for NBC Sports. He has written four books, including the *New York Times* bestseller *The Machine* about the 1975 Cincinnati Reds and the Casey Award Winning *The Soul of Baseball: A Road Trip Through Buck O'Neil's America*. Joe is working on a book on Harry Houdini. He lives in Charlotte with his wife Margo, their two daughters Elizabeth and Katie, and their poodle Westley.

JAMES L. RAY is an attorney who has lived and worked in Center City, Philadelphia for the past 25 years. Born and raised a Yankee fan, jim moved to Philadelphia to attend the University of Pennsylvania Law School. Within a few years, he gave in to the lure of mediocrity and heartbreak that personifies Philadelphia Phillies, and has been a fan ever since. It is both the best and the worst decision he ever made. Jim has written for SABR the past seven years, and his contributions include biographies of Don Mattingly, Lou Gerhig, Mickey Mantle, and Paul O'Neill for the SABR Bio project. Jim has also contributed chapters to several SABR books on the Phillies, Dodgers, and Yankees. Jim has a lovely wife Cindy and two cats, Ivan and Buji. He also enjoys good beer.

E. A. (BETSY) REED grew up in New England, and learned at an early age the dedication required of all true Red Sox fans. Although now a resident of Henderson, Nevada, she and her husband, Peter Simonds, still attend at least three Red Sox games each season.

CINDY THOMSON is a freelance writer and co-author of *Three Finger, The Mordecai Brown Story*, the biography of a Cubs Hall of Fame pitcher. She is also the author of a historical fiction series. The final novel, *Sofia's Tune*, released in 2015. She has written for SABR's BioProject, and contributed to several SABR publications including *Deadball Stars of the American League*, *Detroit Tigers 1984*, *New Century, New Team: The 1901 Boston Americans*, and *The Great Eight: The 1975 Cincinnati Reds*. A life-long Reds fan, she writes full time from her home in Central Ohio where she and her husband Tom raised three sons to root for Cincinnati. She also mentors writers and is a member of the American Christian Fiction Writers and the Historical Novel Society. Visit her online at: http://www.cindyswriting.com.

JOHN THORN, the Official Historian for Major League Baseball, has written many books about the game. He is the editor of the scholarly annual *Base Ball: A Journal of the Early Game*.

JOSEPH WANCHO has been a SABR member since 2005. He serves as the chair of the Minor League Research Committee.

STEVE WEST is a math nerd, a history nerd, and a wannabe writer. Combine these with his love of baseball and the SABR BioProject is right in his wheelhouse. Steve works as a data analyst in the energy industry, messing around with computers and numbers all day long, and comes home and does the same with baseball stats while watching Rangers games at night. Steve (a SABR member since 2006), his wife Marian, and son Joshua are die-hard Rangers fans, which is one reason why Steve is now editor of a BioProject book on the 1972 Texas Rangers.

A lifelong Pirates fan, **GREGORY H. WOLF** was born in Pittsburgh, but now resides in the Chicagoland area with his wife, Margaret, and daughter, Gabriela. A professor of German studies and holder of the Dennis and Jean Bauman Endowed Chair in the Humanities at North Central College in Naperville, Illinois, he edited the SABR books *"Thar's Joy in Braveland!" The 1957 Milwaukee Braves* (2014), *Winning on the North Side: The 1929 Chicago Cubs* (2015), and *A Pennant for the Twin Cities: The 1965 Minnesota Twins* (2015). He is currently working on projects about the Houston Astrodome and Milwaukee's County Stadium, and is co-editing a book with Bill Nowlin on the 1979 Pittsburgh Pirates.

BRADLEY WOODRUM holds an MA Economics from Roosevelt University and an MFA in Creative Writing from the University of Tampa. His writing credits include FanGraphs, The Hardball Times, Baseball Prospectus, ESPN.com, Banknotes Industries, DRaysBay, and the men's bathroom stall in the Council Building at Jacksonville University. Imagining ways to fit dragons and wizards into fantasy baseball by night, Bradley spends his days as a financial analyst and an under-qualified IT technician. Find his self-loathing ruminations on Twitter at @BradleyWoodrum or bother him directly at bradley.woodrum@gmail.com.

PAUL ZINGG came to the Red Sox through Harry Hooper and a lifelong loathing of the Yankees. He even forgives Harry and his teammates for defeating his beloved National League Giants in the 1912 World Series. His baseball books include a biography of Hooper (*Harry Hooper: An American Baseball Life*) and a history of the old Pacific Coast League (*Runs, Hits, and an Era: The Pacific Coast League, 1903–1958*). He is the president of California State University, Chico, home of a perennial participant in the NCAA Division-II World Series.

SABR BioProject Books

In 2002, the Society for American Baseball Research launched an effort to write and publish biographies of every player, manager, and individual who has made a contribution to baseball. Over the past decade, the BioProject Committee has produced over 3,400 biographical articles. Many have been part of efforts to create theme- or team-oriented books, spearheaded by chapters or other committees of SABR.

A PENNANT FOR THE TWIN CITIES:
THE 1965 MINNESOTA TWINS
This volume celebrates the 1965 Minnesota Twins, who captured the American League pennant in just their fifth season in the Twin Cities. Led by an All-Star cast, from Harmon Killebrew, Tony Oliva, Zoilo Versalles, and Mudcat Grant to Bob Allison, Jim Kaat, Earl Battey, and Jim Perry, the Twins won 102 games, but bowed to the Los Angeles Dodgers and Sandy Koufax in Game Seven
Edited by Gregory H. Wolf
$19.95 paperback (ISBN 978-1-943816-09-5)
$9.99 ebook (ISBN 978-1-943816-08-8)
8.5"X11", 405 pages, over 80 photos

MUSTACHES AND MAYHEM: CHARLIE O'S THREE TIME CHAMPIONS:
THE OAKLAND ATHLETICS: 1972-74
The Oakland Athletics captured major league baseball's crown each year from 1972 through 1974. Led by future Hall of Famers Reggie Jackson, Catfish Hunter and Rollie Fingers, the Athletics were a largely homegrown group who came of age together. Biographies of every player, coach, manager, and broadcaster (and mascot) from 1972 through 1974 are included, along with season recaps.
Edited by Chip Greene
$29.95 paperback (ISBN 978-1-943816-07-1)
$9.99 ebook (ISBN 978-1-943816-06-4)
8.5"X11", 600 pages, almost 100 photos

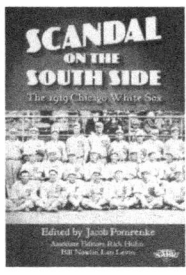

SCANDAL ON THE SOUTH SIDE:
THE 1919 CHICAGO WHITE SOX
The Black Sox Scandal isn't the only story worth telling about the 1919 Chicago White Sox. The team roster included three future Hall of Famers, a 20-year-old spitballer who would win 300 games in the minors, and even a batboy who later became a celebrity with the "Murderers' Row" New York Yankees. All of their stories are included in Scandal on the South Side with a timeline of the 1919 season.
Edited by Jacob Pomrenke
$19.95 paperback (ISBN 978-1-933599-95-3)
$9.99 ebook (ISBN 978-1-933599-94-6)
8.5"x11", 324 pages, 55 historic photos

WINNING ON THE NORTH SIDE
THE 1929 CHICAGO CUBS
Celebrate the 1929 Chicago Cubs, one of the most exciting teams in baseball history. Future Hall of Famers Hack Wilson, '29 NL MVP Rogers Hornsby, and Kiki Cuyler, along with Riggs Stephenson formed one of the most potent quartets in baseball history. The magical season came to an ignominious end in the World Series and helped craft the future "lovable loser" image of the team.
Edited by Gregory H. Wolf
$19.95 paperback (ISBN 978-1-933599-89-2)
$9.99 ebook (ISBN 978-1-933599-88-5)
8.5"x11", 314 pages, 59 photos

DETROIT THE UNCONQUERABLE:
THE 1935 WORLD CHAMPION TIGERS
Biographies of every player, coach, and broadcaster involved with the 1935 World Champion Detroit Tigers baseball team, written by members of the Society for American Baseball Research. Also includes a season in review and other articles about the 1935 team. Hank Greenberg, Mickey Cochrane, Charlie Gehringer, Schoolboy Rowe, and more.
Edited by Scott Ferkovich
$19.95 paperback (ISBN 9978-1-933599-78-6)
$9.99 ebook (ISBN 978-1-933599-79-3)
8.5"X11", 230 pages, 52 photos

THE 1934 ST. LOUIS CARDINALS:
THE WORLD CHAMPION GAS HOUSE GANG
The 1934 St. Louis Cardinals were one of the most colorful crews ever to play the National Pastime. Some of were aging stars, past their prime, and others were youngsters, on their way up, but together they comprised a championship ball club. Pepper Martin, Dizzy and Paul Dean, Joe Medwick, Frankie Frisch and more are all included here.
Edited by Charles F. Faber
$19.95 paperback (ISBN 978-1-933599-73-1)
$9.99 ebook (ISBN 978-1-933599-74-8)
8.5"X11", 282 pages, 47 photos

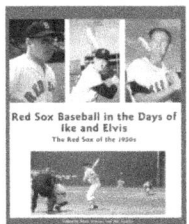

RED SOX BASEBALL IN THE DAYS OF IKE AND ELVIS: THE RED SOX OF THE 1950S
Although the Red Sox spent most of the 1950s far out of contention, the team was filled with fascinating players who captured the heart of their fans. In *Red Sox Baseball*, members of SABR present 46 biographies on players such as Ted Williams and Pumpsie Green as well as season-by-season recaps.
Edited by Mark Armour and Bill Nowlin
$19.95 paperback (ISBN 978-1-933599-24-3)
$9.99 ebook (ISBN 978-1-933599-34-2)
8.5"X11", 372 pages, over 100 photos

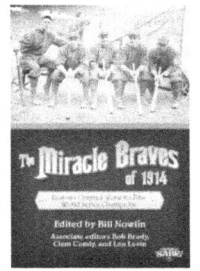

THE MIRACLE BRAVES OF 1914
BOSTON'S ORIGINAL WORST-TO-FIRST CHAMPIONS
Long before the Red Sox "Impossible Dream" season, Boston's now nearly forgotten "other" team, the 1914 Boston Braves, performed a baseball "miracle" that resounds to this very day. The "Miracle Braves" were Boston's first "worst-to-first" winners of the World Series. Includes biographies of every player, coach, and owner, a season recap, and other great stories from the 1914 season.
Edited by Bill Nowlin
$19.95 paperback (ISBN 978-1-933599-69-4)
$9.99 ebook (ISBN 978-1-933599-70-0)
8.5"X11", 392 pages, over 100 photos

SABR Members can purchase each book at a significant discount (often 50% off) and receive the ebook edtions free as a member benefit. Each book is available in a trade paperback edition as well as ebooks suitable for reading on a home computer or Nook, Kindle, or iPad/tablet.
To learn more about becoming a member of SABR, visit the website: sabr.org/join

The SABR Digital Library

The Society for American Baseball Research, the top baseball research organization in the world, disseminates some of the best in baseball history, analysis, and biography through our publishing programs. The SABR Digital Library contains a mix of books old and new, and focuses on a tandem program of paperback and ebook publication, making these materials widely available for both on digital devices and as traditional printed books.

Greatest Games Books

BRAVES FIELD:
MEMORABLE MOMENTS AT BOSTON'S LOST DIAMOND
From its opening on August 18, 1915, to the sudden departure of the Boston Braves to Milwaukee before the 1953 baseball season, Braves Field was home to Boston's National League baseball club and also hosted many other events: from NFL football to championship boxing. The most memorable moments to occur in Braves Field history are portrayed here.
Edited by Bill Nowlin and Bob Brady
$19.95 paperback (ISBN 978-1-933599-93-9)
$9.99 ebook (ISBN 978-1-933599-92-2)
8.5"X11", 282 pages, 182 photos

INVENTING BASEBALL: THE 100 GREATEST GAMES OF THE NINETEENTH CENTURY
SABR's Nineteenth Century Committee brings to life the greatest games from the game's early years. From the "prisoner of war" game that took place among captive Union soldiers during the Civil War (immortalized in a famous lithograph), to the first intercollegiate game (Amherst versus Williams), to the first professional no-hitter, the games in this volume span 1833–1900 and detail the athletic exploits of such players as Cap Anson, Moses "Fleetwood" Walker, Charlie Comiskey, and Mike "King" Kelly.
Edited by Bill Felber
$19.95 paperback (ISBN 978-1-933599-42-7)
$9.99 ebook (ISBN 978-1-933599-43-4)
8"x10", 302 pages, 200 photos

BioProject Books

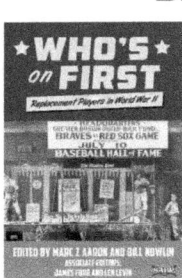

WHO'S ON FIRST:
REPLACEMENT PLAYERS IN WORLD WAR II
During World War II, 533 players made the major league debuts. More than 60% of the players in the 1941 Opening Day lineups departed for the service and were replaced by first-timers and oldsters. Hod Lisenbee was 46. POW Bert Shepard had an artificial leg, and Pete Gray had only one arm. The 1944 St. Louis Browns had 13 players classified 4-F. These are their stories.
Edited by Marc Z Aaron and Bill Nowlin
$19.95 paperback (ISBN 978-1-933599-91-5)
$9.99 ebook (ISBN 978-1-933599-90-8)
8.5"X11", 422 pages, 67 photos

VAN LINGLE MUNGO:
THE MAN, THE SONG, THE PLAYERS
Although the Red Sox spent most of the 1950s far out of contention, the team was filled with fascinating players who captured the heart of their fans. In *Red Sox Baseball*, members of SABR present 46 biographies on players such as Ted Williams and Pumpsie Green as well as season-by-season recaps.
Edited by Bill Nowlin
$19.95 paperback (ISBN 978-1-933599-76-2)
$9.99 ebook (ISBN 978-1-933599-77-9)
8.5"X11", 278 pages, 46 photos

Original SABR Research

CALLING THE GAME:
BASEBALL BROADCASTING FROM 1920 TO THE PRESENT
An exhaustive, meticulously researched history of bringing the national pastime out of the ballparks and into living rooms via the airwaves. Every play-by-play announcer, color commentator, and ex-ballplayer, every broadcast deal, radio station, and TV network. Plus a foreword by "Voice of the Chicago Cubs" Pat Hughes, and an afterword by Jacques Doucet, the "Voice of the Montreal Expos" 1972-2004.
by Stuart Shea
$24.95 paperback (ISBN 978-1-933599-40-3)
$9.99 ebook (ISBN 978-1-933599-41-0)
7"X10", 712 pages, 40 photos

BASEBALL IN THE SPACE AGE:
HOUSTON SINCE 1961
Here we have a special issue of *The National Pastime* centered almost entirely on the Houston Astros (né Colt .45s) and their two influential and iconic homes, short-lived Colt Stadium and the Astrodome. If you weren't able to attend the SABR convention in Houston, please enjoy this virtual trip tour of baseball in "Space City" through 18 articles.
Edited by Cecilia M. Tan
$14.95 paperback (ISBN 978-1-933599-65-6)
$9.99 ebook (ISBN 978-1-933599-66-3)
8.5"x11", 96 pages, 49 photos

NORTH SIDE, SOUTH SIDE, ALL AROUND THE TOWN: BASEBALL IN CHICAGO
The National Pastime provides in-depth articles focused on the geographic region where the national SABR convention is taking place annually. The SABR 45 convention took place in Chicago, and here are 45 articles on baseball in and around the bat-and-ball crazed Windy City: 25 that appeared in the souvenir book of the convention plus another 20 articles available in ebook only.
Edited by Stuart Shea
$14.95 paperback (ISBN 978-1-933599-87-8)
$9.99 ebook (ISBN 978-1-933599-86-1)
8.5"X11", 282 pages, 47 photos

THE EMERALD GUIDE TO BASEBALL: 2015
The Emerald Guide to Baseball fills the gap in the historical record created by the demise of *The Sporting News Baseball Guide*. First published in 1942, *The Sporting News* Guide was truly the annual book of record for our National Pastime. The 2015 edition of the *Emerald Guide* runs more than 600 pages and covers the 2014 season; it also includes a 2015 directory of every franchise, rosters, minor league affiliates, and career leaders for all teams.
Edited by Gary Gillette and Pete Palmer
$24.95 paperback (ISBN 978-0-9817929-8-9)
8.5"X11", 610 pages

SABR Members can purchase each book at a significant discount (often 50% off) and receive the ebook edtions free as a member benefit. Each book is available in a trade paperback edition as well as ebooks suitable for reading on a home computer or Nook, Kindle, or iPad/tablet.
To learn more about becoming a member of SABR, visit the website: sabr.org/join

Join SABR today!

If you're interested in baseball — writing about it, reading about it, talking about it — there's a place for you in the Society for American Baseball Research.

SABR was formed in 1971 in Cooperstown, New York, with the mission of fostering the research and dissemination of the history and record of the game. Our members include everyone from academics to professional sportswriters to amateur historians and statisticians to students and casual fans who merely enjoy reading about baseball history and occasionally gathering with other members to talk baseball.

SABR members have a variety of interests, and this is reflected in the diversity of its research committees. There are more than two dozen groups devoted to the study of a specific area related to the game — from Baseball and the Arts to Statistical Analysis to the Deadball Era to Women in Baseball. In addition, many SABR members meet formally and informally in regional chapters throughout the year and hundreds come together for the annual national convention, the organization's premier event. These meetings often include panel discussions with former major league players and research presentations by members. Most of all, SABR members love talking baseball with like-minded friends. What unites them all is an interest in the game and joy in learning more about it.

Why join SABR? Here are some benefits of membership:

- Two issues (spring and fall) of the *Baseball Research Journal*, which includes articles on history, biography, statistics, personalities, book reviews, and other aspects of the game.
- One expanded e-book edition of *The National Pastime*, which focuses on baseball in the region where that year's SABR national convention is held (in 2015, it's Chicago)
- 8-10 new and classic e-books published each year by the SABR Digital Library, which are all free for members to download
- *This Week in SABR* newsletter in your e-mail every Friday, which highlights SABR members' research and latest news
- Regional chapter meetings, which can include guest speakers, presentations and trips to ballgames
- Online access to back issues of *The Sporting News* and other periodicals through Paper of Record
- Access to SABR's lending library and other research resources
- Online member directory to connect you with an international network of SABR baseball experts and fans
- Discounts on registration for our annual events, including SABR Analytics Conference & Jerry Malloy Negro League Conference
- Access to SABR-L, an e-mail discussion list of baseball questions & answers that many feel is worth the cost of membership itself
- The opportunity to be part of a passionate international community of baseball fans

SABR membership is on a "rolling" calendar system; that means your membership lasts 365 days no matter when you sign up! Enjoy all the benefits of SABR membership by signing up today at SABR.org/join or by clipping out the form below and mailing it to SABR, Cronkite School at ASU, 555 N. Central Ave. #416, Phoenix, AZ 85004.

SABR MEMBERSHIP FORM

	Annual	3-year	Senior	3-yr Sr.	Under 30
U.S.:	❏ $65	❏ $175	❏ $45	❏ $129	❏ $45
Canada/Mexico:	❏ $75	❏ $205	❏ $55	❏ $159	❏ $55
Overseas:	❏ $84	❏ $232	❏ $64	❏ $186	❏ $55

Add a Family Member: $15 for each family member at same address (list on back)
Senior: 65 or older before 12/31/2015
All dues amounts in U.S. dollars or equivalent

Participate in Our Donor Program!
I'd like to desginate my gift to be used toward:
❏ General Fund ❏ Endowment Fund ❏ Research Resources ❏ _____
❏ I want to maximize the impact of my gift; do not send any donor premiums
❏ I would like this gift to remain anonymous.

Note: Any donation not designated will be placed in the General Fund.
SABR is a 501 (c) (3) not-for-profit organization & donations are tax-deductible to the extent allowed by law.

Name _____
Address _____
City _____ ST _____ ZIP _____
Phone _____ Birthday _____
E-mail: _____
(Your e-mail address on file ensures you will receive the most recent SABR news.)

Dues $_____
Donation $_____
Amount Enclosed $_____

Do you work for a matching grant corporation? Call (602) 496-1460 for details.

If you wish to pay by credit card, please contact the SABR office at (602) 496-1460 or visit the SABR Store online at SABR.org/join. We accept Visa, Mastercard & Discover.

Do you wish to receive the *Baseball Research Journal* electronically?: ❏ Yes ❏ No
Our e-books are available in PDF, Kindle, or EPUB (iBooks, iPad, Nook) formats.

Mail to: SABR, Cronkite School at ASU, 555 N. Central Ave. #416, Phoenix, AZ 85004